INEQUALITY AND THE STATE

Inequality and the State

John Hills

OXFORD
UNIVERSITY PRESS

OXFORD
UNIVERSITY PRESS

Great Clarendon Street, Oxford OX2 6DP

Oxford University Press is a department of the University of Oxford.
It furthers the University's objective of excellence in research, scholarship,
and education by publishing worldwide in

Oxford New York

Auckland Bangkok Buenos Aires Cape Town Chennai
Dar es Salaam Delhi Hong Kong Istanbul Karachi Kolkata
Kuala Lumpur Madrid Melbourne Mexico City Mumbai Nairobi
São Paulo Shanghai Taipei Tokyo Toronto

with an associated company in Berlin

Published in the United States
by Oxford University Press Inc., New York

British Library Cataloguing in Publication Data

Data available

Library of Congress Cataloging in Publication Data

Data available

ISBN 0–19–927663–3 (hbk.)
ISBN 0–19–927664–1 (pbk.)

1 3 5 7 9 10 8 6 4 2

Typeset by Newgen Imaging Systems (P) Ltd., Chennai, India
Printed in Great Britain
on acid-free paper by
Biddles Ltd., King's Lynn, Norfolk

Acknowledgements

This book brings together research that I and others have carried out at the ESRC Research Centre for Analysis of Social Exclusion (CASE) at the London School of Economics, much of it supported by core funding from the Economic and Social Research Council. I am very grateful to the research council for this support, and to the Joseph Rowntree Foundation, which funded some earlier pieces of analysis that are drawn on and updated here. Neither of these bodies is responsible for the opinions expressed, however, which are the author's own.

Part of the purpose of this book has been to bring together in a single place analysis that had previously been published in diverse forms in recent years, and to bring it up to date so as to reflect what we know about Britain in 2004. In particular, some parts of Chapters 2, 4, 5, 6, and 8, draw on material that was previously published by the Joseph Rowntree Foundation in my reports on *The Future of Welfare* (1993), *Income and Wealth: A Survey of the Evidence* (1995), *Income and Wealth: The Latest Evidence* (1998), and *Private Welfare and Public Policy* (1999; co-authored with Tania Burchardt and Carol Propper). Material from these publications has been used by kind permission of the Foundation, to which I am most grateful. Similarly, an earlier version of some of the material on public attitudes to poverty and social security was previously published in chapters in the 1999 and 2001 reports of the *British Social Attitudes* survey. I am very grateful to the National Centre for Social Research for permission to use this material, and more generally for access to the data analysed here from the survey for the last twenty years. Parts of Chapter 7 draw on and update material on taxation also used in a chapter in *Public Policy for the 21st Century: Social and Economic Essays in Memory of Henry Neuburger* (Policy Press, 2000). I am very grateful to Policy Press and to my co-editor, Neil Fraser, for permission to do so. Section 8.1 draws on material also in used in a chapter in *The Student's Companion to Social Policy*, edited by Pete Alcock, Angus Erskine, and Margaret May (2003); I am grateful to the editors and to Blackwell Publishing for permission to draw on it here. Figures 2.1 and 10.4 are Crown Copyright and are reproduced by kind permission of the Controller of HMSO and the Queen's Printer for Scotland. I am also grateful to the Data Archive at Essex University and the Department for Work and Pensions for access to data from the Family Resources Survey used in the Households Below Average Income dataset.

Many parts of the book draw on analysis by or with colleagues within CASE, or its associates. I am particularly grateful for permission to use joint work to Karen Gardiner (Section 5.4), Tania Burchardt and Carol Propper (Section 6.4), and Holly Sutherland (Section 9.3). More generally, this book would not have been possible without the help, support, and forbearance of all my colleagues within CASE, and I hope that I have done justice to some of their research in the pages that follow. The whole book has been immensely improved thanks to numerous helpful and perceptive comments from those who have read parts or all of earlier drafts from Tony Atkinson, Fran Bennett, Tania Burchardt, Chris Dobson, Howard Glennerster, Stephen Jenkins, Julian Le Grand, Stephen Machin, Abigail McKnight, Alison Park, David Piachaud, Tom Sefton, Kitty Stewart, and Rachel Smithies. The remaining errors where I have failed to take their always good advice are my own responsibility.

I am also grateful to members of CASE's Advisory Committee and to students of social policy at LSE for their helpful suggestions when presented with some of the material here, particularly from its final chapter; to Julian Sharman and Robert Teasdale of Sharmans in Glenridding for help with internet access and communication; and to Raymond and Jean Young and members of the Iona Community for their hospitality and inspiration while I was working on part of the text.

There are several people to whom I owe more than the normal author's debt. First, Jane Dickson, Effie Gika, and Lucinda Himeur gave enormous and efficient help in preparing the manuscript for publication, and Nic Warner and Irina Verkhova gave IT support of all kinds. Second, this book could not have been completed without the help of Rachel Smithies in the last six months in all parts of the book, but particularly in carrying out the empirical analysis of poverty gaps in Chapter 3, and of the impact of demographic change in Chapter 9, as well as updating earlier work on changing public and private boundaries in Chapter 6 (drawing on work previously carried out by Melissa Cox and Tania Burchardt), and on the intergenerational distribution of social spending in Chapter 8. Nor could this book have come into existence without the continual encouragement and advice of Julian Le Grand in acting as mentor and guardian of its timetable, or the support and patience of Anne Power throughout the last year. I am more than grateful to them all.

John Hills
London School of Economics
March 2004

Contents

I: INCOME INEQUALITY AND POVERTY IN BRITAIN

Contents

II: THE IMPACT OF POLICY

III: WHERE DO WE GO FROM HERE?

List of Figures

List of Figures

List of Tables

Glossary

AHC	After housing costs (net income after deducting costs such as rent and mortgage interest)
BCS70	Birth Cohort Study 1970
BHC	Before housing costs (net income before deducting housing costs)
BHPS	British Household Panel Study
BSA Survey	British Social Attitudes Survey
CASE	Centre for Analysis of Social Exclusion (LSE)
Deciles	Points that cut off successive tenths of the income or earnings distribution
Decile groups	Tenths of the population in order of income
Decile ratio	Ratio between top and bottom deciles (that is, the income cutting off the top tenth of population divided by the income cutting off the bottom tenth of population)
DSS	Department of Social Security
DWP	Department for Work and Pensions
Effective marginal tax rate	Proportion of any extra pound of gross income that is lost in higher tax and/or reduced benefits
Equivalent (or equivalized) income	Income adjusted to take account of needs of different-sized family units income
EU	European Union
FES	Family Expenditure Survey (from 2001–02 known as Expenditure and Food Survey, EFS)
FRS	Family Resources Survey
GB	Great Britain (England, Wales, and Scotland; containing 97.1 per cent of UK population)
GDP	Gross Domestic Product (also referred to as 'national income')
Gini coefficient	Index of inequality, taking value of zero for a completely equal distribution and of 100 per cent (or 1) for completely unequal distribution (that is, one person receives all the income or wealth).
Golden rule	Current Treasury guideline that government borrowing should not exceed government net investment, averaged over the economic cycle
HBAI	Households Below Average Income
Hypothecated	Taxes earmarked for a particular kind of spending
IFS	Institute for Fiscal Studies

IMF	International Monetary Fund
IS	Income Support
Incidence	Who actually ends up effectively paying a tax
JSA	Jobseeker's Allowance
LIS	Luxembourg Income Study
LSE	London School of Economics
Mean	Arithmetic average
Median	Mid-point of any distribution (so half of the population has more and half less than this amount)
MIG	Minimum Income Guarantee (Income Support for pensioners)
NA	National Assistance (now Income Support)
n/a	Not available
NCDS	National Child Development Study
NICs	National Insurance Contributions
NMW	National Minimum Wage
NPI	New Policy Institute
OECD	Organization for Economic Cooperation and Development
OfA	*Opportunities for All*
PC	Pension Credit
Percentiles	Points that cut-off successive hundredths of a distribution
Poverty gap	Amount or proportion by which people counted as poor fall below a poverty line
Progressive	Tax system whereby people with higher incomes pay a greater proportion of their income in tax than people with lower incomes
Quintile groups	Fifths of the population in order of income
Real/real terms	Adjusted for price inflation
Regressive	Tax system whereby people with lower incomes pay a greater proportion of income in tax than people with higher incomes
Relative	Compared with rest of population
S2P	State Second Pension
SERPS	State Earnings-Related Pension Scheme
Social spending	Spending on education, health care, housing, personal social services, and social security (in OECD comparisons also includes cost of employment measures and public service pensions)
Social wage	Benefit to individuals or households from government social spending on services in kind (rather than as cash benefits)
Tax credit	Reduction in tax otherwise payable (but sometimes also payable as 'negative tax' to non-taxpayers)
TME	Total Managed Expenditure

UK	United Kingdom
Unisex	Equal payment for men and women (as in pension contributions or annuity payments)
USA	United States of America
1991–92	Financial year (April 1991 to March 1992)
1991/92	Average of two financial years (1991–92 and 1992–93)

1

Introduction

The evidence and research presented in this book bear on questions that are—or certainly should be—at the centre of politics, not just in Britain but in other industrialized countries. How society's resources are ultimately distributed, and how collective decisions through the state affect that distribution, are very big issues. Even in a country such as the UK with relatively low social spending, a quarter of all of national income is channelled through public spending on services such as health care, education, and social security. Policies related to such spending, now two-thirds of all government expenditure, increasingly dominate domestic politics, especially since many macroeconomic decisions are now taken by independent central banks or are subject to predetermined fiscal rules (such as the 'golden rule' in the UK or the constraints of the Stability and Growth Pact for members of the Eurozone). The other side of the coin—who pays the taxes to finance this and other spending—is of equal if not greater importance, affecting as it does nearly two-fifths of national income in the UK and a greater proportion in most other European Union countries.

The book describes and analyses one of the biggest social changes in Britain since the Second World War: the dramatic widening of the income distribution since the end of the 1970s, the growth of poverty, and the factors that have driven them. It examines how government intervention through social spending (the 'welfare state') and the taxes that pay for it affect this distribution, and why they take the forms they do. Each part of the discussion is set in the context of public attitudes as revealed by the rigorous and long-running *British Social Attitudes* survey (for details see the appendices to the annual volume published by the National Centre for Social Research, such as Park et al. 2002).

Against this background, the book analyses changes in policy since New Labour came to government in 1997 and evidence on their impacts. It then looks at the constraints and pressures on future policies, concluding with a discussion of the dilemmas facing policy-makers as they try to meet competing aims in terms of reducing poverty and inequality, growing demands on social spending, and the constraints and opportunities created by public attitudes.

The book brings together new analysis carried out by the author and colleagues at the ESRC Research Centre for Analysis of Social Exclusion (CASE) at the London School of Economics since it started in 1997. This includes material on topics such as income dynamics, the relationship between public and private welfare provision and finance, the distributional effect of government spending, public attitudes to inequality and social security, and the impact of recent reforms. It covers topics that are often analysed separately, such as income distribution, social spending, and taxation, but which are best understood together. All of these have changed rapidly in recent years. This book provides an up-to-date picture as of spring 2004. To assist the reader, each chapter concludes with a brief summary and a guide to further reading and information sources. A glossary at the front of the book gives a guide to some of the abbreviations and technical terms used.

Inevitably, there are related topics which could have been included but which have not been for reasons of space rather than relative importance. The focus of the book is on the situation in Britain, but it makes frequent comparisons with the situation elsewhere, particularly within the European Union, and the policy dilemmas it sets out are common to many countries, even though the policy mixes may vary. But there are many issues of international inequality and of the position in other countries that it does not cover. Nor does it examine issues of distribution and policy impact at area or neighbourhood level (but for recent work in CASE on this, see Lupton 2003 and Mumford and Power 2003).

The book is about inequality, how the state affects distribution through its spending programmes and through taxation, and what the public thinks of all three. This should not be taken to imply that the only reasons for having a welfare state and for state intervention are to do with distribution; far from it. But the economic efficiency and other arguments for sometimes choosing public rather than private provision of services are discussed in detail elsewhere (Barr 2004; Burchardt and Hills 1997; Burchardt, Hills, and Propper 1999). Nor is public spending the only way in which collective decisions affect who gets what from society's resources—laws, regulation, customs, and norms matter too. But taxation and social spending are two of the most powerful influences we have on distribution, and their impacts on poverty and inequality are central to their appraisal. The aim of this book is to widen understanding of such impacts.

The first part of the book sets out to describe the distribution of income and of wider measures of well-being and disadvantage in Britain today. Chapter 2 describes the distribution of income and its trends over time. Chapter 3 examines the closely related issue of poverty, presenting trends in it and in wider indicators of deprivation and social exclusion. Chapter 4 looks at some of the causes of the rapid growth of inequality between the 1970s and 1990s, and of more recent trends. Chapter 5 presents evidence on income dynamics and on the extent to which the picture is changed if we take account of the way individuals' incomes change over time.

As evidence in several chapters shows, people's knowledge of the distribution of income and their place in it is often very vague, so the first section of Chapter 2 sets out what proportions of the population have incomes at different levels, and which groups are found towards its top and bottom, drawing in particular on evidence from the government's *Households Below Average Income* analysis. The following two sections set out how income inequality has changed in recent decades, showing contrasting trends for the most recent years when looking at the distribution as a whole and the distribution at its very top, and at how these trends contrast with those in other comparable countries, most of which have not experienced as sharp a change as Britain. While most of the attention in the book is on income, a short section gives information about the distribution of wealth, and the way it too has become more unequally distributed in the most recent years. Finally, the chapter looks at public views of inequality in the UK, and at how these match or contrast with those in other countries.

The first section of Chapter 3 discusses what might at first sight seem a simple question: how do we measure the extent of poverty? There is a great variety of methods but little consensus. The second section presents trends in the core measure of poverty in terms of the numbers with low incomes currently presented and used by government, for instance in measuring progress towards the abolition of child poverty within a generation, as promised by Prime Minister Tony Blair in 1999. It includes evidence on the depth of poverty for those falling short of the government's effective poverty line. Many would argue, however, that cash, particularly cash in hand at a single moment, is not by itself an adequate measure of poverty or of whether people can or cannot participate in society. On the one hand, cash is not the only way in which people have, or can fail to achieve, command over material resources. On the other hand, there is more to personal fulfilment, and there are other dimensions in which people can fail to participate in their society, than material consumption. The third section discusses the concepts of 'social inclusion' and 'social exclusion' that have become part of British political discourse in recent years. The fourth section puts the UK evidence in international context, discussing quite how poor Britain's record had become in international terms by the mid-1990s. The final section again presents attitudes survey evidence on what the public as a whole thinks about poverty, shedding light on which measures might resonate with the public and how great they think the problems are.

Chapter 4 looks at why there was such a dramatic widening of the gap between rich and poor in Britain between the 1970s and the 1990s, and at what has now happened to those pressures. Earnings—market incomes from paid work—are a very important part of the picture, but earnings are only part of people's total incomes and explain only part of income distribution. The complexity of this relationship is examined in Section 4.1. The following sections look at the widening distribution of earnings for those in work and at the factors that are suggested to have led to changes in it, such as 'skill-biased technological change' and breakdown of social norms. Section 4.4 looks at other key elements in determining how much income households receive from earnings—the levels of unemployment, worklessness, and economic inactivity. This shows the complexity of the relationship between the levels of unemployment and of poverty, for instance. The final two sections discuss other sources of market income and the impact of tax and benefit policies and of changes in them, such as in the level of cash benefits relative to other incomes.

The evidence surveyed so far in the book is cross-sectional—the picture revealed by successive snapshots of the population. Chapter 5 presents what we now know from longitudinal surveys that track what happens to the same people over time. Its first section discusses what such information can tell us and why it might be useful in formulating policy. The chapter then looks at the extent of income mobility in the UK, using data for the whole of the 1990s, and specifically at evidence on movements into and out of poverty. Section 5.4 looks across the distribution at the overall patterns that these data reveal for the trajectories that people's incomes follow over time. The following sections present evidence on whether income mobility has been changing over time, and at how income mobility and earnings mobility in the UK compare with those in other countries. The final section looks at longer-term links between generations.

The second part of the book examines the impact of welfare policy in different ways. Its three chapters discuss: social spending, its extent, and issues in the design of social security programmes; tax policy and its relationship with social security; and the distributional effects of the two sides of the government budget combined.

Chapter 6 looks at both public and private spending on areas that have traditionally come under the heading of the 'welfare state'. The first section looks at public social spending, its recent trends, and its relationship with government spending as a whole. Section 6.2 looks in more detail at social security—which represents nearly half of social spending—and at issues connected with its changing structure, particularly the balance between 'universal' and means-tested benefits. Section 6.3 compares trends in social spending in the UK with those in other industrialized countries. Section 6.4 looks more broadly at the respective roles of public and private sectors in the areas traditionally considered the domain of the welfare state—education, health care, income maintenance, housing, and personal care. It suggests three ways of distinguishing their roles, depending on who provides a service, who pays for it, and who is in control. It shows how the mix between these roles varies between services, and how these have changed in the last twenty years. Finally, the chapter examines public attitudes to social spending and its distribution, particularly means-testing, perceived problems in the social security system, and whether the views on the welfare state of those using private welfare services differ from those of others. Such views are a crucial part of the context within which policy operates.

Chapter 7 first sets out trends in taxation over the last twenty-five years, how these compare with those in other countries, and the relationship between the totals of tax and public spending. Section 7.2 looks at Britain's overall tax structure, the changing role of tax reliefs and what are now known as 'tax credits', and at how much tax people at different points in the income distribution scale pay. The following section looks at the changing interaction between tax and social security, how the reforms of the last few years have affected incomes, and the implications of these changes for work incentives. The final section presents public attitudes towards taxation in terms of its overall level, its links to particular spending items, and its progressivity—how the proportion of income taken in tax varies with income level. As with other parts of the book, the evidence suggests some important differences between how people think the system works, how they think it ought to work, and how it actually does work.

The book suggests that discussion of either tax or spending in isolation can easily be misleading. Chapter 8 discusses the combined impact of tax and public spending on income distribution, analysing differences between groups defined in different ways. It first discusses the problems faced and choices to be made in this kind of analysis. Section 8.2 then examines the 'vertical' distribution by income group of both social security benefits and other government services in kind—what is sometimes known as the 'social wage'. Section 8.3 compares the distribution of these benefits from social spending with that of the taxes which pay for them in order to judge which income groups gain or lose from the combination. Section 8.4 then examines the effects of using a longer time horizon, and focuses on redistribution over the life cycle. Section 8.5 discusses how different age cohorts or generations have been affected by the UK system as it has evolved so far and may do so in future. Finally, Section 8.6 discusses public attitudes towards the redistributive role of government, and how these have changed over the last twenty years.

The final part of this book looks to the future, starting with the impact of changes in tax and social security policy since the 1997 change of government, then looking at constraints on and challenges for future policy and finally at the dilemmas in designing policy within the context described in the rest of the book.

Chapter 9 looks how policy has been evolving since New Labour was elected in May 1997. Its first section looks at the challenges the Blair government faced in 1997 and at what has been new about 'New Labour' policies since then. The second section outlines the key features of these policies, looking in turn at those connected with labour markets, incomes, social exclusion, and public spending. The third section examines what we know so far about the outcomes of these policies in terms of recent trends in poverty, inequality, and social exclusion, and at what modelling evidence suggests their impact will be, particularly on rates of poverty.

That chapter suggests that progress has been made in tackling some of the problems outlined earlier in the book. However, the pressures on social spending and on distribution do not stand still. Chapter 10 looks at how the constraints and pressures under which policy operates may change in the coming years. First, does economic growth solve the problems or does it increase the pressures? The next section looks at the biggest source of pressure on spending, namely, the ageing population: do we really face a 'demographic time bomb', as some have argued, or can it be defused or coped with in some other way? Within this, the third section examines pressures from rising spending on pensions in particular. The final section discusses a different kind of constraint, particularly relevant to the strategies pursued since 1997, resulting from the spread of different kinds of means-testing, and whether we are reaching the limits to that kind of approach.

The final chapter looks at the policy dilemmas created by these pressures and constraints in the light of the evidence presented in the rest of the book. It highlights some parts of the evidence reviewed in earlier parts of the book that may come as a surprise to readers, and summarizes its central themes. One of these is whether it is possible for policy-makers to resolve the conflicting pressures of public desires for reduced poverty and inequality, growing demands on social programmes as the population ages, and the constraints imposed by the objective of keeping tax rates down. There are few easy ways out, but better public understanding of precisely that fact may be one of the crucial ingredients of any resolution.

I

INCOME INEQUALITY AND POVERTY IN BRITAIN

2

Income Inequality in the UK:
Extent and Trends

2.1 THE CURRENT POSITION

One of the most striking features of the distribution of income is how little most of us know about it. There is a marked tendency for people, however high or low on the income scale they are, to assume that they are in the middle. After all, most of us at work have a boss who is paid a great deal more than we are, and know someone else at work (or out of work) who is worse off. The natural assumption is that we are in the middle. This is illustrated in Table 2.1, which shows where people put themselves on a scale of one to ten when asked in 1999 by the British Social Attitudes (BSA) survey, 'In our society there are groups which tend to be towards the top and groups which tend to be toward the bottom. Where would you put yourself on this scale?' Of course, people answering this question may not have been thinking here in terms only of income, but income is clearly a major factor in people's relative position in modern society. Nor would they necessarily be thinking of equally sized groups, but that might be a natural assumption when presented with ten groups. If so, the results are striking. Only 6 per cent put themselves in the top three groups (where one might expect to find 30 per cent), and only 16 per cent in the bottom three groups. Three-quarters of us— nearly twice what one might expect—put ourselves in the middle four groups. The most popular group is the fifth, just above the middle, where nearly a third of people put themselves.

Asked specifically about which of three income groups they would place themselves in, only 4 per cent of respondents to the 2001 BSA survey said 'high income' (Park et al. 2002: 261). More than half, 53 per cent, said 'middle income', and 42 per cent 'low income'. In the same survey, when respondents were asked what proportion of workers were paid £40,000 or more a year, the median answer was 25 per cent—in other words, half said more, half said less than this (2002: 289). In fact, at the time only 8 per cent of (full-time) workers actually earned as much as this (Taylor-Gooby and Hastie 2002: Table 4.12). On the other hand, people tend to underestimate the actual pay of well-paid professions (see Table 2.9).

It is worth starting, therefore, with a clear picture of what the income distribution actually looks like. Much of the evidence below is drawn from the main

Table 2.1. *Respondents' self-allocation in ten groups 'towards the top or bottom of society', 1999, GB*

Group	% of respondents
Top	0.4
2	1.5
3	4.0
4	10.5
5	31.8
6	18.1
7	14.5
8	8.8
9	5.1
Bottom	2.0

Note: Based on 819 responses; 3.3% did not answer this question.

Source: Jowell et al. (2000: 326).

official income distribution series, the Department for Work and Pensions' (DWP) annual Households Below Average Income (HBAI) analysis. This uses data from the Family Resources Survey (FRS) of Great Britain to calculate a measure of the net income of each individual in the population. The measure is based on the total income of the household to which someone belongs, including market income such as earnings, interest, and dividends as well as cash benefits from the state, but after deducting income tax and National Insurance Contributions. It then adjusts this total—'equivalizes' it, in the statistical jargon—to give a measure of living standards that allows for the greater needs of bigger households but also for the 'economies of scale' that bigger households benefit from (the idea that two people living together can have a higher standard of living than two single people with the same total income). A number of important—and sometimes controversial—assumptions and rules are adopted to construct this measure of net income, including:

- Households are assumed to share resources equally, not just within families but also within households made up of several family units. This may not, of course, be the case: even within an immediate family, some members may end up 'better off' than others.
- Larger households are assumed to live more cheaply than smaller ones.
- The adjustment for family size uses the 'McClements scale', which assumes that children, particularly young ones, have much less of an effect on household living standards than adults.
- There is no adjustment for the extra costs faced by disabled people compared with others (see Table 2.3 and the related discussion).

- Incomes are shown both before housing costs (BHC), such as rent or mortgage interest, and after them (AHC), but do not include the benefits of home ownership or subsidized rents.
- The focus is on household incomes, not expenditure.
- The income figures do not include 'in kind' benefits from ownership of consumer durables or from the 'social wage', that is, the value of public services such as health and education (see Section 8.2).

Each of these assumptions or rules is debatable,[1] as are others, such as the omission of people who do not live in households, the omission of investment income taking the form of capital gains, lack of an allowance for the value of leisure to those who are and those who are not working, the omission of the effect of indirect taxes, the assumption that prices are the same across the country, and the time period over which income is measured (see Chapter 5). Nonetheless, the figures are widely accepted as the most accurate and robust account of income distribution in Britain, and include statistics on a comparable basis since 1979. Part of the picture they reveal for 2001–02[2] is shown in Figure 2.1. This shows how many people can be found at each income level (before allowing for housing costs), and the boundary lines for each tenth of the distribution. The income levels it shows are those for a childless couple (or for other household types adjusted to be the equivalent of this). Median net income for the whole population was £311 per week: half of the population would be judged poorer than a childless couple who had this amount, half richer. The figure shows the characteristic way in which the distribution is skewed, with many people having incomes grouped around and just below the median (mid-point), but a long tail to the right of those having considerably more than the median. Their incomes pulled up the arithmetic average (mean) to £384 per week, nearly a quarter higher than the median. Two-thirds of people are 'below average' in these terms.

It also shows that the income levels that many middle class professionals, including many journalists and other commentators,[3] would regard as unexceptional are easily high enough to take them into the top tenth of the distribution: a childless couple with over £636 per week between them in net income in 2001–02 would be in the top tenth. This cut-off corresponded to pre-tax annual income possibly no greater than £44,000 between the two of them: a childless couple of which one had the starting salary of a university professor and the other had no earnings would be at this point. Perhaps more surprisingly, so would be a childless couple each earning only average adult earnings. The cut-off for the top 5 per cent was £805 per week in net income for a childless couple (corresponding to joint pre-tax income of around £57,000); and the top 1.5 million

---

[1] See Hills (1998a: Section 4) and DWP (2003a: Appendices 2 and 5) for discussion of the effects of alternative assumptions.

[2] For an explanation of the system used in this book for expressing financial years and financial year averages, see the Glossary.

[3] See Wakefield (2003) for a discussion of how high on the income distribution people often referred to as 'middle Britain' actually are.

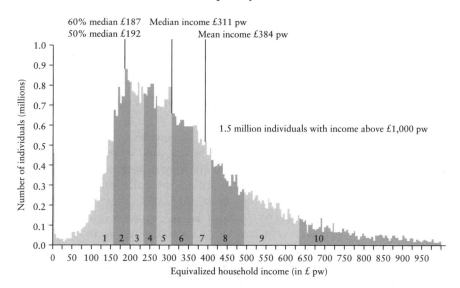

Figure 2.1. *Income distribution, 2001–02, GB*
Source: DWP (2003*a*: Figure 2.1), BHC.

people (2.6 per cent) had net equivalent incomes of £1,000 per week or more. At the other end of the scale, the figure often taken as a poverty line, 60 per cent of median income (see Chapter 3), was £187 per week for a couple (or around £11,300 in gross annual income). One in six, or 17 per cent, of the population had incomes below this in 2001–02.

To help interpret the figures, Table 2.2 shows the net income levels before adjustment for family size which would put people from different household types at particular points in the distribution. Thus, for example, a single person with a net income of £190 per week and a couple with two children and income of £454 per week would all be classed as having median incomes (£311 after adjustment for family size). A single pensioner receiving only the basic state pension of £72.50 in 2001–02, and claiming no other benefits would be just below the cut-off for the poorest 5 per cent. A single person working 38 hours at the minimum wage of £4.10 per hour in October 2001 would have had weekly take-home pay after tax of about £138, putting him or her above 60 per cent of median equivalent income but well below the median itself.

2.1.1 *Family Type*

Figure 2.2 shows the family composition of successive fifths of the 2001–02 income distribution calculated in this way. There are large differences between family types. Lone parents and their children made up 9 per cent of the total population but 17 per cent of the poorest fifth. Overall, 40 per cent of those in

Table 2.2. *Net incomes for different household types corresponding to particular positions in the income distribution, 2001–02, GB (£/week)*

Point in distribution	Equivalent net income *after* adjusting for family size	Corresponding net income *before* adjusting for household size for:			
		Single person	Childless couple	Couple with 2 children (aged 5 and 11)	Single parent with 2 children (aged 5 and 11)
Cut-off for bottom 5%	128	78	128	187	137
Cut-off for bottom 10%	159	97	159	232	170
60% of median	187	114	187	273	200
Median	311	190	311	454	333
Mean	384	234	384	561	411
Cut-off for top 10%	636	388	636	929	681
Cut-off for top 5%	805	491	805	1175	861

Sources: DWP (2003*a*: Tables A2 and C) and author's calculations.

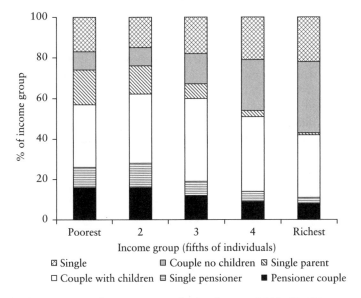

Figure 2.2. *Composition of income groups by family type, 2001–02, GB*
Source: DWP (2003*a*: Table D3), BHC.

lone parent households were in the poorest fifth and 73 per cent in the poorest two-fifths. Although being a pensioner is no longer synonymous with being poor, pensioners were also disproportionately represented in the poorest two-fifths. By contrast, couples without children represented 18 per cent of the whole population but 35 per cent of the richest fifth. Within this group, the best-off tend to be childless couples in their 50s—the 'empty nesters' (although such calculations do not allow for transfers from such couples to family members such as grown-up children no longer living at home, and so may exaggerate their position).

Even if we assume equal sharing within the household, as the HBAI analysis does, the positions of men, women, and children vary. In 2001–02, 25 per cent of children were in the poorest fifth of individuals, and only 13 per cent of them were placed in the richest fifth (DWP 2003a: Table 3.1, BHC). If we look at adults only, 55 per cent of the poorest fifth were women but only 46 per cent of the richest fifth. Research suggests that the equal sharing assumption may be misleading, with the position of children in some ways better than these figures suggest: poor parents often try to protect their children. However, the position of mothers in particular may be worse (Middleton, Ashworth, and Braithwaite 1997; Jarvis and Jenkins 1997c; Goode, Callendar, and Lister 1998).

2.1.2   *Economic Status*

Figure 2.3 shows a comparable breakdown by economic status. Again, there are important variations. Nearly half of the richest fifth were single full-time workers or from families in which a couple both worked full-time, although these family types represented only 25 per cent of the whole population. Eighty-five per cent of the richest households contained at least one full-time earner. Unsurprisingly, families with unemployed heads or spouses (with no other members with earnings) were concentrated at the bottom, as was the much larger residual 'other workless' category, including non-earning lone parents and the long-term sick and disabled. Almost two-thirds of the poorest fifth came from the groups without earnings—these two categories plus those with a head or spouse aged 60 or more. Correspondingly, however, more than one-third of those in the poorest fifth were from families where at least one member had income from work. The figure shows that access to paid work has a huge effect, but there is an important group of people who have paid work but are nonetheless poor.

2.1.3   *Housing Tenure*

Figure 2.4 shows the results of one of the most dramatic social changes in the last two decades: the polarization of housing tenures by income. As the proportion of the population living in social housing has declined, so it has become increasingly concentrated in the poorest groups. In 1979, 42 per cent of all individuals lived in social (local authority or housing association) housing. Of these, just under half were in the poorest two-fifths, but 40 per cent were in the top half of

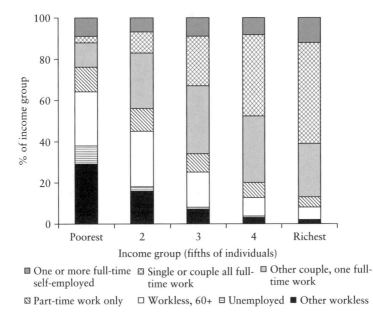

Figure 2.3. *Composition of income groups by economic status, 2001–02, GB*
Source: DWP (2003*a*: Table D4), BHC.

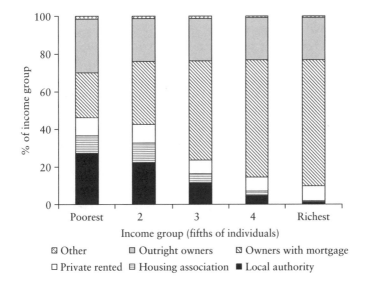

Figure 2.4. *Composition of income groups by tenure, 2001–02, GB*
Source: Derived from DWP (2003*a*: Table 3.2), BHC.

the income distribution (Hills 1998*a*: Figure 9; UK data). By 2001–02, only 19 per cent of the population were living in social housing, but 73 per cent of these were in the poorest two-fifths. Only 2 per cent of those living in social housing were in the top fifth, compared with 13 per cent in 1979.

A main reason for this change has been that those moving into social housing have been much poorer than those moving out (Giles et al. 1996; Burrows 1997). In one sense, this could be seen as a success of policies like the 'Right to Buy' for council tenants and the shift from 'bricks and mortar' subsidies to Housing Benefit, which have been designed to 'target' social housing more effectively on those in greatest need. However, because so much social housing is concentrated in estates, the tenure polarization shown in Figure 2.4 implies geographical polarization, with those on low incomes becoming more concentrated in particular neighbourhoods.

At the same time, the growth of owner-occupation has affected all income groups so that, although social tenants are overwhelmingly likely to be poor, the figure also shows that more than half of the poor are owner-occupiers. On the basis shown, before deduction of housing costs, 52 per cent of the poorest fifth were owners. This does not, however, take account of the benefit to owners of having somewhere to live (or the cost to tenants of paying rent). After housing costs are deducted, which partly corrects for this, a smaller proportion, but still 40 per cent, of the poorest fifth were owners.

2.1.4 *Ethnic Group*

Figure 2.5 shows the proportion of each of five minority ethnic groups within each fifth of the overall income distribution. If income were unrelated to ethnicity, 20 per cent of each group would also be found in each fifth of the overall distribution. Instead, while only 8.6 per cent of the whole population came from ethnic minority households[4] in 2001–02, their members made up 15 per cent of the poorest fifth. They were only 6 per cent of the richest fifth (although this is twice the proportion in 1994–95; Hills 1998*a*: 24). This is despite the age structure of the minority population, which has a much smaller proportion of pensioners, who generally have below average incomes. The figure also shows large differences between minority groups. People from a Pakistani or Bangladeshi background tend to have the lowest incomes, with 60 per cent falling into the poorest fifth and only 7 per cent in the top two-fifths. The other groups are more evenly spread, but are also disproportionately found in the poorest fifth (although this is less true for those from an Indian background).

---

[4] Individuals are classified here according to the reported ethnicity of the 'household reference person' (formerly 'household head'), so no distinction is made between members of households of mixed and of single ethnicity. When Berthoud (1998) examined earlier FRS data, he found that, where households report mixed membership, risks of low income were less than for unmixed minority households.

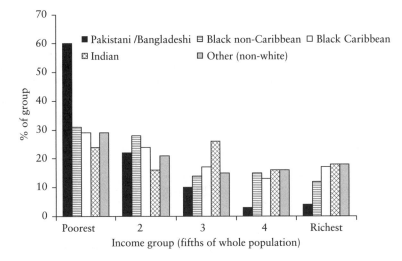

Figure 2.5. *Minority ethnic groups by income group, 2001–02, GB*
Source: DWP (2003*a*: Table 3.1).

Using two years of FRS data from the mid-1990s, Berthoud (1998) looked more closely at the picture and identified five factors contributing to it:[5]

- high rates of lone parenthood among black (Caribbean and African) families, with nearly a quarter of individuals members of lone parent families compared with 6 per cent for white families;
- much higher proportions of families having no earner: Africans, Pakistanis, and Bangladeshis were three times more likely to have no earner in the family than white families;
- lower average earnings for those Caribbean, African, Pakistani, and Bangladeshi families that did have earnings, but higher average earnings for Indian and Chinese families than for white families (however, this advantage is reversed once qualifications and other characteristics are controlled for; Strategy Unit 2001: ch. 4);
- much higher proportions with relatively low net earnings for Caribbean and Pakistani and Bangladeshi families; and
- much higher dependence on means-tested benefits by Pakistani and Bangladeshi families.

2.1.5   *Disability*

The HBAI analysis shows that members of households where one or more members report disability are more likely than others to have low incomes: 25 per cent

---

[5] The definitions he used classify households as belonging to ethnic minorities if any person living there is non-white.

Table 2.3. *Poverty rates and the costs of disability, 1996–97, GB: Percentage of population in households with less than 60% of median income (after housing costs)*

	Unadjusted incomes (including disability benefits)	Income excluding benefits related to the extra costs of disability	Incomes adjusted for estimated additional costs of disability
Non-disabled	23.0	23.1	21.6
Disabled*	35.1	42.2	60.8
All	25.1	26.2	28.1

* Adults reporting an impairment (with OPCS score of 1 or more).
Source: Zaidi and Burchardt (2003: Table 11).

of households containing at least one disabled adult were in the poorest fifth in 2001–02, and 29 per cent of those containing a disabled child (DWP 2003*a*: Table 3.2, BHC). However, this calculation simply takes the total incomes of households with disabled members (including any benefits intended to compensate for the extra costs of disability) and compares those with the incomes of other households. There is a strong argument that, just as we adjust incomes for household size in trying to give a measure more representative of living standards, so we should for additional costs arising from disability (Berthoud, Lakey, and McKay 1993; Zaidi and Burchardt 2003). Doing so makes the position of disabled people substantially worse, as can be seen from Table 2.3. This compares poverty rates (against a standard of 60 per cent of median income, and in this case after deducting housing costs) in 1996–97 for individuals depending on whether they themselves report a disability (if an adult). On the standard methodology, 23 per cent of the non-disabled group were poor but 35 per cent of the disabled group. If we exclude benefits explicitly designed to compensate for extra costs from household income, the poverty rate for disabled adults rises to over 40 per cent. However, Zaidi and Burchardt's analysis suggests that such benefits do not fully achieve the objective of compensating for such costs. Using other indicators of standard of living, they calculate the additional costs implied by different reported levels of disability. The final column shows poverty rates after household incomes (including benefits) are adjusted for additional costs calculated in this way, suggesting that the poverty rate for disabled adults rises to over 60 per cent, compared with 22 per cent for others (some of whom live in households with a disabled member and so are also affected by the adjustment).

2.1.6 *Risks of Low Income*

If we put this kind of information together, the risks of particular groups of being in poverty vary considerably. Table 2.4 shows the groups identified by the HBAI

Table 2.4. *Groups at high risk of low income, 2001–02, GB (% of group below 60% of median income)*

	BHC	AHC
All	17	22
Unemployed	64	75
Other inactive	42	63
Workless, 60+	25	26
Only part-time work	25	33
Single parent	31	53
Single female pensioner	24	24
Children	21	30
Pakistani/Bangladeshi	55	63
Black non-Caribbean	29	45
'Other' (non-white) ethnicity	27	38
Black Caribbean	24	35
Disabled adult in household	24	29
Disabled child in household	23	33
Local authority tenant	34	48
Housing association tenant	28	52
Private tenant	19	40
Inner London	21	33

Note: Table lists groups in which risk of low income on either BHC or AHC basis is greater than one-third above average.

Source: DWP (2003a: Tables 3.5 and 3.6).

analysis as being at high risk (more than one-third above the average risk) of being poor, if a low-income threshold is used of 60 per cent of median income either before or after housing costs. Seventeen per cent of the whole population were poor on this basis in 2001–02 before housing costs, 22 per cent after allowing for housing costs. For most of the groups shown, poverty risk is significantly higher after housing costs: this partly reflects the way in which many are tenants receiving Housing Benefit, which boosts their BHC income, but all or most of which is then needed to cover the rent they pay. By contrast, some owner-occupiers, particularly older ones, can have relatively low housing costs.

Unemployment, or other economic inactivity, is clearly a strong driver: 64 per cent of workless households with an unemployed head or spouse are poor before housing costs, 75 per cent after them. Nearly a third of lone parents and their children are poor before housing costs, more than half after them. Nearly a quarter of female single pensioners are poor on either basis, and 30 per cent of all children were in poor households after housing costs. Overall, much higher proportions of minority ethnic groups were poor, including 24–35 per cent of Black Caribbean people, 27–38 per cent of 'other' non-white ethnic groups,

29–45 per cent of Black non-Caribbean people, and 55–63 per cent of Pakistanis and Bangladeshis. Disability and tenure are also strong factors. Even without any adjustment for the extra needs of households with disabled members, up to a third of them were classed as poor in the HBAI analysis. About half of social tenants were poor after allowing for housing costs, and two-fifths of private tenants. Finally, although poverty risks before housing costs do not vary enormously by region (from 12 per cent in the Eastern region to 21 per cent in Inner London), once they are allowed for one-third of Inner London households are classed as poor.

2.2   RECENT TRENDS IN INCOME DISTRIBUTION

2.2.1   *Changes in Income*

The idea that Britain has become a more unequal society has become so familiar to those looking at the UK income distribution that it is sometimes easy to forget how unusual the rapid growth in income inequality in the 1980s was. For instance, Figure 2.6 shows what happened between 1961 and 1979, based on analysis by Alissa Goodman and Steven Webb (1994), using the same methods as the official Households Below Average Income (HBAI) analysis described above. It shows how much real (after allowing for inflation) incomes changed over the period as a whole, dividing the population into tenths and then comparing the incomes of those in each successive tenth with those of their predecessors eighteen years earlier, both before and after deducting housing costs. The same individuals are not, of course, necessarily in the same part of the

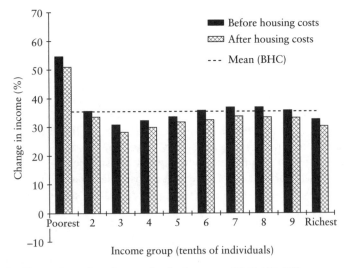

Figure 2.6. *Change in real net income by decile group, 1961–79, UK*
Source: Goodman and Webb (1994).

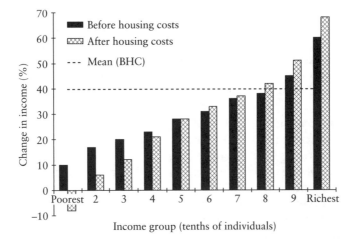

Figure 2.7. *Change in real net income by decile group, 1979 to 1994/95, UK*
Source: DSS (1997: Table A1) (including self-employed).

distribution at each date (as is discussed further in Chapter 5). Income growth shown is between the median incomes for each tenth (that is, the income of the person whose income puts him or her halfway up the group). The figure shows that over the 1960s and 1970s as a whole all income groups benefited from rising incomes, the lowest rising fastest. It was only after 1978 that this pattern broke down.

From 1979 results are available from the official HBAI series. These are available using data from the Family Expenditure Survey (FES) for the UK until 1994/95.[6] Since 1994–95 they have been based on the larger Family Resources Survey (FRS), with more detailed questions on incomes, but covering only Great Britain, thus not including Northern Ireland. The picture revealed by this analysis for the period from 1979 to 1994/95 shown in Figure 2.7 is a remarkable one. On average, real income grew by 40 per cent (BHC) or 42 per cent (AHC), that is, about 2 per cent per year. However, rates of growth were very different across the distribution. Incomes for the highest tenth rose by 60–68 per cent. At the median, incomes grew by about 30 per cent, and incomes for the poorest tenth rose by only 10 per cent before housing costs. After allowing for housing costs, incomes for the poorest tenth were 8 per cent lower in 1994/95 than in 1979. During this period council and housing association rents rose much more than general inflation. For tenants with the lowest incomes, Housing Benefit rose by the same amount. As this is included in income before housing costs, the perverse effect of a rent rise is to give someone receiving Housing Benefit living in exactly the same house a higher income. This effect is removed by looking at income

[6] '1994/95' refers here to the combination of the two financial years 1994–95 and 1995–96, with a mid-point in the Spring of 1995.

after housing costs, which argues for putting more weight on this measure when looking at trends in incomes at the bottom over this period. On the other hand, there are also problems which argue against sole reliance on the AHC measure as it excludes any increases in housing costs that actually correspond to improvements in housing quality and hence living standards. The best picture of what happened to living standards is likely to be somewhere between the two measures.

The more recent picture has been different again. Figure 2.8 shows the income growth for different parts of the distribution since the financial year 1994–95 from the most recent HBAI analysis (now for Great Britain rather than the UK as a whole). Over this eight-year period, growth in average living standards was quite rapid, particularly in the later years: 2.7 per cent per year before housing costs, 3.4 per cent after them. By and large, all income groups benefited in proportion, with the exception of the poorest tenth before housing costs, whose incomes grew by only about 13 per cent. After housing costs, the DWP estimates of growth for the poorest group are subject to particular uncertainty, and put in the range 21–33 per cent. The figure shows the mid-point (a little less than mean income growth AHC for the population as a whole). By contrast with the 1979 to 1994/95 period, proportionate income growth for the top tenth was virtually the same as the mean (although slightly faster than median income growth both BHC and AHC).

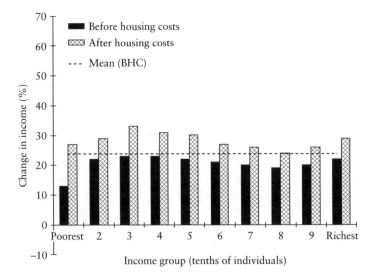

Figure 2.8. *Change in real net income by decile group, 1994–95 to 2002–03, GB*
Note: The AHC figure for the poorest tenth is the mid-point of the range (21–33%) given by DWP.
Source: DWP (2004: Table A1).

2.2.2 *Shares of Income*

Table 2.5 shows what these changes meant for the shares of income received by each tenth of the income distribution between 1979 and 2002–03 both before and after housing costs. In summary:

- Over the whole period, the share of all income received by the bottom half of the distribution fell from 33 to 27 per cent (BHC) and from 32 to 25 per cent (AHC).
- In the 1980s, the shares of both of the top two tenths rose, but in the 1990s only the share of the top tenth continued to rise. The share of the top tenth rose from 21 per cent of the total in 1979 to 28 per cent (BHC) or 29 per cent (AHC) in 2002–03. The top tenth now receives a greater share of total net income than the whole of the bottom half.
- The poorest tenth received only 3 per cent (BHC) or 2 per cent (AHC) in 1990/91, compared with 4 per cent in each case in 1979. Its share stayed roughly constant over the 1990s.

Given the growth in the real value of average incomes over the period, the increase in net income going to the top tenth between 1979 and 2002–03 represents

Table 2.5. *Distribution of income: HBAI series 1979 to 2002–03 (% share of total income received by successive tenths of individuals ranked by equivalent net income)*

	Poorest	2	3	4	5	6	7	8	9	Richest
(a) Before housing costs										
1979	4.3	5.7	6.6	7.6	8.5	9.5	10.7	12.2	14.2	20.6
1981	4.0	5.6	6.5	7.4	8.4	9.5	10.7	12.2	14.5	21.1
1987	3.6	5.0	5.9	6.9	8.0	9.1	10.4	12.2	14.9	24.2
1990/91	2.9	4.5	6	6	8	9	11	12	15	26
1994–95	3	5	6	6	8	9	10	12	15	26
1998–99	3	5	5	6	7	9	10	12	15	27
2002–03	3	5	5	7	7	9	10	12	14	28
(b) After housing costs										
1979	4.0	5.6	6.6	7.5	8.5	9.5	10.8	12.3	14.3	20.9
1981	3.7	5.4	6.3	7.3	8.3	9.5	10.7	12.3	14.7	21.8
1987	2.9	4.6	5.6	6.7	7.6	9.1	10.6	12.3	15.1	25.0
1990/91	2.1	4.1	5	7	7	10	10	12	16	27
1994–95	2	4	5	6	8	9	11	12	16	27
1998–99	2	4	5	6	7	9	11	12	15	29
2002–03	2	4	5	7	7	9	10	12	15	29

Sources: 1979–87: Jenkins and Cowell (1993). 1990/91: DSS (1993: Table A3) and Hansard, HC, vol. 228, cols. 215–16 (8 July 1993). 1994–95 to 2002–03: DWP (2004: Table A3). The figures up to 1990/91 are from the FES (for the UK); subsequent ones from the FRS (for GB). FES-based figures for 1994/95 (averaging two financial years) are virtually identical to those shown in the table for 1994–95.

about 40 per cent of the total growth in real incomes. In other words, for every £100 in additional net real income over the 23-year period for the population as a whole, £40 of this went to the richest tenth.

2.2.3   *Trends in Overall Income Inequality*

The extent to which the period after the late 1970s broke with the rest of the post-war period can be seen from the overall trends illustrated in Figure 2.9. This shows the values of one summary index of income distribution, the 'Gini coefficient'. This takes a value of zero for a completely equal distribution and 100 per cent if one person has all the income and the rest none.[7] The figure shows its value from three different series. The definitions of income used in each vary, so that the levels of inequality shown are not directly comparable (and so the 'Blue Book' series is plotted against a different scale from the other two). However, as can be seen from the overlapping periods, the trends are consistent:

- The oldest, Blue Book, series (for distribution between 'tax units'—couples or single people over the period shown) is based mainly on tax records, and does not adjust for household size. If one allows for a change in definitions in the mid-1970s, it shows inequality in after-tax incomes rising slowly between 1949 and 1964, then falling rather unevenly to a low point in 1975–76 and 1976–77, nearly five percentage points below its maximum. By the final year of the series, 1984–85, however, the increase in the index was already almost enough to take it back to its 1949 level.
- The *Economic Trends* series (for distribution between households) shows a ten percentage point increase between 1978 and its maximum in 1990. By the mid-1990s, it had fallen back by three percentage points, but it then grew again to equal its all-time high in 2001–02. The most recent figure, for 2002–03, shows a sharp drop back to the position of the mid-1990s.
- The *Economic Trends* series is unsatisfactory in some ways.[8] The third series, produced by the Institute for Fiscal Studies (IFS), has the advantages that it shows income distribution between individuals, and uses the HBAI methodology and sources explained in Section 2.1. As with the Blue Book series, this index fell to a minimum in 1977, clearly below the level of the early 1960s.

[7]   There are many different ways of measuring income inequality, of which the Gini coefficient is only one. The Gini coefficient is calculated by ranking the population in order of income, and then drawing a line (a 'Lorenz curve') showing the cumulative share of total income going to successive proportions of the population from the bottom (for example, going to the bottom 10 per cent, or the bottom 20 per cent). If income distribution were equal, this would produce a straight line running at 45 degrees from the horizontal. The Gini coefficient measures how far the actual Lorenz curve falls below this as compared with the extreme case, where virtually everyone has no income—so the 'bottom 99 per cent' would have nothing, and the richest person would have all of the income. See Atkinson (1975) or Cowell (1995) for detailed discussion of this and other inequality measures.

[8]   It gives all households an equal weight rather than each individual, as in the IFS/HBAI series. It is also rounded to the nearest percentage point, which can exaggerate year-to-year changes. Unlike the IFS/HBAI series, it does not allow for changes at the very top of the distribution.

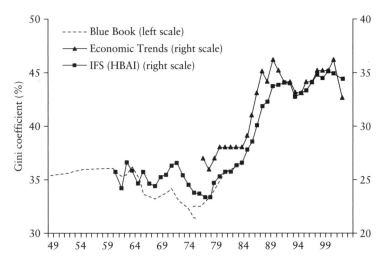

Figure 2.9. *Trends in income inequality, 1949 to 2002–03*

Sources: Blue Book series from Atkinson and Micklewright (1992); *Economic Trends* series from Lakin (2004: Table 27, Appendix 1) and earlier equivalents; IFS (HBAI) series from Clark and Taylor (1999) and Brewer et al. (2004: Figure 2.9) (before housing costs).

Like the *Economic Trends* series, it then rose by more than ten percentage points—an increase twice as big as the previous fall—by 1993. As other indicators show, there was then a short-lived reduction in inequality before it rose again in the second half of the 1990s, in this case reaching an all-time high in 2000–01, from which it had fallen slightly by 2002–03.

These figures tell a consistent story. Incomes became more equally distributed between the mid-1960s and mid-1970s. After the late 1970s, they became more unequal, with particularly rapid increases in inequality in the late 1980s. The increase in inequality in this period was more than twice the scale of the preceding fall, so that income inequality in the early 1990s was much greater than it had been for forty years from the late 1940s. There was a drop in inequality in the mid-1990s (reflecting some real income growth at the bottom at a time when average and higher incomes were growing very slowly in real terms). But after 1995–96, overall income inequality rose again and, depending on the measure used, it at least equalled, if not exceeded, its post-war high by the start of the twenty-first century. The very latest figures for 2002–03 suggest a fall from this, but it is too early to tell whether this will be a sustained trend.

2.2.4 *Incomes at the Very Top*

For much of the post-war period, all measures of income distribution tell the same story, whichever index is chosen. This is particularly true of the great increase in UK inequality in the 1980s: the poor fell behind the middle; the middle fell behind the top; and the top fell behind the very top. As a result, the movements in the numbers with relatively low incomes examined in Chapter 3 mirror those in overall inequality shown in Figure 2.9. As inequality soared, so did relative poverty.

The period since 1998–99 has been a little different. Here the statistics show a slight fall in relative poverty and a significant one in child poverty (see Figures 3.1 and 3.2). At the same time, those in Figure 2.9 show a rise in overall inequality as measured by the Gini coefficient—in shorthand, the gap between rich and poor. A clue to what was happening is given in Table 2.5, which shows the share of the top tenth rising after 1994–95. Unlike the pattern of the 1980s, the most recent period seems to be marked by the poor catching up on the middle to some extent, but the top moving away from the middle.[9] By analogy, one can think of the income distribution as being shaped a little like an onion (seen on its side in Figure 2.1). In the most recent period, the bottom has been squeezed up towards the bulge in the middle where the incomes of most people can be found. But, at the same time, the top of the onion has continued to stretch away from the middle.

Quite how far this stretching process has gone can be seen in the results of a remarkable piece of detective work by Tony Atkinson and colleagues using data drawn from records of income tax (and its predecessors) for the whole of the twentieth century, some results of which are shown in Table 2.6. This shows the proportion of total personal income net of income tax that was going to various groups of the population right at the top of the distribution. By contrast with the data shown so far, the figures are unadjusted for family size, and since 1990 relate to individual income (reflecting the introduction of separate taxation for husbands and wives). They also do not allow for National Insurance Contributions. Together, these factors lead to higher measured inequality. Thus, the top 10 per cent of 'tax units' in 1999 are shown as having 36 per cent of after-tax income in Table 2.6, compared with the 29 per cent share of equivalized net income for the top 10 per cent of individuals shown in Table 2.5.[10] However, the trends are consistent: the increase in the share of the top 10 per cent from the tax records between 1979 and 1999 is 10.1 percentage points, or 7.5 percentage points if the whole of the change between 1989 and 1990 is assumed to be caused by the change in definitions. The equivalent change shown in the HBAI series in Table 2.5 is eight percentage points.

These figures are based on tax records. Particularly when the top rates of income tax were very high indeed (over 90 per cent from the 1940s up to 1979), the very rich with good accountants would have had little trouble in converting

[9] This also explains why recent falls in relative poverty have been faster when measured against 60 per cent of median income than when measured against 50 per cent of mean income.
[10] Note that the HBAI analysis (and figures derived from it) takes account of income tax data for the top 1 per cent of the distribution (through what is known as the 'SPI adjustment', as it uses the Inland Revenue's Survey of Personal Incomes based on tax records, so the series shown in Tables 2.5 and 2.6 are consistent in the income data used for the very top of the distribution.

Table 2.6. *Income shares (%) of the highest income tax payers (after income tax), 1937–1999, UK*

	Top 0.05%	Next 0.05%	Top 0.1%	Next 0.4%	Top 0.5%	Next 0.5%	Top 1%	Next 9%	Top 10%
1937	2.37	1.28	3.65	5.4	9.0	3.6	12.6	23.1	35.6
1949	0.68	0.55	1.23	2.9	4.2	2.6	6.8	22.0	28.8
1954	0.53	0.44	0.97	2.4	3.4	2.3	5.7	20.9	26.6
1959	0.54	0.45	0.95	2.4	3.3	2.2	5.5	20.4	25.9
1964	0.57	0.45	1.02	2.5	3.5	2.2	5.7	20.4	26.1
1969	0.44	0.37	0.81	2.2	3.0	2.0	5.0	20.0	25.1
1974	0.39	0.30	0.69	1.8	2.5	1.8	4.4	20.4	24.8
1979	0.53	0.33	0.86	1.9	2.8	1.9	4.7	21.5	26.2
1984	0.67	0.43	1.10	2.3	3.4	2.2	5.6	24.0	29.6
1989	1.13*	0.70*	1.81	2.9	4.7	2.5	7.1	24.2	31.3
1990	NA	NA	2.21	3.2	5.4	2.6	8.0	25.9	33.9
1993	1.61	0.76	2.37	3.4	5.8	2.7	8.5	26.5	34.9
1997	2.41	0.87	3.28	3.6	6.9	2.9	9.8	25.5	35.2
1999	n/a	n/a	n/a	n/a	7.2	2.9	10.2	26.1	36.3

Note: Figures are based on the shares of different groups of 'tax units' (as proportions of total population of potential tax units). There are two discontinuities in the series: income definitions changed slightly after 1974, and until 1989 married couples counted as one tax unit; since 1990 husbands and wives have been taxed separately and count as separate units. Figures may not add up due to rounding.

* 1988 figures.

Source: Atkinson and Salverda (2003: Table 3UK), based on Inland Revenue Survey of Personal Incomes data.

significant parts of their investment incomes into more lightly taxed capital gains, which would not show up in these figures (a feature that would affect earlier statistics as well, of course). On the other hand, in the last two decades other forms of tax avoidance—such as share option schemes or offshore accounts—have become more popular for the highest-paid top executives, and this will have offset at least part of any tendency for a bigger fraction of total income of the very rich to end up subject to tax and captured by the statistics.

If such caveats are borne in mind, the table shows a startling pattern. Figures on an after-tax basis are available only since 1937. If we look at pre-tax incomes, before the First World War data on 'super tax' suggested that the top 0.05 per cent of the population—sometimes known as 'the top ten thousand'—received more than 8 per cent of total *pre-tax* personal incomes, and the top 0.1 per cent more than 11 per cent of the total (Atkinson and Salverda 2003: Table 2UK). By 1920 these shares had fallen to 6 and 8 per cent respectively, and by 1937 to 4.8 and 6.6 per cent. The equalizing effects of income tax can be seen in Table 2.6: the after-tax share of the top 0.05 per cent in 1937 was 2.4 per cent, while the top 0.1 per cent received 3.7 per cent.

The table shows the rapid fall in the shares of all parts of the top 10 per cent, particularly the top 0.1 per cent, between 1937 and 1949, and its continued fall until 1974. Since then, the story has gone into reverse. If we allow for the change in definitions, the detailed figures show that the shares of the highest groups started growing after 1976 and rapidly after 1978. The increases are striking, and show the extent to which the gains of the top 10 per cent discussed earlier are accounted for by the highest groups. For instance, the share of the top 1 per cent rose by 5.5 percentage points between 1979 and 1999 (4.6 per cent if the change between 1989 and 1990 is discounted), accounting for more than half of the increase in the share of the top 10 per cent. Within this, the majority was actually accounted for by the top 0.5 per cent, whose share of the total more than doubled, rising by 4.4 percentage points (or 3.7 points if the 1989 to 1990 change is discounted). The 0.05 per cent at the very top had by 1997 restored their share to what it had been just before the Second World War. As Atkinson (2002a: 38) summarizes, 'Since 1979, we have seen a reversal [in the declining share of top incomes], with shares of the top income groups returning to their position of fifty years earlier. The equalisation of the post-war period has been lost'.

The implication of the changing shares of after-tax income shown in Table 2.6 is that about a sixth, 17 per cent, of the whole national increase in real after-tax income between 1979 and 1999 went to the top 1 per cent; about 13 per cent went to the top half of 1 per cent.[11] Based on the figures up to 1997, around one pound out of every twenty of the national increase went to the top one-thousandth of taxpayers.

2.3   INTERNATIONAL COMPARISONS OF INCOME INEQUALITY

The growth in income inequality in Britain in the 1980s was exceptional not only in British historical terms but also internationally. The ten percentage point increase in the Gini coefficient between the late 1970s and early 1990s seen in Figure 2.9 corresponds to traversing two-thirds of the international range of income inequality between the most equal Scandinavian countries and the USA. Only New Zealand in the second half of the 1980s had inequality growing as rapidly as the UK did from 1977 to 1990, and this was for a shorter period (Barclay 1995: Figure 2). Figure 2.10 shows more recent data on trends in income inequality in different countries (from the EU and other major industrialized countries) between the mid-1980s and mid-1990s, drawn up on a comparable basis by the Luxembourg Income Study (LIS). By the mid-1990s, inequality in the United Kingdom was greater than in any other country shown,

---

[11] The growth of real household disposable income per capita (61 per cent) between 1979 and 1999 is used as an approximation for the growth in after-tax personal incomes, and it is conservatively assumed that all of the change in shares between 1989 and 1990 was due to the change in definitions.

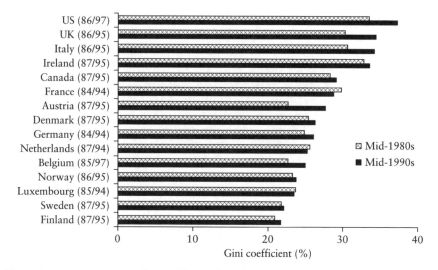

Figure 2.10. *Income inequality in fifteen selected countries in mid-1980s and mid-1990s*
Source: Luxembourg Income Study. www.lisproject.org, 9 June 2003.

apart from the United States.[12] Furthermore, the four percentage point increase in inequality shown in Figure 2.9 for the UK over this period was exceeded only by Austria (from a lower base) and was approached only by Italy and the USA.

Figure 2.10 suggests that rapidly rising income inequality has not been a uniform global phenomenon. It is true that over this period inequality fell in only three of the fifteen countries shown, but in a further six of them the increase in the Gini coefficient was less than one percentage point (and only 1.2 for Germany) over a period of eight to ten years. In a detailed examination of data for nine countries for which year-to-year changes can be distinguished, Atkinson (2003: Table 1) looks at the evidence for three claims about what has been happening to income distribution globally:

- that income distribution has not been constant ('non-glacial change');
- that there is a U-shaped pattern, with inequality falling after the Second World War but recently rising; and
- that income distribution continues to widen.

As might be suspected from Figure 2.10, Atkinson does not find the second and third suggestions—influenced by US and UK experiences in the 1980s and 1990s—confirmed. It is true that eight of the nine countries have experienced significant changes in income distribution (Canada has been more marginal), but the patterns are not universal. The UK, Finland, and the Netherlands do all

[12] Since the LIS analysis uses some different definitions (notably a different way of adjusting for household size) from those used by the HBAI analysis, the figures for the UK in Figure 2.10 are slightly lower than those given in the HBAI/IFS series in Figure 2.9, but the trends are the same.

show evidence of a decline in inequality followed by a rise, as does the USA if the Kennedy-Johnson years in the 1960s are treated as a decline, but for the other five countries there is no clear pattern of this kind. Only in Norway, Finland, and Italy is the most recent pattern one of a significant rise, although there has been a modest rise in the 1990s in the USA, Canada, and West Germany. Right at the top the dramatic increase in the share of the top 1 per cent since the early 1980s shown for the UK in Table 2.6 has also been seen in Canada and (even more dramatically) in the USA. But it has not occurred in France or the Netherlands (Atkinson 2003: Figure 10). In Chapter 4 we examine explanations for the rapid growth of income inequality and relative poverty in the UK; the lack of a consistent international picture revealed by Atkinson's analysis and suggested by Figure 2.10 is an important part of the evidence on possible causes.

2.4   DISTRIBUTION OF WEALTH

This chapter concentrates on the distribution of income—the annual flow of resources to individuals and families. There is not the space to discuss in detail the distribution of wealth—the stock of assets over which people have command.[13] However, it is interesting to compare the levels and trends in income inequality discussed above with some comparable data for the distribution of wealth. Table 2.7 shows long-term trends in the distribution of wealth with the use of one definition, for 'marketable wealth'. This series does not include, for instance, the value of people's accrued pension rights, from either private or public sector. Adding those in would give a rather more equal distribution (Hills 1995: Figure 52).

The most striking thing about the table is quite how unequal the distribution of wealth is. Even without the impact of inheritance or of differential savings rates between richer and poorer people, one would expect wealth to be significantly less equally distributed than income, if only for life cycle reasons: people tend to build up their assets during their working lives and to run them down in retirement. But the degree of inequality is greater than could be explained like this. For instance, earlier tables have suggested that the top 10 per cent of individuals received 28–9 per cent of net income in 2001–02. The top 10 per cent of holders of all marketable wealth in 2001 accounted for twice this proportion: 56 per cent. The data in Table 2.6 suggest that the top 1 per cent of taxpayers received 10 per cent of after-tax income in 1999. By 2001, the top 1 per cent owned 23 per cent of marketable wealth. To summarize the distribution, the Gini coefficient for the distribution of wealth in the table, now 70 per cent, is far higher than that of net incomes, twice the figure for incomes using HBAI definitions shown in Figure 2.9.

The trends shown in the table also differ from those seen above for incomes. Between the 1920s and the 1970s, the figures suggest, like those for incomes,

---

[13] For discussion of the distribution of wealth, see Atkinson and Harrison (1978), Hills (1995: ch. 7), and Banks, Blundell, and Smith (2000).

Table 2.7. *Long-term trends in the distribution of marketable wealth*

	Share of:			Gini Coefficient (%)
	Top 1%	Top 5%	Top 10%	
(a) England and Wales				
1923	61	82	89	—
1930	58	79	87	—
1938	55	77	85	—
(b) Great Britain				
1950	47	74	—	—
1955	44	71	—	—
1961	37	61	72	—
1966	31	56	70	—
1971	29	53	68	—
1976	25	49	65	—
1981	23	46	63	—
(c) United Kingdom				
1976	21	38	50	66
1981	18	36	50	65
1986	18	36	50	64
1991	17	35	47	64
1996	20	40	52	68
2001	23	43	56	70

Sources: (a) Atkinson and Harrison (1978: Table 6.5). (b) Atkinson, Gordon, and Harrison (1986: Table 1). Break in series between 1955 and 1961. (c) Inland Revenue (2003a: Table 13.5).

a trend towards greater equality. In contrast to incomes, however, there continued to be a slow move towards a more equal distribution up to the early 1980s. This was followed by a period when the distribution hardly changed at all, lasting up to the mid-1990s. Indeed, as late as 1995 the Gini coefficient for this series was 65 per cent, compared with 66 per cent nearly twenty years before in 1976, when the series begins. This contrasts with the rapid growth in income inequality at the time. But since then there has been a dramatic increase in the inequality of wealth, at a time when the distribution of income has been more stable. For instance, by 1999 the top 1 per cent had increased their share to 23 per cent of the total, from 17 per cent in 1991. This share, equalled in 2001, is the highest since the UK series began in 1976. If we allow for the change in definitions between the GB and UK series, the shares of the most wealthy groups shown in the table for 2001 are probably as high as they were thirty years before, at the start of the 1970s.

It is interesting to speculate on the reasons for this difference in trends. In a sense, wealth represents 'congealed income', so it is perhaps unsurprising for its inequality to lag behind that of income. It took a while for the increased income inequality of the 1980s to show up in the wealth distribution. With income inequality still at a higher level than before, the effects are still feeding into the wealth distribution. Other factors matter too: the effects of the stock market boom in the late 1990s and the continuing rise in house prices. Changes in the taxation of capital will also have had an effect, with, for instance, a move from what used to be higher rates of tax on investment income than on earnings to the opposite between the 1970s and the 1990s. There have also been much lower rates of tax on large inheritances since the mid-1980s than there were (in theory, at least) in the preceding four decades. On the other hand, capital taxes as whole represented no lower a share of total tax revenue in 1996–97 than they had in 1978–79, and their share had increased by 2002–03 (see Table 7.2).

2.5   PUBLIC ATTITUDES TO INEQUALITY

As income inequality has grown, so has the proportion of the population, as found by the British Social Attitudes survey, saying that, 'the gap between those with high incomes and those with low incomes is too large'. Figure 2.11 shows the percentage who said they agreed with this proposition plotted alongside one of the measures of the inequality of overall income distribution shown in Figure 2.9. Very large numbers say the gap is too large. As inequality grew in the 1980s and early 1990s, so did the numbers saying that the gap was too great,

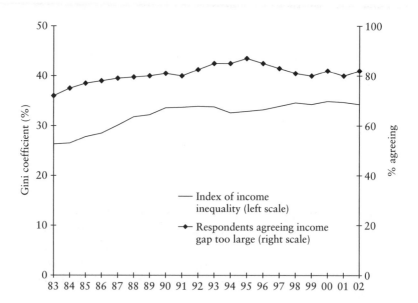

Figure 2.11. *Inequality and attitudes to the gap between rich and poor, 1983–2002, GB*

Sources: British Social Attitudes survey; Clark and Taylor (1999) and Brewer et al. (2004) (see notes to Figure 2.9).

peaking at 87 per cent in 1995. After inequality levelled out in the mid-1990s, the numbers concerned about the gap fell back slightly, but have remained at 80 per cent or more. On a related question, Catherine Bromley (2003: Figure 4.2) shows that the proportion agreeing that 'ordinary people do not get their fair share of the nation's wealth' was somewhat smaller at around two-thirds between 1986 and 1996, in this case falling slightly but remaining at 60 per cent or more between 1999 and 2002.

This concern about inequality extends across social and economic groups. Table 2.8 shows more details of responses to the question about the gap between high and low incomes, in this case from the 2002 BSA survey. There are relatively small differences between groups based on gross household income. While twice as many of those in the highest quarter thought that the gap was 'about right' as in the other groups, this was still only a fifth of them, with three-quarters saying it was too large (very few of any group say the gap is too small). Among those who identify with the Conservative Party, about a quarter thought it was 'about right', but even in this group more than seven out of ten thought that the income gap was too large.

Two other BSA questions show continuing hostility to income inequality over the last decade or more. In 1999, 54 per cent of respondents rejected the idea that 'large differences in income are necessary for Britain's prosperity' and only 17 per cent agreed, down from 26 per cent in 1987 (Jowell et al. 2000: 324; Bromley 2003: Table 4.1). Correspondingly, in 1999, 58 per cent agreed that, 'inequality continues to exist because it benefits the rich and powerful', as many as in 1987, and only 14 per cent disagreed.

Table 2.8. *Views of the gap between high and low incomes in Britain, by income and party identification, 2002, GB (%)*

	Too large	About right	Base
All	82	13	1,148
Gross household income:			
£38,000 and over	74	22	275
£20,000–37,999	86	11	236
£10,000–19,999	87	9	290
Under £10,000	84	7	233
Party identification:			
Labour	88	7	444
Liberal Democrat	84	16	137
Conservative	71	25	284
None	81	12	170

Source: Bromley (2003: Tables 4.2 and 4.3), based on British Social Attitudes survey.

Table 2.9. *Perceptions of annual earnings before tax, 1999, GB*

	What people think cases usually earn (median response)	What people think they *should* earn (median response)	Actual average earnings
Shop assistant	£9,000	£12,000	£10,300
Unskilled factory worker	£10,000	£12,000	£13,100
Skilled factory worker	£15,000	£18,000	£18,000
Doctor in general practice	£35,000	£40,000	£50,800
Solicitor	£50,000	£40,000	£37,900
Owner-manager of large factory	£60,000	£50,000	n/a
Cabinet minister	£60,000	£45,000	£94,200[a]
Appeal court judge	£80,000	£50,000	£139,900
Chairman of large national corporation	£125,000	£75,000	£555,000[b]
'Someone in your occupation'	£15,000	£18,000	£17,600[c]

[a] Amount actually drawn. 'Entitlement' was £111,300.

[b] Figure for 2000 base pay for chairmen, managing directors, and chief executives of UK FTSE 100 companies. Bonuses, incentives, and share options would more than double this.

[c] Median earnings for all full-time workers.

Sources: British Social Attitudes survey (Jowell et al. 2000: 325), based on 819 responses. Actual average earnings (men and women full-time) from ONS (1999) and Review Body on Senior Salaries (2000, 2001).

Another piece of evidence is in Table 2.9, showing how much respondents to the 1999 BSA survey thought that those in particular occupations earned before tax.[14] It also shows what they thought people in those occupations should earn. The responses are consistent with a general desire for more equality of earnings than people think there actually is: the median response is that the lower-paid jobs should be paid more and the higher-paid ones less (with the exception of family doctors, who were believed to be underpaid). Bromley (2003: 85) shows that the responses to this kind of question in 1987 and 1992 showed similar results: '. . . in each year, people saw the size of the gap between the highest- and the lowest-paid occupations as *twice* the size they thought would be appropriate.'

People do not seem to have become more accepting of earnings inequality since the 1980s. It should be noted, however, that both the perceived and the pre-ferred size of the gap has increased somewhat. People thought a chairman of a corporation was paid ten times as much as an unskilled worker in 1987, but

---

[14] The occupations are ranked in terms of these perceptions in the table, but the survey asked about them in a more random order.

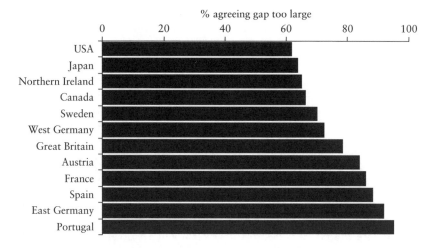

Figure 2.12. *International views of income gap, 1999*
Source: International Social Survey Programme *Social Inequalities III* survey dataset (1999).

ought to be paid only five times as much. In 1999 they thought the ratio was 12.5 to one, but ought to be just over six to one. The preferred ratio did grow over the period but, as we shall see in Chapter 4, by only a fraction of the actual increase in the gap between high and low pay.

As we saw at the start of the chapter, people's perceptions of income distribution are not necessarily very accurate. The last column of Table 2.9 shows how much average earnings actually were (for men and women combined) in each occupation in 1999. In reality, the higher-paid jobs (apart from solicitors) were paid a great deal more than the median respondent thought.[15] People greatly underestimate the extent of inequality between the earnings of particular occupations, but still think that the gap between rich and poor is too great.

Finally, some of these views in Britain can be compared with those in other countries. Of the countries shown in Figure 2.12, Great Britain was in the group where more than three-quarters said that the gap between rich and poor was too large. This was significantly more than agreed in the USA or Japan, although even there the majority agreed as well. It was a smaller proportion than in southern or eastern European countries (including some other countries not shown here), where up to 90 per cent or more agreed.

Data from the regular international survey, the World Values Survey from 1997–99, confirms the greater desire in the UK than in many comparable countries for a more equal distribution of income than there is now. Respondents were asked to put their views on a scale of 1 to 10, with 1 representing greatest

[15] As we saw at the start of the chapter, they nonetheless overstate the proportion that has quite high earnings (over £40,000 in 2001).

agreement with the statement 'incomes should be made more equal', and 10 greatest agreement with the statement 'we need larger income differences as incentives for individual effort'. In Britain, 29 per cent put themselves at the egalitarian end (score of 1 to 3) and 20 per cent at the incentives end of the scale (score of 8 to 10). The mean score was 4.9. Only Finland and what was East Germany had a lower mean score than Britain, while those in other industrialized countries were higher, including Norway and West Germany (both 5.3), Spain (5.4), the USA (5.5), Japan and Australia (5.6), and Sweden (5.8). Intriguingly, only 16 per cent of Swedes put themselves in the three most egalitarian categories, compared with 43 per cent of Finns, reflecting rather different views of the similar low levels of inequality they both have at present (Figure 2.10). At the other end of the inequality scale, people in Britain appear much less content with high inequality than those in the USA. Chapter 8 examines opinions of what should be done about the gap, particularly whether these concerns about inequality are linked to a desire for government to do more to redistribute income between rich and poor.

2.6   SUMMARY

Composition of the Income Distribution

- Three-quarters of lone parents and their children are in the poorest 40 per cent of the income distribution. Pensioners are also disproportionately in the poorest groups. Couples without children are most likely to be at the top.
- Nearly half the richest fifth are single full-time workers or couples both working full-time. Nearly two-thirds of the poorest fifth come from groups without earnings, but more than a third of the poorest fifth do have earnings.
- In 2001–02, 70 per cent of those in social housing were in the poorest two-fifths, compared with under half in 1979. However, between 40 and 50 per cent of the poorest fifth were owner-occupiers, depending on whether housing costs are allowed for.
- Households with disabled members were more likely than others to be poor, even before the additional costs facing disabled people are allowed for. After such costs are allowed for, disabled adults were nearly three times as likely as others to be poor.
- Those from ethnic minority households were 8.6 per cent of the population, but 15 per cent of the poorest fifth. Sixty per cent of people in Pakistani and Bangladeshi households were in the poorest fifth.

Recent Trends In Distribution

- From 1961 to 1979, incomes for all parts of the income distribution rose, the lowest fastest. From 1979 to 1994/95, real incomes rose by 40 per cent on average but by over 60 per cent for the richest tenth. For the poorest tenth they only rose by 10 per cent (before housing costs) or fell by 8 per cent (after housing costs). Since then, the picture has been more mixed, with most income groups benefiting from quite rapid growth in living standards, apart from slower growth for the poorest tenth before housing costs are allowed for.

- By 2002–03 the top tenth received a greater share of total income than the whole of the bottom half. About 40 per cent of the total increase in real net incomes between 1979 and 2002–03 went to the top tenth. If we look at the very top, about 17 per cent of the increase in after-tax incomes between 1979 and 1999 went to the top 1 per cent; about 13 per cent went to the top half per cent.

- Even with the more varied pattern of the 1990s, overall income inequality was greater at the start of the twenty-first century than at any time in the fifty years from the late 1940s.

- Britain's inequality growth was exceptional internationally. Between the late 1970s and early 1990s Britain traversed two-thirds of the range between the more equal Scandinavian countries and the USA. By the mid-1990s, among fifteen industrialized countries only the USA had a higher level of overall income inequality.

- Wealth is much more unequally distributed than incomes. After two decades of stability, the wealth distribution became sharply more unequal after 1995. By 2001, the shares of the top 1 per cent and top 10 per cent appeared to be as great as at any time since the early 1970s.

- More than four-fifths of the British population say that the gap between those with high incomes and those with low incomes is too large. Such concerns became more widespread as inequality grew between the 1980s and 1990s. They are stronger in the UK than in several other countries, particularly than in the USA. They are strong even though highly paid professions are thought to receive considerably less than they actually do.

FURTHER READING

The key official source published annually by the Department for Work and Pensions is *Households Below Average Income: An Analysis of the Income Distribution*, which is now the main current source for statistics on the UK income distribution (www.dwp.gov.uk/asd/hbai.asp).

Two books examining the changes in distribution of income in the UK up to the mid-1990s are *New Inequalities: The Changing Distribution of Income and Wealth in the UK*, edited by John Hills (Cambridge University Press, 1996); and *Inequality in the UK*, by Alissa Goodman, Paul Johnson, and Steven Webb (Oxford University Press, 1997). A summary of the more recent period can be found in *Poverty and Inequality in Britain: 2004* by Mike Brewer, Alissa Goodman, Michal Myck, Jonathan Shaw, and Andrew Shepherd (Institute for Fiscal Studies, 2004).

A comprehensive discussion of the strengths and weaknesses of different measures of income distribution and other indicators of social cohesion, particularly for international comparisons, is *Social Indicators: The EU and Social Inclusion*, by Tony Atkinson, Bea Cantillon, Eric Marlier, and Brian Nolan (Oxford University Press, 2002).

If readers would like to find their own place in the UK income distribution calculated in the way described in Section 2.1, the Institute for Fiscal Studies has an interactive model at www.ifs.org.uk/wheredoyoufitin/.

3

Poverty, Deprivation, and Exclusion

3.1 POVERTY AND DEPRIVATION: HOW CAN WE MEASURE THEM?

How do we measure poverty? When Tony Blair startled the audience at his March 1999 Beveridge lecture by pledging to eliminate child poverty over twenty years (Walker 1999), he may have been under the impression that there was an obvious way of knowing whether 'child poverty' had been eliminated, and how much progress was being made towards that goal. But it took nearly five years for the Department for Work and Pensions (DWP) to produce its final proposals for measuring progress (DWP 2003e), following consultation with representative groups and a battery of opinions from academics and analysts. There are many choices and little consensus (for a survey, see Alcock 1997). Definitions used in academic attempts to measure its extent over the last century have included the following:

- *Subjective assessment by the researcher.* In his study of poverty in York published in 1899, Seebohm Rowntree (1901) asked his investigators to say whether people were 'living in obvious want and squalor', and used these counts to give the overall numbers living in poverty.
- *Budget standards.* At the same time, Rowntree also established a 'primary poverty line', based on the amount of income needed to purchase an austere basket of goods—'the minimum necessaries for the maintenance of merely physical efficiency'—such as the food which was required to meet nutritional standards, set after consultation with scientific experts. The idea was that it would be impossible to argue that people with income below the primary poverty line could avoid 'want and squalor', however efficiently they husbanded their resources. They were then in 'primary poverty'. The others classified as poor were in 'secondary poverty', possibly as a result of 'wasteful' spending (such as on drink or gambling) or simply because the minimal primary poverty line had, in fact, been set too low. In his later work in the 1930s, he dropped the 'obvious want and squalor' criterion as too subjective and expanded his budget-standards approach to calculate the income needed to meet the 'human needs of labour' (which went beyond purely physical needs). Some countries use a 'minimum income standard' based on this kind of budget standards approach to produce official counts of poverty (Veit-Wilson 1998).

- *Social security standards.* In their classic study *The Poor and the Poorest*, Brian Abel-Smith and Peter Townsend (1965) used national data from the Family Expenditure Survey to compare household incomes and spending with the minimum that was supposed to be guaranteed by the National Assistance (now Income Support) system. As well as the basic National Assistance rates, claimants could then get extra payments for exceptional needs, and were allowed to keep some earnings without benefit being cut. Allowing for such extras, Abel-Smith and Townsend argued that anyone with an income below 140 per cent of the basic National Assistance rates was poor by official standards. Official measures of the number of 'low income families' based on this approach were published up to the 1980s (with those between 100 and 140 per cent of the scale rates sometimes described as 'on the margins of poverty').

- *Relative income measures.* A problem with the social security standards approach is that, if the system is made more generous, more people are counted as poor (or fewer, if rates become meaner). To avoid this, the then Department of Social Security started in the 1980s to publish measures based on the shape of the income distribution in its Households Below Average Income (HBAI) series (see Section 3.2 for findings from it). Such figures include, for instance, the numbers with less than half of that year's average income or, as is more commonly now used for official purposes, with less than 60 per cent of median income.[1] These are examples of 'relative poverty' measures, as the poverty line moves with contemporary income levels.

- *Real income measures.* The HBAI statistics also give the numbers with incomes below proportions of the average at some earlier date, adjusted simply for price inflation. Such measures are sometimes described as 'absolute poverty' measures, as they show the numbers below a fixed line that is not based on contemporary incomes or living standards.[2] The official poverty line in the USA is of this kind, based originally on spending patterns in the 1960s and adjusted from year to year simply for price inflation.[3] The European Union uses both relative and real income measures of the 'risk of financial poverty' as part of its comparison of progress between countries in achieving social cohesion (Atkinson et al. 2002).

---

[1] As explained in Chapter 2, the median income is that of someone exactly half way up the income distribution between rich and poor, as opposed to the usual 'average' (mean) income, which divides the total income of the population by the number of people in it. During the 1990s, poverty lines based on 50 per cent of the mean and 60 per cent of the median had very similar values. By 2001–02, the median had fallen to 81 per cent of the mean (Table 2.2), and so 60 per cent of the median was slightly below 50 per cent of the mean.

[2] However, this terminology risks confusion with the notion of 'absolute poverty' as used in United Nations debates, for instance, referring to severe deprivation in relation to basic needs (Gordon et al. 2000: 9).

[3] It might be noted, though, that median US incomes rose very little between the mid-1970s and the mid-1990s, so for a long period the US poverty line did not move far from what a relative standard would have produced.

- *Participation standards.* While robust figures can be produced using the approaches based on incomes, and they give very useful information on trends over time and comparisons between countries, it is hard to escape a degree of arbitrariness: why set the line at, say, 60 per cent of median income, not 55 per cent or 65 per cent? In his monumental study *Poverty in the United Kingdom*, Peter Townsend (1979) pioneered an alternative approach, looking at people who were deprived in the sense of lacking the items or activities that he regarded as necessary for participation in normal activities and consumption. He also argued that below a certain income level—a 'threshold of deprivation'—the number of items people lacked accelerated and that this could be used to measure poverty 'objectively', based on concepts of relative deprivation.
- *Consensual deprivation measures.* The items in such lists of 'necessities' are, however, set by the researcher, and so open to challenge as based simply on the researcher's opinion. To get round this, in their work for a 1980s television documentary series *Breadline Britain*, Joanna Mack and Stewart Lansley (1985) carried out a national survey asking a sample of the population as a whole what they saw as 'necessities'. They then counted as poor respondents who reported that they lacked three or more items that the majority of the population regarded as 'necessities' (because they could not afford them rather than because they did not want them).[4] Two subsequent surveys have generated comparable data, including the Poverty and Social Exclusion Survey of Britain (PSE survey) in 1999 (Gordon and Pantazis 1997; Gordon et al. 2000).
- *Combined low income and deprivation.* Using Irish data, Brian Nolan and Christopher Whelan (1996) suggested that it was the combination of low income and deprivation in the sense of lacking essential items that yielded the clearest distinction between those in 'poor' and 'not poor' groups. This was carried through by the Irish government to form the basis of the 'consistent poverty' measure that it has used in setting its targets for poverty reduction. Statistical analysis of the 1999 PSE survey by David Gordon et al. (2000) produced a similar measure for Britain, to 'identify poverty as a scientific phenomenon rather than just drawing an arbitrary line', resulting in a measure based on the lack of two or more necessities (identified by a majority of the population) and having a 'low income'.[5]
- *Subjective measures*: having an income which is below the amount that the respondent himself or herself says is enough to avoid poverty. This kind of measure has been used more extensively in other countries, but was included in the 1999 PSE survey (Bradshaw and Finch 2003).

[4] Note that this approach excludes as poor those who say they do not want an item, but could not afford it even if they wanted it. Others might argue that such people were nonetheless poor, despite their austere aspirations.

[5] Or, at least, not having an income high enough to be classed as having recently 'risen out of poverty', using a 'high income' threshold that excluded only those in about the top quarter of incomes overall. The method showed a sixth of those classed as 'poor' as having incomes in the top 40 per cent of the income distribution (Gordon et al. 2000: Table 4).

Each of these approaches brings its own insights, but equally each arguably has serious limitations, depending on the purpose for which it is being used.

- Subjective assessment by the researcher has obvious problems in that it represents one person's opinion, possibly based on only cursory investigation.
- Budget standards approaches are in one sense more 'scientific', but still represent the standards set by an expert (or panel of experts) as what they see as minimum needs in the context of their own time. These may or may not be in line with more general views.
- Using the government's own minimum income standard embodied in social security gives a measure of success against its explicit objectives, but embodies the paradox described above that, under a more generous government which raised benefit levels, 'poverty' would rise as the standard did, with the reverse under a mean government.
- Measures based on relative incomes are now widely used in Britain and across Europe, and give robust information on trends over time. They have been the nearest that the UK has to an official poverty line.[6] However, cash income does not capture everything about people's living standards; they may have different needs from others, or may have sources of income not counted by conventional measures. Drawing a cut-off is generally arbitrary, and there are many choices that could be made for it. Ultimately these kinds of measures are essentially a description of the income distribution, and may or may not accord with what people generally think of as 'poverty'. They are also vulnerable to the 'Irish paradox': in the late 1990s in Ireland overall incomes were rising very rapidly, but incomes at the bottom rose less fast than the average. The poor were a lot better off in real terms than they had been, but relative poverty still rose. This jarred with public perceptions of what poverty constituted, since it had not adjusted upwards as fast as average living standards. Equally, in times of recession a fall in relative poverty may be of cold comfort if the poor are actually getting poorer in real terms.
- Measures based on real incomes—of the kind used as the official poverty line in the USA—avoid this problem but have the opposite one. Few would argue that Rowntree's primary poverty line drawn in 1899 would tell us much about poverty in Britain in the twenty-first century, and even over shorter periods perceptions of poverty clearly do change as living standards rise (see Section 3.5).

[6] For instance, initial progress towards the government's aim of the abolition of child poverty is being measured against whether the number of children living in households with less than 60 per cent of contemporary median income is cut by a quarter in the six years up to 2004–05 (see Chapter 9). For this initial target, the government is looking at trends in both the before and after housing costs measures of income. In its new proposals for measuring further progress in reducing child poverty (DWP 2003e) it has suggested looking at the before housing costs measure only, and switching to the use of a different equivalence scale that puts more weight on the needs of younger children, on the grounds that this provides comparability with statistics for other European countries. Looking at only before housing costs tends to show a lower rate of child poverty than after housing costs. The change in equivalence scale will lead to an increase in the number of children counted as poor.

- Researcher-defined lists of 'necessities' get round some of the failure of income to capture living standards, but still involve subjective assessments of what should be on the list, and arbitrariness in deciding how many items someone has to lack to count as deprived.
- Consensual measures as pioneered by the Breadline Britain approach avoid the first of these problems, and capture changing public standards of what constitute necessities as overall living standards change. But they still involve some arbitrariness: why lacking three items, not two or four, and what was in the list to start with?
- Combining low income and deprivation measures can produce a more robust separation between who is poor and who is not, and can produce helpful information at times when living standards are changing very rapidly. However, the statistical techniques used to produce a combined measure are not transparent. Nor do they necessarily produce comparable trends over time. If the items used to define the deprivation side of the measure are left unchanged, such measures become essentially absolute standards, but there is no easy way of adjusting the list of necessities from year to year, and no easy way of producing standards on this basis that allow comparison across countries (see Atkinson et al. 2002: 120–3 for a discussion).
- Asking people whether they themselves are poor (to produce a 'subjective measure') might seem the most obvious approach; after all, they are in the best position to understand their own situation, and many would argue that the opinions of the poor themselves are what matters. However, others might say that some people have unrealistic views of their own needs and unreasonably class themselves as poor. Equally, there may be people who, although nearly everyone else would see them as 'poor', would not apply that label to themselves, either as a result of pride or through having adjusted to a low standard of living ('adaptive expectations'). As we saw in Table 2.1, only 2 per cent of the population see themselves as being in the bottom of ten groups in society.

Finally, all of the measures outlined above are designed to measure the extent of poverty—to produce 'poverty head-counts'. But for many purposes we may be as interested in its depth: are most poor people just below the line or deeply in poverty? A partial solution to this is to look at the numbers below lines set at different degrees of severity, such as lacking two, three, or four essential items in the case of deprivation measures, or below different proportions of the average in the case of relative income measures. An alternative, where the data allow, is explicitly to measure 'poverty gaps': how far below an income threshold the typical poor person lies. Some information along these lines is presented in Section 3.2. Equally, we may be interested in how long poverty lasts, its duration. Some measures, such as those based on deprivation (lack of necessities), may reflect circumstances over a longer period than that given by a snapshot of income, which can be an advantage. Chapter 5 looks in detail at issues connected with income mobility and poverty duration.

Table 3.1. *Measures of the extent of poverty in Britain*

Researcher	Date	Area	Finding
Subjective researcher assessment			
Booth (1892)	1880s	London	31% poor
Rowntree (1901)	1899	York	28% 'in obvious want and squalor' (primary plus secondary poverty)
Budget standards			
Rowntree (1901)	1899	York	10% in 'primary poverty'
Rowntree (1941)	1936	York	4% below 1899 primary poverty line in real terms
	1936	York	8% below 'Class A' poverty line (same relative level as 1899 primary)
	1936	York	18% below Human Needs of Labour standard
Social security standards			
Abel-Smith and Townsend(1965)	1953	GB	1.2% below National Assistance (same relative level as Rowntree's 1936 Class A line)
	1960	GB	3.8% below National Assistance (NA)
Townsend (1979)	1968–69	GB	6.1% below Supplementary Benefit (SB)
DSS[a]	1979	UK	6% below SB
	1992	UK	8% below Income Support (IS)
Abel-Smith and Townsend (1965)	1953	GB	7.8% below 140% NA
	1960	GB	14.2% below 140% NA
Townsend (1979)	1968–69	GB	27.9% below 140% SB
DSS[a]	1979	UK	24% below 140% SB
	1992	UK	33% below 140% IS
Relative income measures (HBAI)			
Goodman and Webb(1994)	1961	UK	11% below half mean income
DSS (1995)	1979	UK	8–9% below half mean
DSS (1995)	1991/92	UK	21–25% below half mean
DWP (2003a)	1996–97	GB	18–25% below half mean
	2001–02	GB	19–23% below half mean
DWP (2003a)	1996–97	GB	18–25% below 60% median
	2001–02	GB	17–22% below 60% median
Fixed real income measures (HBAI)			
DWP (2003a)	1979	UK	30–32% below 60% 1996–97 median
	1991/92	UK	23–27% below 60% 1996–97 median
	2001–02	GB	11–15% below 60% 1996–97 median

Table 3.1. (*Continued*)

Researcher	Date	Area	Finding
Participation standards			
Townsend (1979)	1968–69	GB	23% below 'deprivation standard'
Consensual deprivation measures (Breadline Britain)[b]			
Mack and Lansley (1985)	1983	GB	14% of households lack 3+ 'necessities'
Gordon and Pantazis (1997)	1990	GB	21% of households lack 3+ 'necessities'
Gordon et al. (2000)	1999	GB	24% of households lack 3+ 'necessities'
Combined low income and deprivation (PSE survey)			
Gordon et al. (2000)	1999	GB	26% lack 2+ necessities and have 'low income'
Subjective poverty (PSE survey)			
Bradshaw and Finch (2003)	1999	GB	20% with income below level they say needed to keep out of poverty

[a] Cited in Oppenheim and Harker (1996: Figure 2.1).

[b] *Breadline Britain* figures are for households, that is, they give the proportion of households that are poor; results taken from Gordon et al. (2000: 52). All other figures give the proportion of individuals that are poor.

Such problems do not mean that the products of such measures are 'wrong', but rather that care has to be applied when using them, depending on the question being asked. Table 3.1 summarizes some of the results of studies using different approaches to measuring the extent of poverty over the last century. What is immediately apparent is that different approaches, even at the same date, produce widely varying figures for the extent of poverty (deliberately so in some cases, as they are designed to capture different levels of severity). Some also suggest differences in trends over time. For instance, using a fixed real line between 1899 and 1936, 'primary poverty' in York fell from 10 per cent to 4 per cent, but using a line with the same value relative to average incomes it fell only to 8 per cent. Between 1979 and 2001, the proportion of the whole population with income below a relative standard doubled, but against a fixed real line the proportion fell by up to two-thirds.

But there is some apparent reassurance in the figures too: for instance, in the 1990s the relative income, deprivation, and subjective measures could all be said to suggest that around a fifth of the population were poor, and that the rapid growth of poverty seen in the 1980s had at least slowed, if not reversed. Such reassurance is, however, somewhat punctured by Table 3.2. This shows Jonathan Bradshaw and Naomi Finch's analysis (2003) of the Poverty and Social

Table 3.2. *Overlaps between different poverty definitions,*
1999, GB (% of whole population)

	Deprived	Not deprived	All
(*a*) With low income (below 60% of median)			
Subjective poverty	5.6	3.4	9.0
Not subjective poverty	1.8	7.7	9.5
All with low income	7.4	11.1	18.5
(*b*) Above low-income threshold			
Subjective poverty	5.5	5.0	10.5
Not subjective poverty	4.0	67.0	71.0
All above low income	9.5	72.0	81.5

Note: Totals differ slightly from those quoted in text as a result of rounding.
Source: Bradshaw and Finch (2003).

Exclusion survey, which allows comparison of who is classed as poor on three different bases, but using exactly the same sample. Of this sample, 18.8 per cent had low relative incomes (below 60 per cent of the median, the measure on which most official attention now focuses); 17.2 per cent were deprived (in the sense of lacking four or more popularly defined necessities, a stricter criterion than that used in Table 3.1); and 19.6 per cent had incomes below the level they themselves had said was needed to keep a 'household such as the one you live in out of poverty' ('subjective poverty'). In aggregate, one might think that the measures were telling a similar story—between a sixth and a fifth of people were poor in Britain in 1999. But the table shows that the measures only partly overlap. Fewer than 6 per cent are classed as poor on all three measures, but a third is classed as poor on one measure or another. The different measures are correlated in that anyone classed as poor on one is much more likely than otherwise to be classed as poor on another, but the correlation is evidently not very close: nearly half of those with relatively low incomes think of themselves as poor, but just over half do not; two-fifths of those with relatively low incomes lack four or more necessities, but three-fifths do not.

That there is some difference is hardly a surprise, given the issues listed above. Some may only just have had a drop in income, but might still have the resources to keep up consumption of necessities. If the income drop is temporary, consumption levels or deprivation scores may be the best guide to their living standards but, if the drop is permanent, income will give the better guide to their longer-run position. Others may have lived at such a low standard for so long among others in the same situation that they might not see themselves as poor, even if others would, and so on. But the absence of more overlap is still striking. The measures are evidently capturing different things. But we then face a dilemma: a multiplicity of measures is hard to interpret, and runs the danger that commentators or politicians may pick and choose whichever best serves the argument of the moment.

Which we want to use will depend on our purpose. To identify a group that is clearly poorer than the rest of the population at a point in time, the combined deprivation and income measures developed in Ireland (Nolan and Whelan 1996) and applied in the UK by the PSE survey (Gordon et al. 2000) have strengths. However, the statistical techniques used do not necessarily generate figures showing consistent trends over time. A combination of a deprivation and a low-income test (not necessarily derived from statistical tests) also has political attractions: if someone is poor on both, it is hard to argue that he or she is 'undeserving'. But to show consistent trends over time, and to make robust comparisons between countries, we are often forced back to examining cash incomes, despite the limitations of this approach.

Faced with this dilemma, while needing to give substance to Tony Blair's 1999 pledge to eradicate 'child poverty' over twenty years, the government has come up with a measure with three parts:

- 'absolute low income': measuring numbers with incomes below a fixed real line (based on 60 per cent of median income in 1998–99);
- a 'combined material deprivation and low income measure': lacking particular items (to be adjusted periodically, as living standards rise) and having income below 70 per cent of the contemporary median; and
- 'relative low income': numbers below 60 per cent of contemporary median income.

The DWP (2003*e*: 1) suggests that 'poverty is falling when all three indicators are moving in the right direction' and that 'Success in eradicating poverty could, then, be interpreted as having a material deprivation child poverty rate that approached zero and being amongst the best in Europe on relative low incomes'.

In the circumstances, this seems a sensible—and demanding—compromise. It essentially follows the 'tiered' approach suggested by Layte, Nolan, and Whelan (2000) after reviewing Irish experience with setting poverty targets. The first indicator—a 'US style' poverty line—gives a minimal (but, by itself, weak) test that things are not moving in the wrong direction. The second—an 'Irish-style' measure—picks up what many would see as progress even at times when average living standards are rising fast. The third—a 'European-style' measure—gives the most robust (and toughest) test of long-term progress.

Section 3.5 examines evidence of how some of these ideas relate to what the population as a whole thinks is meant by 'poverty'.

3.2 TRENDS IN NUMBERS WITH LOW INCOMES

3.2.1 *How Many People are Poor?*

As a result of the changes in income distribution described in Chapter 2, the proportion of the population with low incomes relative to the average—and hence counted as 'in poverty' under a relative income measure—rose sharply

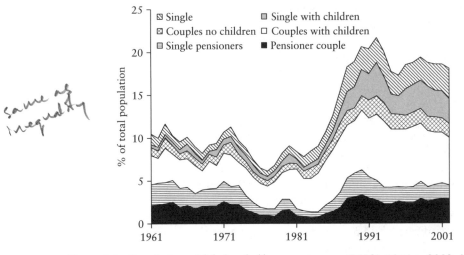

same as inequality

Figure 3.1. *Population with below half average income (BHC), 1961 to 2002–03*

Note: GB figures since 1994–95; UK figures earlier.

Sources: 1979 to 1991 derived from Goodman and Webb (1994); 1991/92 and 1992/93 from DSS (1995: Tables B1 and F1); 1994–95 to 2001–02 from DWP (2003a: Table D7.2 and p. 37); 2002–03 from DWP (2004: Table D7.2 and p. 37).

between the late 1970s and the early 1990s, since when it has fallen rather unevenly. Figure 3.1 combines recent information from the official HBAI analysis (see Section 2.1) with Institute for Fiscal Studies (IFS) figures on the same basis from 1961. To give consistency across the whole period, the figure shows the proportion of the population with below half of mean income (rather than below 60 per cent of median income used in the rest of this chapter; for most of the period, the two indicators give similar results). During the 1960s roughly 10 per cent of the population had incomes below this threshold (before housing costs). Between 1972 and 1977 the number fell back to a low point of 6 per cent in 1977. It then rose sharply, peaking at 21 per cent in 1991/92, before falling back to 17 per cent in 1995–96, but stabilizing at around 18–19 per cent since the late 1990s, still more than three times the level of 1977. On an after-housing-costs basis the changes are more dramatic, with a rise from 7 per cent to 25 per cent below half average income between 1977 and 1991/92, falling back to 23 per cent in 2002–03. It should be noted that poverty on this basis fell up to 1977, giving the lie to the notion that 'relative' poverty can never be reduced.[7]

Figure 3.1 also shows how the composition of the low-income population has changed. At the start of the period many of those with relatively low incomes were pensioners. But the bulk of the growth in numbers after 1977 came from

---

[7] As, for instance, implied by the title of Norman Dennis's *The Invention of Permanent Poverty* (1997).

non-pensioners, especially couples and single people with children. By 2002–03, three-quarters of the low-income population were non-pensioners, compared with just over half in the late 1960s. Nonetheless, it can be seen that in 2002–03 just under 5 per cent of the population consisted of pensioners who were also poor, the same proportion as in 1961. Pensioner poverty may be a smaller part of the overall poverty problem than it used to be, and the proportion of pensioners who are poor may have fallen, but there are just as many poor pensioners as there were two generations ago.

Trends like those in Figure 3.1 are often used to measure the numbers 'in poverty', implicitly using a poverty line which moves with the country's prosperity. As discussed in Section 3.5 below, this does appear to reflect majority conceptions of what is meant by 'poverty', but others take the view that poverty should rather be measured against a fixed real or absolute standard, unaffected by changes in contemporary living standards. Even if one does not take this view, movements in the numbers below fixed real thresholds are still of interest for the reasons discussed in the last section.

Figures 3.2(a) and 3.2(b) respectively contrast the proportions since 1979 of the whole population and of children with incomes both below the relative measure of 60 per cent of contemporary median income and below a fixed threshold of 60 per cent of median income as it was in 1996–97 in real terms. The proportion of the whole population below the relative line of 60 per cent of contemporary median income follows much the same course as the total shown in Figure 3.1. Only 12 per cent of the population were poor on this basis in 1979, but this had reached 21 per cent by 1991/92. The proportion fell in the first half of the 1990s, but has remained between 17 per cent and 18 per cent since 1994–95. By contrast, the numbers below the fixed real threshold grew more rapidly in the 1979–1981 recession, from 30 per cent to 33 per cent: as median incomes were falling, the small rise in relative poverty meant a much larger rise against a fixed real threshold. By 1991–92, median incomes had grown by a third, so, despite the rise in relative poverty, the proportion below the fixed threshold was down to 23 per cent. It stagnated again in the recession of the early 1990s, before falling again. The fall was quite fast through New Labour's first years in office, from 18 per cent in 1997–98 to only 10 per cent in 2002–03.

The figures for children in Figure 3.2(b) show a similar but more accentuated story. In relative terms, child poverty had risen from less than 10 per cent in the late 1960s (Gregg, Harkness, and Machin 1999: Figure 1) to 12 per cent in 1979. It peaked at 27 per cent in the early 1990s. Since then it has fallen unevenly, down to 21 per cent in 2001–02 and 2002–03, compared with 25 per cent in 1996–97, the year before New Labour came to power. Against the fixed real threshold, nearly as many, 30 per cent, of children were below the line in 1992/93 as in 1979, despite a growth of nearly 40 per cent in average incomes over the period. Numbers have fallen since then. Notably between 1996–97 and 2001–02, the proportion more than halved, from 25 per cent to 12 per cent. Chapter 9 examines these changes since Labour came to office in more detail.

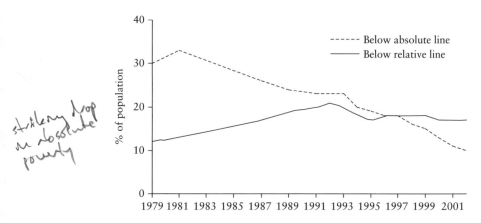

*striking drop
in absolute
poverty*

Figure 3.2. *(a) Proportion of population below relative and real income thresholds, 1979 to 2002–03*

Notes: Relative threshold is 60% of contemporary median. Real threshold is 60% of 1996–97 median. GB figures since 1994–95; UK figures earlier.

Source: DWP (2004: Tables H1 and H5), BHC.

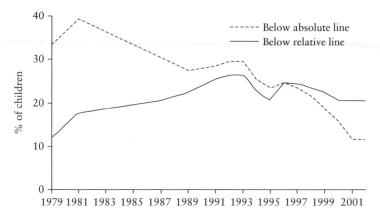

Figure 3.2. *(b) Proportion of children below relative and real income thresholds, 1979 to 2002–03*

Notes: Relative threshold is 60% of contemporary median. Real threshold is 60% of 1996–97 median. GB figures since 1994–95; UK figures earlier.

Source: DWP (2003a: Tables H2 and H6), BHC.

Looking at the trends presented in the two figures, we can distinguish five periods:

• the 1979 to 1981 recession, when poverty rose in both relative and absolute terms, particularly for children;

• the 1981 to 1991 period, when poverty fell in absolute terms, but relative poverty rose rapidly as the poor were left behind the rest of the population;

- the 1991 to 1993 recession, when both changed little: living standards of both the poor and the middle of the distribution stagnated;
- a brief period in the mid-1990s when both absolute and relative poverty fell: overall living standards were growing slowly and the poor were catching up. The gains in relative poverty were partly reversed by 1996–97; and
- the period from 1996–97 up to the most recent figures for 2002–03, during which overall relative poverty fell slowly (but more rapidly for families with children), combined with a rapid fall in poverty against a fixed real line, particularly for children. In this period, typical living standards rose quite fast, but those of the poor rose a little faster.

Only the periods 1993–1995 and 1996–2000 would count as 'successful' in terms of the government's new tests of whether child poverty was falling, described at the end of Section 3.1.

3.2.2   How Far Short do the Poor Fall?

The numbers just described tell only part of the story: there is all the difference in the world between a society where a fifth have incomes just below a particular threshold, and one where the same proportion is not only below the threshold but is well below it. Simply crossing a threshold from just below to just above may mean very little, and poverty head-counts of the kind shown can be positively misleading in some circumstances (although the HBAI analysis shows that the kinds of trends since 1979 discussed above are not, in fact, very sensitive to the precise threshold chosen). One way of enriching the statistics is, therefore, to look at how far those counted as poor fall short of the poverty line: what is the 'poverty gap'? In constructing a measure of this kind, one problem is that the data for the very lowest incomes are not very robust, but would have a large effect on any measure of the aggregate or average amount by which the poor fall short. Table 3.3 therefore gives estimates of the median poverty gap, the proportion of the poverty line by which the 'typical' poor individual falls short of it. Such numbers are not yet published officially in the UK, although the European Union has recommended that they should be collected (Atkinson et al. 2002).

The table shows that in the late 1970s and early 1980s the median poverty gap was smaller than in the 1990s—typically someone in poverty was then about 12–14 per cent below the poverty line, compared with 18–24 per cent below it in the 1990s. In other words, as the numbers in poverty increased rapidly in the 1980s, so did the depth of poverty. Since the early 1990s there has been much less of a clear pattern—in fact, the figures are rather stable. In so far as there has been a reduction in the overall level of relative poverty since the early 1990s (Figures 3.1 and 3.2), this has been accompanied by neither deeper nor shallower poverty for those left behind. The trends in the numbers in poverty therefore tend to understate the growth of the problem in the 1980s, but give a fairer impression in the 1990s.

Table 3.3. *Poverty gaps, 1979 to 2001–02*

	Median poverty gap as a percentage of the poverty line (60% of median income)	
	Before housing costs	After housing costs
FES results (UK)		
1979	13.2	14.4
1981	12.1	13.9
1987	14.9	18.0
1990/91[a]	20.0	23.0
1994/95[b]	18.9	22.9
FRS results (financial years, GB)		
1994–95	17.6	22.9
1996–97	17.8	23.6
1998–99	18.7	23.5
2000–01	19.8	23.7
2001–02	18.9	24.0

[a] 1990 and 1991 calendar years combined.

[b] 1993–94 and 1994–95 financial years combined.

Source: Author's calculations using HBAI dataset.

3.3   SOCIAL EXCLUSION

Until the late 1990s, the term 'social exclusion' was an unfamiliar one in the UK. It might have been encountered by people reading European Commission documents, sometimes interpreted as a convenient euphemism for the word 'poverty' at a time when the then British and other governments might have objected to its use referring to problems affecting all member states. Otherwise its main appearances would have been in academic documents, particularly those linked to continental European debates. But since 1997 the phrase has become much more common. Indeed, combating social exclusion has been one of New Labour's key aims, as witnessed by the establishment in late 1997 of the Social Exclusion Unit (SEU), originally within the Cabinet Office, reporting directly to the Prime Minister (but now within the Office of the Deputy Prime Minister), as well as the establishment of 'social inclusion networks' by the Scottish Executive. But the new familiarity does not mean that people are talking about the same thing.

In their extensive review of the way the term has come to be used, Tania Burchardt, Julian Le Grand, and David Piachaud (2002*a*) trace its use from Max Weber through to France in the 1970s, where 'les exclus' were those who fell though the net of social protection, and its later extension to include those affected by long-term unemployment. For some, 'social exclusion' is something affecting the most marginal, a subset of the poor, affected simultaneously by different kinds of deprivation (see, for instance, Room 1999). In this kind of interpretation, the issue is that problems of income poverty are compounded by other kinds of disadvantage, or indeed are a reflection of those disadvantages.

The SEU (1997) takes a somewhat wider view in its description of its remit, describing social exclusion as a

...short-hand label for what can happen when individuals or areas suffer from a concentration of linked problems such as unemployment, poor skills, low income, poor housing, high crime, bad health and family breakdown.

The government's annual Opportunity for All (OfA) reports include more than fifty indicators to monitor its 'strategy to tackle poverty and social exclusion' (DWP 2002*b*, 2003*b*). The indicators used cover not only low income but also educational attainment, mortality rates, smoking, teenage conceptions, employment, housing standards, rough sleeping, drug use, pension scheme membership, fear of crime, burglary rates, and fuel poverty. Some of these are measured at the individual or household level, others across deprived areas. Earlier, the independent New Policy Institute (NPI) started publishing a set of fifty 'poverty and social exclusion indicators', many of which are also now tracked by the OfA series. The NPI indicators include low income, receipt of means-tested benefits, worklessness, low pay, low educational qualifications and lack of training, children experiencing parental divorce, conceptions at less than 16 years of age; drug use, physical and mental health problems, mortality and suicide, housing problems, lack of financial services, and dissatisfaction with the local area. A summary of recent trends in both the official OfA and NPI indicators is given in Chapter 9, as well as very recent findings on aspects of material deprivation and financial hardship from the new Families and Children Survey (Tables 9.3 and 9.4).

The study by Tony Atkinson et al. (2002) for the European Union on what indicators should be used to compare progress in member states towards greater social inclusion also takes a multi-dimensional approach, identifying indicators within five main fields that should be covered: material deprivation (including low income), lack of education, lack of productive role, poor health, and poor housing (2002: 70).

It has to be said that the older phrase 'multiple deprivation' would cover much the same set of problems, at least in so far as they overlap. But there is another aspect, beyond multi-dimensionality, that the Dutch social scientist Jos Berghman (1995) suggests makes the concept of social exclusion distinct from deprivation, the implication that dynamics are involved. 'Exclusion' and its counterpart 'inclusion' are words referring to processes. Atkinson (1998) stresses two further aspects of the notion: relativity and agency. First, exclusion is a relative notion: people are excluded from a particular society at a particular time (in contrast to absolute poverty measures that focus on ability to purchase a fixed basket of goods that might have been regarded as adequate at another place or time). Second, agency matters: inability to control major aspects of one's life is an important aspect of exclusion, while the phrase carries the implication that someone else, or some other aspect of society, may be responsible for exclusion occurring. Finally, while 'poverty' is most commonly thought of as an individual (or household) phenomenon, Burchardt, Le Grand, and Piachaud (2002*a*) argue that the concept of social exclusion is multi-layered: exclusion can operate at different levels—individual, household, community or neighbourhood, local, national, or even global.

These five aspects—multiple dimensions, dynamics, relativity, agency, and multiple layers—suggest that what makes social exclusion distinct is that it is a wider concept than income poverty, although income poverty remains central to it. Synthesising previous studies, Burchardt, Le Grand, and Piachaud (2002*b*) identify four dimensions of participation as central to measuring the extent of social exclusion in Britain in the 1990s: consumption (the capacity to purchase goods and services), production (participation in economically or socially valuable activities), political engagement (involvement in local or national decision-making), and social interaction (integration with family, friends, and community). More colloquially, this could be taken to measure participation in terms of what people get out, what they put in, having a say, and having someone to listen. Table 3.4 shows results from their analysis of trends in the extent of social exclusion in Britain in the 1990s against particular thresholds in each of their four dimensions, with the use of the (sometimes limited) data available from the British Household Panel Study (BHPS). Of course, choice of a different threshold would change the results for each dimension,[8] and the results in this table simply give the position at one moment rather than incorporating any dynamic component. They are also restricted to the working-age population. They do indicate, however, that in three of the dimensions things did not appear to be getting worse, at least, between 1991 and 1998. As far as their 'consumption' dimension (based on relative income poverty) is concerned, this confirms what we saw in Figure 3.2 (a). For their 'production' dimension, there is little change over the period (which contrasts with the more rapid fall in officially measured 'unemployment'—see Figure 4.8). Lack of social interaction appears to fall over the period. On the other hand, lack of political engagement—heavily affected by lower turn-out in the 1997 general election—is greater at the later date shown than the earlier one.

What is more striking in their findings, however, is the comparatively low correlation between these four dimensions. For instance, in the 1997 wave of BHPS data only 0.1 per cent of respondents were counted as 'excluded' on all four of the

---

[8] The thresholds used were:

Consumption: equivalized net household income below half the population mean.

Production: not employed, self-employed, in education, or caring for family or relatives.

Political engagement: did not vote in general election and not a member of a campaigning organization.

Social interaction: in one of five respects lacks anyone to turn to for support.

For further details and justification, see Burchardt, Le Grand, and Piachaud (2002*b*).

Table 3.4. *Exclusion at a point in time, by dimension, 1991–1998, GB*
(% of working-age population)

Year	Consumption	Production	Political engagement	Social interaction
1991	16	13	n/a	12
1992	17	14	17	n/a
1993	17	14	n/a	10
1994	17	14	n/a	n/a
1995	15	13	n/a	9
1996	15	13	n/a	n/a
1997	16	12	21	9
1998	n/a	12	n/a	n/a

Source: Burchardt, Le Grand, and Piachaud (2002*b*: Table 3.2).

Table 3.5. *Low income and exclusion on different dimensions, 1997, GB (%)*

Income quintile group*	Production	Political engagement	Social interaction
Bottom	46	28	28
2	24	23	21
3	15	18	19
4	9	17	17
Top	6	14	16
All	100	100	100

* Income groups for equivalent net household incomes of working-age population.
Source: Burchardt, Le Grand, and Piachaud (2002*b*: Table 3.5).

dimensions with these thresholds, and only 2.3 per cent on three or four of them. This does not mean that they are unrelated. As Table 3.5 shows, those with lower incomes are much more likely than others to lack any 'productive activity' on these definitions, and are also less likely to be politically engaged or have someone to turn to for social support. However, the overlap is a long way from complete. This is not necessarily a surprise (by contrast with, for instance, Table 3.2, where the measures are all attempting to measure something more closely related). The dimensions of exclusion measured in Table 3.4 appear to be distinct: inclusion (or lack of it) in one is no guarantee of inclusion (or lack of it) in another.

The advantage of using panel data of the kind produced by the BHPS for this kind of analysis is that it allows analysis of whether people who fall below a threshold in one year do so in other years. In their analysis, Burchardt, Le Grand, and Piachaud find that exclusion on each of their four dimensions is significantly correlated with exclusion on the same dimension in the previous year; but, again, the correlation is not perfect. Over time people move above and below the thresholds used. For instance, as Table 3.4 showed, around 13 per cent of the working age population lacked 'productive activity' (work, training, or caring responsibilities) in the 1990s. However, only 3 per cent were continuously in the position for the eight years examined. This does not mean that this was randomly spread through the population: 70 per cent of the working-age population were never without productive activity, and 10 per cent were without it for four or more of the eight years (Burchardt, Le Grand, and Piachaud 2002*b*: Table 3.7). This is far more continuity than one would see if people moved in and out of work randomly, for instance. Finally, Burchardt, Le Grand, and Piachaud combined the information about all four dimensions of exclusion, and all of the eight years for which data were available in the survey (2002*b*: Table 3.9). The results showed the following:

- Nearly two-thirds (63 per cent) of the working age population were 'excluded' at some point in the period on at least one dimension. Only a third of the sample was entirely untouched by exclusion.
- However, continuous 'exclusion' in all dimensions is rare. By the time data from three successive waves had been examined, only 0.1 per cent of the sample was below all of the possible thresholds in all three years. By the time periods of four years or longer were examined, none of the sample was below all of the four thresholds for all of the years.

Taken together, such findings suggest that, although low income does predict that people are less likely to be participating in society in other ways, it is by no means the whole story. We need to examine other dimensions of participation as well. This is not only because lack of participation acts as an indicator of lack of resources (as in Townsend's 1979 formulation of relative deprivation), but because we may care about lack of participation arising because of other barriers than simply material ones. The findings also suggest that understanding patterns over time adds to what can be learnt from 'snapshots' of people's circumstances at a particular moment (Chapter 5 looks in more detail at one aspect of this, the dynamics of incomes).

3.4   INTERNATIONAL COMPARISONS OF RELATIVE POVERTY AND WIDER MEASURES

The Luxembourg Income Study (LIS) allows comparison of relative income poverty rates on a consistent basis. Table 3.6 presents results for the most recent year available from the LIS dataset. For most countries this is 1999 or 2000, but for some it is as early as 1994, so relative positions for exactly the same year may vary slightly. With that caveat, the position of the UK in the late 1990s was poor:

- Only the USA and Ireland had higher relative poverty rates overall.
- Only the USA had a worse relative child poverty rate. Four countries, three in Scandinavia, had rates which were less than half that in the UK. However, more recent data from a different source suggests that between 1998 and 2001 the UK's child poverty rate moved from being the worst in the European

Union to below that in Italy, Ireland, Spain, and Portugal (DWP 2003*e*: Figures 1 and 2).

• Only Ireland had a worse poverty rate for its elderly population than the UK. In all countries except Luxembourg, poverty rates for the elderly were higher than the average and were surprisingly high in Scandinavia.

The final column of the table shows the proportion of the population in severe poverty. The UK did very well on this kind of comparison in the late 1970s and early 1980s. Deborah Mitchell (1991: Table 4.1) found the UK then to have the lowest poverty rate against a threshold of 40 per cent of mean income out of the ten countries she examined. The UK still does not do quite as badly as it does against more generous thresholds, but the recent figure of nearly 6 per cent below 40 per cent of median income is still the fourth highest shown in Table 3.6 (equal with Denmark), albeit well below the US, where 11 per cent of the population were in severe poverty on this measure.

These figures compare poverty rates against a national standard. In a recent piece of analysis, UNICEF's Innocenti Research Centre in Florence not only included a comparison of relative child poverty rates—showing much the same picture as the table—but also showed child poverty rates against a fixed international standard (based on the US poverty line, converted using Purchasing Power Parities and using consistent income definitions). This analysis showed that in these terms the child poverty rate of 29.1 per cent in the UK in the mid-1990s

Table 3.6. *International comparison of relative poverty rates, 2000 and late 1990s (% of population)*

Country (year)	Below 60 % of population median			Below 40% of median
	All	Children	Elderly	
United States (2000)	23.8	30.2	33.3	10.8
Ireland (1996)	21.8	23.6	41.5	4.0
United Kingdom (1999)	21.3	27.0	34.9	5.7
Italy (2000)	19.9	26.5	22.2	7.3
Canada (1998)	19.7	23.8	21.5	7.6
Denmark (1997)	17.1	14.5	30.5	5.7
Belgium (1997)	14.4	13.7	22.7	3.3
Austria (1997)	14.2	17.3	22.7	3.3
France (1994)	14.1	14.3	18.5	3.4
Germany (2000)	13.1	11.2	21.2	4.9
Netherlands (1999)	12.7	14.8	12.8	4.6
Luxembourg (2000)	12.5	18.3	10.5	1.4
Finland (2000)	12.4	8.0	24.8	2.1
Norway (2000)	12.3	7.5	28.9	2.9
Sweden (2000)	12.3	9.2	21.2	3.8

Source: Luxembourg Income Study. www.lisproject.org, 10 February 2004.

was below only that in Italy and Spain (out of twelve EU members). It was much higher than in most of Europe, and twice the 13.9 per cent figure in the USA (UNICEF 2000: Figure 2).[9] In other words, despite being a comparatively rich country, which ought to help their living standards, a larger proportion of British children were poor against an absolute international standard than in most comparable countries. Given the halving in child poverty against a roughly comparable absolute standard shown in Figure 3.2 (b) between 1996–97 and 2001–02, the UK's position may now have improved on this measure by comparison with the US, at least, if not other countries.

Finally, Britain is not alone in studying trends in a wider range of social indicators of the kind discussed in Section 3.3. Since the Lisbon summit in March 2000, member states of the European Union have been committed to achieving greater social cohesion. This is to be achieved through what the EU calls the 'open method of coordination': member states choose their own policies, but the results of these are to be monitored through a common set of agreed indicators. For the future, these will be based on a set agreed at the EU summit in Laeken, Belgium, in December 2001, largely following the recommendations of the specialist advisory group chaired by Tony Atkinson (Atkinson et al. 2002). The full set includes ten 'level one' indicators, covering relative poverty, income inequality, lack of education or training for 18–24-year-olds with low qualifications, unemployment, inequalities in health, and poor housing. Other indicators will also be collected and published on a comparable basis to add depth to the picture given by the lead indicators.

It will be some time before the data are available to implement these recommendations in full. In the short term, however, Eurostat already publishes a set of eight interim indicators that correspond to most of the future lead indicators. The recent position of the UK in respect of seven of these is shown in Table 3.7.[10] These slightly more recent figures than those in Table 3.6 show the UK's position somewhat more favourably, particularly with the inclusion of more southern European countries. For the first two indicators—relative poverty and persistent poverty—the UK was sixth worst out of the fifteen, below Ireland and the four southern countries. For income inequality, it was fourth. Perhaps surprisingly given the UK's low unemployment rate, it had the highest proportion of children living in jobless households (including those early retired due to sickness, and lone parents), and the second highest after Belgium of adults living in jobless households (see Section 4.4 for further discussion). Only for long-term unemployment—on the narrow definition—and for early school-leavers does the UK come out below the EU average (as the sixth and fifth best of the fifteen respectively). Such figures show some of the effects of recent improvements in relative poverty,

---

[9] The US figure is lower than that conventionally given by the US government, as the income definitions used by UNICEF allow for income items such as food stamps.

[10] The eighth is on regional differences in unemployment rates. See Stewart (2003) for a discussion of the problems with this approach, and for a comparison at regional level across Europe of a wider set of indicators.

Table 3.7. *European Union social cohesion indicators (%)*

	At risk of poverty (2001)[a]	Persistent poverty (2001)[b]	Income inequality (2001)[c]	Children living in jobless households (2003)[d]	Adults living in jobless households (2003)[e]	Long-term unemployment (2002)[f]	Early school-leavers (2003)[g]
EU 15	15	9	4.4	9.8	9.6	3.0	18.1
Ireland	21	13	4.5	*10.8*	*8.5*	1.3	12.1
Portugal	20	15	6.5	*5.1*	*5.3*	1.8	41.1
Greece	20	14	5.7	*4.5*	9.0	5.1	15.3
Italy	19	13	4.8	*7.0*	9.7	5.3	24.6
Spain	19	10	5.5	*6.1*	7.2	3.9	29.8
UK	17	10	4.9	17.0	10.9	1.1	*16.7*
France	15	9	4.0	*9.3*	*10.4*	2.8	13.3
Belgium	13	7	4.0	*13.8*	14.2	3.5	*12.4*
Luxembourg	12	9	3.8	*2.8*	*6.3*	0.8	*17.0*
Austria	12	7	3.5	*4.4*	*7.5*	0.8	*9.5*
Germany	11	6	3.6	*9.3*	*10.0*	4.0	12.6
Finland	11	6	3.5	n/a	n/a	2.3	9.9
Denmark	11	5	3.1	n/a	n/a	0.9	10.0
Netherlands	11	5	3.8	7.2	8.1	0.7	*15.0*
Sweden	10	n/a	3.4	n/a	n/a	1.0	9.0

  [a] Individuals with equivalent net income below 60% of national median.
  [b] Individuals with income below 60% of national median in current year and in two or three of preceding three years.
  [c] Quintile share ratio of equivalent disposable income.
  [d] Share of population aged 0–17 living in households where no one is working.
  [e] Share of population aged 18–59 living in households where no one is working (excluding those in households consisting solely of students aged 18–24).
  [f] Unemployed over one year (as percentage of total active labour force).
  [g] Proportion of 18–24 year olds with lower secondary education not in full-time education or training.

Note: Figures in italics are provisional.

Source: Eurostat. www.europa.eu.int, 10 February 2004.

and confirm that income distribution is not the whole story, but do little to temper the view that the UK still does poorly in international comparisons of poverty and social cohesion.

3.5   PUBLIC ATTITUDES TO POVERTY

So far this chapter has presented a number of different ways in which the extent of 'poverty' and related concepts can be measured, and trends in some of them. In formulating policy, it is clearly important to understand how the potential measures relate to public attitudes: if politicians promise to reduce—or even end—'poverty', what is it that people will expect to see falling?

3.5.1   *What is Poverty?*

Table 3.8 gives a first check on how well different definitions of poverty match public attitudes. Since the mid-1980s, the British Social Attitudes (BSA) survey

Table 3.8. *Definitions of poverty, 1986–2000, GB*

% who say in poverty if someone had....	1986	1989	1994	2000
...enough to buy the things they needed, but not enough to buy the things most people take for granted	25	25	28	27
...enough to eat and live, but not enough to buy other things they needed	55	60	60	59
...not enough to eat and live without getting into debt	95	95	90	93
Base	1,548	1,516	1,167	3,426

Source: British Social Attitudes survey.

has periodically asked whether people in Britain would be 'in poverty' in certain circumstances. Clearly for most people, being unable to afford the things most people have and take for granted does not constitute 'poverty', but nor is poverty simply about not having enough to 'eat and live'. It is about also being able to afford other things that people 'need'. These results have changed little from when the same questions were asked in earlier years of the survey, suggesting that these attitudes are very stable.

Indeed, poverty as 'being unable to afford necessities' is almost a tautology. Such a definition does not by itself tell us what these 'things people need' are, whether they change over time, or how many people lack them. However, the results do suggest that most people would have sympathy for something related to the Breadline Britain approach of measuring poverty by first asking the population what they think of as 'necessities' and then finding out how many people are unable to afford them. Analysing earlier results of this kind, Peter Taylor-Gooby (1995) interpreted them as suggesting that only a small number think of poverty in relative terms. But the key question is whether what constitute 'the things people need' change over time with rising living standards. The other evidence surveyed below suggests that they do, as do the responses to the three surveys following the Breadline Britain approach (Gordon et al. 2000: Table 12). For instance, in the 1983 Breadline Britain survey only 43 per cent of those surveyed thought a telephone a necessity, so it did not make the majority list. By 1990, 56 per cent, and in 1999, 72 per cent, thought that it was. Similarly, in the 1983 and 1990 surveys fewer than 40 per cent thought that the ability to 'have friends and family round for a meal, snack or drink' (how often was unspecified in the questionnaire) was a necessity; by 1999, 65 per cent thought that it was. This kind of pattern is repeated for many other items (particularly when one compares the 1983 and 1990 surveys), but there are exceptions: having 'new, not second-hand clothes' was seen as a necessity by nearly two-thirds in 1983 and 1990, but by only 50 per cent in 1999, only just remaining in the majoritarian list of necessities.

A second indication of what people mean by poverty and how widespread they think it is comes from what they say about their own experiences. When asked by the 2000 BSA survey to look back over their lives, judging by the standards of that time, only 51 per cent said they had never lived in poverty, with a further 17 per cent saying they had done so only rarely. A third of respondents said they had lived in poverty more frequently: 23 per cent 'occasionally', 7 per cent 'often', and 3 per cent 'most of the time'. Just over a quarter said they had experienced poverty as a child, and 37 per cent as an adult (including 13 per cent as both).

These numbers mirror findings on movements in and out of low income from the British Household Panel Study in the 1990s (see Chapter 5). For instance, if one looks at the first ten years of the survey, an identical 51 per cent never had incomes below a poverty line of 60 per cent of each year's median income, but 15 per cent did so for five or more of the years, 8 per cent for seven or more years, and 2 per cent for all ten years (DWP 2003a: Table 7.6). The reported experiences of 'poverty' from the British Social Attitudes survey suggest that this kind of pattern matches public perceptions of their own experience. The pattern supports poverty definitions that would include around a fifth of the population in the 1990s.

Beliefs about what constitutes 'poverty' vary to some extent with people's own experience and other factors, such as political identification, as can be seen in Table 3.9. Conservative identifiers are the least likely, and Labour identifiers the most likely, to take the most generous definition of poverty in the first column; but the differences are not large, and for all three political groupings the median view is the central one, focused on 'needs'. There is more variation by people's own reported experience of poverty and their own assessment of their current income. Two-fifths of those 'finding it very difficult' on their current income favour the most generous interpretation, compared with only 23 per cent of those 'living comfortably' on their current income. There is almost as big a gap between those who say they have never been in poverty and those who say they have experienced it 'often' or 'most of the time'.

Of course, causality can go both ways here. Those closest to poverty may have the most generous (or realistic) view of what is needed to avoid it. Alternatively, the people with the most generous interpretation of poverty may also be those who are most likely to count themselves as poor at any given level of income, or find it as being too little to manage on. Either of these could generate the pattern seen in the last two panels of the table. However, those finding it difficult or very difficult on their current incomes are also much more likely to report low cash incomes than others, suggesting that their difficulties are not only the result of their high aspirations.

3.5.2   *Perceptions of Trends in the Extent of Poverty*

The BSA survey suggested to respondents that 'Some people say there is very little real poverty in Britain today. Others say there is quite a lot. Which comes closest to your view?' In 1994, 28 per cent had said that 'very little real poverty'

Table 3.9. *Definitions of poverty, by political leanings and own circumstances, 2000, GB (%)*

% who agree that someone is in poverty if they have...	... enough for needs, not things most take for granted	... enough to eat eat and live, not other needs	... not enough to eat and live without debt	Base
All	27	59	93	3,426
By party identification				
Conservative	22	55	93	937
Liberal	23	65	97	341
Labour	30	63	92	1,394
By own experience of poverty				
Never	22	54	92	1,646
Rarely/occasionally	30	65	93	1,381
Often/most of the time	38	67	94	393
By assessment of current income				
Living comfortably	23	59	93	900
Coping	27	58	93	998
Finding it difficult	33	62	92	276
Finding it very difficult	40	67	95	114

Source: British Social Attitudes survey.

came closest to their view, but 71 per cent preferred the statement that there was 'quite a lot'. 'Quite a lot' is not very precise, but this response is again not inconsistent with the proportions of around a fifth during the 1990s suggested by the (relative) measure of numbers below half of average income and the Breadline Britain counts (see Table 3.1). More to the point, the proportion saying that there was 'quite a lot of real poverty' had risen from 55 per cent in 1986 and 63 per cent in 1989. This is clearly inconsistent with a widespread belief in a fixed real poverty line, which would have implied falling numbers in poverty by the mid-1990s.

Table 3.10 shows that by 2000 there had been a small shift back, with 35 per cent now saying there was very little real poverty, and a reduced number, but still a majority—62 per cent—suggesting that there was quite a lot. This suggests there may have been some decline in public perceptions of the extent of poverty in the second half of the 1990s (or in views of what constitutes 'quite a lot'). Again, however, this small change does not seem consistent with the rapid fall indicated by measures using a fixed real income threshold.

Beliefs about the extent of poverty also vary by political identification and personal experience. Table 3.10 shows that nearly half of Conservative identifiers, but only a third or fewer of Liberal and Labour identifiers, thought that there is 'very little' real poverty in Britain today. Meanwhile, three-quarters of those who count themselves as having experienced poverty often or most of

Table 3.10. *Perceptions of level of poverty in Britain, by political leanings and own circumstances, 2000, GB (%)*

	Very little real poverty	Quite a lot of poverty	*Base*
All	35	62	*3,426*
By party identification			
Conservative	46	51	*937*
Liberal Democrat	34	65	*341*
Labour	30	69	*1,394*
By own experience of poverty			
Never	41	56	*1,646*
Rarely/occasionally	30	68	*1,381*
Often/most of the time	26	73	*393*
By assessment of current income			
Living comfortably	39	58	*900*
Coping	35	62	*998*
Finding it difficult	24	74	*276*
Finding it very difficult	20	80	*114*

Source: British Social Attitudes survey.

the time, or who are finding it difficult to manage on their current incomes, say that there is 'quite a lot'. Again, it is not possible to determine from this alone whether it is experience that is driving a realistic assessment, or a generous assessment which leads to the gloomy view of people's own experience. Interestingly, however, this kind of gradient is not apparent when people's responses are divided according to their reported gross household income. There is little difference between those in the top and bottom quarters of the population by income in how much poverty they think there is.

Two further sets of questions give more clues about people's views of trends. Table 3.11 shows that in both the 1986 and 1989 surveys half of respondents said that they thought poverty had increased over the previous ten years. By 1994, more than two-thirds thought that poverty had increased over the previous ten years, but in 2000 this had halved: only just over a third thought it had increased since 1990, with a similar number thinking it had stayed the same. A growing number, but still only a fifth, now thought that it had fallen.

Comparing these results with the trends in the measures shown in Figures 3.1 and 3.2 suggests that most people certainly do not seem to have a fixed real poverty line in mind. If they had, they would have been reporting constant or slowly falling poverty in the 1980s and more rapidly falling poverty in the 1990s. Rather, they seem to have in mind a poverty line that rises in real terms in some way over time. There is also a feeling that poverty increased less rapidly in the 1990s than it had from the mid-1980s. Neither finding contradicts the

Table 3.11. *Perceptions of trends in poverty in Britain over past ten years,*
1986–2000, GB (%)

	1986	1989	1994	2000
Increasing	51	50	68	37
Staying at same level	30	31	24	38
Decreasing	15	16	6	20
Base	1,548	1,516	1,167	3,426

Source: British Social Attitudes survey.

Table 3.12. *Feelings about household's present income, 1986–2002, GB (%)*

	1986	1989	1994	1998	2000	2002
Finding it very difficult	8	6	6	4	4	3
Finding it difficult	18	17	16	12	11	13
Coping	49	49	49	46	42	45
Living comfortably	24	27	29	37	43	39
Base	3,100	3,029	1,167	3,146	2,292	1,184

Source: British Social Attitudes survey.

pictures given by the trends in the purely relative and Breadline Britain lines
(see Table 3.1), but these data do not allow us to choose between them.

However, another series of responses, shown in Table 3.12, gives a rather
different picture for trends over time. One might expect notions of 'poverty' to
be closely related to whether people can manage on their incomes. But when
asked about their feelings about their own household's current income in 1986,
a quarter of respondents said that they were finding it 'difficult' or 'very
difficult'. In 1989 and 1994 this proportion had changed little, but by 1998 only
16 per cent gave this response (with similar proportions in 2000 and 2002).
If 'finding it difficult' on one's own income was close to people's feelings about
what constitutes poverty, these trends would suggest a somewhat faster decline
in the 1990s than the purely relative measure, although not as fast as that
implied by a fixed real line (which would also suggest a continuing fall after
1998, which these numbers do not). They would not be consistent with the
upward trend over the 1990s in the Breadline Britain measure.

3.5.3   Adequacy of Benefits

A final piece of evidence on people's implicit poverty lines can be gleaned
from another series of BSA questions, which explore how people perceive the
adequacy of benefits in keeping people out of poverty. Responses show that
there are important differences between what people think of the adequacy of

Table 3.13. *Whether benefits are enough to live on, 2000, GB (%)*

	Really poor	Hard up	Enough to live on	More than than enough	Don't know
25 year old unemployed woman on:					
State benefits	10	46	31	3	10
£52 after rent	13	55	28	3	1
Unemployed single mother, one child, on:					
State benefits	17	51	23	2	7
£95 after rent	10	43	41	5	1
Pensioner living alone on:					
State pension and other benefits	20	57	19	1	3
£82 after rent	8	40	48	4	1

Base: 3,426

Source: British Social Attitudes survey.

social security benefits when asked about them in the abstract, and what they think when they are told the specific amounts. This is confirmed in the findings for 2000 shown in Table 3.13. When asked simply about a 25-year-old unemployed woman living alone whose income consists solely of state benefits, more than half, 56 per cent, describe her as 'really poor' or 'hard up', while a third say she has enough or more than enough to live on. But when the actual amount of benefit, £52 per week after rent, is specified, the proportion saying this is not enough to live on rises to 68 per cent (mostly as a result of a decline in the number who 'don't know' when asked just about 'state benefits'). Interestingly, the pattern is something of the reverse for the single mother and single pensioner shown in the table. Sixty-eight per cent think a single mother whose only income is from state benefits is really poor or hard up, and 77 per cent think this of a single pensioner. When the actual amounts are specified, these proportions fall to 53 per cent and 48 per cent respectively. This kind of difference is in line with findings in previous surveys (Hills and Lelkes 1999). It suggests that people's mental image of benefits for the unemployed is that they are more generous than they really are, but that the reverse is true for pensions.

To return to implicit poverty lines, from the results for a single woman, £52 per week was below what most people thought was enough to live on in 2000. On the other hand, just over half thought that the £82 for a single pensioner was enough to live on. The poverty line on which policy now tends to focus at present—60 per cent of median income—worked out at £84 per week in 2000 (after housing costs) for a single person, and £111 for a single parent with a child aged 4 (DWP 2002a: Table 2.2). The British Social Attitudes findings are consistent with these kinds of amounts—the closest we have to an official 'poverty line'—as reflecting at least median views.

Such results also allow exploration of variations in views between different population groups. Analysing 1998 BSA data, Hills and Lelkes (1999: Table 1.9) found, for instance, that pensioners were a little less likely than others to say that people of the kind shown in the table were 'really poor' or 'hard up', and so may have a somewhat lower implicit poverty line. This could reflect the way people use their own past living standards as a reference point (although the effect is not large).

In summary, the different pieces of evidence reviewed so far in this section generally suggest public support for the pictures given by 'relative' poverty definitions of the kind generated by the HBAI statistics, or unable to afford 'necessities' as in the Breadline Britain measures. They are not consistent with the picture given by measures using fixed real income thresholds. The levels of income at which most people say benefit recipients would not have enough to live on also appear to correspond to the income cut-offs on which most attention now focuses in measuring trends in relative poverty.

3.5.4 *Whose Responsibility is Poverty?*

In general then, people appear to be concerned about poverty and believe that it is quite widespread and has grown since the 1980s. Believing that poverty exists and has grown does not, however, necessarily mean that people see it as government's responsibility to do something about it—or within its capabilities. After all, it might be people's own fault that they are poor.

Table 3.14 shows that ascribing 'living in need' simply to laziness or lack of will-power on the part of the poor is the view of a minority, but one which grew from 15 per cent to 23 per cent during the economic recovery between 1994 and 2000. At the same time, the proportion blaming 'injustice in our society' for poverty fell from 30 per cent to 21 per cent. This could reflect a belief either that there is now a fairer society as a result of policy changes in the second half of the 1990s, or that with a better economy those left behind are more likely

Table 3.14. *Reasons why people live in need, 1986–2000, GB (%)*

	1986	1989	1994	2000
Because of laziness or lack of will-power	19	19	15	23
Because they have been unlucky	11	11	15	15
It's an inevitable part of modern life	37	34	33	34
Because of injustice in our society	25	29	30	21
None of these/don't know	8	7	8	7
Base	*1,548*	*1,516*	*1,167*	*3,426*

Source: British Social Attitudes survey.

to have themselves to blame. A third of the population sees poverty as an inevitable part of modern life, although this is slightly less than the numbers doing so in 1986.

Some fatalism is also reflected in views about future trends: in 2000, 41 per cent said that they thought poverty would increase over the next ten years, 38 per cent that it would stay the same, and only 18 per cent that it would fall. This does not suggest great faith in the current government's anti-poverty strategy (despite the progress reported in Chapter 9), but it is at least more optimistic than respondents were in the past, when up to half thought poverty would rise over the following ten years (45 per cent in 1986, 44 per cent in 1989, and 54 per cent in 1994) and few that it would fall (only 10 per cent in 1994).

It is instructive to investigate some of these views by respondents' characteristics. Table 3.15 shows the variations in beliefs about why people live in need by political identification and experience of poverty. Some of the biggest contrasts come in the proportions blaming 'injustice in our society'. For instance, nearly twice as many Labour and Liberal identifiers (25 per cent) as Conservatives (13 per cent) do so. By contrast, Conservatives, those who say they have never experienced poverty, and those currently living comfortably or coping on their incomes are more likely to blame laziness or lack of will-power. There is much

Table 3.15. *Why people live in need, by party identification, own experience of poverty, and assessment of current income, 2000, GB (%)*

	Laziness/ lack of willpower	Unlucky	Inevitable part of modern life	Injustice in our society	*Base*
All	23	15	34	21	*3,426*
By party identification					
Conservative	28	14	38	13	*937*
Liberal Democrat	18	14	35	25	*341*
Labour	20	15	34	25	*1,394*
By own experience of poverty					
Never	25	15	35	18	*1,646*
Rarely/occasionally	22	15	35	22	*1,381*
Often/most of the time	18	19	29	29	*393*
By assessment of current income					
Living comfortably	24	15	35	17	*900*
Coping	25	13	33	21	*998*
Finding it difficult	19	15	31	31	*276*
Finding it very difficult	12	22	31	31	*114*

Source: British Social Attitudes survey.

less variation when it comes to seeing it as inevitable or a matter of bad luck—across all the groups about half blame one or other of these.

On this question, we can make a direct comparison with attitudes elsewhere in the European Union, thanks to the findings of a Eurobarometer poll carried out in the Autumn of 2001, shown in Table 3.16. The wording of the questions varies slightly from that in the BSA questions, and the response rate to the survey was particularly poor in some countries, including the UK, where it was only 21 per cent. Nonetheless, the UK findings are very close to those from the 2000 BSA. The recent changes in UK views shown in Table 3.14 have taken the UK out of line with most other European countries. The proportion blaming laziness or lack of will-power is higher in the UK than in any of the countries apart from Portugal. Notably, four of the six countries where people are most likely to blame laziness on the part of the poor—Portugal, the UK, Greece, and Ireland—also had four of the six highest relative poverty rates in Europe in 2001 (Table 3.7). Conversely, the proportion blaming 'much injustice in our society' is lower in the UK than in any of the others apart from Denmark and the Netherlands. The latter two countries are much more equal in income terms than the UK, and have much less relative poverty, which may be why they tend not to blame injustice (although

Table 3.16. *European Union views of why there are 'people that live in want', 2001 (%)*

	Laziness/ lack of willpower	Unlucky	Inevitable part of modern progress	Much injustice in our society	None of these
Portugal	29	18	10	34	3
UK	23	21	22	19	5
Austria	22	13	24	30	7
Greece	20	14	25	33	4
Denmark	19	28	31	13	6
Ireland	18	23	29	23	7
Belgium	18	18	24	31	4
Germany (West)	17	12	25	33	4
France	16	16	19	40	5
Italy	15	19	16	36	6
Finland	15	13	23	43	2
Germany (East)	14	10	19	50	4
Spain	12	24	19	35	4
Netherlands	12	23	23	19	14
Sweden	9	13	27	42	5
All	18	18	22	31	6

Source: Gallie and Paugam (2002), based on 2001 *Eurobarometer* poll.

Swedes and Finns are amongst the most likely to blame injustice for the poverty they do have, despite having among the lowest rates in Europe).

Despite the UK's rather different position from most of the rest of Europe, fewer than a quarter of respondents to either survey attribute poverty to individual laziness. By implication, anti-poverty policies could be popular—but that depends on issues about their structure as well (see Chapters 6 and 8 in particular).

While a direct comparison between the UK and the USA on such a question is not possible, the 1995–1997 World Values Survey does suggest a much greater difference between US attitudes to poverty and those in four of the European countries also covered in Table 3.16[11] than there is between the UK and the rest of the EU. When asked to choose between two reasons why people live in need—because of 'laziness and lack of will-power' or because 'society treats them unfairly'—61 per cent of US respondents opted for the former, but only 8–20 per cent of the European respondents. When asked whether government was doing too much or too little for people in poverty in their country, 33 per cent of US respondents said 'too much', but 5 per cent or fewer of the Europeans. This may partly be because 70 per cent of US respondents believed that 'most poor people in this country have a chance of escaping from poverty' (as opposed to 'little chance'), but only 8–53 per cent believed this in the European countries (the Germans being the least optimistic on this score). This contrast in beliefs is despite the longer actual durations of poverty in the USA than in Germany (see Table 5.9).

3.6 SUMMARY

- A wide variety of measures has been used to measure the extent of poverty in Britain over the last century. Each brings insights but, equally, has weaknesses. While some of the different measures suggest similar levels of poverty overall, and similar upward trends in it over the last two decades, detailed analysis shows that even within the same survey the measures do not always overlap and they classify different people as 'poor'. Care is needed in deciding which to use, depending on the question being asked, and a single measure is unlikely to tell the whole story.
- During the 1960s roughly 10 per cent of the population had incomes below half the contemporary average, falling to 6 per cent in 1977. The proportion peaked at over 20 per cent in 1991/92, fell to 17 per cent in 1995–96, but has stabilized at around 18–19 per cent since the late 1990s.
- Child poverty more than doubled in relative income terms between 1979 and the early 1990s. Since New Labour came to power it has fallen.

[11] The available data are for what were East and West Germany, Finland, Spain, and Sweden. The results were downloaded from www.worldvaluessurvey.org/services/index.html on 19 January 2004.

- Against fixed real income standards, overall and child poverty fell rapidly in the periods between 1993 and 1995, and after 1996–97. Against one fixed real income standard, child poverty halved between 1996–97 and 2001–02.
- As the numbers in relative poverty grew rapidly in the 1980s, so did the depth of poverty. In the late 1970s and early 1980s, a typical poor person fell 12–14 per cent short of the poverty line. In the 1990s the shortfall has been between 18 per cent and 24 per cent.
- In recent figures for fifteen countries, only the USA and Ireland had higher relative poverty rates overall than the UK; only the USA had a worse relative child poverty rate; and only Ireland had a worse relative poverty rate for its elderly population. Despite living in a comparatively rich country, a larger proportion of British children were poor against an absolute international standard in the mid-1990s than in comparable countries (apart from Italy and Spain within the EU).
- Recently attention has been focused on wider ways in which people may not be fully participating in society, and so affected by 'social exclusion'. If we look at longitudinal data, broad indicators of social exclusion in four key dimensions did not worsen between 1991 and 1998. Few people were below thresholds in all four dimensions at the same time, although having a low income was associated with a greater chance of 'exclusion' on the other dimensions. Very few people were continuously below a threshold in each dimension, but being below it in one year was associated with a higher chance of being below it the next. Over eight years, two-thirds of the working-age population was touched by exclusion in some form at some time.
- As well as having a comparatively high relative poverty rate in European terms (although now below southern European countries as well as Ireland), the UK also has high persistent poverty, high income inequality, and a particularly high proportion of the population living in jobless households. Long-term unemployment and early school-leavers are lower than the European average, however.
- The majority of the British population is more generous in its assessment of what poverty means than a pure subsistence line. Consistently, most people see poverty as being about being unable to afford necessities that go beyond just being able to eat and live. Evidence suggests that new items are seen as 'necessities' over time as overall living standards rise.
- Many more people say that there is 'quite a lot of real poverty in Britain today' than say there is 'very little'. Trends in responses are inconsistent with widespread support for a fixed real poverty line (as used in the USA).
- Similarly, beliefs about trends in the extent of poverty in the 1980s and 1990s are consistent with relative measures, including that its growth levelled off in the 1990s.
- During the second half of 1990s there was a sharp fall in the numbers of people who said they found it 'difficult to manage' on their current income. If this were related to feelings about poverty, it would give a more optimistic picture than purely relative measures over this period.

- The levels of income at which most people say benefit recipients would not have enough to live on roughly correspond to the income cut-offs on which most attention now focuses in measuring trends in relative poverty.
- Fewer than a quarter of the British population blame 'laziness or lack of will-power' on the part of the poor for poverty. This is, however, more than in the early 1990s, and is higher than in nearly all other EU countries. A fifth blame 'injustice in our society', significantly fewer than in the early 1990s, and one of the lowest proportions to do so in the EU.
- In the mid-1990s, a much higher proportion of the US population blamed poverty on the laziness or lack of will-power of the poor than did Europeans, and a much higher proportion in the USA believed that their government did too much to help the poor, partly reflecting more optimistic US beliefs about the chances of escaping poverty.

FURTHER READING

An introduction to issues in measuring poverty can be found in *Understanding Poverty* by Peter Alcock (Macmillan, 1997) and of the concepts involved in *Poverty* by Ruth Lister (Polity Press, 2004). A discussion of the concept of social exclusion and different aspects of it is in *Understanding Social Exclusion*, edited by John Hills, Julian Le Grand, and David Piachaud (Oxford University Press, 2002).

A detailed discussion of the issues involved in choosing indicators of poverty and inequality commissioned to inform the European Union's monitoring of its commitments to achieve social cohesion is given in *Social Indicators: The EU and Social Inclusion* by Tony Atkinson, Bea Cantillon, Eric Marlier, and Brian Nolan (Oxford University Press, 2002). The Department for Work and Pensions' recommendations for measuring progress in reducing child poverty can be found in *Measuring Child Poverty* (December 2003; www.dwp.gov.uk/consultations/consult/2003/childpov/final.pdf).

The many studies putting forward different approaches to measuring poverty include:

- *Poverty in the United Kingdom* by Peter Townsend (Penguin, 1979).
- *Poor Britain* by Joanna Mack and Stewart Lansley (George Allen and Unwin, 1985).
- *Resources, Deprivation, and Poverty* by Brian Nolan and Christopher Whelan (Oxford University Press, 1996).
- *Poverty and Social Exclusion in Britain* by David Gordon et al. (Joseph Rowntree Foundation, 2000).
- *Households Below Average Income* (published annually by the Department for Work and Pensions, www.dwp.gov.uk/asd/hbai.asp).
- *Bare Necessities: Poverty and Social Exclusion in Northern Ireland* by Paddy Hillyard et al. (Democratic Dialogue, 2003) is of particular interest in showing the results of different approaches to poverty measurement within a single survey.

4

Why Has the Income Distribution Changed?

4.1 THE COMPOSITION OF HOUSEHOLD INCOME

The previous two chapters described a huge social change: the rapid increase in income inequality and relative poverty in Britain that took effect between the late 1970s and the early 1990s. The growth of overall income inequality has not been reversed and, although relative poverty was falling by the end of the 1990s, it was still much higher than in the 1960s and 1970s. This chapter looks at the factors that contributed to that change, and some of the explanations that have been put forward. A starting point is that earnings represent around two-thirds of gross (pre-tax) household incomes, so what happens to them is clearly crucial to what happens to overall income inequality. Income inequality increased in both the UK and the USA between the 1970s and the 1990s at the same time as earnings dispersion—the gap between low and high pay—widened dramatically in both countries. This makes it tempting for commentators to focus only on what has happened to earnings dispersion, as if that (sometimes with a focus only on male earnings) was the only determinant of income distribution, and to assume that fundamental changes in the modern labour market have made rising inequality inevitable. However, we have already seen that Britain's experience was not typical of other industrialized countries: while others have experienced rising inequality, this has not been global, and none experienced as large a change as the UK.

One reason for this is that earnings, and their distribution, are only part of total income. The individual income measures used in Chapters 2 and 3 were based on *net household income*, with particular assumptions about sharing within households and economies of scale in living costs. As Figure 4.1 illustrates, the distribution of net household incomes results not just from inequality *within* particular components of income (such as earnings of household members, investment income, occupational pensions, and state benefits), and their relative sizes, but also from the way in which different components are *associated* with each other. Thus, the distribution of gross household earnings depends not only on the distributions of male and female earnings but also on how employment (that is, having earnings at all) of one partner is related to that of another, and on whether high earners tend to have high-earning partners, and

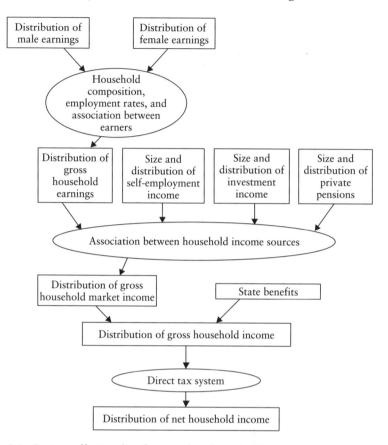

Figure 4.1. *Factors affecting distribution of net household incomes*
Source: Hills (1996a: Figure 1.3).

so on. Similarly, the distribution of gross household market income depends not only on the relative sizes and distributions of each of its components but also on whether, for instance, those with high investment incomes have high or low earnings.

The overall shape of the distribution can alter both as a result of changes in the distribution of each component—such as a widening gap between high and low earnings—and as a result of changes in the association between components—for instance, the polarization between 'no-earner' and two-earner couples. Theoretically, the gap between low and high pay for individual earners could widen, but without there being any change in net household income distribution—for instance, if high-earning wives were married to low-earning husbands and vice versa, or if changes in taxation and state benefits offset the changes in pre-tax earnings.

Figure 4.2. *Composition of income by household income group, 2001–02, UK*
Source: Lakin (2003: Table 14, Appendix 1).

For different parts of the income distribution, particular components of income or links in the chain shown in the figure are of more or less importance. Figure 4.2 shows the importance of different sources of gross household income across the distribution in 2001–02 (with each household given equal weight here, in contrast to the Households Below Average Income, HBAI, analysis used in Chapters 2 and 3).[1] Wages and salaries were 66 per cent of household income on average, but less than a quarter for the poorest two-tenths of households. State benefits accounted for 15 per cent of all gross income, but 60 per cent of the income of the poorest two-tenths. Means-tested benefits were nearly a quarter of income for the poorest tenth (although this was down from more than a third for the equivalent group in the mid-1990s). Market incomes other than earnings (such as private pensions or investment income) were around a sixth of income for all groups, apart from the top tenth, for which they made up 30 per cent, resulting in earnings being a smaller share for the top tenth than for the rest of the top half. These differences in income composition mean that changes in the relative values of different income sources—for instance, of benefits in relation to earnings—have large effects on the overall distribution.

---

[1] The equivalence scale used to adjust for household size also makes a difference: if larger households were assumed to have smaller economies of scale in living costs, wages would be more important lower down the distribution, for instance.

4.2   EARNINGS DISTRIBUTION

The gap between high and low pay has widened considerably in the UK since the late 1970s. Figure 4.3 summarizes what has happened to the dispersion of full-time weekly earnings between 1968 and 2003, using data from the *New Earnings Survey* (NES). When one interprets these data, it should be remembered that the NES is based on information from payments of National Insurance Contributions and therefore tends to omit the lowest earners, particularly part-timers, with weekly pay below the lower limit for it to count towards National Insurance rights.[2]

The figure shows three series:

- the 'decile ratio'—the ratio between the cut-off points below which the lowest tenth of male earners fall (the 'bottom decile') and above which the highest tenth come (the 'top decile');
- the decile ratio for women with full-time work; and
- the ratio between the median earnings (earnings of the 'typical worker') for women and men working full-time.

For men, the figure shows a slight narrowing in the dispersion of earnings between 1968 and 1977, followed by a substantial and almost continual widening right up to the most recent figures (another data source, the Labour Force Survey, suggests that earnings dispersion widened somewhat less fast than the NES figures show between 1994 and 2001; Machin 2003: Table 12.1a). In the late 1960s and early 1970s, the men just into the highest paid tenth earned two and a half times as much as those at the top of the bottom tenth; by 2003, the equivalent men earned three and a half times as much. This quarter century of rising dispersion ended a century or more of apparent wage rigidity, at least for manual male workers: in both 1886 and 1978, the bottom decile of male *manual* earnings was 69 per cent of the median for manual workers, while the top decile only rose from 143 per cent to 146 per cent of the median (Hills 1995: Table 4). Note that the introduction of Britain's first National Minimum Wage (NMW) in April 1999 coincided with what was only a temporary halt in the growth of this measure of dispersion, not a fall in it. At its introduction, the NMW was 44 per cent of male median hourly earnings (Low Pay Commission 2003: Table 6.3), well below the cut-off for the lowest tenth. Only around a sixth of the 1.5 million workers directly affected by the NMW in 2001 were men working full-time (2003: Figure 2.1). In fact, low male full-time weekly earnings did grow slightly relative to the middle between 1998 and 2002, but top earnings continued to grow relative to the middle of the distribution, so the ratio between top and bottom shown in the figure grew.

[2] See Wilkinson (1998) and Low Pay Commission (2003: Appendix 3) for discussion of statistics for the low-paid. A recent Office for National Statistics review of earnings statistics found that about 1.6 million low-paid jobs were not covered by the New Earnings Survey.

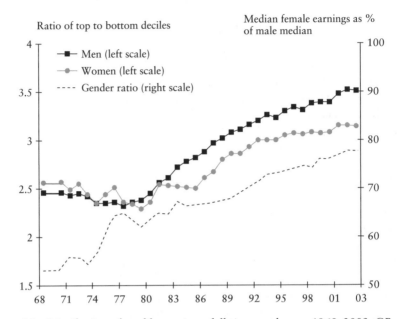

Figure 4.3. *Distribution of weekly earnings, full-time employees, 1968–2003, GB*
Source: ONS (2003: Table A28) and earlier equivalents.

The steady growth in male earnings dispersion change seen in Figure 4.3 already contrasts with the movements in overall income distribution described in Chapter 2, which also started widening at the end of the 1970s, but which followed a much more uneven path in the 1990s. Evidently, male earnings cannot be the only explanation of the changes in income distribution.

Figure 4.3 shows that female full-time earnings dispersion started widening rather later, in the mid-1980s, but has also continued to widen since then, so that its level in 2001 was the highest yet seen, although not as high as the equivalent for men. Again, since the introduction of the NMW in 1999, the bottom decile has stabilized as a percentage of the median, but the top decile has continued to grow relative to both.

Given the tendency in modern Britain for well-paid women to be married to well-paid men and the preponderance of couples with two full-time earners at the top of the distribution, the widening dispersion for men and women will have reinforced each other in contributing to overall *household* income inequality.

The figure also shows (against the right-hand scale) the rise in median female *full-time* weekly earnings relative to those of men since 1968. The ratio—only 54 per cent before the equal pay legislation of the mid-1970s—was 62 per cent in 1979, but since then has risen slowly to reach over 78 per cent by 2003. The 'gender gap' in full-time weekly pay has halved in the last thirty years, but the typical full-time woman worker is still paid a fifth less than a typical man. Desai et al. (1999) looked in detail at the factors associated with the changing gender gap in hourly wages. The gap for full-time workers was 43 per cent in 1975–77, of which only eleven percentage points could be explained by different characteristics such as education, age, industry, or region. The balance of thirty-two points was attributable to lower 'rewards' for given characteristics for women compared with men or unexplained factors. By 1993–95 the gap was down to 24 per cent, of which nineteen points reflected differential rewards or was unexplained. So factors implicated in potential discrimination had diminished, and this explained most of the change. But for women working *part-time*, the gap in hourly earnings compared with men working full-time had *increased*, from 46 per cent to 55 per cent, reflecting a growing penalty on part-time work, after controlling for characteristics.

Susan Harkness and Jane Waldfogel (2003) examine in more detail the relationship between the gender gap in pay (comparing men and women) and the 'family gap' (comparing women with and without children), contrasting the position in the UK with that in six other countries in the early to mid-1990s. Looking at hourly pay, they show that UK women with children receive only 70 per cent of men's pay, less than in the other six countries (where the ratios range from 76 per cent in the US to 92 per cent in Australia). This reflects by far the biggest family gap: women with children in the UK are paid 13 per cent less than women without children. In turn, this is mainly explained by the high proportion of UK mothers who work part-time, and the large penalty on part-time work. If one looks only at full-time workers, the overall UK gender gap falls to 18 per cent (16 per cent for women without children and 21 per cent for women with children), in the middle of the international range. Part of this reflects the overall inequality of wages in Britain: in other countries women tend to come equally far down the overall earnings distribution but, because earnings dispersion is less, the effect on relative pay is smaller. Remarkably, non-mothers in Sweden are *further* down the combined earnings distribution than in the other countries, and mothers almost as far down as in the UK, but the gender gap in pay is one of the smallest because Swedish pay differentials in general are small.

Figure 4.4 looks at trends in earnings dispersion in a different way. It shows real hourly earnings (from the NES) between 1975 and 2001 at different points in the combined earnings distribution for all employees, men and women, full- and part-time. At 2001 prices, the real wage (that is, adjusted for price inflation) at the bottom decile (the employee a tenth of the way from the bottom of the distribution) grew from £3.44 an hour in 1975 to £4.45 an hour in 2001, or by 29 per cent, with virtually no growth at all between 1975 and 1985. At the median, real hourly earnings grew by 41 per cent, from £5.62 to £7.92. But the top decile of hourly wages grew by 76 per cent, from £9.96 to £17.56. The value of the real increase in hourly wages at the top decile was seven and a half times that at the bottom decile.

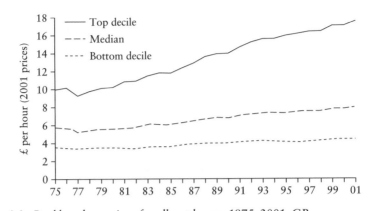

Figure 4.4. *Real hourly earnings for all employees, 1975–2001, GB*
Source: McKnight (2002: Figure 7.4), kindly updated by the author (based on New Earnings Survey Panel Dataset).

The rise in earnings dispersion has meant that more of those in work are affected by low pay when their earnings are measured against the median. For instance, Abigail McKnight (2002: Figure 7.1) shows that the proportion of all employees whose hourly wages are below two-thirds of the median (on NES data) rose from 12 per cent in 1977 to 21 per cent in 1998. At the same time, the links between low pay and poverty have strengthened over time—only 3–4 per cent of low-paid full-time workers were in households in poverty (against a line of half mean income) in the 1970s and early 1990s, but this had risen to 13 per cent by the 1990s. Looking at all of those paid less than 60 per cent of median hourly wages in 2000–01 (including part-timers), Sutherland, Sefton, and Piachaud (2003: Table 8) show that *half* of them are in households in poverty (against a 60 per cent of median income line). As Figure 2.3 showed, in 2001–02 a third of those in the poorest fifth of the income distribution were in households where someone had income from work.

Finally, Figure 4.5 shows the rise in earnings dispersion at the very top of the distribution. Atkinson and Voitchovsky (2004) analysed what had happened to the cut-offs for the top parts of the earnings distribution for all workers (including part-timers, unlike Figure 4.3). The bottom line shows the cut-off for the top tenth, rising from 1.7 times median earnings in 1977 to 2.1 times in 2001. This was a gain of 22 per cent over the period (contributing half of the rise in the decile ratio shown in Figure 4.3). But the top groups of earners gained even more. In 1977, someone with 2.9 times median earnings was just in the top 1 per cent; by 2001 the equivalent cut-off was 4.8 times, 63 per cent higher. For the top half a per cent the rise was from 3.4 times to nearly *six times* the median, 75 per cent higher. Growth at the very top has continued to be very fast since 1995. As we saw in Chapter 2, to understand the growth in inequality in Britain in the last quarter century it is important to look *within* the top 10 per cent.

Have to compare with pre-1975 trends

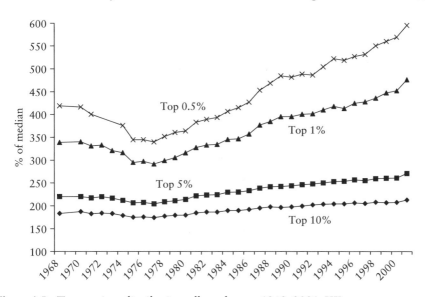

Figure 4.5. *Top earnings distribution, all employees, 1968–2001, UK*
Source: Atkinson and Voitchovsky (2004: Figure 2).

4.3   WHY HAS EARNINGS DISPERSION WIDENED?

The rise in earnings dispersion for twenty years after the mid-1970s was also a notable feature in the USA, its effects there even more striking given the stagnation or slow growth in real *median* earnings and substantial falls in real earnings for the lowest paid (Mishel and Bernstein 1994: Table 3.7). However, as Figure 4.6 (based on OECD data) shows, earnings dispersion between 1980 and 2000 (or similar periods) did not change in the same way everywhere. The decile ratio (for men and women combined) rose by as much in the Netherlands (from a lower base) and New Zealand as in the UK, and by twice as much in the USA. But in three of the countries the decile ratio fell, and in the other three it grew only slowly. Explanations of changing earnings dispersion have to take account of such differences.

In terms of explanation, one feature stands out: widening wage differentials are associated with, but by no means entirely explained by, increasing returns to skills and educational qualifications. Figure 4.7 shows the way in which possession of qualifications was associated with greater wage premiums in the mid-1990s than in the mid-1970s.[3] For instance, men with a degree had weekly earnings 73 per cent greater than those with no qualifications in the earlier period, but 93 per cent higher in the later one. Note that this occurred *despite* a substantial increase in the

---

[3] The premiums shown to some extent overstate rates of return to education. They control for neither individual ability nor age, but the young unqualified group is much smaller (and more selected by ability) than in earlier generations.

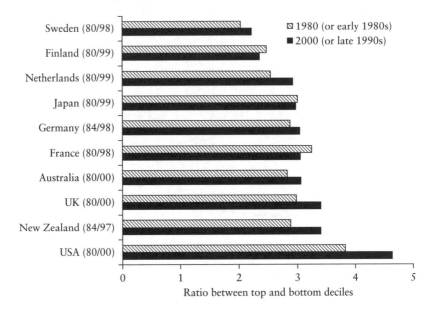

Figure 4.6. *International trends in wage differentials*

Source: OECD labour market statistics data base, www.OECD.org, 30 June 2003; figures for men and women.

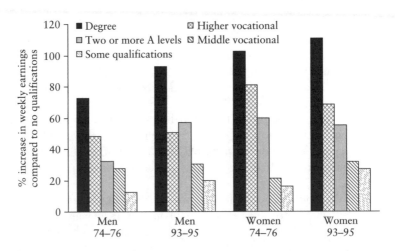

Figure 4.7. *Impact of qualifications on earnings, 1974–6 to 1993–5*
Source: Machin (1999: Table 11.4).

supply of workers with degrees over the period. Premiums also increased for men with lower qualifications compared with those with none. For women, the premium on a degree and lower and middle vocational qualifications increased, but not for higher vocational qualifications or A levels by themselves.

A leading explanation of this is that technological change has increased the returns to higher levels of skill—what has become known as 'skill-biased technological change'. Reviewing evidence from across industries and countries, Stephen Machin (2001) points to five factors consistent with this hypothesis:

- The bulk of the change in wages going to higher-skilled workers is seen *within* industries, and cannot be explained by, for instance, the declining role of manufacturing.
- Skill demand has risen faster in more technologically intensive workplaces.
- Workers using computers at work appear to receive a wage premium.
- Faster changes in skill demand are concentrated in similar industries in different countries.
- Skill upgrading is occurring in more technology-intensive developing countries, not just developed ones.

Machin (2001: 774) concludes:

The array of evidence that has been accumulated seems to be in line with the notion that technological changes that have occurred in recent years seem to be strongly linked to the relative demand shifts and increases in labour market inequality seen in many countries.

An alternative suggestion is that the changes result in part from more open global trade with developing countries with large amounts of unskilled labour— hence depressing its 'price', the wages of unskilled workers. Robert Reich (1991), later US Labor Secretary under President Clinton, stressed the way in which increasingly integrated world trade has enhanced the bargaining power of some (already well-paid) workers, but reduced that of routine production workers in industrialized countries. Adrian Wood (1994) also argued that the growth in income inequality in the North was associated with increasing trade with the South. However, Machin (2001) argues that trade flows between developed and developing countries do not seem large enough to explain the changes; that the industries in which trade has increased fastest are not those with the labour-market shifts favouring the higher-skilled; that increasing returns to skill are seen *within* developing countries; and that skill-upgrading is happening in industries that do not trade across international borders. All of these factors suggest that a simple model, at least, of the effect of greater trade does not account for increasing skill premiums in developed economies.

If changing technology is the driver of rising earnings dispersion, and rising earnings dispersion the driver of rising income inequality, there is a temptation to accept that rising income inequality is in some way inevitable. But Figure 4.6 showed that what has happened to earnings dispersion is not the same in all countries. To start with, labour market institutions—unions, national wage bargaining systems, and minimum wage legislation—matter as well. As unions declined in importance and minimum wages were eroded in both the US and the UK in the 1980s, wage inequality grew. By contrast, in other countries where they did not, or where centralized wage bargaining was important, wage differentials did not widen so much. However, supporters of the proposition that changes in the supply and demand for skilled and unskilled workers explain what has happened to relative earnings and to income inequality point to the much higher levels of unemployment in continental European economies than in the US or the UK. This leads to a proposition so influential in international institutions such as the IMF and the OECD that Tony Atkinson (2002*b*) has labelled it the 'Transatlantic Consensus'—a single cause (either technological change or more open trade) can explain *both* greater earnings inequality in the USA and UK *and* higher unemployment in continental Europe. In the former, lower demand for unskilled workers has led to lower pay; in the latter, minimum wages and more generous social security benefits have stopped this but left unskilled workers 'priced out' of jobs. Either way, there is little to stop inequality rising.

Atkinson challenges this 'consensus' on several grounds. To start with, even if the purely supply- and demand-based explanations of rising earnings inequality are correct, this does not mean that *income* inequality has to move in the same way. As discussed in Section 4.6, the structure of taxes and transfers from government has a major impact on household incomes. This can also be seen clearly at an international level. As Figure 2.10 illustrated, income inequality has not changed in the same way at all in different countries in recent years. Part of the reason for this lies in the impact of government: for example, in Canada the Gini coefficient for market incomes rose by five percentage points between the late 1970s and the mid-1990s, but inequality of *disposable* incomes did not rise at all; in Britain, not only did inequality of market incomes rise twice as much as in Canada, but inequality of disposable income rose by as much as that of market income (Atkinson 2002*b*: Figure 2.5; see also Figure 4.10 below).

Atkinson's challenge goes further than this. He shows that, in simple models of international trade, demand shifts of the kind described by those favouring the trade explanation might lead *either* to unemployment in economies with effective floors to wages *or* to widening earnings inequality in market-driven ones, but not to both at the same time. For this to occur, the world has to be much more complex than suggested by simple models of supply and demand for labour. In any case, it is a huge simplification to talk of a divide between 'skilled' and 'unskilled' labour: in reality there is a spectrum of skill, and relative wages in the UK have changed all the way along this spectrum, not just, or even most, for the unskilled.

Andrew Glyn (2001: 712) adds an empirical challenge to the 'consensus'. Reviewing evidence for changes in relative earnings and employment rates from across the OECD countries in the 1980s and 1990s, he concludes that for the least qualified '...the extent to which their relative employment rates have declined has *not* been closely tied to the extent to which their relative wages have declined. This refutes the idea that lack of wage flexibility is the dominant explanation for differences in the degree of job loss at the bottom of the labour market'. An interesting addition to the story is provided by Daron Acemoglu (2003). He suggests that the labour market institutions that have resisted rising wage dispersion in continental Europe have, as a result, encouraged investment in technologies that have increased the productivity of less-skilled workers. This means that technological change has been less 'skill-biased' than in, say, the USA.

Atkinson's greatest challenge is to suggest that relative earnings do not simply reflect market demand and supply, but that social factors are important too. In particular, he suggests that in the past there were 'reputational costs' to receiving pay that was far above the average. In everyday language, senior managers who paid themselves too much would be seen as just plain greedy. So long as most people followed social norms which constrained high pay, breaking those norms was very conspicuous, and so meant a high reputational cost. But once such constraints began to break down, and enough others had broken previous norms, the cost to the next manager of breaking them became much lower— 'they are all doing it, so why shouldn't I?' In the US, Robert Reich (1991: 223–4) points to the way in which pay differentials within US corporations in the 1950s and 1960s looked like those within integrated institutions like the army; by the 1990s, the routine production workers of large corporations were no longer necessarily in the same country or even continent as their top managements, with no social contacts binding the two together. Privatization and 'contracting out' in the public sector may similarly have broken such norms and connections between high- and low-paid workers. In this view of the world, pay relativities were strongly influenced by pay norms up until the late 1970s, not simply by supply and demand, but changes in social attitudes since then (in Anglophone countries, at least) have resulted in much weaker constraints on high pay being driven upwards by market pressures. In the UK case, if one looks back at Figures 4.3 and 4.4, it is as if the elastic bindings snapped in the early 1980s, and the highly paid have continued to accelerate away ever since.

4.4 UNEMPLOYMENT, WORKLESSNESS, AND ECONOMIC INACTIVITY

Overall income inequality is as much a matter of people being without income from work as of dispersion between low and high pay for those who are in work. Higher unemployment usually means more people dependent on state benefits and hence—in the UK, at least— living at a standard well below those in work. Even if benefit levels themselves are unchanged, a larger number receiving them and hence on low incomes means a lower standard of living for those at a certain distance from the bottom—for instance, in the middle of the poorest tenth or fifth.

However, the relationship between unemployment and income inequality is not straightforward, as can be seen by comparing the unemployment rates shown in Figure 4.8 with levels of income inequality (such as those shown in Figure 2.9). Unemployment rose in the mid-1970s, when inequality was still falling. Both rose rapidly in the first half of the 1980s, but inequality continued to rise just as fast after 1986, when unemployment fell. Unemployment leapt again between 1990 and 1993, by which time inequality had begun to level out.

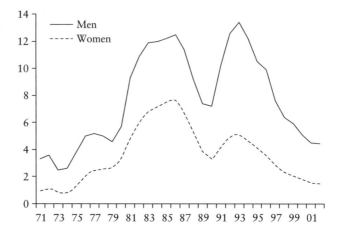

Figure 4.8. *Unemployment rates, 1971–2002, UK (%)*

Note: Annual averages of claimant unemployment (using current definitions; seasonally adjusted).
Source: ONS website (dataset Imsum 11).

Since then unemployment has fallen rapidly to levels last seen thirty years ago, but inequality has remained near its post-war peak.

Part of the explanation is that inequality measures include what is happening at the top of the distribution, while the impact of unemployment is mostly at the bottom. But even here the relationship between unemployment and poverty is not what might be assumed. Figure 4.9, updated from analysis by Burgess, Gardiner, and Propper (2001), traces how (claimant) unemployment and relative poverty (the proportion of the population with below half mean income, as in Figure 3.1) have moved since 1971. Each point shows the unemployment rate (horizontal axis) and poverty rate (vertical axis) for the year indicated. One might have expected the two to rise and fall together: greater unemployment would mean more people on benefits, and at risk of relative poverty. But the figure shows nothing like this: between 1973 and 1977, the two move in opposite directions; then unemployment rises rapidly without much change (in fact a slight fall) in relative poverty; after 1983 unemployment stabilizes but relative poverty leaps in the second half of the 1980s, and relative poverty continues to rise while unemployment falls up to 1990; relative poverty stabilizes again in the early 1990s, while unemployment rises; and finally unemployment falls back through the 1990s to the levels it started at in the early 1970s, but with relative poverty remaining more than twice as high as it was in most of the 1970s.

This diagram is a further reminder of the complexity of the relationship between the labour market, inequality, and poverty. First, the poverty rate shown is for the whole population: a quarter of those included in it are pensioners, whose poverty rate relative to average incomes might not be expected to move up and down with unemployment (and, in fact, can move in the opposite

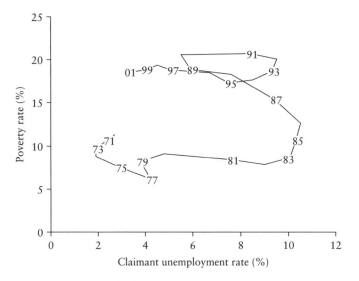

Figure 4.9. *Unemployment and relative poverty, 1971 to 2001–02, UK*
Source: Burgess, Gardiner, and Propper (2001) updated (using same sources as Figures 3.1 and 4.8).

direction if pensioners have fixed incomes, while average earnings rise in booms when unemployment is falling). But the relationship between unemployment and poverty just for those of working age is fairly weak too: looking at the 1990s only, using individual data from the British Household Panel Survey (BHPS) for those aged 16 to 55, Burgess, Gardiner, and Propper (2001) show that the relationship implies that a doubling of unemployment from 5 per cent to 10 per cent would be associated with a rise of only one percentage point in the relative poverty rate. What happens to those who remain *working* in recessions matters as well as what happens to those who lose their jobs. In particular, when one looks at *relative* poverty, slow growth or falls in average earnings hold down the poverty line against which incomes are measured.

Another factor is that the unemployment rate shown in both Figures 4.8 and 4.9 is for those who are without work and classed as unemployed while receiving benefit. Many others are of working age and without work, and at risk of poverty, but without being classed as 'unemployed'. Table 4.1 shows that 'worklessness' has followed a different pattern from unemployment. The male unemployment rate shown in Figure 4.8 may have been 10 per cent in both 1981 and 1996, but the proportion of (working age) workless households nearly doubled, from 11 per cent to 19 per cent. The falls in numbers of workless families in both the late 1980s and the late 1990s were much less marked than those in unemployment. By 2002, although the *employment* rate—the proportion of working age adults in work—was the highest for the years shown, worklessness was still far higher than in the 1970s. By 1996, three-quarters of workless

Table 4.1. *Household worklessness, 1975–2002, GB (%)*

	Workless households (working age)	Working age adults in workless households	Children in workless households	Households where all adults work	Employment rate
1975	6.5	4.3	n/a	56.7	76.9
1981	10.9	7.8	11.0	52.4	73.1
1987	16.4	11.8	17.5	54.5	72.7
1993	18.7	13.8	20.8	58.2	72.7
1996	19.3	14.2	21.5	60.7	74.6
1998	17.9	13.1	20.0	63.0	76.5
2000	16.9	12.3	17.9	65.2	77.3
2002	16.8	12.2	18.3	65.7	77.3

Source: Gregg and Wadsworth (2001: Table 1; 2003: Table 2.1).

households were poor, and they accounted for more than half of all non-pensioners in poverty (Gregg and Wadsworth 2001: Table 4). This is a particularly important driver of child poverty and explanation of why the child poverty rate in the UK is so high in international terms—a fifth of all children in the UK were in households without income from work in the mid-1990s, the highest of eighteen OECD countries surveyed by Paul Gregg and Jonathan Wadsworth (2001: Figure 3), and more than double the OECD average.

High worklessness is partly driven by rising lone parenthood and the relatively low (in international terms), but now rising, employment rate for lone parents, as well as an increase in single adult households. However, Gregg and Wadsworth's analysis suggests that these account for only a quarter of the rise in workless households. It also results from the polarization that has occurred within two-adult households between those where *both* work and those where *neither* works—the phenomenon of 'more work in fewer households'. They show that in the mid-1970s more than a third of working age households contained one adult who worked and one who did not, and only 7 per cent had no adult in work. By 2001, only a sixth of households had a mix of working and non-working adults, and a sixth had no adult in work. Part of the explanation lies in shared characteristics of partners, whose skills, age, and location may make finding a job hard for each of them. But this explains only part of what is going on. Other research suggests that the benefit system has an impact too, particularly the way in which the family means-test in Income Support (or what is now called income-tested Jobseeker's Allowance) affects the second earner in a couple once his or her entitlement to non-means-tested unemployment benefits runs out (McKay, Walker, and Youngs 1997; Gallie, Marsh, and Vogler 1994). Having a working partner has a major positive effect on someone's returns to low-paid work.

If we look at the impact on overall income inequality, the increase in female labour force participation that has contributed to the rise of the two-earner couple has had different effects at different times (Harkness, Machin, and Waldfogel 1996; Hills 1995: 50–1). Up to the 1970s, it was the wives of relatively well-paid men whose employment increased most rapidly, tending to increase household income inequality. In the 1980s, however, the wives of less well-paid (but employed) men tended to catch up. This tended to slow inequality growth *among* couples with work, but contributed to the growing gap *between* them and other population groups, such as pensioners, lone parents, or the unemployed.

An important part of the rise in worklessness that is not registered as 'unemployment'—economic inactivity—has been among older men, particularly those with low skills and/or health problems. As Stephen Nickell (2001: 623) puts it, '...the huge decline in the relative demand for unskilled workers has outstripped the fall in their relative supply. This has led directly to significant falls in their relative pay and very large increases in their unemployment, inactivity, and sickness and disability rates'. Faggio and Nickell (2003) show that the inactivity rate for men aged 55–64 rose from 14 per cent in 1977–78 to between 36 per cent and 40 per cent twenty years later (although it was down slightly by 2002). For men of this age with low skills (in the bottom quarter of men by qualifications), the rate rose from 15 per cent to 50 per cent over this period. For those reporting a 'limiting long-standing illness', the rise was from under 40 per cent to nearly two-thirds. Even among men aged 25–54, by 2000 half of those both with low skills and reporting chronic illness were economically inactive. This is an aspect of a wider problem: Tania Burchardt (2000) found that disabled people made up *half* of the total of those not employed and looking for work. Once out of work, older workers and disabled people find it much harder to get back into work than others. Nigel Campbell (1999: 44) calculated that in the first half of the 1990s a 45–49 year-old man not in employment had a chance of under a quarter of *ever* working again in a year-round job (with employment rates now higher for those over 50, the chances will have improved since then). Burchardt (2000) shows that the proportion of disabled people who get into work in a year is only a sixth of that for non-disabled people, and that a third of disabled people who do so are out of work again by the following year (compared with only a fifth for others).

4.5   OTHER SOURCES OF MARKET INCOME

The composition of household income has changed since the late 1970s. Table 4.2 shows that back in 1978 wages and salaries (excluding income from self-employment) accounted for nearly two-thirds of household market income (on national accounts definitions, which differ from those used in Figure 4.2). By 1996, when this series ends, this had fallen to only 54 per cent. By contrast, incomes from self-employment, private pensions, and life insurance had all become more important. State benefits rose over the period as a whole, reflecting, for instance, greater

Table 4.2. *Composition of household income, 1978–1996, UK (%)*

	Wages and salaries	Self-employment	Rents, dividends, interest	Private pensions and life insurance	State benefits, etc.	Income in kind
1978	65.8	8.9	4.9	5.3	14.1	1.1
1982	60.7	8.4	6.5	6.7	16.5	1.1
1986	57.1	9.7	7.7	7.9	16.0	1.7
1990	57.4	9.9	10.0	8.5	12.5	1.5
1994	54.7	10.3	6.5	11.0	16.2	1.4
1996	54.1	10.2	7.0	11.7	15.7	1.3

Source: ONS (1997: Table 4.9) and earlier equivalents.

numbers of pensioners, but also rose and fell with the economic cycle.[4] This changing balance affected the overall income distribution—generally tending to increase inequality—because, as Figure 4.2 showed, the importance of these other income sources varies greatly across the distribution. Most straightforwardly, the detailed figures from which Figure 4.2 is drawn show that 48 per cent of all investment income in 2001–02 went to the richest tenth of households. The rise in the share of 'rents, dividends, and interest' in the 1980s directly contributed to the increase in overall inequality. Since then the picture is less clear. As a result of lower inflation in the 1990s, *nominal* interest rates have fallen, and so some investment incomes fell. However, the sharp increase in wealth inequality at the end of the 1990s discussed in Section 2.4 will have fed back into income inequality.

Similarly, 56 per cent of self-employment income in 2001–02 went to the top tenth of households, so growth in this has also contributed to growing inequality. This has been compounded by a growth in low-income self-employment—as Figure 2.3 showed, the self-employed are disproportionately found at *both* the top *and* the bottom of the income distribution. There is, for instance, a significant group of people with low incomes classed as 'self-employed', in some cases resulting from arrangements such as 'contracting out', which allows previous employers to avoid the additional costs of direct employment. Stephen Jenkins (1995) found that self-employment incomes were the largest single contributor to overall inequality growth in the period 1971 to 1986. This reflected the rising numbers of, and growing inequality among, the self-employed, and greater correlation between high incomes from self-employment and other sources. Similarly, Alissa Goodman and Steven Webb (1994) found that the growth in self-employment and in the dispersion of self-employment incomes were important contributors to the overall growth in inequality between 1979 and 1991.

[4] Data on household income composition from survey data suggests that some of these trends may have reversed after 1996, with earnings making up a larger share in 2001–02 than in 1996–97 (Lakin 2003).

Finally, an important social change of the last twenty years has been the emergence of a group of relatively high-income pensioners with significant incomes from occupational pensions. This has led to a pattern of income polarization *within* the pensioner population. On the one hand, there is still a substantial group of pensioners almost entirely dependent on state benefits—either the basic state pension or the means-tested minimum given (if it is claimed) by what is now called the 'guarantee element' of Pension Credit (previously Income Support, or the 'minimum income guarantee'). As Figure 4.11 below shows, until the most recent years, the value of the basic pension has slipped further and further behind average earnings, but the means-tested minimum has lost less of its relative value. On the other hand, as Figure 2.2 showed, the maturing of occupational pensions has meant that 11 per cent of the richest fifth of the population are now pensioners.

Table 4.3 shows the growth in inequality between pensioners during the overlapping periods 1979 to 1996–97, and 1994–95 to 2001–02. The figures in each panel show the changes in real income for those put in successive fifths of the distribution of income for pensioner couples and single pensioners respectively. In the first period, real pensioner income grew faster than for the population as a whole, but the difference over the period was much greater at the top. A new generation with good occupational pensions was replacing an older one with lower incomes. Lower income pensioners in 1996–97 were better off than their predecessors, but by less (and by less than average income growth). Over the second period, the growth in pensioner income has been more balanced, with the poorest fifths of pensioner couples and single pensioners keeping up with the average (and continuing to gain relative to the population as a whole, whose equivalent incomes after housing costs grew by 27 per cent).

Table 4.3. *Growth in real net pensioner income by income group, 1979 to 2001–02 (%)*

	Fifths of the couple or single pensioner income distribution					Overall mean
	Bottom fifth	Second fifth	Middle fifth	Fourth fifth	Top fifth	
Pensioner couples						
1979 to 1996–97	31	51	63	76	93	69
1994–95 to 2001–02	26	29	28	26	20	29
Single pensioners						
1979 to 1996–97	22	28	46	78	84	61
1994–95 to 2001–02	37	34	48	44	27	33

Note: Figures are after housing costs, from FES for UK for 1979 to 1996–97; from FRS for GB for 1994–95 to 2001–02. Figures show growth in quintile group median for relevant group of pensioners.

Source: DWP (2003f: Tables 16 and A16).

4.6   THE IMPACT OF POLICY: BENEFIT LEVELS AND TAXATION

What governments do through the operation of the tax and transfer (benefit) system has a considerable impact on the distribution of people's disposable incomes, which varies between countries and over time. The distributional impact of the UK's current system is analysed in detail in Chapter 8, but an indication of the way in which government has contributed to slowing or accelerating the growth of inequality can be seen in Figure 4.10. This presents Gini coefficient indices of inequality (see Section 2.2) for household income measured in various ways from the Office for National Statistics' (ONS) *Economic Trends* series. It compares the inequality of market incomes with that of gross income (including cash benefits and tax credits), disposable income (after direct taxes), and post-tax income (after indirect taxes are allowed for).[5] The series for disposable incomes is that also shown in Figure 2.9. Note that in these series each household, regardless of size, counts as a single unit, not each individual as in the HBAI statistics.

4.6.1   *Social Security Benefits*

The benefit system has a large equalizing effect. Throughout the period, the inequality index for gross incomes (including benefits) was much lower than that for market incomes. However, the relationship between the two has varied over time. Between 1977 and 1984, the growth in market income inequality was much faster than that in gross incomes: the benefit system appears to have restrained the growth in income inequality. Between 1984 and 1991, the reverse was the case, and inequality in gross incomes grew faster—benefits were no longer having this restraining effect. In the first half of the 1990s, market incomes became somewhat more unequal, but inequality in gross incomes declined. In the second half of the 1990s, market income inequality was relatively stable, while inequality of gross incomes rose. An important contributor to these patterns has been the relative value of cash benefits. In the second halves of the 1980s and 1990s, market incomes were rising in real terms, but the real values of many benefits were frozen, with the result that inequality in gross incomes rose more rapidly than that in market incomes, as those dependent on benefits were left behind (see Chapters 6 and 9 for discussion of more recent developments).

Different parts of the benefit system have been treated in different ways. Figure 4.11 shows what has happened since 1971 to the values of four example benefits: the single basic state retirement pension; Income Support (or its equivalent) for single pensioners; unemployment benefit (now Jobseeker's Allowance,

---

[5] The ONS also publishes a series for 'final incomes', including the effects of public services 'in kind'. This is not included here, as it would be misleading as a guide to living standards without also allowing for differences in households' needs for health care, for instance. The distributional effect of in-kind services is discussed in Chapter 8.

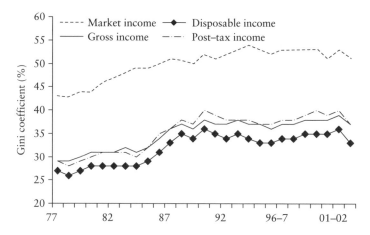

Figure 4.10. *Taxes, benefits, and household income distribution, 1977 to 2002–03, UK*
Source: Lakin (2004: Table 27, Appendix 1) and earlier equivalents.

JSA) for single people; and Income Support for single people aged 25–60. The top panel shows their values in real terms, the lower one values relative to average adult earnings (note that the indices for prices and earnings used by DWP in these two series are applied at different points within the year, so the two diagrams show slightly different patterns over time). The basic pension increased significantly in real terms between 1971 and 1983, after which the early 1980s policy decision to link most benefit levels to prices rather than to earnings or other incomes took effect, and the real value of the pension stayed much the same until the end of the 1990s, when it rose again. This meant, however, that it fell from 26 per cent of average earnings in 1983 to 18 per cent by 1990, and 16 per cent by 2002. By contrast, the real value of Income Support has increased steadily since 1976, with particularly large increases since 1998. As a result, the value of the means-tested minimum for a single pensioner was almost as great in relation to average earnings in 2002 as it had been in 1971 (see Hills 2004 for a more detailed discussion of changes in state pensions since 1978).

The decline in the relative value of Unemployment Benefit since its link with the pension was broken in 1973 has been even greater, particularly since the early 1980s, falling from 21 per cent of average earnings in 1979 to 12 per cent by 2002. In this case the values of non-means-tested and means-tested benefits converge by the end of the period.

Benefit levels are only one indicator of the generosity of the benefit system. Wider availability of benefits or a higher rate of take-up of entitlements can also have major effects. However, the figures illustrate the implications of current policy towards benefit uprating, that benefits should be linked to prices rather than any measure of general income growth, a policy which has, as a default, been that of

(a) Real values (£/week, April 2002 prices)[a]

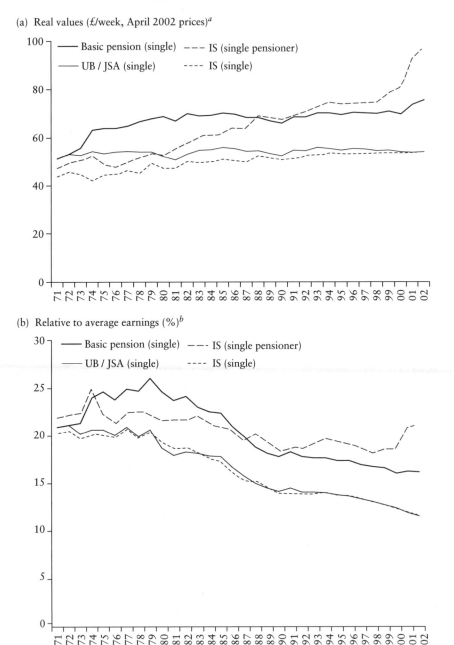

(b) Relative to average earnings (%)[b]

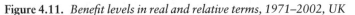

Figure 4.11. *Benefit levels in real and relative terms, 1971–2002, UK*

[a] Cash value of benefit in month uprated adjusted by average value of price index between upratings.
[b] Cash value of benefit in month uprated adjusted by average earnings index at April that year.

Source: DWP (2003g: Table 5.11).

New Labour's predecessors since the early 1980s and has continued to be that of the government since 1997 (but with some important exceptions, the effects of which are discussed in Section 7.3 and in Chapter 9). When general living standards are rising, those dependent on price-linked benefits inevitably fall behind the rest of the population, which increases inequality.

4.6.2   *Direct Taxes*

Figure 4.10 also gives a measure of the impact of taxation. That of direct taxation can be seen by comparing the index for disposable income (the main focus of the analysis in Chapter 2) with that of gross income. After direct taxes are allowed for, incomes are less unequal than before them, but the difference in the two indices remains at around three percentage points for the entire twenty-four year period shown. At first sight this is surprising, as one might expect the rapid growth in the inequality of market incomes to have pulled the better-off into higher income tax brackets, implying slower growth in inequality after allowing for taxes than before them. However, this 'automatic' dampening effect of direct taxes has been cancelled out by 'discretionary' tax changes, such as the cuts in higher rates of income tax in the 1980s that had the opposite effect to dampening, boosting high incomes and implying faster growth in inequality of income after allowing for taxes (Hills 1995: 58–61). In some other countries, such as France and Germany, taxation appears to have slowed the growth in inequality, but in the UK and USA discretionary tax changes in the 1980s meant that it did not. Indeed, in the USA inequality grew faster after for taxation was allowed for than before it (Gardiner 1997; Atkinson 2002*b*: Figure 2.5).

Chapter 7 discusses the overall structure of taxation as it is now. As far as the changes over the last two decades are concerned, three periods can be distinguished:

- *From 1978–79 to 1992–93:* Over this period cuts in the top rates of income tax, failure of tax allowances to keep up with income growth, increasing use of National Insurance Contributions, and introduction of the Poll Tax (officially, the 'Community Charge') to fund local government all tilted the direct tax burden away from those with high towards those with average and lower incomes. If, for instance, the rules of the 1978–79 tax system (adjusted for income growth) had been applied to people in 1992–93, the richest tenth would have been about 10 per cent *worse* off than they were under the actual 1992–93 system, and the poorest tenth about 20 per cent *better* off.[6] These discretionary changes cancelled out what would otherwise have been the

---

[6] Derived from Hills (1995: Figure 35), based on analysis in Redmond and Sutherland (1995). This assumes that people's pre-tax incomes would have remained the same even if the 1978–79 tax system had been restored. This is unlikely for the highest investment incomes, at least, given that in theory the earlier system involved tax rates of up to 98 per cent on investment income but only 30 per cent on capital gains. The straightforward accountancy manoeuvres that avoided the highest rates were no longer so important by the end of the 1980s.

automatic effect of the tax system in slowing down the impact of the rapid growth in inequality in market incomes.

- *From 1992–93 to 1997–98:* Tax policy in this period was much less regressive. First, the Poll Tax was abolished in April 1993 and replaced by the less regressive Council Tax. Between 1992–93 and 1994–95 taxes increased sharply overall, but most as a proportion of income for the top half of the income distribution. Tax reductions from 1994–95 to 1997–98 reined back the increase for those with higher incomes but, if one looks at the period as whole, the overall effect—compared with having kept the 1992–93 system indexed for inflation—was to reduce incomes for the top six tenths of the income distribution by about 1 per cent, while having a neutral effect on the bottom four tenths (Hills 1998a: Figure 18).

- *Since 1997–98:* The overall impact of tax, tax credit, and benefit changes since New Labour was elected is examined in Chapter 9. Taken as a whole, they imply a significant redistribution of income towards those with low incomes, compared with what would have happened if the system inherited from the Conservatives had simply been adjusted for price inflation. However, at a time when overall living standards have been rising rapidly, the changes were not enough—in New Labour's first term, at least—to prevent inequality measures of the kind shown in Figure 4.10 for disposable income rising.

4.6.3   *Indirect Taxes*

Finally, Figure 4.10 shows that, after the estimated impact of *indirect* taxes is allowed for as well, 'post-tax' incomes are usually as unequal as gross incomes. Inequality in post-tax income grew faster than that in disposable incomes in the 1980s, but since then the two have moved together. Indirect tax changes, particularly their greater role in the tax system as a whole, therefore appear to have had a *disequalizing* effect in the 1980s, but to have been more neutral in the 1990s. Sutherland, Sefton, and Piachaud (2003: Figure 13) suggest that, in the period from 1997 to 2002–03, indirect taxes rose by an amount equivalent to around 0.4 per cent of income for most income groups, but by more than 1 per cent for the poorest tenth. This regressive impact (for instance, from increasing taxes on tobacco) partly offset the progressive effect of New Labour's direct tax and benefit changes.

4.7   SUMMARY

- The increasing gap between low pay and high pay has been a key contributor to rising income inequality in Britain in the last two decades, but income inequality is not explained by earnings dispersion alone—changes in other components of income can offset or compound its effects. In the 1980s, most of these factors pushed in the same direction: towards greater income inequality. Since the 1990s, the situation has been more complicated, with some factors pushing in one direction, some in the other.

- At the bottom of the distribution, state benefits are 60 per cent of gross income. For the richest tenth, market income other than earnings is 30 per cent of gross income. Changes in the relativities between benefits or investment income and earnings therefore affect the overall income distribution.

- In the 1970s, men at the cut-off for the top tenth of full-time earnings had two and a half times the weekly pay of those at the cut-off for the bottom tenth. By 2003 the ratio was three and a half times. The continuous growth of male earnings dispersion throughout the 1980s and 1990s followed a different pattern from income inequality.

- Female full-time earnings dispersion started growing later than that for men, but had also reached record levels by 2001, still somewhat lower than for men.

- The very highest earners have had even greater gains than those on the margins of the top tenth. The cut-off for the top half a per cent of earners grew from 3.4 times median earnings in 1977 to nearly six times in 2001.

- Earnings dispersion grew as fast in some other countries as in the UK between 1980 and 2000, and in the USA twice as fast. But in some countries dispersion narrowed or grew only slowly: there was no uniform global pattern.

- A feature of rising earnings dispersion has been that the extra wages received by those with higher qualifications have risen, despite their increasing numbers.

- A leading explanation is that technology has changed in the last two decades in ways that increase demand for skilled workers and reduce it for unskilled ones. Some analysts also point to more open trade with developing countries as a contributory factor, but the evidence for this is disputed.

- Even if such changes affected all countries equally, this would not mean that nothing could be done to stop *income* inequality rising. The tax and benefit system can offset rising earnings dispersion. In some countries it has done so; in the UK and USA it has not.

- Wage determination is not a simple matter of market supply and demand. Social norms can also affect differentials. One explanation of rising earnings differences in the UK is that such norms have broken down since the 1970s, and social constraints that used to apply to high pay have been eroded.

- Levels of unemployment also affect income distribution, but over the last twenty years unemployment, inequality, and poverty have not moved directly together in the ways that might have been expected.

- One reason is that incomes of the non-working age population matter too. Another is that relative poverty measures are affected by income growth of the working population during recessions and booms.

- An important factor in the UK is that 'worklessness', including people outside the labour market, grew much faster than unemployment, and has fallen back less fast. Economic inactivity rates for men aged 55–64 rose from 14 per cent in the late 1970s to up to 40 per cent in the late 1990s.

- The number of workless households is an important explanation of child poverty in the UK. This is not just because of high rates of lone parenthood, but also because there has been a progressive polarization for two-adult households between those where neither works and those where both work.
- Employment incomes are a smaller share of household incomes than in the past. The rising shares of the total from investment and self-employment incomes have contributed to growing inequality. Another contributor has been growing income polarization within the pensioner population.
- Inequality measures based on gross incomes (including cash benefits) have followed a different pattern from market incomes. In the late 1970s and early 1980s, benefits appeared to restrain inequality growth, but they have not done so since benefits were in general linked to prices rather than incomes in the early 1980s. Those dependent on such benefits have fallen behind the rest of the population, particularly when average incomes were growing strongly in the second halves of the 1980s and 1990s.
- Allowing for direct taxes makes—perhaps surprisingly—little difference to inequality growth over the period. In the 1980s, the way in which direct taxes might automatically have slowed inequality growth was offset by discretionary tax changes that shifted the tax burden from those with high to lower and middle incomes. Tax policy in the mid-1990s was less regressive. (The impact of policy since 1997 is examined in Chapter 9.)
- Increases in indirect taxes in the 1980s widened inequality after allowing for them. Increases in them since 1997 have also partly offset the progressive effect of other tax and benefit changes.

FURTHER READING

Different factors contributing to the growth in overall income inequality between the 1970s and 1990s are covered by Chapters 6–10 of *New Inequalities: The Changing Distribution of Income and Wealth in the UK* edited by John Hills (Cambridge University Press, 1996).

Two very useful sources on what has happened to the labour market in the past two decades are: a special issue of the *Oxford Bulletin of Economics and Statistics*, 63 (2001), on 'The Labour Market Consequences of Technical and Structural Change'; and *The Labour Market under New Labour* edited by Richard Dickens, Paul Gregg, and Jonathan Wadsworth (Palgrave Macmillan, 2003).

Tony Atkinson's 'Is Rising Income Inequality Inevitable? A Critique of the "Transatlantic Consensus" ' is chapter 2 in *World Poverty: New Policies To Defeat an Old Enemy* edited by Peter Townsend and David Gordon (Policy Press, 2002).

For analysis of the effects on income distribution of recent changes in tax and benefit policy, see: *Poverty in Britain: The Impact of Government Policy Since 1997,* by Holly Sutherland, Tom Sefton, and David Piachaud (Joseph Rowntree Foundation, 2003); and 'Social Security Under New Labour: What Did the Third Way Mean for Welfare Reform?' by Mike Brewer, Tom Clark, and Matthew Wakefield, *Fiscal Studies*, 23/4 (2002).

5

Income Dynamics and Social Mobility

5.1 WHY EXAMINE INCOME DYNAMICS?

Chapter 2–4 have been concerned with the ways in which income distribution and other aspects of inequality have changed over time. This analysis has been based on comparing the results of successive cross-sectional surveys. In effect, we have been comparing annual snapshots of the population. This is very revealing of the extent to which British society has been transformed in the last quarter century. But it does not tell us what has happened to *individuals* over time. After all, it would be possible to have a society where the overall distributions of income and earnings stayed exactly the same from year to year, but where people were swapping places: some individuals would be getting much better off and others getting poorer. Under the surface of the aggregate statistics, it would not be a static society at all. To get under this surface, we need surveys that follow the same individuals over time: what are known as longitudinal data. Here the UK is now in a very favourable position. One of the most exciting developments of recent years has been research on income dynamics, particularly as a result of analysis of the British Household Panel Study (BHPS), a survey that has been tracking people's circumstances from year to year. In addition, the UK has two longer-running studies each of which has been looking at a group of people regularly since they were born. Those surveyed in the National Child Development Study (NCDS) were born in March 1958; those in the Birth Cohort Study (BCS70) in 1970. Both groups were interviewed most recently in 2000. These studies allow analysis of the links between childhood circumstances and adult outcomes and of how they are changing between the generations, as well as of the links between the circumstances of one generation and of their children. A new cohort study—the Millennium Cohort—is now following a group of children born in 2000–01.

Such data are invaluable for several reasons:

- The results of cross-sectional surveys may be misleading in certain ways. For instance, those shown as poor may not stay poor for very long. If what we are seeing is, for instance, simply a short gap in income between jobs, no great hardship may be associated with it. More generally, the data collected for income in a single week or month may not be a good guide to someone's living standards over longer periods, such as a year.

- On the other hand, long periods of low income may imply more serious problems than would be expected simply from knowing someone had a low income at a particular date. Savings are likely to be run right down, opportunities for 'tiding over' loans exhausted, and consumer durables may need to be replaced.
- Correspondingly, we may look very differently at periods of low income when people are studying or at the start of what will be a well-paid career from those when income is unlikely to recover—for instance, near or during retirement.
- It may be most effective to differentiate policies towards those with low income depending on its duration. We may also be interested in whether policy itself has a dynamic or persistent effect, and whether it changes the risks of favourable or adverse events happening or simply moderates their effects when they do.
- If one of the aims of policy is to give people equal opportunities and life chances, *lack of* economic or social mobility may be a marker for inequalities in opportunity. Understanding the links across people's lifetimes and between generations may shed light on the most effective ways of breaking continuities in disadvantage.

However, whether finding a great deal of mobility is a 'good thing' in itself is unclear. On the one hand, seeing people trapped in low incomes with little chance of escape would be worrying. Indeed, when the first British data on short-term income mobility became available, the then Social Security Secretary, Peter Lilley (1996), hailed them as meaning that the picture of people trapped in poverty had been 'blown apart'. As we shall see in Section 5.3, the longer-term picture is more complex, and less reassuring, than this, but the point remains that persistent poverty will usually be more of a concern than temporary poverty.

On the other hand, for others 'mobility' may not be so desirable. After all, in many circumstances people are prepared to pay insurance premiums or other savings costs precisely to *avoid* fluctuations in incomes. And, if we are looking at mobility in relative terms, every instance of upward mobility must be balanced by another downward. The former may be popular; the latter may well be uncomfortable for those experiencing it.

5.2   HOW MUCH MOBILITY IS THERE? INCOME DYNAMICS IN THE 1990S

Thanks to the British Household Panel Study, we now know far more about how people's incomes change over time than we did just a few years ago. This survey has been tracking the same people since 1991, interviewing them each year about their incomes, jobs, family circumstances, and other aspects of their lives. By the tenth wave (2000), there was complete information on household income at every wave for about 5,600 people. Since the results presented in this section and the next two draw heavily on this source, some limitations of using any survey of this kind should first be noted:

- Although BHPS does collect some information for the whole period between surveys, the income information refers to the most recent month (or other payment interval) at intervals of a year apart. There may be considerable movement *within* the year that is not captured by this approach, and the months available may be atypical of the rest of the year.
- The longer the time period studied, the more likely it is that respondents may drop out of the survey. This *attrition* can be a problem, not just because sample numbers get smaller but also because those who stay in may be atypical of the population as a whole. People who move frequently may be hard to track, for instance. Although 'weighting' is used to correct for this kind of bias, the longer the survey runs the harder it is to do so. For very long runs, 'survivor bias' also becomes a problem as, for instance, only particular groups of the initially elderly survive.
- Any income survey involves a degree of uncertainty about the data collected. When one compares two observations a year apart, what looks like a change in income may simply be the result of different observations or reporting errors from an unchanged level.
- In particular, those seen with low incomes in one year may tend to be those for which the random measurement error—or indeed genuine random variation—happens to be downwards that year, while for those with high incomes the opposite may be true. If one examines the same cases a year later, even if underlying circumstances have not changed, it is more likely that the lower income cases will have gone up and the higher ones down. This may give a spurious impression of a move towards greater equality over the period (Atkinson, Maynard, and Trinder 1983: Figure 5.2).
- Since the 1990s were in some ways a special decade, with falling unemployment through much of it, patterns seen then may not be reproduced at other stages of the economic cycle.

The most straightforward way of looking at mobility is a *transition matrix* showing where people from, for instance, the poorest tenth end up a year later. If there were complete immobility, all the positive entries would be on the 'leading diagonal' (the same tenth in both years) and would equal 100. By contrast, if people's income rankings each year were random, all of the entries in a ten-by-ten matrix would equal 10. The less mobility there is, the greater the numbers on the leading diagonal will be. Where actual results fall between the extreme cases gives an idea of how much mobility there is. Whether it represents 'a lot' or 'a little' depends to some extent on prior expectations.

For instance, Table 5.1 shows Sarah Jarvis and Stephen Jenkins' comparison (1997*a*) between the income group of individuals between the first and second years of BHPS (1991 and 1992). Of those in the poorest tenth in 1991, 46 per cent were also in it a year later. If all the numbers in bold are added together,

Table 5.1. *Income mobility between 1991 and 1992, GB*

Initial income group (tenths of individuals) in 1991	Percentage of each initial income group ending up in each income group in 1992									
	Poorest	2	3	4	5	6	7	8	9	Richest
Poorest	46	21	15	5	4	5	3	1	0	2
2	23	39	20	11	4	1	1	1	0	1
3	12	19	28	22	8	3	3	2	2	1
4	7	9	19	27	20	9	5	2	0	2
5	2	4	11	15	30	22	7	5	2	1
6	3	5	5	10	17	25	18	10	5	2
7	3	1	2	4	11	20	36	14	6	3
8	2	1	2	2	2	11	19	34	17	6
9	4	2	2	2	2	6	8	23	41	13
Richest	2	1	1	1	1	2	3	7	24	58

Source: Jarvis and Jenkins (1997*a*).

36 per cent of the sample were in the same tenth a year later, compared with 10 per cent in the random model or 100 per cent with complete immobility. Seventy-one per cent are on the leading diagonal or the two diagonals next to it. In other words, nearly three-quarters of the sample were in either the same income group or a neighbouring one a year later.

The table shows that more than half of the poorest tenth 'escape' from it by the next year. This might be taken to imply that much poverty is only temporary, and so less of a problem than might be feared. However, the table also shows that 67 per cent of them remain in either the poorest or the next-poorest tenth. Only a third move further. For the poorest fifth as a whole, 65 per cent are still there one year later and 85 per cent are in either the poorest or the next-poorest fifth. Taking these figures together suggests that around one-third of low income is in some sense transient, but two-thirds is not. As this kind of research shows, there is considerable income mobility from year to year, but little of it is long-range.

Even so, repeating this process often enough could mean that the income groups would become completely mixed up. It might be thought that, if only 65 per cent of the poorest fifth stay in it the next year, then with repeated attrition only 42 per cent would be left by Year 3, and only 2 per cent by Year 10. However, even if people's incomes move completely at random, some of those who escape would drop back again. Eventually, a fifth of each initial income group would be found in each finishing group. However, the results in Table 5.2—which looks at people's positions in 2001 depending on which fifth they started in back in 1991—do not show this at all. More than two-fifths of those who started in the poorest fifth were either back there or still there ten years later.

Table 5.2. *Income mobility between 1991 and 2001, GB*

Initial income group (fifths of individuals) in 1991	Percentage of each initial income group ending up in each income group in 2001				
	Poorest	2	3	4	Richest
Poorest	41	26	16	10	7
2	24	30	22	16	8
3	15	22	25	22	16
4	12	13	22	29	24
Richest	9	8	16	24	45

Source: DWP (2003*c*: Table 4).

Table 5.3. *Repeated low income: Random model and actual data*

Number of times in poorest fifth	Percentage of individuals		Percentage of low-income observations accounted for	
	Random model	BHPS 1991–94	Random model	BHPS 1991–94
None	41	64	—	—
1	41	13	51	17
2	15	9	36	22
3	2.5	7	9.6	26
4	0.2	7	0.8	35

Note: Low income in this table taken as being in poorest fifth.

Source: Own calculations based on Jarvis and Jenkins (1997*b*: Table 1).

Such results show that low income is *not* a random phenomenon. Low-income observations are linked. For instance, from the first four waves of BHPS one can plot how often different individuals (with income data for all four years) are found in the poorest fifth. Table 5.3 compares the observed pattern with what one would expect if income movements were random. The BHPS data are very different. In the BHPS 64 per cent of individual cases never enter the poorest fifth (compared with 41 per cent at random), and 14 per cent of individuals are in the poorest fifth three or four times out of four (compared with only 3 per cent at random). Moreover, 61 per cent of low-income *observations* (being in the poorest fifth in any given year) are accounted for by the individuals who are in the poorest fifth three or four times, compared with only 10 per cent in the random model. In other words, repeated low income accounts for a far greater proportion of the low income seen in cross-sections than would be expected if movements were random.

5.3   WHO ESCAPES FROM POVERTY? WHO REMAINS POOR?

5.3.1   *Exiting and Re-entering Poverty*

Stephen Jenkins (1998) has described British income mobility as reflecting a 'rubber band model'—people can move around to some extent from year to year but many are pulled back to the same position, as if held in place by a rubber band. Two of the mechanisms by which this works are shown in Figures 5.1 and 5.2, based on analysis of nine waves of the BHPS by Stephen Jenkins and John Rigg (2001). The first shows the rate at which people *exit* from poverty (equivalent income below 60 per cent of the contemporary median) depending on how long they have already been poor. The figure shows two things. First, there is a huge variation in people's chance of escape even in the first year, depending on their characteristics. On average more than half of those seen in poverty for the first time would no longer be poor a year later. But of people with favourable characteristics—a young, well-qualified two-earner couple with no children, for instance—90 per cent would escape. By contrast, a non-working single parent with low qualifications would have only a 30 per cent chance of escape in the first year. By itself, this would mean that exit rates from poverty would be lower for groups that had already been poor for a while; those with a high chance of escape would most likely have gone, leaving behind those less likely to do so. But

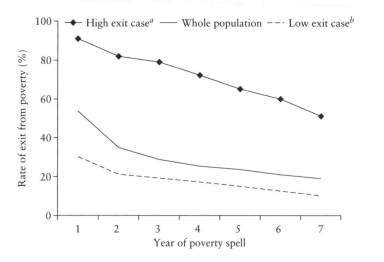

Figure 5.1. *Poverty exit rates by duration of poverty, GB (where household head aged under 60)*

[a] 'High exit' case is household head aged under 30, with A levels or higher qualifications, no children, two adults, both working.

[b] 'Low exit' case is single adult with two children (one under 6 years of age), no A levels, and not working.

Source: Jenkins and Rigg (2001: Figure 4.1).

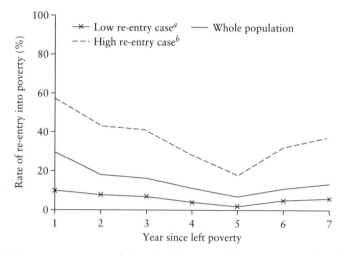

Figure 5.2. *Poverty re-entry rates by length of time since left poverty, GB (where household head aged under 60)*

[a] Low re-entry case is same as high 'exit case' in Figure 5.1.
[b] High re-entry case is same as low exit case in Figure 5.1.
Source: Jenkins and Rigg (2001: Figure 4.5).

Figure 5.1 shows that more than this is going on: even if one looks only at people with the same characteristics, exit rates decline the longer people have already been poor. The chance of escape in the next year for the case with a low exit rate to start with falls to only 10 per cent by their seventh year in poverty. In other words, the longer one has been poor, the more slowly will one escape.[1]

But second, even when people do escape from poverty, they have a higher chance of dropping back into it than those who were not previously poor. Figure 5.2 shows that on average 30 per cent of those who have just escaped poverty drop back in again the next year—and of those with unfavourable characteristics, nearly 60 per cent drop back in within a year. These rates compare with an overall entry rate into poverty for all those starting outside it the previous year of 8 per cent (Jenkins and Rigg 2001: Table 3.11). The main message to policy-makers from the figure is that it is not enough to concentrate on helping people out of poverty and then hoping they will stay out; what happens afterwards is equally important. The figure also shows that staying out of poverty helps: by the time the lone mother with a high re-entry rate has been out of poverty for four years, her risk of re-entry has dropped to 30 per cent. In this sense, success breeds success.[2]

---

[1] Technically, this is known as 'duration dependence'. Strictly, the observation could still reflect the impact of unobserved differences between those who remain a long time and those who escape, even if their main characteristics are the same.

[2] Figure 5.2 shows, however, that after five years of escape from poverty re-entry rates appear to increase. It is unclear why this should be, and Jenkins and Rigg (2001) report that this is not seen in other analysis of this kind. It may simply reflect the rather small sample sizes available of those who started in poverty but were still out of it five years later.

5.3.2 *Persistent Poverty*

Despite these continuities, there is enough mobility to make *continuous* poverty rather unusual, particularly over long time periods. For instance, DWP analysis of BHPS data suggests that 18 per cent had incomes below 60 per cent of the median in 1991, but only 6 per cent had incomes below this level for all four years from 1991 to 1994. If the time is extended to ten years, only 2 per cent were poor in every year from 1991 to 2000 (DWP 2003*a*: Table 7.6; 2003*c*: Table 6). That only a minority of the poor are *continuously* so does not, however, stop most being *repeatedly* poor. The same analysis shows that, in successive four-year periods starting in the 1990s, a total of 19 per cent were poor in at least two of the four years and 11 per cent in either three or four years. If one looks over all ten years, 15 per cent were poor for at least five of the years and 8 per cent for seven or more of the ten years. Thus, even if being poor for fewer than half of the years was seen as not being a particular problem, the extent of more persistent poverty is a comparable problem to the numbers suggested by a single snapshot.

The other side of this coin, however, is that quite large numbers experience poverty at one time or another—over the ten-year period, nearly half (49 per cent) were observed in poverty at least once on this definition—although, as Table 5.3 showed, people who are poor for a only short time do not account for a large proportion of the poverty observed at any one time. In the frequently used analogy, in a hospital ward the short-stay cases may account for the majority of new cases entering the ward, but most of the beds will be taken up by the minority of patients who stay a long time.

Whether people are persistently poor or are at risk only of short-term poverty depends on their characteristics. Table 5.4 shows the likelihood of different patterns of repeated poverty (income below 60 per cent of median) over the first nine waves of the BHPS. In this analysis, 53 per cent of the whole population are shown as never poor over the nine years, and a further 13 per cent poor only once. Two-thirds of the population are either never poor or experience only transitory poverty. The table also shows three other patterns:

- 'long-term persistent poverty', in which people are poor for at least seven out of the nine waves: 8 per cent in all;
- 'short-term persistent poverty', in which people are either poor in any two consecutive waves or are poor between three and six times (separated by at most one wave): a further 19 per cent of the population; and
- 'recurrent poverty': other cases with more than one poverty observation, 6 per cent of the total.

Looking at different kinds of people (in terms of their characteristics in 1991) reveals some interesting differences. For instance, single pensioners were twice as likely as the average to be poor in 1991, but more than twice as likely to experience long-term persistent poverty. More than half of lone parents and their children were poor in the 1991 wave, and 27 per cent of them experienced

Table 5.4. *Poverty persistence by family type and economic status, 1991–1999, GB*

	Proportion poor in 1991	Poverty pattern over nine waves of BHPS[*]				
		Never poor	Poor once	Recurrent poverty	Short-term persistent	Long-term persistent
All	20	53	13	6	19	8
Children	25	45	13	7	25	10
Couple, no children	8	66	15	3	14	3
Single, no children	14	62	15	3	17	3
Couple with children	18	56	12	6	20	6
Single with children	51	19	13	12	29	27
Pensioner couple	27	47	11	6	22	13
Single pensioner	40	30	15	11	25	20
One or more full-time self-employed	18	44	18	7	27	4
All adults work FT	2	83	9	1	7	1
Couple, one FT, one PT	3	70	14	2	13	0
Couple, FT	9	61	14	3	18	5
Single or couple, PT only	34	31	20	10	32	7
Head / spouse 60+	36	37	13	9	24	17
Head / spouse unemployed	66	13	13	14	33	28
Other	49	20	15	12	30	23

Note: Family type and economic status as in 1991.

[*] Poverty is taken as income below 60 per cent of contemporary median. 'Long-term persistent poverty' is poverty in at least seven waves. 'Short-term persistent poverty' is either poor in two consecutive waves or three to six observations of poverty (separated by at most one wave). 'Recurrent poverty' is other cases with more than one poverty observation.

Source: Jenkins and Rigg (2001: Tables 2.1, 2.3, and 2.4).

long-term persistent poverty. On the other hand, while 14 per cent of single non-pensioners were poor in 1991, only 3 per cent went on to experience long-term persistent poverty. Those initially in a household with a self-employed earner had a poverty rate in 1991 similar to the average, but only 4 per cent experienced long-term persistent poverty. Two-thirds of those initially unemployed were poor in 1991, and 28 per cent persistently poor in the long-term.

These patterns of persistence and repetition help our understanding of what seeing someone with a low income in one year can imply for their experience over a longer period. But it does not transform our impression of which groups are at risk of poverty. This can also be seen in Table 5.5, which looks at repeated poverty in four years in the mid-1990s. There are some differences when one looks at those within the poorest 30 per cent at any one time and those with persistent low income (taken here as being in the bottom 30 per cent at least three out of the four years, and never out of the bottom 40 per cent). For instance,

Table 5.5. *Characteristics of those with low and persistently low income, 1995–1998, GB*

	% of whole population	% of poorest 30% at any one time	% with persistently low income[*]
By family type			
Couple with children	36	35	33
Couple without children	21	10	5
Single with children	7	13	15
Single without children	16	12	7
Pensioner couple	10	13	17
Single pensioner	10	17	21
By tenure			
Owner-occupied	69	48	43
Social rented	22	41	48
Private rented	8	10	8
By economic status			
Fully employed	29	7	6
Partially employed	25	21	15
Workless	14	34	37
Pensioner	17	27	35
Self-employed	15	11	6

[*] In poorest 30% for at least three out of four years (including first) and in poorest 40% in remaining year.

Source: DSS (2000*a*: Table 8.8), based on BHPS data.

couples without children are a tenth of those with low income at any one time, but only a twentieth of those with persistently low income. Lone parents and their children, pensioners, social tenants, and the workless are all over-represented amongst those with persistently low income. But these are exactly the same groups as one would focus on even if one had only the snap-shot data shown in the middle column.

In summary, analysing data for people's incomes over a period of years does not greatly change our impression of the scale of the overall 'poverty problem', nor of which groups are most at risk. It shows that there are relatively few people who are remorselessly poor for year after year. In that sense, Britain does not have an 'underclass'. However, many 'escapes' from poverty are only temporary, and particular groups suffer both from longer durations of poverty, and have greater chances of falling back into it, if they do escape.

5.4   WHAT PATTERNS DO PEOPLE'S INCOMES FOLLOW?

Two-dimensional transition matrices of the kind shown in Tables 5.1 and 5.2 compare people's positions between just two years. But what we have seen about poverty exit and re-entry rates suggests that what happens in between matters.

It may be helpful for policy-making to understand why people follow different trajectories over a number of years, and then perhaps identify factors or policies that might help some onto a more positive trajectory. To do that, we need to understand the data in a more complex way, over a series of observations. In addition, we would like to know whether observed movements reflect large changes or are just 'wobbles', with income changing just enough to take people across some dividing line between one income group and another but not representing any substantial change. In other words, it is important to distinguish the genuine 'movers' from those who are simply 'shakers'.

To shed light on this, John Rigg and Tom Sefton (2004) analysed incomes over ten waves of the BHPS. Their analysis extends that presented using four waves of BHPS data in Gardiner and Hills (1999). The income definition used is very close to the measure used in the DWP's HBAI analysis (before housing costs). In the first wave Rigg and Sefton divided the observations into percentile groups, with a hundredth of the (weighted) sample in each group. In subsequent waves the group boundaries were taken from the initial percentiles, increased in line with *average* income growth, so they refer to them as 'quasi-percentiles'. If the overall shape of the distribution remained unchanged, there would still be a hundredth of the sample in each group in later waves. On the other hand, if, for instance, those with low incomes had above-average income growth, relative poverty would fall and so would the number in the bottom groups. This would be reflected in trajectories that tended to rise over time. This seems preferable in principle to simply taking actual percentile groups in each subsequent wave (in which the same circumstances would not be reflected in rising trajectories).[3] An individual could therefore be in any of a hundred groups in each of ten waves.

They then divided the sample cases between six different broad kinds of trajectory which these combinations might represent, as illustrated in Figure 5.3. The definitions used for different kinds of movement require cases to cross a certain number of percentile boundaries, and so ignore the effects of small variations—wobbles—in someone's position in the distribution between one year and another:

- *Flat* trajectories, with a stable position in the distribution over all ten waves—cases in which all observations are within a band of plus or minus fifteen quasi-percentiles of their mean.[4] An example might be a single pensioner with an income protected against inflation, but otherwise fixed.
- *Flat with 'blips'*, in which all but one or two observations are within a band of this kind: in other words, a basically stable position with only temporary

---

[3] An alternative would be to take the percentiles of the initial wave of data and adjust them for inflation only. This would give a measure of mobility against absolute income standards, as opposed to the movements against a relative income standard in Rigg and Sefton's results.

[4] The 15 percentile criterion for movement is the same as that used in Gardiner and Hills's analysis (1999) of four waves, but was validated by showing a small group of people a range of possible patterns to see which they would describe as 'flat', and so forth. In terms of transition matrices of the kind shown in Table 5.1, it is equivalent, on average, to requiring cases to cross two decile group boundaries to count as movement.

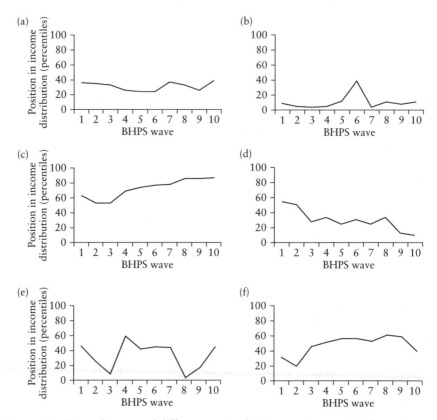

Figure 5.3. *Example cases of different types of income trajectory (a) Flat trajectory, (b) Blipping trajectory, (c) Rising trajectory, (d) Falling trajectory, (e) Fluctuating trajectory, and (f) Other trajectory*

Source: Rigg and Sefton (2004).

deviations. This would include someone who was in work with similar pay in most years but was out of work on benefits in one of the years.

- *Rising* trajectories, in which there is upward movement over the period as a whole of at least fifteen quasi-percentiles (allowing some temporary downward movements provided that the overall trend is positive and statistically significant). This might include someone at the start of his or her working career, or a middle-aged couple whose children had left home.

- *Falling* trajectories, in which equivalent criteria are met but the overall trend is downwards: for instance, someone reducing working hours and then retiring onto a lower income.

- *Fluctuating trajectories* in which there are at least three substantive movements alternating up and down over the ten years.[5]

---

[5] Rigg and Sefton (2004) take a difference between the (local) peak and trough of at least 22.5 quasi-percentiles as being substantive.

Table 5.6. *Income trajectories by type, GB (% of cases)*

Trajectory type[a]	Four waves of data[b]	Ten waves of data	Random dataset (ten waves)[c]
Flat	45.6	24.3	0.0
Flat with blip(s)	13.1	23.8	1.1
Rising	11.3	12.6	4.1
Falling	13.1	14.3	3.8
Fluctuating	—	12.6	88.2
Other	17.0	12.5	2.8

[a] For definitions, see text and Figure 5.3.
[b] Waves 1–4 (where cases have income information for all ten waves).
[c] Based on Monte Carlo analysis with 10,000 randomly generated observations.

Source: Rigg and Sefton (2004: Table 1), based on BHPS data.

- *Other* trajectories, covering all possibilities not covered by the five types described above.

Table 5.6 shows the results of this exercise, giving the proportion of cases falling into the different 'trajectory types' over both the first four waves[6] and over the full ten waves. It also shows the results generated by an entirely random dataset of 10,000 cases over ten waves. After all, if there are enough cases some of them will apparently be following a consistent pattern, even if this has been generated only randomly. But what the exercise shows is that only 9 per cent of the random cases would fall into the first four categories over ten waves, compared with three-quarters of the actual cases. This confirms what should be obvious: people's incomes are *not* the result of an annual lottery. History matters, and people's income trajectories are generally regular, even over a period as long as ten years. Looking at the four-year results shows that the trajectories are, if anything, *flatter* than one might have expected from the single year transitions shown in Table 5.1. Nearly 60 per cent of cases follow a flat trajectory or one that is basically flat with a single blip, over four years, while about a quarter are classified as rising or falling. Over the longer ten-year period, fewer remain flat but, strikingly, nearly half of the cases remain categorized as either flat or 'flat with blips'—confirmation that Jenkins's 'rubber band model' applies to many people, not just those with low incomes but across the distribution as a whole. Slightly more cases are now shown as rising or falling with this longer perspective than over four years. Only a quarter of the cases are in the fluctuating category (which, as can be seen, can easily result from random movements) or in the residual 'other' group.

Rigg and Sefton's analysis shows that different kinds of individual, and those at different stages in their lives, are more likely to follow some trajectories than

[6] Four waves are too short for the 'fluctuating' category to be distinguished (so such cases are in the 'other' category), and only a single 'blip' is allowed.

Table 5.7. *Differences in income trajectories by initial life-stage characteristics, GB*

	More likely than average trajectories[a]	Less likely than average trajectories[b]
Life stage		
Children	Rising	
Young and single	Rising	
Single parent	Rising	Flat
Young couple, no children	Falling	Rising
Couple, older children	Rising	Falling
Older couple, no children	Falling	Rising
Older, single		Rising
Pensioner couple	Flat	Rising/fluctuating
Single pensioner		Rising
Economic Status		
Self-employed	Fluctuating/other	Flat
All adults FT employed		Fluctuating
One FT/one PT	Rising	Fluctuating
PT work only	Fluctuating	
Head/spouse 60+	Flat	Rising/falling/fluctuating
Head/spouse unemployed	Rising	Falling
Other	Rising	Falling
Income group		
Poorest fifth	Rising	Falling
Second fifth	Rising	Falling
Third fifth		Flat
Fourth fifth		Rising
Richest fifth	Falling	Rising

[a] At least 150% of average probability of following trajectory type.

[b] Less than 67% of average probability of following trajectory type.

Source: Based on Rigg and Sefton (2004: Tables 2 and 3).

others. Table 5.7, presents a broad summary of some of their findings in identifying the types of cases that are much more or less likely than average to be following particular trajectories. The most common differences relate to the falling and rising trajectories. Children, young people, single parents and their children, couples with older children, those initially unemployed, and those with low incomes are more likely to have incomes rising over the ten years—all for reasons that it is easy to understand. By contrast, young *and* older couples without children, and those with high incomes are more likely than average to be falling. Incomes of pensioner couples are the most likely to be flat (40 per cent of cases) and least likely to be rising (3.5 per cent). Single parents and their children have the least stable incomes—fewer than 14 per cent of cases are classed as flat. The initially self-employed have the least predictable incomes—nearly half of them are classed as fluctuating or 'other', compared with a quarter of the whole population. Rigg and Sefton show that certain life cycle events are an important predictor of rising or falling trajectories. Even after other characteristics are controlled for, partnership formation and children becoming independent are the most important predictors of rising trajectories; having children and retirement are the most important predictors of falling trajectories. Rigg and Sefton conclude that life cycle factors have a very important impact on income trajectories. While this impact is generally less strong than that of labour market factors, life cycles are almost as important in driving rising and falling trajectories.

This approach also allows distinctions to be made between individuals who experience poverty in a way that goes beyond simply counting how many times over the ten years they are counted as poor. Table 5.8 shows the trajectory types from Table 5.6 broken down depending on whether the cases experience poverty or not. 'Poverty' is taken here as being within the bottom fifth of the distribution. 'Poor flat' cases are those in which half or more of the time is spent in the bottom fifth; 'blips out of poverty' are in or close to poverty for most of the time, but with one or two (in the ten-wave results) upward blips out of it, while blips out

Table 5.8. *Poverty-related income trajectories over four and ten waves, GB*

Trajectory type		Four waves[*]		Ten waves	
		% of cases	% of low income observations	% of cases	% of low income observations
Flat	Poor	9.0	42.5	5.5	24.3
	Non-poor	36.6	1.7	18.8	2.3
Blips	Out of poverty	1.9	8.1	6.9	21.8
	Into poverty	2.2	5.2	4.9	4.2
	Non-poor	9.0	—	12.0	—
Rising	Out of poverty	4.7	10.5	5.8	10.9
	Non-poor	6.6	—	6.8	—
Falling	Into poverty	5.1	13.3	6.8	11.4
	Non-poor	8.0	—	7.5	—
Other	Repeated poverty	4.1	11.7	7.8	18.8
	Occasional poverty	5.2	7.1	8.3	6.3
	Non-poor	7.7	—	8.9	—
Poor flat		9.0	42.5	5.5	24.3
Other problematic poor		11.6	33.1	22.2	53.3
Less problematic poor		13.2	24.4	20.2	22.4
Non-poor		66.2	—	52.1	—

[*] Cases with income information for all ten waves.

Source: Rigg and Sefton (2004: Table 7), based on BHPS.

of poverty are the reverse of these; cases which are rising out of or falling into poverty start or end in the poorest fifth respectively; 'other occasional poverty' involves one (within four waves) or one or two years (out of ten) in the poorest fifth; while 'repeated poverty' is more frequent than this (but not 'poor flat').

In earlier research using four waves of BHPS data, Karen Gardiner and I had found that 'poor flat' cases were 9 per cent of the total but accounted for just over 40 per cent of all observations of someone having a low income, and that those with only 'blips out of poverty' were 6 per cent of the total but accounted for a further 20 per cent of low-income observations (Gardiner and Hills 1999: Table 6). Using slightly different definitions, Rigg and Sefton similarly found over four years that 9 per cent of cases were 'poor flat', accounting for more than 40 per cent of low-income observations. On their definitions—which allow more cases to be classed as rising or falling—blips out of poverty were less common but still accounted for 8 per cent of low-income observations. Over the longer ten-year period, fewer than 6 per cent of cases were 'poor flat', but these still accounted for nearly a quarter of low-income observations, and nearly as many were accounted for by blips out of poverty.

When the earliest data of the kind shown in Table 5.1 were published, some drew the conclusion that Britain had dramatic income mobility with few people remaining poor for long. What can now be seen from Table 5.8 is that, even over ten years, nearly half of all low-income observations are accounted for by people who are essentially poor throughout the ten years, with temporary respite at most.

Going further, one might regard low-income observations that result from the cases which are 'rising out of poverty', 'blips into poverty', or 'other occasional poverty' trajectory types as less problematic than the others—they would be consistent with either transitory poverty or poverty which the individual had escaped by the end of the period. Table 5.8 shows that, over the first four years of the BHPS, less than a quarter of observed low income was accounted for by such 'less problematic' trajectories. Three-quarters of low-income observations were still a problem even in these terms. If the analysis is extended to ten years, while the proportion of observed low income accounted for by poor flat cases falls from 43 per cent to 24 per cent, the overall proportion accounted for by problematic cases stays just as high, and in fact rises slightly.

If one looks at any cross-section, therefore, for three-quarters of those seen as poor at that moment this will still represent a 'problem', despite the dynamics. At the same time, any cross-section will show some people whose trajectories are, in fact, unfavourable over the longer term as not being in poverty at that particular moment—for instance, those in a temporary blip out of poverty or those with repeated poverty seen in one of the years they are out of it. If one allows for these cases, the number of people affected by longer-term poverty will only be a little—between a tenth and a fifth—smaller than the number seen as poor at any one time.

5.5   IS MOBILITY INCREASING OR DECLINING?

With ten years of data from the BHPS, it is now possible to begin to see if there is any sign that income mobility and poverty durations have changed over time. The short answer is that, over the 1990s at least, there is little sign of any change at all. For instance, the DWP's analysis of eleven waves of data compares the numbers of times individuals experience poverty on different definitions within successive four-year periods (2003c: Table 5). Thus, between 1991 and 1994 the results show 66 per cent as never being below 60 per cent of median income, 14 per cent below it once, 8 per cent below it twice, 7 per cent three times, and 5 per cent in all four years. The figures are almost identical in the 1995–98, and 1998–2001 periods, but with a slightly larger number (68 per cent) in the 'never poor' group. The same is true of one uses an alternative poverty line of 70 per cent of median income, or looks at the numbers of times people are in the bottom 20 per cent or 30 per cent. The numbers falling in each group change only by the odd percentage point. If there is a movement, it is towards a little *less* mobility in the most recent two four-year periods than at the start of the 1990s.

In the DWP analysis, the only figure that does change significantly over the ten years is the incidence of persistent poverty over four years for children: between 1991 and 1994, 20 per cent of children were below 60 per cent of median income for at least three out of the four years; this fell to 17 per cent for periods starting after 1992, and to 16 per cent for most periods starting from 1994 (DWP 2003c: Table 6). With this exception—itself reflecting the fall in child poverty on an annual basis from around 26 per cent at the start of the 1990s to around 23 per cent by the last four years (1998 to 2001)—the rate of income mobility seems to have been remarkably *immobile* over the 1990s, despite the large changes in the economic cycle over the decade.

Unfortunately, there is no equivalent of the BHPS for earlier decades with which one could compare the 1990s to give direct evidence on whether mobility rose during the period through which cross-sectional inequality increased so fast. There are, however, two sources of indirect evidence.

First, one earlier survey does allow examination of income transitions between 1978 and 1979. This is the combination of the then Department of Health and Social Security's Family Finances Survey and its follow-up Family Resources Survey (not to be confused with the current survey of the same name). This looked only at families with children, focusing on those with income after housing costs below 140 per cent of each family's Supplementary Benefit scale rate in 1978. Looking at those representing the poorest 10 per cent of families with children, Ruth Hancock found that 43 per cent had escaped from it after a year (Hancock 1985; reanalysed in Hills 1998a: Table 4). This compares with, say, the 54 per cent leaving the poorest tenth between 1991 and 1992 shown in Table 5.1. However, the earlier results are in terms of numbers of families, the later ones in terms of numbers of individuals. If one looks only at families with children within the BHPS, the escape rate from the poorest tenth is somewhat faster: from 52 per cent to 60 per cent depending on the years chosen in the early 1990s, significantly more than the 43 per cent in the earlier survey. This does suggest there may have been a rise in mobility at the bottom. Even so, the increase in mobility does not appear to be of the scale required to offset very much of the growth in cross-sectional inequality over the period (and the results are hard to compare because mobility varies over the economic cycle, which was in a boom in the late 1970s but in recession in the early 1990s).

Second, much more complete longer-term information on how individuals' *earnings* have changed over time since the 1970s is available from the New Earnings Survey Panel Dataset (which draws on linked records from a sample of national insurance records). Richard Dickens (2000) constructed a mobility index for year-to-year movements in the earnings distribution (abstracting from age effects) during 1974–94. His results show a clear *decline* in earnings mobility over the period. However, the mobility index appears correlated with inflation, which fell over the period. One might expect this, given that that the pattern of annual settlements could lead to much greater variation in people's position in the earnings distribution from observation to observation in times of rapid inflation. Allowing for this, Dickens still finds that the mobility index fell by 22 per cent for men and by 11 per cent of women. There was certainly no evidence of an *increase* in mobility. He reaches the overall conclusion that 'The low paid are worse off both in terms of the relative wage they receive, *and* in terms of the opportunity to progress out of the low pay trap' (Dickens 2000: 31).

Using the same dataset, but for the slightly more recent period of 1977 to 1997, Abigail McKnight (2000) comes to similar conclusions. Comparing mobility in three sub-periods, she finds that male earnings mobility was lower between 1991 and 1997 than it was between 1977 and 1983. As a result, averaging earnings over a number of years has a *smaller* effect in reducing earnings inequality than it used to. There was some improvement in earnings progression for low-paid women over the period, but this was not enough to offset the growth in cross-sectional earnings inequality. Overall, long-term earnings inequality increased by more than cross-sectional inequality.

5.6   INTERNATIONAL COMPARISONS OF INCOME MOBILITY

Finding comparable data to make international comparisons of income mobility is also hard, although there is now a growing body of evidence that suggests that income mobility in the UK, in the 1990s at least, was lower than in some other countries. For instance, Table 5.9 shows comparisons made by the Organization for Economic Cooperation and Development (OECD) of the proportion of poverty (incomes below *half* the national median) in six countries that was accounted for by people experiencing it infrequently or repeatedly. Two countries (the Netherlands and Sweden) had low poverty rates over the period

Table 5.9. *International comparison of poverty durations, early 1990s (%)*

	Netherlands (91–96)	Sweden (91–96)	Germany (91–96)	Canada (90–95)	USA (89–93)	GB (91–96)
Average poverty rate	6.1	7.4	10.2	11.4	14.2	20.0
Poor at least once	12	12	20	28	26	38
(a) Share of individuals experiencing some poverty* for different numbers of years out of six						
One year	48	41	46	36	33	26
2 years	21	22	19	27	19	19
3 years	12	13	12	14	11	14
4 years	8	9	8	9	10	13
5 or 6 years	12	15	16	14	27	28
Average number of years poor	*2.2*	*2.4*	*2.4*	*2.4*	*3.0*	*3.1*
(b) Share of total poverty observations accounted for by those experiencing different numbers of years poor						
One year	22	17	19	15	11	8
2 years	19	18	16	22	12	12
3 years	16	16	15	18	11	13
4 years	14	14	13	15	13	17
5 or 6 years	29	35	36	30	52	50

* Poverty based on income below 50% of median.

Source: Oxley, Dang, and Antolín (1999: Table 1).

studied, two (Germany and Canada) had somewhat higher rates, while the USA and Britain had the highest rates. The panel datasets used for this analysis show a lower poverty rate for the USA than might have been expected from the more detailed cross-sectional data presented in Chapter 3. The panel results should be treated with some caution, therefore.

As can be seen, there is quite a large difference between the USA and Britain on the one hand and the remaining four countries on the other. Of those who did experience some poverty within a six year period, only 26 per cent did so for just one out of the six years in Britain, compared with nearly half in Sweden, Germany, and the Netherlands, and around a third in Canada and the USA. More than a quarter in both Britain and the USA who experienced some poverty did so for five or six out of the six years, nearly twice as many as in the other countries. As a result the number of years (out of six) for which those who were poor experienced it averaged three or more in Britain and the USA compared with 2.4 in the other four countries. Even more strikingly, *half* of all poverty observations came from those poor for five or six years in Britain and the USA, but only around a third in other countries. Not only is relative poverty high in international terms in Britain and the USA, but when it does occur it is more likely to be long-term or repeated.

Similarly, in a comparison of earnings mobility over a six year period (1986 to 1991), an OECD study found that initially low-paid workers (paid less than 65 per cent of median earnings) remained low-paid for a year longer on average in the USA and UK than in France, Germany, and Italy, and two years longer than in Denmark (OECD 1997: Table 2.5c).

Bradbury, Jenkins, and Micklewright (2001) look more specifically at child poverty dynamics using a variety of data sources for seven countries in the early 1990s. This shows a more mixed picture. For instance, *fewer* children in the UK are in households with incomes in the poorest fifth in all five years out of five than in Germany, Hungary, or the USA (2001: Table 4.4). On the other hand, on relative child poverty (if one uses a line of half median income), the UK does less well. First, it has a higher *entry* rate into poverty for children who were not poor before than in the three other countries. Second, it has a lower *exit* rate than Germany: in the UK 38 per cent of children poor on this basis exit poverty each year, but in Germany 52 per cent of them do so (2001: Table 4.6). That will drive longer durations in the UK. However, the exit rates in the UK are still higher than in Hungary and the USA, which will mean shorter child poverty durations than in those countries.

5.7 LONGER-TERM CONTINUITIES AND SOCIAL MOBILITY

All of the evidence surveyed so far is about relatively short-term income mobility, within periods of up to ten years. But we are also very interested in longer-term mobility. How does people's economic position change over their whole lives? In particular, how does the position of children relate to that of their parents? Here we do not have evidence which compares with that generated by surveys such as BHPS, but we do have some useful indications from a variety of other sources.

First, there is a long-standing body of research comparing the social class of children with that of their parents, based on occupation (although for married women, particularly in earlier periods, this may mean the occupation of their husbands). Some of the results of this are shown in Table 5.10, which looks at people born in decades up to the 1950s (with their own social class measured at age 35 or older). The table shows a decreasing number of both men and women who end up in a lower social class than their parents, particularly for men born in the 1950s, only 13 per cent of whom moved downwards. By contrast, those experiencing upward mobility increased, reaching 42 per cent for men born in the 1940s and 1950s and 36 per cent for women born in the 1950s.[7] This asymmetry reflected what has become known as the 'more room at the top' phenomenon: during the period from the 1940s to the 1970s, the proportion of jobs classed as being in the higher occupational groups increased considerably— there were more white collar, 'middle class' jobs. This allowed room for more

---

[7] Movements between classes III, IV, and V/VI are treated in this analysis as 'horizontal'.

Table 5.10. *Absolute social mobility for those born between 1890 and 1959, GB (%)*

	Downwardly mobile	Horizontal movement	Stable	Upwardly mobile
(a) Men				
Born pre-1900	20	10	43	27
1900–09	21	11	39	29
1910–19	20	12	38	30
1920–29	17	9	35	39
1930–39	18	10	34	38
1940–49	19	11	28	42
1950–59	13	10	35	42
(b) Women				
Born pre-1900	30	15	31	24
1900–09	32	17	29	22
1910–19	30	18	26	27
1920–29	28	21	28	23
1930–39	27	22	22	29
1940–49	26	22	20	32
1950–59	27	20	17	36

Source: Heath and Payne (2000), quoted in PIU (2001), based on data from British Election Surveys for social classes of parents and children aged 35 and over.

children to move upwards (in 'absolute terms') by comparison with their parents.

There are indications, however, that this process stopped after the end of the 1970s (PIU 2001). There was slower growth in the number of professional and managerial jobs, and a contraction in skilled manual jobs (which had allowed upward mobility for the children of unskilled manual workers). John Goldthorpe and Colin Mills (forthcoming) use data from cross-sections of the adult population between 1973 and 1992 to suggest that, for men, 'Over the later decades of the twentieth century, the previous tendency for rates of total, and especially of upward, mobility to rise has been halted, and, if anything, it is downward rather than upward mobility that has become more frequent'. For women, they find evidence that upward mobility has continued to increase. However, when they examine rates of mobility in people's *relative* social class position they find 'little compelling evidence of these rates changing in a way indicative of increased—or decreased—fluidity within the British class structure', which confirms that it was the changing sizes of social classes that allowed the trends shown in Table 5.10, rather than increased mobility in people's relative positions.

While this kind of evidence does not tell us about what was happening to the relative *income* position of children by comparison with that of their parents, the social mobility it shows was accompanied by the fall in income inequality between the 1940s and the 1970s. The evidence that such processes have slowed for more recent generations accompanies the period during which income inequality has risen (although the two do not necessarily have to move in step). We also now have more concrete evidence for what has happened to links between the earnings or incomes of parents in one generation and that of their children covering those born between the 1950s and 1970. The data that help us here are taken from the long-running cohort studies, which have been following the same group of people since they were born. One of these is the National Child Development Study (NCDS), which covers all the children born in two weeks in mainland Britain in March 1958. Table 5.11 shows analysis by Stephen Machin (1998). It relates the earnings of men and women in the sample when they were aged 33 to those of their fathers back in 1974. If there were no link, all the figures in the table would be 25—regardless of fathers' income, a quarter of the sons and daughters would be in each earnings group. As it is, only 6 per cent of sons with fathers who were in the top quarter in 1974 had earnings in the bottom quarter for men aged 33 in 1991. More than half were in the top quarter— twice what would be expected at random. More than a third of sons of men in the bottom quarter are also in the bottom quarter in 1991, and only 13 per cent are in the top quarter. The lower panel shows a similar pattern for daughters: nearly half of the daughters of high-paid fathers were themselves high-paid at age 33, and 37 per cent of those whose fathers' earnings had been in the bottom quarter were themselves in the bottom quarter for 33-year-old women.

So there *are* intergenerational links in earnings position, but they are by no means rigid. On Machin's analysis, about half of the child's earnings position seems to be linked to parent's earnings—but half does not. Like a glass that is either half empty or half full, this kind of link can be seen as depressing in the ways in which it suggests lack of equality of opportunity, or as cheering in the

Table 5.11. *Earnings of fathers and of children (born in 1958), GB (%)*

Father's earnings group (by quarter in 1974 when children were aged 16)	Child's adult earnings group (quarters) in 1991 (at age 33)			
	Bottom	Second	Third	Top
(a) Sons				
Bottom	34	30	24	13
Second	29	31	25	14
Third	30	24	24	21
Top	6	15	27	52
(b) Daughters				
Bottom	37	32	19	12
Second	27	31	26	16
Third	23	22	31	25
Top	13	16	24	48

Source: Machin (1998), based on NCDS.

ways it makes clear that later outcomes are by no means predetermined. After all, more than a third of the sons, and nearly a third of the daughters, whose fathers' earnings were in the bottom quarter had ended up in the top half of the earnings distribution by the time they were in their thirties.

But what is more clearly depressing is that these kinds of links appear to be getting *stronger* over time. First, the link between parents and children's earnings shown in Table 5.11 is stronger than Atkinson, Maynard, and Trinder (1983) found in their pioneering study of the links between parents interviewed by Seebohm Rowntree in 1950 and their children interviewed in the late 1970s. Second, we now have evidence from a cohort of children born in 1970 that can be compared directly with that for those born in 1958. First, Table 5.12 shows Abigail McKnight's comparison of how the earnings of the two groups in their mid-twenties related to the incomes of their parents (net household income) when they were each aged 16. The data on the 1970 cohort do not allow direct comparison between parents' and children's earnings of the kind possible for the 1958 cohort. The columns of the table therefore show the proportion of each group by parental income ending up in each fifth of the hourly wage distribution. As with Table 5.11, there are clear continuities between the 1958 cohort and their parents: 28 per cent of those whose households were poor (measured against a line of half average income) when they were aged 16 had earnings in the bottom fifth when they were 23, compared with only 17 per cent of those with average or higher household incomes at 16. The lower panel suggests that these links are indeed stronger for the later cohort: 30 per cent of those with poor parents now end up low-paid (at age 26), and only 12 per cent end up in the highest fifth of wages (compared with 15 per cent for the earlier cohort). So, not only were those in the later cohort more likely to be poor when aged 16 (as child poverty had risen significantly by 1986), but also childhood poverty was more

Table 5.12. *Links between childhood poverty and earnings in adulthood, 1958 and 1970 cohorts, GB (%)*

Household income group (age 16)	Child's adult hourly wage group (fifths)				
	Bottom	Second	Third	Fourth	Top
(a) Cohort born in 1958 (age 23)					
Average income or above	17	19	20	21	22
Below average	22	21	19	19	18
Below half average	28	22	18	17	15
(b) Cohort born in 1970 (age 26)					
Average income or above	13	16	20	24	26
Below average	26	23	20	16	14
Below half average	30	25	17	16	12

Source: McKnight (2002: Table 7.3).

strongly linked with later low pay. By contrast, the proportion of the children of those with average or above-average income at 16 whose earnings were in the top fifth when they were in their twenties rose from 22 to 26 per cent.

We also now have information on what had happened to the 1970 cohort by the time they were aged 30 (in 2000) that we can compare directly with what we know about the earnings of the 1958 cohort when they were 33. Table 5.13 shows analysis by Jo Blanden et al. that does this (unlike Table 5.11, it uses parental household income when the children were 16 to give comparability between the two datasets). The findings are clear: the proportion of sons and daughters from lower-income families when they were 16 who end up with low earnings in their thirties has risen, and the proportion of those who end up with above-average earnings has fallen. The same reduction in mobility has occurred for those with high childhood incomes: 42 per cent of the sons and 40 per cent of the daughters in the 1970 cohort whose parents were in the top income group had the top earnings at age 30, compared with 34 per cent and 35 per cent respectively for the earlier cohort.

Table 5.13. *Parental income and earnings in adulthood, 1958 and 1970 cohorts, GB (%)*

Parental net income group (quarters)	Child's adult weekly earnings group (quarters)			
	Bottom	Second	Third	Top
(a) Sons born in 1958 (aged 33)				
Bottom	30	29	24	17
Second	28	25	26	20
Third	23	24	25	29
Top	19	22	25	34
(b) Sons born in 1970 (aged 30)				
Bottom	39	28	19	14
Second	25	29	29	16
Third	22	23	27	28
Top	14	20	25	42
(c) Daughters born in 1958 (aged 33)				
Bottom	26	28	27	18
Second	29	26	25	21
Third	27	22	26	26
Top	18	24	22	35
(d) Daughters born in 1970 (aged 30)				
Bottom	33	26	25	15
Second	31	29	22	18
Third	23	26	27	27
Top	13	19	26	40

Source: Blanden et al. (2002: Tables 6a and 6b).

So, while the social class evidence gives a picture of increasing upward mobility between the generations as far as their occupations are concerned (in absolute terms) that lasts up to those born in the 1950s, the cohort data suggest that income mobility between the generations has been declining since then. For those now in their thirties, who their parents were matters more than it used to. Blanden et al. (2002) suggest that this is driven by education: the economy may be more 'meritocratic' in the sense that educational qualifications are more important than they used to be in driving earnings (see Chapter 4), but the qualifications people end up with depend more than they used to on the incomes of their parents. They suggest that

. . . this fall in mobility can partly be accounted for by the fact that a greater share of the rapid educational upgrading of the British population has been focussed on people with richer parents. This unequal increase in educational attainment is thus one factor that has acted to reinforce the link between earnings and income of children and their parents.

By contrast, Goldthorpe and Mills (forthcoming) suggest that, as far as social class (rather than income) is concerned, 'there is no evidence for the period [1973 to 1993] of the role of education in mobility processes increasing in importance: it would rather appear to decline'. Either way, there is no evidence that education has acted in the most recent decades to *reduce* the links between people's socio-economic position and that of their parents.

5.8   SUMMARY

- Data on income mobility show that those who are poor in any one year are not necessarily the same as those who are poor the next. However, this does not mean that concerns about the widening cross-sectional inequality can be dismissed on the grounds that it is offset by mobility.
- Only 36 per cent of individuals were in the same tenth of the income distribution in both 1991 and 1992. However, nearly three-quarters were either in the same tenth or a neighbouring one a year later. Of the poorest tenth in the first year, 54 per cent had escaped it a year later. However, two-thirds were still in the poorest fifth, and two-thirds of the poorest fifth as a whole stayed there.
- Income mobility is mostly short-range. Some people drop back after an initial escape and others stay where they are. The longer people remain in poverty, the more slowly they escape it. Those who have just left poverty are more likely to drop back into it than those who have been out of it for a longer time. As a result, more than two-fifths of those who started in the poorest fifth in 1991 were either still there or back there ten years later.
- For policy, it is therefore important to look at what can be done once people escape poverty to help them stay out, not just at how to promote exit from poverty.

- Continuous low income over a long period is unusual, but repeated poverty in a number of linked spells is not. Only 2 per cent of the BHPS sample were poor in *every* year from 1991 to 2000. However, 8 per cent were poor for seven or more of the ten years, and 15 per cent for at least half of the years.

- Those experiencing persistent poverty are disproportionately those who start as lone parents and their children, pensioners, social tenants, and the workless. These are the same high risk groups as seen in cross-sections, but the extent of their additional risk is greater looking at poverty over time.

- Most people's incomes do not follow the chaotic trajectories one would expect at random. Over a ten-year period, nearly half of the BHPS sample follow trajectories that are basically flat (with no more than two years when they have a 'blip' in income).

- Nearly half of low-income observations are accounted for by people who are essentially poor throughout a ten-year period. Less than a quarter of observed low income is accounted for by those with trajectories that may be less problematic than others (representing either transitory poverty or poverty that is later escaped).

- Over the 1990s, mobility patterns within successive four-year periods changed little, with the exception that persistent child poverty appears to have fallen.

- Direct comparisons with earlier periods are not possible, but one piece of evidence suggests that exit rates from low income for families with children were lower in the late 1970s than in the early 1990s. More generally, however, earnings mobility appears to have fallen since the 1970s, at the same time as earnings became more unequal.

- Evidence from comparable international surveys suggests that poverty in the UK (and the USA) is more likely to take the form of long-term or repeated poverty than in countries such as the Netherlands, Sweden, Germany, and Canada. Low pay also appears to be longer-lasting in the USA and UK. Children appear to escape poverty more slowly in Britain than in Germany, but more quickly than in the USA.

- Evidence from people's occupational social class by comparison with their parents suggests an increasing amount of upward social mobility over the twentieth century up until children born in the 1950s, but that this process may now have stopped. It appears to have been allowed by changing social class sizes rather than by an increase in mobility between *relative* social positions.

- If one compares cohorts born in 1958 and 1970, the link between the earnings of children in their twenties and those in their thirties has become more strongly linked to the incomes of their parents when they were teenagers: inter-generational mobility appears to have fallen over the period. A significant part of the reason for this appears to be stronger links between qualifications and earnings, but also stronger links between parental income and their children's qualifications.

FURTHER READING

The extent and patterns of mobility revealed by the first nine years (1990 to 1999) of the BHPS are analysed in *The Dynamics of Poverty in Britain* by Stephen Jenkins and John Rigg (Department for Work and Pensions Research Report 157, 2001). Each year the DWP's volume on *Households Below Average Income* also contains a chapter analysing BHPS results, drawing on a separate analysis, *Low-Income Dynamics*, published the previous year on the DWP website www.dwp.gov.uk.

The analysis of income trajectories discussed in Section 5.4 is presented in more detail in *Income Dynamics and the Life Cycle: Evidence from ten waves of the British Household Panel Survey* by John Rigg and Tom Sefton (CASE paper 81, 2004; http://sticerd.lse.ac.uk/case/publications/).

International evidence on the extent and patterns of income mobility can be found in: *The Real Worlds of Welfare Capitalism* by Robert Goodin, Bruce Heady, Ruud Muffels, and Henk-Jan Driven (Cambridge University Press, 1999); *The Dynamics of Child Poverty in Industrialised Countries*, edited by Bruce Bradbury, Stephen Jenkins, and John Micklewright (Cambridge University Press, 2001); and in *Poverty Dynamics in Six OECD Countries*, by Howard Oxley, Thai-Thanh Dang, and Pablo Antolín (OECD, 1999).

A classic early study of links in circumstances between parents in the 1950s and their children in the 1970s is *Parents and Children: Incomes in Two Generations* by Tony Atkinson, Alan Maynard, and Chris Trinder (Heinemann Educational Books, 1983).

More recent evidence can be found in *Changes in Intergenerational Mobility* by Jo Blanden, Alissa Goodman, Paul Gregg, and Stephen Machin (Centre for the Economics of Education Discussion Paper 26, 2002). A general survey of recent evidence on social mobility, *Social Mobility: A Discussion Paper* by the Performance and Innovation Unit (2001), can be found on the 10 Downing Street website www.number-10.gov.uk/files/pdf/socialmobility.pdf.

II

THE IMPACT OF POLICY

6

Social Spending and the Boundaries Between Public and Private Sectors

6.1 WHAT HAS HAPPENED TO SOCIAL SPENDING?

In the financial year 2002–03, UK social spending as shown in Figure 6.1 totalled £263 billion, exactly one quarter of national income (GDP). Social security as a whole made up just under half of this total, with the biggest single item, National Insurance pensions, costing £47 billion (see Section 6.2 for more details). Spending on health care was the second biggest item, costing £66 billion, while education spending was £54 billion. Spending on personal social services—including items such as residential and home care for the elderly—has grown quite fast in recent years, reaching nearly £16 billion in 2002–03, but that on housing (excluding means-tested housing benefits) had dwindled to under £5 billion.

On top of this direct spending, the state also contributes to the cost of social provision through various forms of tax reliefs and allowances, and more recently through 'tax credits'. These are discussed in detail in Section 7.2, but are taken into account in the analysis of public funding of private provision in Section 6.4. For the moment it should be noted that tax credits can in principle be treated in two ways: as spending items, equivalent to cash benefits, or as reductions in what would otherwise be someone's tax liability, and hence outside public spending. The official figures for social security spending shown in Figure 6.1 include only those tax credits received by people who would not otherwise be taxpayers. Figure 6.6 gives a more detailed breakdown of social security, including tax credits received by taxpayers.

The statement that social spending represents about a quarter of national income could have been made at almost any time in the last thirty years. Figure 6.2 shows the long-term pattern of spending on the three largest welfare services, education, health care, and social security. After reaching around a tenth of national income in the 1930s, this total fell back during the Second World War, before starting thirty years of continuous growth in the post-war welfare state, taking spending on these three services to 20 per cent of national income in 1976–77.

But since then the total has been roughly constant. Figure 6.3 presents the picture of the last twenty-five years in more detail. This measure—which is what matters for our ability to pay for it—shows that there has not been the continuous

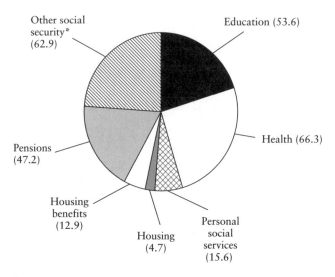

Other social
security*
(62.9)

Education (53.6)

Health (66.3)

Pensions
(47.2)

Housing
benefits
(12.9)

Housing
(4.7)

Personal
social
services
(15.6)

Figure 6.1. *Government social spending, 2002–03, UK (£ billion) (total spending of £263 billion)*

* 'Other social security' includes tax credits in excess of someone's tax liability (but not the part offset against tax liabilities).

Source: HM Treasury (2003*b*: Table 3.5).

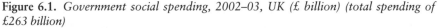

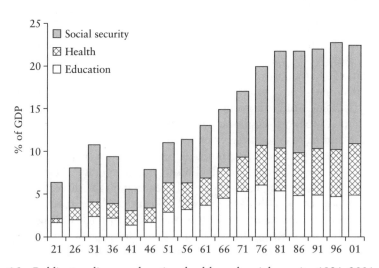

□ Social security
⊠ Health
□ Education

% of GDP

25

20

15

10

5

0

21 26 31 36 41 46 51 56 61 66 71 76 81 86 91 96 01

Figure 6.2. *Public spending on education, health, and social security, 1921–2001*

Note: Figures are for financial years (apart from education to 1946 and health to 1936).

Sources: Hills (1992: Table 2) for figures until 1981–82 (GB). HM Treasury (2003*b*: Table 3.4) for figures from 1986–87 (UK).

growth some might have expected. When people talk about the 'inexorable growth of the welfare state', they are talking about a period that ended a generation ago, at the time of the early 1970s oil crisis and the 1976 International Monetary Fund (IMF) visit to the UK. But nor is there the savage retrenchment depicted by others following the election in 1979 of Prime Minister Margaret Thatcher. Rather, the total has kept within a relatively narrow band either side of its average of just under 24 per cent of GDP over these years, fluctuating up and down within the range of 21–26 per cent depending in large part on the state of the economy. Notably, the 24.5 per cent total in the year before the Conservatives left government, 1996–97, was just over a percentage point of GDP higher than they had inherited from 1978–79. The total in New Labour's sixth year of government, 2002–03, was only half a percentage point of GDP higher than this, the growth since 1999–00 only just reversing the decline in New Labour's first two years of austerity (see Chapter 9 for more discussion). As Howard Glennerster (1998) has described it, this has been 'welfare with the lid on': the upward pressures arising from new needs and new expectations have collided with political pressures to keep down or cut taxation to produce a kind of stalemate (see Chapter 10).

However, within the total, particular items have fared differently, as can be seen in the figure and, within the context of public spending as a whole, in Table 6.1. *Social* spending has remained roughly constant as a share of GDP since the mid-1970s while total public spending *has* fallen as a share of GDP (see Figure 7.4). As a result, social spending rose from half of total government spending (on the

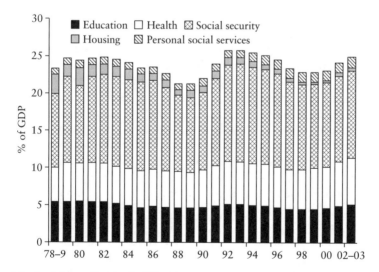

Figure 6.3. *Social spending in the UK, 1978–79 to 2002–03*

Sources: HM Treasury (2003b: Table 3.4) for figures from 1985–86; other figures from earlier equivalents.

Social Spending

Table 6.1. *Composition of public spending, 1978–79 to 2002–03, UK*

	Percentage of Total Managed Expenditure[a]			£ billion	% of GDP
	1978–79	1996–97	2002–03	2002–03	2002–03
Education	11.6	11.5	12.7	53.6	5.1
Health	10.0	13.3	15.7	66.3	6.3
Social security (excluding housing benefits)	20.5	26.6	26.2	110.1	10.5
Housing benefits	1.2[b]	3.8	3.1	12.9	1.2
Housing	5.8	1.5	1.1	4.7	0.4
Personal social services	1.8	3.1	3.7	15.7	1.5
TOTAL SOCIAL SPENDING	50.8	59.7	62.6	263.4	25.0
Defence	9.7	6.7	5.9	25.0	2.4
Other services	23.1	20.1	22.4	94.5	8.9
Debt interest (gross)	9.5	8.9	5.1	21.3	2.0
Other	6.9	4.6	4.0	16.9	1.6
TOTAL MANAGED EXPENDITURE	100	100	100	421.0	39.9

[a] 1978–79 and 1996–97 figures on cash basis; 2002–03 figures on resource basis (with use of capital assets taken into account). 1978–79 total for TME taken from HM Treasury (2003b) and figure for 'other' adjusted accordingly.

[b] 1978–79 figures for housing benefits adjusted to be comparable with current definitions with use of totals from Hills (1998b: Table 5A.1).

Source: HM Treasury (2003b: Tables 3.1, 3.2, 3.4 and 3.5; 1997b, Table 3.2).

current key measure of 'Total Managed Expenditure', TME)[1] in 1978–79 to nearly 60 per cent in 1996–97 and 63 per cent in the most recent year. It is not surprising that domestic politics is increasingly dominated by social policy questions. Over the period as a whole, both health and social security spending have increased their shares. Education spending declined as a share of both national income and public spending until 1999, but since then has been recovering. Indeed, as Figure 6.3 shows, by 2002–03 the total of education and health spending, at 11.4 per cent of national income, had reached its highest ever level.

The table identifies two clear 'losers' in shares of public spending: defence down from nearly a tenth in 1978–79 to under 6 per cent in 2002–03; and debt interest— particularly since 1996–97, an important pay-off to New Labour's initial austerity. The share of housing spending—mainly subsidies for the rents of council and housing association tenants, and payments for new construction—has also fallen dramatically since the early 1970s. As the table shows, however, part of the decline in housing spending represents a switch between classifications. As general subsidies to keep gross rents down were cut in the 1980s, so low-income tenants became entitled to larger amounts of housing benefit from what is now the social security

[1] See Section 7.1 for a description of what is included in TME.

budget (Hills 1998*b*).[2] But even allowing for this, the share of total spending going to housing spending including benefits has fallen by two-fifths.

But perhaps the most striking change in public spending in the last thirty years has been in public investment. The high levels of net public sector borrowing in earlier periods and their more recent falls have to be seen against the background of what was once substantial new public investment. Figure 6.4 shows the longer-term pattern for both public sector net borrowing (PSNB) and public investment net of depreciation of existing assets (PSNI). The figure makes plain the contrast between two periods of high borrowing, the mid-1970s and the mid-1990s. In the former, high public borrowing was mainly to finance high public investment. After 1975–76, both fell rapidly, with net borrowing briefly negative in the late 1980s, while net investment fell to near zero—gross investment was barely above depreciation. The huge increase in net borrowing, reaching nearly 8 per cent of GDP in 1992–93 and 1993–94, did not correspond to a surge in investment but rather to the effects of current spending rising as recession bit, combined with taxes cut ahead of the 1992 election on the strength of what turned out to be wildly optimistic revenue forecasts. By contrast, between 1998–99 and 2000–01 net public borrowing was negative, while net investment began to grow from its very low base.

The relationship between these two totals has been given much greater importance by the current government through its adoption of the 'golden rule' in designing its fiscal policies, which states that over the economic cycle net

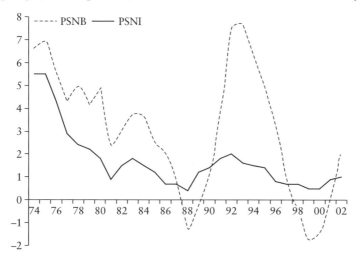

Figure 6.4. *Public sector net borrowing and net investment, 1974–75 to 2002–03, UK*
Notes: PSNB: public sector net borrowing; PSNI: public sector net investment.
Source: HM Treasury (2004: Tables C24 and C25).

---

[2] It can also be argued that the accounting flows of subsidy shown in the public spending total are a poor measure of the subsidy going to tenants in economic terms. These have fallen less fast (Hills 1998*b*; Sefton 2002).

borrowing should be no greater than net capital spending, a rule which appeared to be being met in the late 1990s for the first time since the early 1970s. One idea behind this rule is equity between the generations: if we are to pass debts on to our children, we should pass on assets too. Another is that of long-term sustainability. Either way, it is argued this generation of policy-makers should not be running the public finances in such a way that later generations will be forced to raise taxes higher than their present levels without any benefit in terms of later public services. Another way of looking at this is through the public sector's balance sheet, that is, the balance between its assets and its liabilities. Recent official estimates of this are shown in Figure 6.5 for the same period since 1974–75.

Part of what drives this picture is what we have already seen: the balance between public borrowing and capital spending. But a more detailed look shows that the pattern is more complicated than this. In particular, throughout the 1970s, public sector debt was *falling* as a proportion of GDP, despite the high levels of net borrowing. The reason for this was inflation. With public debt denominated in cash, its real value fell as prices rose. In inflation-adjusted terms, the public sector was not actually borrowing for much of this period. At the same time it was investing, so the net worth of the public sector rose from 40 per cent of GDP at the start of the 1970s to peak at 78 per cent in 1974 (HM Treasury 2000: Table C23). This continued a trend of improvement in this measure since at least the late 1950s (Hills 1996*b*: Table 4.1). Through the 1980s, the picture was more mixed, with debt falling in relation to national income but assets falling too (partly as a result of privatization). In the first half of the 1990s, net worth fell dramatically, reflecting high borrowing at a time of lower inflation but also low net investment (and continuing privatization). In the four years after 1998–99 the pattern was reversed, with net debt

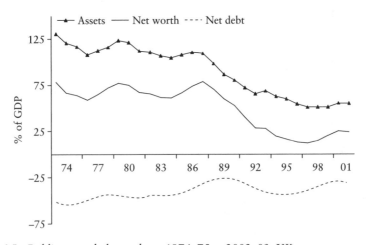

Figure 6.5. *Public sector balance sheet, 1974–75 to 2002–03, UK*

Sources: HM Treasury (2000: Table C23) for figures to 1986–87; HM Treasury (2004: Table C24 for figures from 1987–88).

falling, assets rising, and net worth rising from the equivalent of 12 per cent to 25 per cent of GDP.

However, the public sector has other assets and liabilities beyond those shown in Figure 6.5. The largest of these liabilities is the promises it has made to pay pensions in the future. The capitalized value of people's rights to the basic pension alone—£1,126 billion at the end of 2000—exceeds a year's national income, which would turn the net worth of the public sector negative throughout the period shown (Inland Revenue 2003*a*: Table 13.4). Then again, the Thatcher government started the 1980s with the prospect of substantial oil revenues from the North Sea. By the early 1990s, revenues equivalent to a windfall asset of more than a third of a year's national income had been used up. Their virtual disappearance puts the comparative stability of public sector net worth in the 1980s in a different light. Section 8.5 looks further at issues of inter-generational equity related to social spending in particular.

6.2 SOCIAL SECURITY SPENDING AND STRUCTURE

The largest part of social spending remains that on social security, but this is perhaps the least understood part of public spending. The overall composition of the £119.2 billion spent in the UK in 2002–03 (including the full cost of personal tax credits) is shown in Figure 6.6, broken down in two ways: first, between kinds of benefit, and, second, between different kinds of beneficiary (for the £109.9 billion spent in Great Britain, excluding tax credits). It distinguishes three kinds of

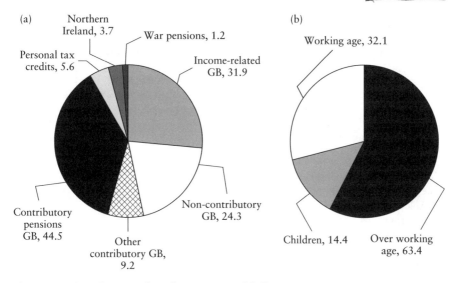

Figure 6.6. *Social security benefits, 2002–03 (£ billion)*
(a) UK spending by type of benefit (total of £119.2 billion including tax credits)
(b) GB cash benefit spending by age group (total of £109.9 billion)

Source: DWP Benefit Expenditure Tables.www.dwp.gov.uk/asd/asd4/expenditure.asp.

benefit:

- *contributory pensions and other benefits*, to which people are entitled if they are simultaneously affected by a particular 'contingency' (such as old age, sickness, or unemployment) *and* have a satisfactory record of paying National Insurance Contributions while at work (or, in certain cases, have been 'credited in' to entitlement, without actually having made contributions—for instance, while in some kinds of education, or for some purposes when caring for children or others);
- *non-contributory (sometimes called universal) benefits*, which depend only on being affected by a particular contingency, such as having children (for Child Benefit) or being disabled on certain criteria and hence having additional needs; and
- *means-tested or income-related benefits*, which go to those whose income (and possibly other resources) is below a particular level, as well as meeting other criteria.

An immediate point is the extent to which social security is dominated by pensions and other benefits for the elderly. Benefits for those over working age were 63 per cent of overall social security spending, and those aimed at children were 14 per cent, with less than a third going to those of working age.

This breakdown would come as a surprise to most people. Table 6.2 shows the responses when the British Social Attitudes (BSA) survey asked people in 2001 what they thought represented the largest and second largest parts of social security spending. Seventy-one per cent thought that benefits for the unemployed were the largest or next largest item, even though they actually made up only a twentieth of the total.

Table 6.2. *Perceptions of the relative size of social security spending, 2001, GB*

	Largest amount amount of money (% of respondents)	Next largest amount of money (% of respondents)	Least amount of money (% of respondents)	Actual spending on these areas 2001–02 (% of total)
Retirement pensions	28	20	24	49[a]
Children	11	22	14	8–16[b]
Benefits for disabled people	4	9	39	25
Benefits for unemployed people	44	27	3	5
Benefits for single parents	13	22	17	Less than 8[b]

[a] Benefits for people over working age (excluding disability benefits).

[b] Spending directly on children was 8% of the total, with a further 8% on 'families', much of which was for lone parents and their children.

Sources: Taylor-Gooby and Hastie (2002), based on British Social Attitudes Survey (based on 3,287 respondents). Spending figures from DSS (2000b: Table B3).

This misconception about where spending on cash benefits goes has important political consequences, as benefits for the unemployed are the least popular part of the social security budget. Indeed, when the BSA survey asked people in 1998 what they thought should happen to different kinds of social security spending, it was *only* on benefits for the unemployed that most people wanted lower spending. Large majorities favoured higher spending on carers, pensioners, disabled people, and low-paid parents with children, even if this meant higher taxes (Hills and Lelkes 1999: 17). But despite the popularity of the items that, in reality, make up the lion's share of the social security budget, 'social security' is a very low priority item within public spending—only 6 per cent of respondents to the survey in 2001 put it as their first or second priority for public spending (Taylor-Gooby and Hastie 2002: Table 4.2). The misperception that unemployment benefits are what social security spending is about greatly tightens the political constraints on the budget as a whole. Section 6.5 examines other aspects of public attitudes to social security and the welfare state more generally (and Section 7.4 examines attitudes towards the overall level of tax and public spending).

The structure of social security has changed considerably over time. Figure 6.7 shows how social security spending as a share of national income has changed over the 55 years since the post-war Attlee government reformed social security (drawing on many recommendations from the 1942 Beveridge report, *Social Insurance and Allied Services*). Most of the growth in the thirty years after 1948 was accounted for by contributory benefits, particularly contributory pensions. They reached a peak of 6.5 per cent of national income more than twenty years ago, in 1983. However, the subsequent growth of social security spending has come from a combination of non-contributory contingency-based benefits and means-tested benefits (and, most recently, tax credits, which mix means-tested and universal elements). Contributory benefits and pensions are a much smaller

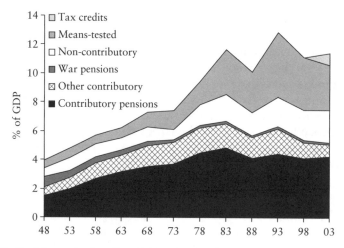

Figure 6.7. *Social security benefits, 1948–49 to 2003–04, UK*

Source: DWP Benefit Expenditure Tables, www.dwp.gov.uk/asd/asd4/expenditure.asp.

share of the total than they used to be. At their peak in the 1960s and 1970s, contributory benefits accounted for 70 per cent of all social security spending. By 2003–04, they were less than 45 per cent of the total.

This pattern is no accident. In the last thirty years, when governments of the left have been in power arguments in favour of inclusion have been predominant, non-contributory benefits have been expanded, and contribution conditions have been softened to 'credit in' people with low earnings or interrupted work histories. When governments of the right have been in power, particularly in the 1980s, contribution conditions have been made tougher and the emphasis has been on focusing limited resources on the poorest through means-testing. New Labour has done both (Hills 2003).

The extent to which social security in particular, and indeed welfare services in general, are universal or are targeted on the poor via means-testing affects stigma and whether people claim what they are entitled to ('take-up'). In today's language, universal services may be more 'inclusive' than means-tested ones. This is not a new debate. Lecturing in 1967, Richard Titmuss (Alcock et al. 2001: 117) argued that the key parts of post-war welfare legislation—establishing the National Health Service (NHS), the National Insurance system, family allowances, and free secondary education until age 15—all embodied a principle of universalism:

> One fundamental historical reason for the adoption of this principle was the aim of making services available and accessible to the whole population in such ways as would not involve users in any humiliating loss of status, dignity or self-respect. There should be no sense of inferiority, pauperism, shame or stigma in the use of a publicly provided service; no attribution that one was being or becoming a 'public burden'.

It is perfectly possible for systems entirely based on means-tested or on universal benefits to have identical effects on people's net incomes and hence on income distribution (Hills 2002b: Figure 13.3). In terms purely of cross-sectional inequality of cash incomes after their impact, there may be nothing to choose between them. But in terms of the way people are treated, there may well be very great differences, with only the poor subject to means tests. Systems designed only for the poor may become 'poor services', while services of no relevance to powerful groups may lose out in the competition for resources.

There is not, however, a simple dichotomy between services that go to all equally and those which only go to the poorest; there are many options in between. If one looks just at social security, the UK system includes benefits where the amounts paid relate in a wide variety of ways to other elements of current income and indeed to past income:

- means-tested benefits, paid only to those whose current income from other sources is low. Examples include Income Support, Housing Benefit, or the amounts paid through the most generous part of the new Child Tax Credit;
- 'affluence-tested' benefits, which are paid to all except those with high incomes. An example is the part of Child Tax Credit (worth £10.45 per week in

2003–04) going to all those with children *except* those with joint incomes of over £50,000;

- flat-rate benefits paid to those in certain circumstances, regardless of their income, such as Child Benefit;
- flat-rate benefits for which entitlement depends on past National Insurance Contributions, such as the basic state retirement pension; and
- National Insurance benefits designed to replace past earnings in part, and so which are *higher* for those who had greater earnings in the past, and so paid higher National Insurance Contributions. Many Continental social insurance systems run on this principle, and until the 1980s British unemployment and invalidity benefits had earnings-related additions. Today, only the earnings-related part of the State Second Pension embodies this principle (and even here recent reforms mean that over the next fifty years the State Second Pension will become steadily more and more flat-rate and less related to past earnings; Hills 2004).

A consequence of means-testing can be that stigmatized services or benefits fail to reach all of their targets because of lack of take-up by those entitled. Targeting by means-testing can be efficient in one sense—achieving the result that only those who are the prime focus of policy benefit—but inefficient in another, if those who are the intended beneficiaries miss out. Table 6.3 shows official estimates by the Department for Work and Pensions (DWP) of the extent to which people claimed the means-tested benefits they were entitled to in 2000–01. The estimates are given in two ways. 'Case-load take-up' gives the proportion of people estimated to be entitled to a benefit who claimed it. 'Expenditure take-up' measures the proportion of the available cash that is, in fact, claimed. Because those entitled to larger amounts are typically more likely to claim than those entitled to only small amounts, expenditure take-up is usually higher than case-load take-up. Take-up for the universal Child Benefit and the basic state retirement pension is generally believed to be near 100 per cent. But for the means-tested benefits it is clear that take-up falls short—in some cases quite a long way short—of this. For instance, around 30 per cent of

Table 6.3. *Take-up estimates for means-tested benefits, 2000–01, GB*

	Case–load take-up (%)	Expenditure take-up (%)
Income Support (non-pensioners)	86–95	91–97
Minimum Income Guarantee (pensioners)	68–76	78–86
Housing Benefit	87–94	91–96
Council Tax Benefit	70–76	73–80
Jobseeker's Allowance (income-based)	62–71	67–78

Source: DWP (2003*d*).

pensioners who were entitled to a top-up from what was then known as the Minimum Income Guarantee failed to claim it, leaving around a fifth of the amount available unclaimed. For Council Tax Benefit and the means-tested part of Jobseekers' Allowance, at least a fifth of the amount available also went unclaimed.

Similarly, the in-work means-tested benefit that used to be paid to low-income families with children, Family Credit, had a case-load take-up of 72 per cent in 1999 and an expenditure take-up of 81 per cent (Marsh et al. 2001). Family Credit was replaced by the Working Families Tax Credit (WFTC) in October 1999 (and in turn by the Child and Working Tax Credits in April 2001) with a larger group of people entitled, and new administrative systems. Initial take-up of WFTC was lower than the old Family Credit, 62–5 per cent by case-load and 73–8 per cent by expenditure in 2000–01, according to the Inland Revenue. However, by 2001–02 these numbers had risen back up to 71–4 per cent and 80–5 per cent respectively (Inland Revenue 2003*b*: Tables 1 and 2).

Such figures indicate one kind of cost of 'targeting': failure to reach some of the targets, some of whom are left below what is intended to be the state's minimum income level as a result and are among those in deepest poverty. Even where people do claim such benefits, to do so they may have to suffer Titmuss's 'humiliating loss of status, dignity or self-respect', adding to the 'hassle factor' involved in form-filling and time spent getting through the bureaucratic machinery. Such 'costs of claiming' to recipients can be estimated by looking at the take-up behaviour of those entitled to larger and smaller amounts of benefit. For instance, Pudney, Hernandez, and Hancock (2002) suggest that the implicit 'cost of claiming' for pensioners entitled to means-tested benefits in the late 1990s averaged between £2 and £4 per week, compared with average payments in the group studied of £21 per week. In other words, costs of claiming were between a tenth and a fifth of the cash received.

When one thinks about trends in social spending and its relationship with income distribution, the differences discussed above in the structure and effectiveness of different kinds of benefit need to be borne in mind. They also affect public views of social security and of the welfare state as a whole, imposing potential constraints on policy (Section 6.5).

6.3 INTERNATIONAL COMPARISONS OF SOCIAL SPENDING

Comparing social spending between countries is difficult. This is partly because the role of public spending varies from country to country: in one, an objective may be achieved directly through state spending, whereas in another the same end may be achieved through some form of tax concession, with little difference in overall impact. Unfortunately, however, we do not have statistics of the kind described for the UK in Section 6.4 below that would allow us to make a comparison of welfare activity as a whole between countries, taking account of

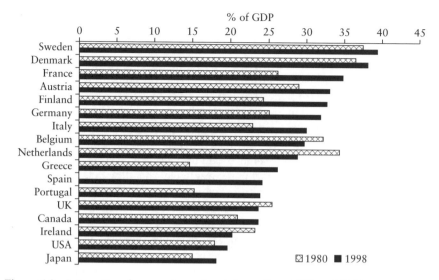

Figure 6.8. *International comparison of social spending, 1980 and 1998*

Sources: OECD social expenditures database and OECD (2001*a*) and earlier equivalents, apart from UK; UK figures from Figure 6.3 (adjusted to include active labour market measures and public service pensions).

private as well as public spending. Comparisons are also difficult because the statistics themselves may be measuring different things.[3]

This kind of comparison has to be treated with care, but there are nonetheless some striking features visible in Figure 6.8. The figures shown are for spending on health care, education, and social security. Unlike those shown earlier, they include pensions to public servants and spending on 'active labour market measures' (such as employment programmes for the unemployed). First, the UK's social spending is not large by comparison with other industrialized countries, and its relative position in this particular league table has been falling over time. Among these countries (EU members apart from Luxembourg and the other large industrialized countries in the G7), the UK came thirteenth out of seventeen in 1998, but would have come seventh out of sixteen in 1980. While the fact that UK spending actually fell in relation to GDP over this period is a product of the particular years used (see Figure 6.3), it is striking that social spending was growing over the period in all but three of the other countries shown (Belgium, the Netherlands, and Ireland). The fall in the UK's

---

[3] For instance, the figures for other countries used in Figure 6.8 come from the Organization for Economic Cooperation and Development (OECD) database of social spending, but not those for the UK. This is because the OECD's figures, drawn from Eurostat data on 'social protection', show a figure for 'public' spending on pensions in the UK that includes payments which are actually from private pension schemes. This is corrected for in Figure 6.8 in the UK case, but it is likely that similar or other problems of definition affect the figures for other countries as well.

relative position reflects the way in which, while 'the lid has been on' in the UK, the share of national income used for social spending has tended to grow elsewhere.

A second notable feature is just how wide the range is. Countries at similar levels of economic development have chosen very different routes, with social spending now ranging from less than a fifth of national income in Japan and the USA to more than a third in France, Denmark, and Sweden. It might be thought that this reflects straightforward differences in political preferences. However, the comparisons of attitudes towards poverty and inequality shown in Chapters 2 and 3 (for example, Figure 2.12 and Table 3.16) do not suggest that this is a straightforward explanation for low social spending in the UK, at least. Nor does it seem to come directly from stronger concerns about the cost of public spending in the UK than in other EU countries, at least, as can be seen from the figures from the early 1990s in Table 6.4.

It is striking that in 1992 UK respondents were *least* likely to agree that 'social security is too costly to society' among the countries shown, with three-quarters of them rejecting the statement. The table shows some tendency for respondents in low-spending countries such as Greece and the UK to be more likely to reject the statement, and those in high-spending ones such as the Netherlands, Italy, and France to be more likely to agree. To this extent there seems a desire for convergence. There are, however, exceptions, notably Spain and Portugal, where low spending seems to accompany little appetite for an increase.

Table 6.4. *EU attitudes to social security spending, 1992*

	Social security as % of GDP	'Social security is too costly for society. Benefits should be reduced and contributions should be lowered'		
		Agree	Disagree	Balance
Netherlands	19.2	40	54	−14
Italy	18.4	50	38	+12
France	18.4	46	51	−5
Belgium	16.9	47	47	0
Denmark	16.0	41	56	−15
Luxembourg	15.5	33	66	−33
Germany	14.6	25	68	−43
Spain	14.4	48	36	+12
Greece	14.3	27	57	−30
UK	13.5	17	73	−56
Ireland	12.1	32	55	−23
Portugal	9.9	47	44	+3

Sources: Spending figures from OECD database, apart from UK, which is from HM Treasury (2003a: Table 3.4), including net public service pensions (from 1993–94 level). Attitudes from Ferrera (1993: Table 3).

6.4 ANALYSING PUBLIC-PRIVATE BOUNDARIES

So far, this chapter has concentrated on public spending. But this gives only a partial view of how 'welfare' needs are met by both private and public sectors, and conveys only part of what the public sector itself does. In certain obvious respects, the private sector has had an increasing role over the last two decades: council housing has been sold under the Right to Buy; non-profit housing associations have taken over other council housing and have provided most of the new 'social housing'; private care homes for the elderly are a larger share of the total than local authority-run ones; private pensions are far more important for many earners than those from the state; major political battles have been fought over privatization, contracting out, and introducing charges for those users of public services judged able to afford them.

Such broad trends give an impression of a growing role for the private sector in welfare activity. However, the developments are very varied. Owner-occupation has grown, but part of this used to be publicly financed through tax relief. Private residential care places for the elderly have grown, but much of this is paid for by local authorities. Housing associations are outside the public sector, but most of the accommodation they provide is both publicly financed through Housing Benefit and publicly allocated by local authority homelessness referrals and waiting lists. Whether something is 'public' or 'private' can depend on exactly what question is being asked. In earlier work on which this section is based, Tania Burchardt, Carol Propper, and I (1999) identified three kinds of question:

- *Provision*: is the provider of the service a public or a private sector body?
- *Finance*: does the public sector pay for the service directly through tax-financed spending or indirectly through benefits or tax relief?
- *Decision*: can individuals choose for themselves the provider used or the amount of service, or are these decided for them by the state?

This three-way classification generates eight possible combinations, illustrated in the diagram shown in Figure 6.9. The sectors in the top half of the circle are publicly provided, those on its right-hand side are publicly financed, while those in the inner circle are under public decision. To take each sector in the top—publicly provided—half:

- *inner right*: the 'pure public' sector, with public finance, provision and decision; for instance, Child Benefit;
- *outer right*: publicly financed and provided services, but with private decisions on whether to use them; for instance, payments into the State Second Pension (which people can 'contract out' of);
- *inner left*: services that are publicly provided and decided upon but financed privately; for instance, rent paid individually (without the use of Housing Benefit) for a council house, or other services with 'user charges'; and

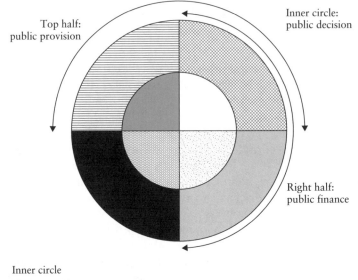

Figure 6.9. *Classification of public and private welfare activity*
Source: Burchardt (1997).

- *outer left*: publicly provided services, but with private finance and decision; for instance, pay-beds in NHS hospitals.

Correspondingly, those in the lower half are privately provided services:

- *inner right*: publicly financed and controlled services from private providers; for instance, contracted-out services such as hospital catering or Housing Benefit payments to housing association tenants;
- *outer right*: publicly financed services from private providers with private decisions; for instance, tax relief for private pensions;
- *inner left*: privately financed and provided services, but with public decisions; for instance child support payments or user charges for contracted-out home care; and
- *outer left*: the 'pure private' sector, with private finance, provision, and control; for instance, unassisted places at private schools.

6.4.1   Service by Service Changes 1979–1999

Using this typology, we can chart the changing welfare mix from 1979 until 1999. Figures for spending in real terms in 1979, 1995, and 1999 in each sector within each of the eight categories are given in Table 6.5 (for detailed sources and methods, see Smithies forthcoming *b* and Burchardt 1997).

In *education*, the striking change was the fall in the 'pure public' sector from two-thirds (66 per cent) to just over half (54 per cent) of the total. The 'pure private' sector more than doubled from 8 per cent to 20 per cent, driven by growing private spending on things like driving lessons and leisure courses as well as university fees paid privately, and greater spending on private schools, reflecting higher fees as well as slow increases in pupil numbers. More important is the publicly financed and controlled, but privately provided, sector, containing public grants to independent establishments like universities and further education colleges, as well as contracted-out local authority spending on education. This also grew over the period up to 1995, as did the publicly financed but privately provided and controlled sector, containing government spending on tuition fees in higher and further education. Notably, after 1995 the latter fell back as changes in funding for higher education came into force.

Within *health* services, the pure public sector has remained dominant, but even in 1979 private provision of publicly financed and controlled services represented 18 per cent of the total (21 per cent by 1999). The biggest part of this sector is general medical services provided by GPs. The pure private sector increased from 9 per cent to 13 per cent between 1979 and 1995 (after which it stabilized), reflecting rapid growth in both consumers' expenditure on over-the-counter medicines, spectacles, and so forth, as well as private medical insurance. Other sectors also grew but remained relatively small, including: tax relief on private medical insurance in 1995 (publicly financed but privately provided and controlled); patient charges for dental services and prescriptions (publicly provided and controlled but privately financed); and pay-beds (publicly provided but privately financed and decided on).

Of all the services, *housing* started in 1979 with the largest pure private and smallest pure public sector. With growing owner-occupation and some revival of private renting, the pure private sector provided more than two-thirds of all housing in 1995 and 1999, measured in terms of its annual rental value.[4] In both 1979 and 1995, public finance for private housing under private control represented another 12–13 per cent of the total, with Housing Benefit for private

---

[4] The allocation between sectors is made on the basis of imputed rents and spending on repairs and maintenance for owner-occupiers, and economic subsidies for tenants, including the annualized value of Right-to-Buy discounts (see Sefton 2002). In effect, the method allocates the annual rental value of the stock between sectors. For the 1999 numbers in Table 6.5, the estimates of economic and imputed rents are based on rents in the private sector. For the earlier years, when there were few uncontrolled market rents, assumed returns on capital values were used to estimate these (for comparability over time, the numbers for 1999 in Table 6.6 and Figure 6.10 also use the capital values method).

Table 6.5. *Public and private welfare activity, 1979–80, 1995–96, and 1999–2000, UK (£ billion, 1999–2000 prices)*

Provision:	Public provision				Private provision				All
Finance:	Public finance		Private finance		Public finance		Private finance		
Decision:	Public	Private	Public	Private	Public	Private	Public	Private	
(a) 1979–80									
Education[a]	17.1	—	—	0.1	6.1	0.8	—	2.1	26.1
Health[b]	20.0	—	0.2	—	5.2	—	0.4	2.5	28.4
Housing[c]	7.4	—	3.8	—	0.4	5.4	0.4	23.9	41.3
Income maintenance[d]	52.2	8.9	—	—	—	12.5	—	17.7	91.3
Personal care services[e]	3.8	—	0.5	—	0.6	—	0.03	0.4	5.3
TOTAL	100.5	8.9	4.5	0.1	12.3	18.7	0.8	46.6	192.3
(b) 1995–96									
Education	22.8	—	—	0.3	9.9	1.5	—	5.8	40.0
Health	34.6	—	0.2	—	10.8	0.3	0.9	7.0	54.1
Housing	8.3	—	3.3	—	2.2	8.9	1.4	48.5	72.6
Income Maintenance	85.9	4.5	0.03	—	—	20.7	—	20.6	131.7
Personal care services	6.9	—	0.6	—	5.6	—	0.8	2.4	16.3
TOTAL	158.5	4.5	4.1	0.3	28.5	31.4	3.1	84.3	314.7
(c) 1999–2000									
Education	22.2	—	—	0.3	10.2	0.8	—	8.1	41.3
Health	42.3	—	0.1	—	13.6	0.2	0.9	8.3	65.7
Housing[f]	14.2	—	3.3	—	6.1	9.5	1.2	59.0	93.3
Income Maintenance	89.0	5.7	0.3	—	—	18.4	—	24.7	138.1
Personal care services	8.0	—	0.8	—	6.2	—	1.6	2.5	19.1
TOTAL	175.7	5.7	4.5	0.3	36.1	28.9	3.7	102.6	357.5

[a] Education: current expenditure only. Does not include student maintenance or pre-school education.

[b] Health: some estimates necessary on contracting out, especially for 1979–80.

[c] Housing; based on estimates of current rental value of all dwellings. Effects of rent controls on private properties not included.

[d] Income maintenance: figures for pensions are contributions, except for basic state pension, which is cost of pensions in payment.

[e] Personal services: some expenditure split between 'own provision' and 'contracted out' on basis of volume of service rather than cost. 'Pure private' expenditure estimated for all years.

[f] 1999–2000 estimates of economic rents and imputed rents based on structure of market rents (rather than returns on capital values as in earlier years). Figures derived from Sefton's estimates (2003) for 2000–01 adjusted to 1999–2000 values.

Sources: Burchardt (1997) and Burchardt, Hills, and Propper (1999) updated (see Smithies forthcoming *b*).

tenants taking over from mortgage tax relief as the largest part of this, and other important contributions from Income Support for Mortgage Interest and the annualized value of Right-to-Buy discounts. However, this had fallen to 10 per cent by 1999, as mortgage interest tax relief was reduced (and later abolished). The growth of housing associations can be seen in the publicly financed and controlled but privately provided sector (rents financed by subsidy or Housing Benefit) from 1 per cent to 7 per cent of the housing sector. Most strikingly, by 1995–96 the pure public sector—council housing paid for through Housing Benefit and subsidy—represented only 12 per cent of all housing provision. However, by 1999 increases in subsidy in economic terms (only partly reflecting a different method of estimation) meant that the pure public sector was 15 per cent of the total (compared with 18 per cent in 1979).

In contrast to the other sectors, the size of the pure public sector actually grew within *income maintenance and social security* to two-thirds of the total. This reflected a near-doubling in the real cost of non-pension social security (if we exclude Housing Benefit and other items included elsewhere) to £50 billion, plus growth with ageing of spending on the basic pension and related items to £39 billion. With higher rates of contracting out of SERPS, there was a switch towards private pension providers but with public finance from tax reliefs and rebates by 1995, but this had fallen back by 1999. The pure private sector—mainly private pension contributions net of tax reliefs, with some private welfare insurance—grew in real terms over the period but fell slightly from 19 per cent to 18 per cent of the total as the public sector elements expanded faster.

Finally, contracting-out reduced the share of *personal care services* in the pure public sector from 70 per cent to 42 per cent of the total.[5] Correspondingly, the publicly financed and controlled but privately provided sector—containing items such as local authority spending on contracted-out residential care and (in 1995 particularly) Income Support for residents of independent care homes—grew from 11 per cent to 32 per cent. User charges for contracted-out services also become more important, and the size of the pure private sector (private spending on residential and non-residential care) nearly doubled to 13 per cent of the total.

6.4.2 *Welfare Activity as a Whole*

As this discussion shows, what happened to welfare activity over twenty years under mostly Conservative governments was far more complicated than might have been expected from a simple model of 'privatization'. There was a relative decline in what might be thought of as the immediate post-war 'Morrisonian'

---

[5] Informal care is not included in the table because of the difficulties in putting a meaningful monetary value on the time and energy of informal carers. Putting a value of £7 per hour on informal carers' time (reflecting then local authority wage rates), Laing and Buisson (1995) suggested a value of £41 billion in 1994–95 (£46 billion at 1999–2000 prices), nearly three times that of all the formal services shown in Table 6.5. Even valued at the minimum wage (£3.60 per hour in 1999), informal care would be greater in value than formal services.

welfare state, that is, the pure public sector, and a rise in the pure private sector. But there were exceptions to this—the increasing importance of general social security—and important changes in some of the mixed sectors in particular services. The totals in Table 6.5 compare the real spending on welfare activity as a whole in our eight classifications in 1979–80, 1995–96, and 1999–2000. A first point is that overall welfare activity grew by 86 per cent in real terms, but within this total growth rates differed considerably between sectors. In particular, the pure private sector more than doubled in real terms from £47 billion to £103 billion (at 1999–2000 prices), and there was rapid percentage growth in the other three sectors involving private provision.

The changing overall welfare mix is illustrated in Figure 6.10. What this brings out—perhaps surprisingly—is how gradual the shifts were over this period. Welfare activity was already very mixed in its composition in 1979–80, with the pure public sector making up only 52 per cent of the total. This fell, but only to 49 per cent in 1999–2000 (the same proportion as in 1995–96). Meanwhile, the pure private sector did increase significantly from 24 per cent, but still only to 29 per cent. Some of the trends seen *within* services shown in Table 6.5 offset each other, as does the changing relative size of each. The general shift away from the Morrisonian welfare state seen in education, health, housing, and personal services is mostly offset by the growing real value of state-provided and state-financed social security. The role of the private sector is particularly large within housing. If this is excluded, there was virtually no change at all in the role of the pure public sector (falling from 62 per cent to 61 per cent of all activity in the other four sectors), and the rise in the share of the pure private sector was only from 15 per cent to 17 per cent of the total.

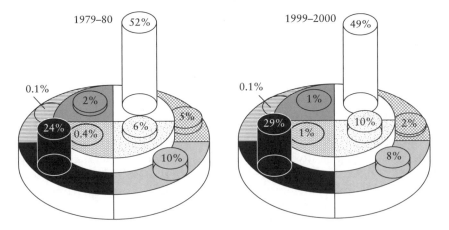

Figure 6.10. *Total welfare activity, 1979–80 and 1999–2000, UK*

Note: 1999–2000 figures use comparable method for calculating housing subsidies and imputed rents to that used for 1979–80 (as in Table 6.6). Key to sections of diagrams as for Figure 6.9.

Source: Burchardt (1997) updated (see Table 6.5).

Perhaps the clearest message from the figure is that the effect of 'privatization' was more to raise the importance of the bottom half of the diagram (private provision, which rose from 41 per cent to 48 per cent) than that of the left-hand side (private finance, which rose from 27 per cent to 31 per cent). This is explored further in Table 6.6, which compares the scale of total public finance and public provision with overall welfare activity, also showing conventional measures of 'public spending'. As a share of national income, public finance grew over the twenty years from 23.8 per cent to 26.6 per cent, but 'public spending' actually fell slightly (from 23.1 per cent to 22.9 per cent of GDP). The difference reflects the greater use of tax reliefs over the period (as well as some

Table 6.6. *Total welfare activity, 1979–80, 1995–96, and 1999–2000, UK*

	Public finance	Public provision	All welfare activity	(Public spending)
1979–80 (£ billion)				
Education	24.0	17.1	26.1	(30.7)
Health	25.2	20.3	28.4	(26.3)
Housing	13.2	11.2	41.3	(19.2)
Income maintenance	73.6	61.1	91.3	(55.1)
Personal services	4.4	4.3	5.3	(5.1)
TOTAL	140.4	114.0	192.4	(136.2)
1995–96 (£ billion)				
Education	34.2	22.8	40.0	(40.3)
Health	45.7	35.1	54.1	(45.4)
Housing	19.4	11.6	72.6	(18.0)
Income maintenance	111.1	90.4	131.7	(90.1)
Personal services	12.5	7.5	16.3	(9.9)
TOTAL	222.9	167.4	314.7	(203.7)
1999–2000 (£ billion)				
Education	33.2	22.2	41.3	(40.9)
Health	56.1	42.7	65.7	(50.2)
Housing	27.6	16.6	92.0	(14.8)
Income maintenance	113.1	95.0	138.1	(92.2)
Personal services	14.2	8.8	19.1	(12.1)
TOTAL	244.2	185.3	356.2	(210.2)
Total as per cent of GDP				
1979–80	23.8	19.4	32.7	(23.1)
1995–96	27.4	20.6	38.7	(25.0)
1999–2000	26.6	20.1	38.7	(22.9)

Note: Public spending figures exclude tax reliefs, include capital spending and in education, student maintenance grants, and use cash-flow definitions of housing subsidies. Other housing figures use economic definitions (on comparable basis for all three years).

Sources: Table 6.5; Glennerster and Hills (1998: Table 8A.1); HM Treasury (2003b: Tables 3.2 and 3.5).

effects of definitional differences). Meanwhile, despite the trends discussed above, public provision increased slightly as a share of GDP, but private provision increased faster. As a result, overall welfare activity grew from 33 per cent to 39 per cent of GDP, despite the lack of any growth in conventionally measured public social spending. The lid may have been on government spending, but not on overall demand for the areas traditionally covered by the welfare state. Chapter 10 discusses further the tendency for demand for these areas to expand as society becomes more affluent, and the implications of this for public policy.

6.5   PUBLIC ATTITUDES TO SOCIAL SECURITY AND PRIVATE PROVISION

The ability of governments to use social security and other forms of social spending to affect income distribution and to meet other objectives is constrained not only by public attitudes to distribution but also by attitudes towards particular policy instruments. This section presents evidence on four aspects of these: means-testing; incentives; fraud; and the relationship between the use of private services and attitudes towards public spending.

6.5.1   *Means-testing*

One of the main controversies surrounding social security in particular and welfare policy in general is the extent to which services should be delivered on a universal or a selective, particularly means-tested, basis. Survey evidence suggests a general public preference against means-testing. Table 6.7 gives results from the 2001 British Social Attitudes (BSA) survey in which people were asked about the treatment which 'very high' as opposed to 'very low' earners should receive, that is, the extremes of the income range. Despite this, for unemployment, three-quarters backed the idea of flat-rate benefits. Only one in ten might

Table 6.7. *Public attitudes to benefits and earnings, 2001, GB (% of respondents)*

	Benefits for a very high earner compared to a very low earner should be:			
	Higher	Same	Lower	None
Unemployment benefit	10	76	10	2
State retirement pension	13	74	9	3
Disability benefits*	4	67	21	5
Child benefit	1	55	23	18

  * For disability benefits, the contrast is between those with very high and very low *incomes*.
Source: Park et al. (2002: 259), from British Social Attitudes survey (3,287 respondents).

back restoration of supplements related to past earnings of the kind abolished in the UK in the 1980s (but which remain common in Continental social insurance-based systems). Only slightly more backed some form of means-testing, with lower benefits for (previously) high earners. Attitudes to pensions are much the same, with just under three-quarters backing flat-rate state pensions, and for disability benefits (although here a quarter backed some form of means-testing).

Opinions are more divided when it comes to benefits for children. In 2001, just over half favoured flat rate benefits (as Child Benefit actually operates), but two-fifths thought that they should be lower for 'very high' earners. Indeed, in 1998, a narrow majority had thought that they should be *lower* or not given at all to the high earners (Hills and Lelkes 1999: 14).

Qualitative research exploring these opinions suggests that, for much of what the welfare state does, there is deeply held public support for state provision that is equal, or goes to all if they have particular needs, regardless of income, and hostility to means-testing on a variety of grounds. In some cases, as with the state pension, this reflects a direct belief that people have 'paid in' to an actual fund, so they are all entitled. In others, such as the NHS or education, it is a less tangible belief that the system should run as a 'club' into which people pay what they can but are then entitled to help from it depending only on their needs (Hedges 2004). An exception is help with the costs of children, where strong arguments are put both for equal treatment and for some form of means-testing.

The unpopularity of means-testing reflects not necessarily concern about economic disincentives from the high combined marginal tax and benefit withdrawal rates it can create, but can reflect perceptions of equity. Like the prodigal son's brother in the Christian New Testament, many people resent the idea that someone who has worked or saved hard can end up little or no better-off than someone who has lived, if not riotously, at least in idleness. As a not atypical low-income pensioner put it to Alan Hedges in his research on attitudes to redistribution,

When me dad died she had his pension from British Steel, and because she was 8p over on her pension, and having me dad's pension, she couldn't get no family support, she couldn't get nothing. She'd have been better off if she hadn't've got me dad's pension, 'cos she would've been able to get help—but me dad had worked for that pension, and she were entitled to it. But she got penalised for it. (Hedges forthcoming: section C2.5)

6.5.2 *Disincentives*

The high effective marginal tax rates that characterize much means-testing (see Section 7.3) cause a problem for political support for the welfare system because of the way they are *assumed* to affect people's behaviour, regardless of whether they actually do so. Figure 6.11 shows responses to the BSA survey since 1983 to three questions about the impact of benefits and the welfare state. First, for the whole period, around a third of respondents agreed that 'the welfare state encourages people to stop helping each other'. The most recent responses to

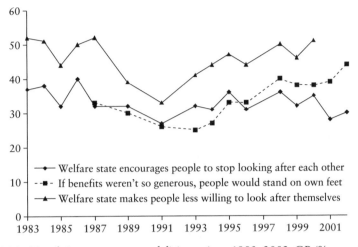

Figure 6.11. *Trends in concerns around disincentives, 1983–2002, GB (% agreeing with each statement)*

Source: British Social Attitudes survey.

this question show somewhat less agreement than before: by 2002, 30 per cent agreed, but slightly more, 31 per cent, disagreed. By contrast, two other questions about disincentive effects show increasing levels of agreement since the early 1990s. By 2002, 44 per cent agreed that 'if welfare benefits weren't so generous, people would learn to stand on their own two feet', and only 30 per cent disagreed. This was a large change from the early 1990s: in 1993, only 25 per cent agreed with this statement, and more than half, 52 per cent, disagreed. Even higher levels of agreement had been reached with the third question by the last time it was asked in 2000. By then more than half, 51 per cent, agreed that, 'the welfare state makes people nowadays less willing to look after themselves', and only a quarter disagreed. This was a reversal of the position in the early 1990s, when more disagreed than agreed, but represented a return to that of the early 1980s. The overall picture appears to be that concerns about incentives expressed in these ways have generally been high over the last twenty years but diminished in the early 1990s. Since then, as the economy has recovered, and perhaps as governments have been perceived to be less harsh towards claimants, they have become more acute.

This kind of evidence, combined with that reported in Chapters 2 and 3 (and in Chapter 8) suggests that many people share two sets of attitudes with competing implications: that something should be done to raise low incomes and that many benefits are too little to live on (see for instance Table 3.13 and Section 8.6), but also that the welfare system reduces work incentives. Figure 6.12 shows how people have responded to the BSA survey since 1983 when they have been asked to say which of the following two statements comes closer to their own view: 'Benefits for the unemployed are too low and cause

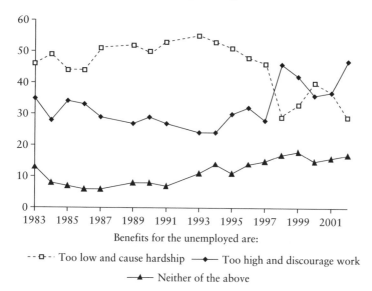

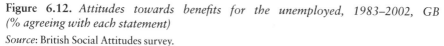

Benefits for the unemployed are:

- - □ - - Too low and cause hardship   —◆— Too high and discourage work

—▲— Neither of the above

Figure 6.12. *Attitudes towards benefits for the unemployed, 1983–2002, GB (% agreeing with each statement)*

Source: British Social Attitudes survey.

hardship', and 'Benefits for unemployed people are too high and discourage them from finding jobs'. Up to the 1996 survey, the balance lay consistently with the first of these. Around half favoured the statement that benefits were too low compared with less than a third favouring the 'too high' option (and around a tenth agreeing with neither). But the 1998 survey gave a dramatically different result, with nearly half then favouring the 'too high' option and only 29 per cent saying they were too low. The responses to the partial BSA survey carried out in early 1997 and shown in the figure suggest that most of the switch occurred *after* the 1997 election. By 2000 the positions had changed back, with the 'too low' option regaining a narrow lead, but by 2002 nearly half of the respondents again favoured the statement that benefits were too high and discouraged work.

These swings are hard to explain. They do not (unlike others discussed below) reflect changes in the economy: unemployment itself showed no such wild swings over the 1996–2002 period, continuing to fall steadily (Figure 4.8). Analysis of the survey shows that the likelihood of someone agreeing with the statement that unemployment benefits are too high is greater if they believe that the system creates disincentives to work, and also if they believe the system is subject to widespread fraud and abuse (Hills 2001). So the trends shown in Figure 6.11 (and Figure 6.13 below) go some way to explaining the change in the balance of views shown in Figure 6.12 (and the decline in support for higher spending on welfare benefits for the poor shown in Table 8.3). However, they cannot explain the dramatic switches in the balance between 1996 and 2002 in Figure 6.12.

In earlier analysis of the results up until 2000 (Hills 2002*a*), I suggested that a possible explanation of the changes—particularly given that it was people who identified with Labour whose views had changed most—was the high prominence which government ministers had given in 1998 to problems with benefits for the unemployed in the run-up to publication of the welfare reform Green Paper. The Green Paper itself stressed 'fundamental problems' of people being trapped on benefit and of fraud (DSS 1998: 9). For some Labour identifiers, hearing these kinds of statements from a Labour, as opposed to a Conservative, government may have shifted the balance of their opinions from those held up to early 1997. By 2000, the political prominence of these issues had declined, and views appeared to be reverting to where they were before. However, it is hard to explain the swing *back* in 2002 in this way. Perhaps what this illustrates is the difficulty people face when asked to choose between two statements *both* of which they tend to agree with. Which comes out on top is a narrow decision, making the results volatile. Whatever the explanation, the data show that perceptions of disincentives matter and go some way to explaining why benefits for the unemployed are such a low priority item within public spending (see Section 6.2).

6.5.3   *Fraud*

Another source of concern with social security in general, and means-tested benefits in particular, is fraud. This is not only because it increases costs and uses up scarce resources but also because perceptions of it being substantial undermine public support for the system. Reviewing the evidence on the extent of fraud, particularly affecting Income Support for the unemployed, Robert Walker and Marilyn Howard (2000: 101) concluded that

On the basis of this official evidence, between 7% and 11% of claimants would appear to be engaged in fraud at any one time. While these figures are not insignificant they nevertheless suggest that the vast majority of benefit recipients, even long-term recipients, are not found to be engaged in fraud.

A recent DWP estimate is that the combined cost of both fraud and overpayments by error was £1.1 billion for Income Support and Jobseeker's Allowance in the year to September 2001, and £2 billion for benefits as a whole (DWP 2002*c*). If this is correct—and, of course, if it were possible to measure fraud accurately, it would be easier to stop it—total fraud would represent less than 2 per cent of the total social security budget. Note that the DWP estimates (Table 6.3) that between a fifth and a third of the amount people *could* claim from the benefit that is most subject to suspicion of fraud, income-tested Jobseekers' Allowance, is not actually claimed. The non-take-up of just this one benefit would then amount to between £2.3 billion and £4 billion in 2001–02, greater than the Department's estimates of fraud and overpayment by error across the whole of the social security budget.

However, as Figure 6.13 shows, public perceptions are that fraud is widespread, and some of these perceptions have grown significantly since the early 1990s,

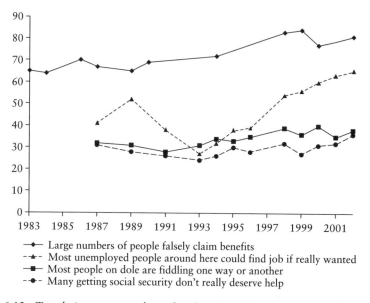

Figure 6.13. *Trends in concerns about fraud in the welfare system, 1983–2002, GB (% agreeing with each statement)*

Source: British Social Attitudes survey.

particularly in relation to benefits for the unemployed. First, around a third of the population agree with two very strong statements. In 2002, 36 per cent agreed that 'many people who get social security don't really deserve any help'. This is only a little higher than over the previous twenty years, but the 2002 survey was the first time that more respondents agreed with this statement than disagreed (Sefton 2003). Slightly more, 38 per cent, agreed that, '*most people* on the dole are fiddling in one way or another' (emphasis added). Agreement with this sweeping statement has again increased since the early 1990s, and more have agreed with it than have disagreed since the mid-1990s.

The other two statements command even wider support. First, more than two-thirds of respondents to the BSA survey have agreed that 'large numbers of people these days falsely claim benefits' since the late 1980s, and this had risen to around four-fifths by the end of the 1990s. The most dramatic change has, however, come in the final series, and this is clearly related to the state of the economy. Back in the recession of the early 1990s, only just over a quarter of the population agreed that 'around here, most unemployed people could find a job if they really wanted one'. But, as unemployment has fallen, so the proportion believing this has risen, reaching nearly two-thirds, 65 per cent, by 2002. Of course, the survey respondents live all over the country, so this response does not mean that they necessarily believe that those claiming in other areas could get a job easily, but it still shows increasing unease with benefits for the unemployed.

Not only do people think that social security fraud is widespread, they also take an unsympathetic view of it. For instance, in the 1998 BSA survey more then half (53 per cent) of respondents said that it was 'seriously wrong' to give incorrect information about oneself to get benefits, and virtually none thought that it was only 'a bit wrong'. By contrast, only 19 per cent thought that it was 'seriously wrong' to give incorrect information about one's income in order to pay less tax, and over a quarter regarded it as only 'a bit wrong' (Hills and Lelkes 1999). In the 2001 survey, only 21 per cent agreed that 'a lot of false benefit claims are the result of confusion rather than dishonesty', compared with 51 per cent who disagreed (although this was down at little from the 58 per cent disagreeing when asked the same question in 1999). A somewhat larger number, 36 per cent, agreed that 'the reason that some people on benefit cheat the system is that they don't get enough to live on', but 41 per cent disagreed (again, slightly down from 45 per cent disagreeing in 1999). And, when asked in 2001 whether it was more important for government to 'stop people claiming benefits to which they are not entitled' or to 'get people to claim benefits to which they are entitled', 56 per cent put combating fraud first, but only 34 per cent put promoting take-up first.

These views relate to benefits for the unemployed in particular, but they affect views of social security as a whole because such benefits are widely believed to be a much larger part of social security spending than they actually are (Table 6.2).

6.5.4   *Effects of Private Welfare Use on Attitudes to Public Welfare*

As Section 6.4 demonstrated, there is no sharp dichotomy between 'public welfare' and 'private welfare': services can be mixed between the two in terms of their provision, finance, and who decides what happens. But nor, as it turns out, is there a great distinction between those who use private welfare and the rest of the population, and this affects people's attitudes. When Tania Burchardt and Carol Propper (1999) investigated who uses private welfare, they found:

- The proportion of the population who use *only* private welfare services is small. In the mid-1990s, about one in ten of the population had private pensions, lived in privately owned housing (including their own), and used private medical care. Only one in twenty used private medical care or had private medical insurance at the same time as living in private housing and using private education for their children (or were privately educated themselves).
- Not only do people use the private sector for some services and the public sector for others, but also those who use the private sector for a service at one time often use the public sector for it at another. For instance, some people use state primary schools for their children, private schools between ages 11 and 16, but then state sixth form colleges (and state-funded universities). Those using private medical care one year may use the NHS the next, or even within the same year.

As a result, Burchardt and Propper argued that any 'private welfare class' in Britain is not large. There are few people for whom state services are irrelevant. Equally, there are many who use some private services—even if housing is excluded, more than half of the population use some form of private health care, pension, or education (Burchardt and Propper 1999: Table 6).

This mixture of use may go some way to explaining their finding that private welfare use was not, as some had suggested, associated with opposition to the welfare state or its expansion. If this were true, as use of private welfare increased (which it has done slowly), the larger numbers 'opting out' might then see themselves as having little to gain from extra welfare spending, which would tighten the political constraints on governments that wanted to increase it. Burchardt and Propper did find that those who used private health care and private education expressed less support for free universal provision than others. However, the differences were not large, nor necessarily statistically significant. Most strikingly, they found little evidence from panel data that actually *using* private health care changed people's support for the NHS to any great degree; if anything, they found it was experience of using either kind of health care, public or private, that was associated with a (small) shift away from supporting free health care for all but an increase in numbers objecting to wealth allowing people to buy medical priority (Burchardt and Propper 1999: Table 9).

More recent evidence has been analysed by Tom Sefton (2003) and is presented in Table 6.8. This shows the proportion of BSA respondents in 2001 who would support an increase of 1p in the pound in the rate of income tax to pay for different public services (told that this would cost taxpayers £100 per year on average). In the case of more spending on the NHS, there was virtually no difference between those who have and do not have private medical insurance—more than four-fifths

Table 6.8. *Attitudes towards higher public spending by whether respondent is user of private welfare, 2001, GB (% of respondents)*

% who would support a 1p increase in income tax to pay for higher spending on ...	Strongly in favour	In favour	Neither	Against	Strongly against	Base
National Health Service:						
No private medical insurance	38	44	9	6	2	886
Private medical insurance	43	42	6	6	2	228
Schools:						
State education only	18	55	14	10	2	1,381
Child or self went to private school	23	49	11	14	3	276
Pensions:						
Not retired, mainly state pension	18	50	16	12	2	369
Not retired, mainly private pension	12	48	21	17	2	812
Retired, state pension only	36	40	11	13	1	338
Retired, private pension	31	34	13	21	1	72

Source: Sefton (2003).

of both groups favoured higher spending. In the case of schools, almost as many of those who went to a private school or used one for their children supported higher spending on state schools as others (although at the same time slightly more private school users were opposed to it than others). For pensions, it is not whether people are contributing to or receiving a private pension that matters; the main difference comes between those who are and are not retired. The large majority in all four groups said they would favour the tax increase to pay for higher pensions, but among the retired groups around a third said that they were *strongly* in favour of this, compared with less than a fifth of the non-retired.

These findings suggest that the reasons for private welfare use may have relatively little to do with people's ideology, and more to do with whether the state offers a good enough service for them. Some of the examples of strong support for additional state spending on education from those who use private schools reflects frustration with the quality of state education: they would use it if they thought it was better. This kind of pragmatism is one reason why private service use varies between sectors: people's choice to use either sector or both depends on the structure of *state* provision (Burchardt, Hills, and Propper, 1999: 56–60). First, it matters whether a private service can be used as an *addition*, or has to be an *alternative*, to what is available from the state. If the former, one might expect many people to combine a fairly small amount of private spending with use of the basic state service—the private sector would be broad, but not very deep. If health care is taken to include dentistry and eye care, it fits this model. If the latter, one might expect a relatively small number of people to be spending quite a lot privately—the private sector would be deep rather than wide. Private schooling fits into this model: it is hard for children to attend state and private schools simultaneously (although they can do so at different stages, and 'extras' such as evening tutors can be added to state schooling).

This suggests part of why the attitudes of those using private welfare towards state provision differ little from others, even without appealing to altruism. Where people are *adding* privately to a basic state service that they also use, their attitudes will depend on the balance they see between the taxes they pay and the value for money of the public service they receive. Where the private alternative is expensive, private users may support greater public spending which would allow them to reduce their private additions (provided they would not pay too much through taxation). On the other hand they will feel the reverse if the public service is seen as poor value for money—as it may be if it comes in a fixed and inflexible form, while the private sector offers choices which they value (as, for instance, in housing provision).

Where the private sector is an *alternative* to a public service, there may be strong pressures from some private users to increase public spending but from others to reduce it. Those remaining with a public service somewhat below what they would like may well favour a large increase in public spending, both to achieve the level of service they want and to avoid potentially having to make an expensive decision to opt out. On the other hand, those who choose private services that are well above the level provided by the public sector will see little return for themselves from greater public provision, and may oppose it. This kind of difference between widely used public services and those that are residualized helps to explain the differences between favourable attitudes of private education users to state education spending shown in Table 6.8 and unfavourable ones of owner-occupiers to higher spending on social housing (Hall, Emmerson, and Brook 1998: Figure 8.3).

6.6 SUMMARY

- Public spending on 'the welfare state' represented exactly a quarter of national income in 2002–03. This total has remained much the same–fluctuating between 21 per cent and 26 per cent of GDP largely with the economic cycle— for the last thirty years. As a share of overall public spending, social spending has become more important, rising from about half of the total in 1978–79 to 63 per cent in 2002–03.
- Within this total, spending on health care has become more important, as did social security spending until the mid-1990s. Personal social services have been growing rapidly, but still represent a small part of the total. Education spending declined as a share of national income between 1978–79 and 1997–98, but has recently recovered to the level of the early 1990s. Housing has become a much less important part of government spending.
- The public sector improved its position in terms of the balance between assets and liabilities between the later 1950s and the mid-1970s. However, its net worth fell considerably during the 1990s, from the equivalent of three-quarters of a year's GDP in 1988–89 to only just over 10 per cent in 1998–99. Since then its position has been improving.
- Within the largest part of welfare spending, social security, spending on pensions and other benefits for those over working age is the largest item, representing 63 per cent of cash benefits. Although benefits for the unemployed are only a twentieth of the social security budget, 71 per cent the population think that they are the largest or second largest item in it.
- Over the last twenty years, the growth in social security spending has come from means-tested and non-contributory contingency benefits. Contributory benefits within the National Insurance system have declined from 70 per cent of all social security in the 1960s and 1970s to under 45 per cent in 2003–04.
- While 'universal' benefits such as the state retirement pension or Child Benefit are claimed by virtually all of those entitled to them, some means-tested benefits have take-up rates of only four-fifths or less of the amount to which people are entitled.
- Public social spending is smaller in relation to national income in the UK than in all other European Union countries, apart from Ireland. The way in which the share of social spending in the UK has remained roughly constant over the last twenty years contrasts with an increase in most other comparable countries, so that the UK has fallen down this league table.

- However, public social spending captures only one part of welfare activity. The roles of public and private sectors can be analysed more broadly according to three key dimensions of the split between sectors: finance, provision, and control.

- If we look at the overall mix of provision across education, health care, income maintenance, housing, and personal care between 1979 and 1999, public *finance* grew while public spending did not. Total public and private welfare activity grew faster still, to reach nearly 40 per cent of GDP by 1999 (or nearly 30 per cent of GDP if housing is excluded).

- The shifts in the welfare mix have been relatively slow. Welfare activity was already very mixed in its composition in 1979–80, with the 'pure public' sector (with public finance, provision, and control) making up only 52 per cent of the total. This fell, but only to 49 per cent, in 1999–2000, after twenty years dominated by Conservative administrations. Within a growing overall total, the private sector has become more important, especially in terms of private provision. By 1999, the 'pure private' welfare sector had grown to 11 per cent of national income (5 per cent if housing is excluded).

- Asked about how benefit entitlements should relate to people's incomes, more than two-thirds say that benefits for retired, disabled, or unemployed people should be flat-rate. About half say this for benefits for children, but up to half say they should be lower for those with higher incomes.

- Whether or not disincentives from benefits actually affect behaviour, beliefs that they do constrain policy. Such concerns increased in the 1990s. Concerns about disincentives from unemployment benefits now tend to outweigh concerns about their inadequacy.

- Despite government estimates that fraud is small by comparison with total social security spending (and is smaller than unclaimed entitlements), public concerns about fraud in the social security system are high and have also been rising.

- Few people use only private welfare. Those using one private service often use the public sector for another, or for the same service at another time. Private welfare users have similar attitudes to social spending to others. Using private welfare does not in itself appear to generate hostility to welfare spending.

- The way in which people can or cannot combine public and private welfare affects attitudes. Where the two sectors are alternatives, attitudes of private users can polarize between those wanting greater public provision so it can reach the standard they want, and those opposing it because they see no potential benefit.

FURTHER READING

For detailed discussion of policy towards the welfare state, including public spending between the 1970s and the end of the 1990s, see *The State of Welfare: The Economics of Social Spending* edited by Howard Glennerster and John Hills (2nd edn., Oxford University Press, 1998).

A comprehensive overview of the economics of public welfare is in *The Economics of the Welfare State* by Nicholas Barr (4th edn., Oxford University Press, 2004). For a discussion of public spending and how it is financed, including developments up to 2003, see *Understanding the Finance of Welfare* by Howard Glennerster (Policy Press, 2003).

A comparison between countries of the pressures on the welfare states and the reasons for differences and similarities in their evolution can be found in *The New Politics of the Welfare State* edited by Paul Pierson (Oxford University Press, 2001).

The relative roles of private and public sectors are explored in *Private Welfare and Public Policy* by Tania Burchardt, John Hills, and Carol Propper (Joseph Rowntree Foundation, 1999). Tania Burchardt and Carol Propper also look at who uses different kinds of private welfare and the relationship between private welfare use and attitudes in 'Does Britain have a Private Welfare Class?', *Journal of Social Policy*, 28/4 (1999), 643–65.

Several of Richard Titmuss's classic essays on 'divisions of welfare' and the respective roles of public and private welfare are reprinted in *Welfare and Wellbeing* edited by Peter Alcock et al. (Policy Press, 2001, especially Part 2, chapters 1 and 2).

7

Tax and Welfare

7.1 THE LEVEL OF TAXATION AND PUBLIC SPENDING

Tax revenue has represented between one-third and two-fifths of total national income over the last quarter century. How much tax should be levied on different kinds of activity or individuals is one of the central decisions of British politics—hardly surprising, with £12,500 to be raised every second.

Much discussion treats tax as if it were simply a loss to those who pay it and to the economy as a whole rather than a vital mechanism to ensure that collective aims can be met and to achieve ends that the market would fail to deliver. The tax system is not there only—or indeed mainly—as a redistributive mechanism. Its role is also to finance the provision of goods and services from which everyone benefits.[1] The overall level of tax is largely determined by the amount of government spending, while the effect of government on distribution can be understood only by looking at tax and spending together. Analysing their joint impact is becoming even more important as the government increasingly uses the tax system through a widening use of 'tax credits' instead of what were formerly social security benefits.

However, tax and spending are often discussed in isolation from one another, by separate specialists and without much reference to the other side of the government coin. The impact of this is also seen in public understanding. As the Fabian Society's Commission on Taxation and Citizenship (2000: 55) put it, '. . . the link has collapsed in people's minds between themselves and the taxes they pay, *and* between those taxes and the public services they are spent on'. To understand fully the impact of trends in public spending discussed in the previous chapter, it is necessary also to ask where the revenue has come from and what the effects of how it is raised are.

Figure 7.1 shows how the tax ratio (total tax and National Insurance Contributions as a share of national income, GDP) has varied since 1978–79. A first point to note is how narrow in some ways the variation is. From an inherited

---

[1] It can also have the function of correcting the price mechanism in situations where markets fail, for instance, because of 'externalities'—benefits or costs which are imposed on others without a price being paid by those responsible. This is sometimes described as 'taxing bads' rather than 'goods'. As an example, city centre 'congestion charges' are a way of ensuring that those who use congested roads pay a price reflecting the problems they cause for others, with the intention that some will change their behaviour. This aspect of taxation is not discussed further here.

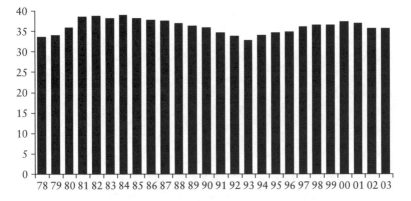

Figure 7.1. *Tax ratio, 1978–79 to 2003–04, UK (total taxes and NICs as % of GDP)*
Source: HM Treasury (2004: Tables C10 and C24).

level of just over 33 per cent, the Conservative government under Mrs Thatcher took tax to nearly 39 per cent of GDP in 1982, near the lowest point of the recession. The ratio fell back through both the recovery of the late 1980s and the recession of the early 1990s, reaching a low point in 1993–94 of 33 per cent, before rising again through the recovery of the later 1990s to reach over 37 per cent in 2000–01. Its level in 2003–04, 35.7 per cent of GDP, was less than one percentage point higher than in 1996–97, the year before New Labour came into office (HM Treasury 2004: Table C10). Plans at the time of the 2004 Budget projected tax revenues rising above 37 per cent of GDP by 2005–06, and above 38 per cent by 2007–08.

There is little clear trend over the period (or indeed, if one looks further back to the start of the 1970s), despite the political sound and fury. Until the mid-1990s, some of the movements relate to the economic cycle, with a tendency for the ratio to fall in economic booms as the denominator, national income, grows rapidly (for instance, the late 1980s) and to rise in recessions (notably the mid-1970s and early 1980s). But politics or the driving force of the public finances can buck such trends, as with the tax-cutting policies set in the run-up to the 1992 election and the subsequent rise in taxes to rein back public borrowing afterwards. The initial rise in the ratio under Labour was associated with falling public borrowing, in line with the Treasury's aim of following the 'golden rule' (see Chapter 6), which states that over the economic cycle borrowing should be only for net investment. The planned rise in the ratio after 2003–04 is driven by the increases in spending discussed in Chapter 6.

One result of this comparative stability over the last quarter century is that the UK has moved from having a somewhat above-average level of taxation among industrialized countries to having a below-average one. Figure 7.2 shows that by 2001 Britain's tax ratio put it tenth out of the eighteen countries listed (the fifteen European Union countries and the three other G7 major economies—the USA,

Canada, and Japan). A similar ranking in 1980 would have put the UK ninth out of these eighteen, above Italy (Townsend 2002: Table 6). As Figure 7.3 shows, the UK has gone from the mid-point of the international range in 1980 (with Sweden the highest and Spain the lowest) to below the mid-point twenty-one years later (with Sweden still the highest at 51 per cent, but Japan now the lowest at 27 per cent).

The scale of variations between countries is far greater than the range over time in the UK. Five of these countries had tax ratios eight or more percentage

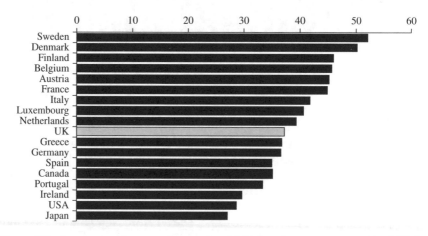

Figure 7.2. *International range of tax ratios, 2001 (total tax revenues as % of GDP at market prices)*

Source: OECD (2003).

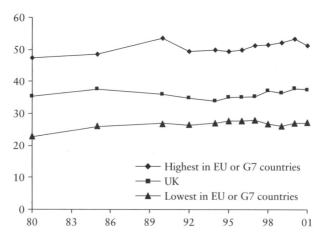
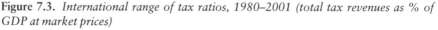

Figure 7.3. *International range of tax ratios, 1980–2001 (total tax revenues as % of GDP at market prices)*

Sources: OECD (2003); Townsend (2002: Table 6).

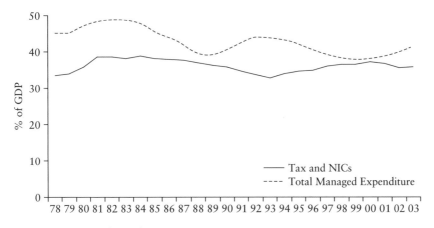

Figure 7.4. *Taxes and spending, 1978–79 to 2003–04, UK*
Source: HM Treasury (2004: Tables C10, C11, C24, C25).

points of GDP above that in the UK in 2001, while the lowest, Japan, was ten points below it. Only five of the seventeen other countries had ratios within the 33–39 per cent of GDP range to which British tax revenues have been confined for the last quarter century. Whatever it is that has constrained this measure of the size of the state in Britain, it is clearly not an iron law of the economics of modern societies. Other countries—some more successful economically, others less so—have made very different choices.

One of the drivers behind the trends in the UK has, of course, been the level of public spending. Alongside tax revenues, Figure 7.4 shows the evolution over the same period of the main measure of public spending on which policy now tends to focus, Total Managed Expenditure (TME). This combines central and local government current and capital spending (with proceeds from privatization counted as a negative item, significantly reducing it in the second half of the 1980s) and includes spending by publicly owned corporations beyond their trading revenues as well (a much smaller part of the economy now than in the past).[2]

For most of the period, tax revenues were well below either measure of public spending, with particularly wide gaps at the start of the period shown and in the early 1990s. Most of the gap has to be covered by borrowing. Only in the late 1990s did the two come into much closer balance (the implications of this for the public sector's balance sheet were discussed in Chapter 6). In contrast to the

---

[2] The measure includes depreciation of publicly owned capital as a spending item, amounting to £15 billion in 2003–04 or 1.3 per cent of GDP (HM Treasury 2004: Table C11). When one looks at the public accounts it should be remembered that this counts as a revenue item too, deriving from the capital the public sector owns rather than being financed by tax or borrowing. It also has to be deducted when *net* investment—the extent to which the state is adding to its capital stock—is measured.

stability of the tax ratio, over the period as a whole there was a trend towards lower public spending as a share of GDP (which had started in 1975–76, when TME reached a peak of nearly half of GDP). Alongside this, there are clear swings with the economic cycle, with spending on some items such as social security rising in recession, and with the denominator, national income, shrinking in the worst recessions.

7.2   THE STRUCTURE OF TAXATION

When people talk about what is happening to tax, they often focus on income tax, and particularly on the *rates* of income tax—for instance, the 22 per cent 'basic rate' which most people pay on any additional income, or the 40 per cent paid on the top slice of income by people with taxable income (after allowances) of more than £30,500 (2003–04 system). The Thatcher government is thought to have been 'tax cutting' principally because it reduced income tax rates, even though, as Figure 7.1 shows, the total tax ratio rose thanks to increases in other tax rates such as those of Value Added Tax (VAT) and National Insurance Contributions (NICs). The Blair government's pledge before the 1997 election, repeated in 2001, was, similarly, not to increase income tax *rates*; indeed, the basic rate was cut in April 2000. This has not prevented a rise in the tax ratio, nor some people paying more income tax (as allowances such as mortgage interest relief or the Married Couples' Allowance were abolished), even before NIC rates were increased in April 2003.

Yet, as Table 7.1 shows, income tax (net of tax credits) is responsible for less than a third of all tax revenues. The rest comes from a variety of somewhat less

Table 7.1. *Taxes and National Insurance Contributions, 2003–04, UK*

	£ billion	% total
Income tax (net)*	114.3	28.7
National Insurance Contributions	72.2	18.1
Corporation tax	28.7	7.2
North Sea	1.2	0.3
Capital taxes	11.2	2.8
Value Added Tax	69.7	17.5
Fuel and Vehicle Excise Duty	27.5	6.9
Alcohol and tobacco	15.7	3.9
Other indirect	8.0	2.0
Council tax and business rates	37.3	9.4
Other	12.3	3.1
TOTAL	398.2	100

  * Figure is net of £4.8 billion of tax credits received by taxpayers and offsetting tax liability (some of which are strictly against corporation tax). Totals may not add up due to rounding.

Source: HM Treasury (2004: Table C8).

politically visible sources, notably VAT and NICs (each more than one sixth of the total). Conventionally, the first five items in the table are often described as *direct* taxes—individuals and businesses pay them according to the amounts of income they receive—while taxes like VAT or those on fuel, cars, alcohol, and tobacco are described as *indirect* taxes—tax is collected by businesses as they sell goods and services, and the amounts people pay do not depend on their incomes.

As a country, Britain makes greater use of indirect taxes than many. Of the countries listed in Figure 7.2, only three (Denmark, Greece, and Portugal) raised more of their revenue from taxes on 'goods and services' in 2001 (OECD 2003). The UK also raised more of its revenue from property taxes (such as Council Tax) than any other OECD country, 12 per cent on the OECD definitions in 2001, compared with an OECD average of only 5 per cent. Most other countries raise much more from social security contributions, the equivalent of our National Insurance Contributions. On average, European Union countries raised 28 per cent of revenue from social security contributions in 2001, compared with only 17 per cent in the UK, with the proportion being more than twice as high in France and Germany. This reflects the much greater importance (and generosity) of social insurance in those countries as a way of funding items such as pensions.

Over the Conservative years from 1979 to 1997, direct taxes became less and indirect taxes more important. This was mostly, as Table 7.2 shows, because VAT rose from 9 per cent to 17 per cent of the total, mirroring the increase in the main *rate* of VAT from 8 per cent to 17.5 per cent. Labour has traditionally been linked to preferring direct taxes and Conservatives to indirect taxes. Since

Table 7.2. *Tax composition, 1978–79 to 2003–04, UK*

Type of tax	Share of total tax revenue (%)		
	1978–79	1996–97	2003–04
Income tax[a]	32.9	25.6	28.7
National Insurance Contributions[b]	21.1	17.4	18.1
Corporation Tax[c]	6.9	10.2	7.2
Capital taxes	2.0	1.9	2.8
VAT	8.6	17.2	17.5
Other indirect	17.6	14.6	12.8
Rates/Council tax	10.1	9.3	9.4
North Sea	0.9	0.9	0.3
Other[d]	—	2.9	3.1
All	100	100	100

[a] Net of tax credits offset against tax in 2003–04.

[b] Includes NI surcharge in 1978–79.

[c] Includes Advance Corporation Tax in 1978–79 and 1996–97.

[d] Includes National Lottery 'good causes'.

Sources: Kay and King (1980: Table 1); HM Treasury (1997a: Table 4A.1); HM Treasury (2004: Table C8).

1996–97, there has indeed been a shift towards a greater share of revenue coming from income tax (although also to markedly less from corporation tax). These political preferences reflect the assumption that direct taxes are more progressive (take a higher share of income from the rich) on the one side, and the idea that indirect taxes interfere less with freedom on the other. The first of these is generally (although not necessarily) true. The second is much more debatable. Any tax, whatever it is called and however it is collected, puts a 'wedge' between people's income and the (pre-tax) value of the goods and services they purchase. It does not really matter very much in the end whether someone has an income of £100, pays £20 income tax, and then buys £80-worth of VAT-free goods or alternatively has a tax-free income of £100 and buys goods for £100, including £20 of VAT. Both kinds of tax mean that people can consume less from the market than otherwise (in return for the services provided through the state). Both change the pattern of returns to, and costs of, different kinds of behaviour.

7.2.1   *Tax Reliefs*

As discussed in Chapter 6, one way in which the public sector can contribute to the cost of particular activities is through special tax reliefs or exemptions. The scale of these can be very large, as shown in Table 7.3. For instance, the official estimate of the value of income tax concessions for pension schemes in 2002–03 was nearly £14 billion. This compares, for instance, with direct spending of about £45 billion on the basic and second state pensions that year. Equally, without the 'zero-rating' of food, VAT revenues could have been more than £9 billion, 15 per cent, higher. The abolition of the income tax relief that used to be given for mortgage interest payments, and of some of the tax concessions for pension schemes, have been important revenue sources since 1997. On the other hand, tax credits have become much more important (taking the form of the Working Families Tax Credit and the Children's Tax Credit in 2002–03, before the April 2003 reforms). These changes affect what is counted as public spending, and what as lower revenue. In the past, when low-paid families received Family Credit, this was a social security payment, and counted in public spending. Now, when similar families receive help from tax credits, this counts as lower tax, not as spending (provided that they would otherwise have been taxpayers; for non-taxpayers the credits still count as public spending).

Care is needed in interpreting figures of the kind shown in Table 7.3, however. To value a tax relief, the tax people actually pay must be compared with what they would have paid in the absence of the relief. If food and other items were not free from VAT, would prices stay the same, would people spend the same, and would the VAT rate really stay at 17.5 per cent, for instance, which is what the table assumes?

Calculating the value of pension fund tax reliefs is even more complex. The figure of £14 billion in the table is arrived at by taking the tax relief that is being given as people make contributions into pension schemes and deducting the tax that those now receiving pensions are paying (and which they would not be if they

Table 7.3. *Major tax expenditures and reliefs, 1996–97 and 2002–03,*
UK (£ billion)

	1996–97	2002–03
Income tax		
Occupational and personal pension schemes	12.8	13.7
Mortgage interest	2.4	—
Personal Equity Plans	0.6	0.6
Individual Savings Accounts	—	0.8
Working Families Tax Credit	—	6.3
Children's Tax Credit	—	2.3
(*Income tax revenue—gross*)	*(71.5)*	*(113.3)*
Value Added Tax		
Zero-rating:		
Food	7.5	9.4
New dwellings	2.1	3.4
Domestic passenger transport	1.4	1.8
Books etc.	1.2	1.5
Lower rate on domestic fuel	1.5	1.9
Exemption of rent	3.3	3.1
(*VAT revenue*)	*(46.7)*	*(63.6)*

Sources: HM Treasury (2003a: Table A3.1) and earlier equivalents; Inland Revenue (1997: Table 1.6); HM Customs and Excise (1997).

were spending savings accumulated in other ways). On the one hand, this probably overstates the value of the tax concession, as today's pensioners are receiving less—and so paying less tax—than today's contributors can look forward to. On the other hand, simply looking at income tax understates the tax advantages of pension saving, as this leaves out the advantage of employer contributions to occupational or private pensions also being free of National Insurance Contributions.

Pensions illustrate another feature of tax reliefs: their value varies with people's circumstances. Income tax relief is worth more to someone who would otherwise be paying 40 per cent tax than to someone paying 22 per cent tax. The relief would be worth nothing at all to a non-taxpayer. It would be more progressive, and some would argue fairer, if, instead of giving incentives to save in pensions through tax reliefs, there was a flat rate 'matching' contribution made by the government, paid at the same proportion of contributions for all (Agulnik and Le Grand 1998).

7.2.2 *The Distributional Impact of Taxation*

Indirect taxes are not necessarily regressive (forming a greater share of the income of the poor) and direct taxes are not necessarily progressive. The Poll Tax (which was used to raise revenue for local government in the late 1980s) was a direct tax, but was highly regressive, despite the partial rebates given to those

Table 7.4. *Tax as share of gross income, by income group, 2001–02, UK (%)*

	Households by tenth of equivalized disposable income										
	1	2	3	4	5	6	7	8	9	10	All
Income tax[a]	3.3	3.1	5.2	8.3	9.4	11.0	12.9	14.1	15.9	19.8	13.8
Employee NICs	1.2	1.2	2.0	2.7	3.7	4.2	4.6	5.0	5.1	3.2	3.8
Local tax (net)[b]	9.1	6.0	5.1	4.6	4.1	3.6	3.2	2.8	2.3	1.5	3.0
All direct	13.6	10.4	12.3	15.6	17.2	18.9	20.6	21.8	23.3	24.5	20.7
VAT	15.1	9.1	7.7	7.3	7.3	6.8	6.6	6.0	5.5	4.2	6.1
Tobacco	4.1	2.5	2.0	1.7	1.7	1.5	1.0	0.8	0.5	0.2	1.0
Alcohol	2.2	1.2	1.0	1.1	1.0	1.1	1.0	0.8	0.8	0.5	0.9
Fuel and VED	4.2	2.8	2.4	2.5	2.4	2.4	2.2	2.1	1.8	1.0	1.9
Employer NICs	3.7	2.3	1.9	1.7	1.6	1.4	1.4	1.3	1.2	0.8	1.3
Other indirect	10.4	6.5	5.5	5.0	4.6	4.1	4.0	3.4	3.2	2.3	3.8
All indirect	39.7	24.4	20.5	19.3	18.5	17.2	16.3	14.3	13.0	9.1	15.0
TOTAL	53.3	34.7	32.7	34.9	35.7	36.1	36.9	36.1	36.3	33.6	35.6

[a] In this table WFTC is treated as part of gross income, not a deduction from income tax.

[b] Local taxes, fuel duties and Vehicle Excise Duty (VED) are those levied directly on households. Those levied on businesses are part of other indirect taxes.

Source: Lakin (2003: Table 14 in Appendix 1).

with low incomes. Certain kinds of consumption—'luxuries'—do represent a greater share of income for the rich than the poor—for instance, meals out, recreation, holidays, and financial services, including saving—and could be more progressive to tax than a proportional share of income.

However, in practice, indirect taxes clearly are much less progressive than direct taxes. Table 7.4 shows figures for 2001–02 derived from the annual Office for National Statistics (ONS) analysis of the impact of different kinds of taxation by income. The figures are for the amount of tax people end up paying, and so incorporate the effects of the tax reliefs and exemptions discussed above. Figure 7.5 summarizes the picture. The most striking finding is that the British tax system is *not*, on this analysis, progressive. Overall, the taxes allocated by ONS represent 36 per cent of household gross income (including income from cash benefits as well as from market sources). But for the richest tenth of households they are below this, and for the poorest tenth they are much higher.[3] In particular, indirect taxes represent 35 per cent of gross income for the poorest tenth, but only 9 per cent for the richest. As is well known, taxes on tobacco are strikingly regressive, now taking more than twenty times the proportion for the poorest tenth than for the richest,[4]

---

[3] If the Working Families Tax Credit was treated as negative income tax for all recipients, including the poorest, income tax would be reduced to 1.5 per cent of gross income for the poorest tenth, and the total tax on this group to 51.7 per cent of gross income.

[4] The figures for tobacco and alcohol in particular are subject to some uncertainty, as people under-report consumption of them to the spending surveys that such results are derived from. The incidence shown assumes that under-reporting is constant across income groups, which may not be true (and that the same is true of the use of 'bootlegged' consumption on which UK duties have not been paid).

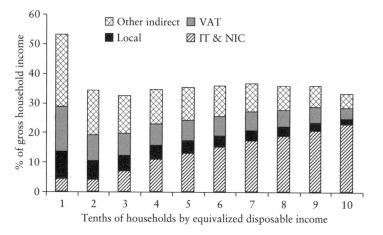

Figure 7.5. *Tax by income group, 2001–02, UK*
Source: Table 7.4.

but taxes on fuel and cars are also regressive, as is the much larger VAT (despite the zero-rating and exemptions described above). Within the direct taxes, local taxes (Council Tax) are also very regressive, even after account is taken of rebates for those with low incomes and discounts for single people. National Insurance Contributions are progressive for most of the range, but not at the top (as a result of the 'Upper Earnings Limit' for employee contributions). Only income tax is progressive throughout the distribution.

It is hard to make such analyses definitive; to do so, one has to have a clear idea of the *incidence* of a tax: who is really worse-off compared with what would have happened without the tax? In the ONS calculations, the NICs that employers pay (as a percentage of the earnings of their employees) are classed as an addition to their costs, and are assumed to be borne by consumers, creating their regressive impact. One could argue just as plausibly that they are as much a wedge as income tax is between gross labour costs to employers and net pay to employees and so should be treated in the same way. If this were done, they would be shown as more progressive than the employee NICs at the top of the table (because employer contributions are not subject to the earnings limit beyond which employee contributions are levied only at 1 per cent—£610 per week in 2004–05). If we allow for such uncertainty, the clearest conclusion is that, for most of the income range, the British tax system is roughly *proportional*: one way or another, most income groups pay about the same share of income in tax. But it is so only because of the contribution of income tax and NICs.

Indirect taxes, by contrast, are regressive. Three factors drive this:

- People with higher incomes save more (and savings are not subject to indirect taxes—and are not likely to be).

- More of the consumption of those with lower incomes goes on heavily taxed items like tobacco (despite the VAT exemption of necessities like food and lower rates on fuel).
- Many indirect taxes are set as lump sum amounts (such as TV or vehicle licences or the part of tax on wine that is a fixed amount per bottle whether cheap or expensive).

Table 7.5 shows more detailed results from a different analysis of the same data source, showing for particular items the estimated tax paid by the richest and poorest fifths (Sutherland, Sefton, and Piachaud 2003). In the case of tobacco, the poorest pay more than the richest, and for TV licences they pay the same. But the disposable (after direct taxes) household incomes of the poorest group are less than a fifth of those of the richest—only stamp duty (mostly on house purchase) and air passenger duty are broadly neutral by comparison, while all the other indirect taxes listed are regressive in varying degrees. Looking in more detail at why the poorest fifth are estimated to pay such a high proportion of income in indirect taxes, the authors show that this proportion is particularly high for single people and couples without children in this group: their spending is particularly high in relation to their reported incomes, perhaps reflecting what may be transitory poverty for some of them, but lack of adjustment to circumstances for others. By contrast, the family types within the poorest fifth that are more like to be in persistent poverty (lone parents and pensioners) have lower reported spending, particularly on the more heavily taxed items, and so pay a lower proportion of income in indirect taxes.

Table 7.5. *Distributional impact of indirect taxes, 2000–01, UK*

	Average tax paid (£/year)		Ratio of tax paid by bottom fifth to that paid by top fifth
	Bottom fifth	Top fifth	
Tobacco duty	298	243	1.2
TV licence fee	104	105	1.0
Betting tax	91	120	0.8
Alcohol duty	138	363	0.4
VAT	1,136	3,158	0.4
Motoring taxes	298	847	0.4
Insurance premium duty	18	60	0.3
Stamp duty	30	167	0.2
Air passenger duty	8	44	0.2
TOTAL	2,119	5,104	0.4

Note: Totals may not add up due to rounding.

Source: Sutherland, Sefton, and Piachaud (2003: Table 18).

7.3   THE INTERACTION BETWEEN TAX
AND SOCIAL SECURITY

The need to look at tax and spending systems together becomes most acute when one is trying to understand the position people are left in after the combined effects of both tax and social security on their incomes, particularly after the recent reforms that have turned what used to be social security benefits into 'tax credits'. First, it is useful to recognize that there are several different ways of achieving what may be the same result, and for some purposes it may not matter what we call them. If, for instance, the aim is that poorer people should end up with higher net incomes than they would otherwise receive, with the cost borne by those with higher incomes, several routes are possible, and can give similar results if designed in the right way:

- flat-rate benefits (in cash or kind) going to all, financed from general taxation;
- means-tested benefits, paid only to those with low incomes, and withdrawn as gross incomes rise (requiring less taxation to pay for them);
- tax allowances, which exempt the first part of someone's income from tax— even with a single rate of tax on the 'taxable income' which remains, the result is progressive to a degree, as the exempt amount is a greater share of income for the poor than for the rich. By and large, the UK income tax system with its long 'basic rate' band operates like this; and
- tax credits, whereby tax is worked out on taxable income first, but the amount due is then reduced by the amount of the credit. Credits can be flat-rate (as used to be the case for the tax 'allowance' for married couples in the UK as run in the late 1990s), or can be worth more for those with lower incomes (as is the case for the Child Tax Credit introduced in April 2003). They can give benefits only to those who would otherwise have paid tax, at the most reducing tax liabilities to zero, or they can be 'payable', in new British government jargon ('refundable' in US terminology), so that, if the calculation results in a 'negative tax liability', people get a payment from the state (again, this is how the Working and Child Tax Credits operate).

For some economists, what matters in all of this is the end result, not what we call the stages of calculation on the way: how do net incomes at the end of the exercise compare with gross incomes before it; and if someone's gross income is a pound higher, what is the change in his or her net income (that is, what is the 'effective marginal tax rate')? But for others—notably, the general public and the politicians making the relevant decisions—what the systems are called and how they are run does seem to matter. There are, for instance, asymmetries in public attitudes to tax evasion and to social security fraud, the former being regarded more leniently (see Section 6.5). If the resentment of the gross tax taken off people is only partly assuaged by what they get back out of the system, using tax credits and tax allowances will be less unpopular than having higher gross taxes that finance more universal benefits. Describing the part-equivalent in the USA to the new tax credits in the UK, the US Earned Income Tax Credit, as a 'tax cut for the working poor' was a politically appealing slogan for Bill Clinton. On the other hand, systems which treat the poor in one way (as recipients of means-tested benefits which they alone receive) and the better-off in another (paying tax for which they get nothing tangible back) may well violate principles of inclusion to which many also subscribe.

Against that background, the changes of the last few years have had a substantive effect on people's incomes and on the incentives which they face that goes beyond labelling and administration. This can be seen by comparing Figures 7.6 and 7.7. The first of these shows how tax and benefit system of 1997–98 affected a one-earner couple with two children, who were also tenants.[5] In that system, regardless of income level, they would have received Child Benefit of £23.25 per week (at 2003–04 prices). Their take-home pay would have grown less rapidly than gross pay as a result of National Insurance Contributions and income tax (although liability was reduced by the effects of the then Married Couples Allowance). If working more than sixteen hours per week,[6] they would

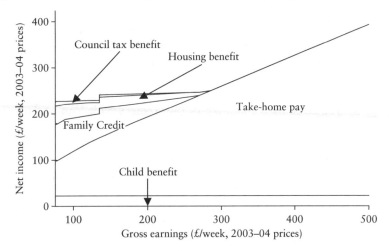

Figure 7.6. *Gross and net income under 1997–98 system*

Note: One earner couple with two children younger than 11 years, rent £60, council tax £16.

Source: Author's calculations.

[5] To give a comparison with Figure 7.7, the various elements of the 1997–98 system have been adjusted for price inflation to 2003–04 prices by using the same amounts as 'statutory' indexation would have applied (16 per cent for tax allowances and bands, and 11.1 per cent for the social security benefits that are adjusted with inflation excluding housing). Rent is assumed to be £60 per week and Council Tax £16 per week. Chapter 9 discusses whether this kind of comparison using only inflation-adjustment of the old system is appropriate in understanding the effects of recent reforms, or whether the relevant comparison for some purposes would be with the previous system adjusted for growth in incomes or earnings.

[6] It is assumed in Figures 7.6–7.8 that the earner is working for sixteen or more hours per week. It is also assumed that, by earnings of £135 per week, they would be working thirty hours or more, which brings a jump in entitlement to Family Credit in the 1997–98 system or to the Working Tax Credit in 2003–04.

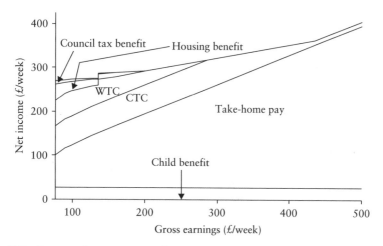

Figure 7.7. *Gross and net income under 2003–04 system*

Note: One earner couple with two children younger than 11 years, rent £60, council tax £16. CTC: Child Tax Credit. WTC: Working Tax Credit.

Source: Author's calculations.

have been entitled to a social security benefit, Family Credit, paid to the mother. If their income after all of this was low, they would also have been entitled to claim Housing Benefit to help with rent, and Council Tax Benefit. As can be seen, over a considerable range of gross income, net income would hardly have risen at all. With gross earnings of £75 per week, their net income would have been £227. With gross earnings of £275, net income would only have risen to £248: a £200 increase in earnings would have left them only £21 better off (before any resultant increased costs of working such as transport or childcare are allowed for).

Over this income range the couple faced an 'effective marginal tax rate' of nearly 90 per cent. This created what had become known as the 'poverty trap'. The help that the system gave to those with very low incomes from work obviously helped them considerably, but the way it was structured meant that it was very hard for them then to make themselves any better-off by working more or finding better-paid work. This resulted from the combination of direct taxation (income tax and National Insurance Contributions) and sharply means-tested social security benefits, which were withdrawn rapidly as other incomes rose. Thus, in the worst part of the poverty trap shown in Figure 7.6 (where the top line showing total net income is flattest), the effective marginal tax rate could reach 97 per cent.[7] This was because for each extra £10 of income:

- £1.00 would be paid in higher NICs.
- £2.30 would be paid in higher income tax.

[7] In fact, at various points the effective marginal tax rate could be over 100 per cent—for instance, at the point when people's incomes took them over the threshold for paying National Insurance Contributions. Note that the administration of the system meant that these kinds of change did not necessarily happen at once; for instance, Family Credit was fixed for six months at a time.

- £4.69 would be lost from lower Family Credit (70 per cent of the £6.70 increase in take-home pay).
- £1.31 would be lost from lower Housing Benefit (65 per cent of the £2.01 increase in income allowing for Family Credit).
- £0.40 would be lost from lower Council Tax Benefit (20 per cent of the £2.01).
- Only 30 pence would be left as the increase in net income.

By 2003–04, a series of reforms had changed the situation facing this type of family (which are among the biggest beneficiaries from New Labour's reforms) to give the position shown in Figure 7.7. Income Support (IS) for non-working families was significantly higher than in 1996–97, but the more generous treatment of low-paid working families had also opened up a clearer gain from work. First, the universal Child Benefit was more generous in real terms—now £26.80 for a two-child family. Various changes to income tax and national insurance contributions largely cancelled one another out.[8] The main change, however, was the transformation of what had been Family Credit into the combination of the Child Tax Credit and the Working Tax Credit. As can be seen by comparing the two diagrams, these are both more generous for those with the lowest incomes than their predecessor and extend over a wider income range. This extension results from a lower rate of withdrawal of the credits as income rises (37 per cent of gross income, compared with around 50 per cent under the old system). For very low-income tenants, some of the advantage of the new tax credits is lost through lower Housing Benefit and Council Tax Benefit. For them, the biggest effect is a reduction in the earnings level at which they escape from the sharpest means-testing.

Overall, the poverty trap is now shallower, but it is also wider. This can be seen more clearly in Figure 7.8, which compares the total net incomes from the two systems at each level of earnings. Between earnings of £200 and £285 per week, the slope of the 2003–04 line is more clearly upwards—there is a clearer gain from higher earnings. But, from about £285 per week to about £435, the new system has a shallower slope than the old. In other words, the new system extends *quite* high effective marginal tax rates (70 per cent once Housing Benefit is exhausted)[9] up to what is about 90 per cent of average adult full-time earnings.

This illustrates an inescapable trade-off. The aim of the system is that, for those with the lowest gross incomes, net incomes should be considerably higher than those delivered by the market, but that this should not happen for those with average or higher incomes. Somewhere between the very low incomes on

[8] These included a cut in the basic rate of income tax to 22 per cent; replacement of a wider initial 20 per cent band with a narrower 10 per cent band; abolition of the Married Couple's Allowance; abolition of the 'entry fee' for National Insurance Contributions and a rise in the threshold for paying NICs, but an increase in the contribution rate to 11 per cent.

[9] However, those whose incomes increase by only a fairly small amount (less than £2,500 in 2003–04), will not in fact have their tax credits cut in the tax year when the increase occurs, so for a time effective marginal tax rates are lower than the 70 per cent figure.

the left of the diagram and the average earnings levels on the right, the line *has to be* flat to some degree: the implied disincentives have to go somewhere. The implicit choice in the systems which applied in Britain for thirty years from the early 1970s until the end of the 1990s was that these disincentives should be concentrated in as narrow an income band as possible. This minimized the 'cost' by concentrating help on the poorest, and also meant that those with earnings much more than half the average were clear of means-testing. The downsides can also be seen from Figure 7.8. Not only was the poverty trap very severe for those affected by it, but also there was a wide earnings range over which people were hardly any better-off in work than out of work, as can be seen by the comparison with the Income Support level shown in the figure for a non-working family in the 1997–98 system (£211 per week, after adjusting for inflation and including help with housing costs). Someone in work up to at around half average earnings would only be little more than £30 better-off (even before allowing for costs of working) than someone out of work.

The 2003–04 system involves a different choice for these trade-offs. First, it can be noted that there has been a significant gain for those with the lowest incomes, whether in work or out of work. In a change which has not been given much publicity (but which has been very important for the overall impact of the reforms on poverty levels), real net income out of work shown by the line for Income Support in 2003–04 has been increased by more than £40 per week. This is almost as much as the net improvement of the position of those in work with earnings up to £200 per week. Over this range, incentives to work have, in fact, increased only a little. But over the next earnings range the gains from the reforms for those in work accelerate, reaching up to £70 per week (over a quarter) by comparison with the old system, and the gap between incomes in and out of work starts increasing much earlier. Up to this point, the new system simultaneously does

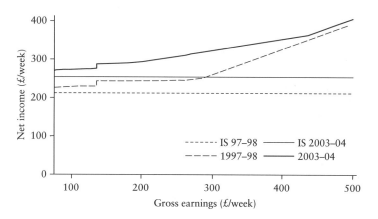

Figure 7.8. *Net incomes under 1997–98 and 2003–04 systems (2003–04 prices)*
Source: Author's calculations.

more to reduce poverty, and improves—or at least does not damage—work incentives. Over the next range of earnings, net incomes have also been improved but effective marginal tax rates have risen too.

The overall effect on work incentives depends on whether there is a larger effect from a smaller number being affected by very sharp disincentives at the bottom or from a greater number of people being affected by somewhat milder disincentives (see Figure 10.7 and Table 10.5 in Chapter 10). Analysis so far suggests that the net effect of the reforms up to 2000 on labour supply were positive on balance (Brewer et al. 2003).

The new system differs from the old in other ways, too, that do not affect the economics of net benefits and incentives. First, as with other parts of the income tax system, the amount of tax credits people are entitled to depends on income over the whole year rather than that over a shorter period. Second, it is run by the Inland Revenue as part of the tax system rather than by the Department of Work and Pensions as part of the benefit system. One intention of this is to reduce the stigma attached to receiving assistance. But, unlike other parts of the income tax system—run automatically by employers through the 'Pay as You Earn' (PAYE) system—receipt of tax credits still requires completion of special forms, and is vulnerable to take-up problems (see Section 6.2). Third, the Working Tax Credit is paid via the wage packet—partly to reinforce the message that 'work pays'—although the more valuable part of the package, the Child Tax Credit, has now reverted to being paid automatically to the 'main carer' (usually the mother), as used to be the case under the old Family Credit (but which had to be specifically opted for by couples under the intermediate Working Families Tax Credit system between 1999 and 2003).

But, perhaps most significantly, the April 2003 reforms involved an important unification of the treatment of those in and out of work. As far as support for children is concerned, those out of work and in low-paid work receive exactly the same amounts of Child Tax Credit—£65.95 in the case illustrated with two children—and this does not depend on hours of work (although the Working Tax Credit still requires sixteen or more hours per week). This has the potential to make transitions into work significantly easier than they used to be. It also changes the options available to some people, notably lone parents, in terms of the incomes that result from working just a few hours, as the requirement of working at least sixteen hours per week now only applies to the Working Tax Credit, not to the support coming through the Child Tax Credit.

7.4 PUBLIC ATTITUDES TO TAX LEVELS AND STRUCTURE

7.4.1 *Overall Levels of Tax and Public Spending*

As far as the overall level of taxation is concerned, conventional political wisdom through the 1980s and 1990s was that voters want lower taxes and will vote for parties that promise them. It is true that, when asked in 2000 about particular taxes in isolation, majorities said that each of income tax, VAT, and duties on petrol, alcohol, and cigarettes, was 'too high' or 'much too high' (Commission on Taxation and Citizenship 2000: Table 2.1). But when respondents were confronted with the trade-off between tax and social spending, their responses are rather different. One of the consistent findings from the British Social Attitudes survey (and from other polls) is, as Table 7.6 shows, that since the late 1980s there has been a clear majority for *increased* public spending on 'health, education and social benefits', even if this means higher taxes. Only a tiny proportion of the population opts for lower taxes and lower spending on these items. Nearly two-thirds of respondents continued to choose the increased tax and spending option in 2002. Analysis of the 1998 survey shows that, even among respondents who identified with the Conservative Party, a narrow majority (51 per cent) preferred increased taxes and spending on these items. Seventy per cent or more of Labour and Liberal Democrat identifiers wanted higher spending, and only 25 per cent of either group wanted the current levels (Hills and Lelkes 1999). In principle, people would appear to want to increase the share of tax and public spending in the British economy.

However, simply wanting *more* tax and spend does not necessarily mean *much* more. Heath and Curtice (1998) show that until 1994 a majority saw Labour as being to their left on the balance between tax and spending: people wanted more spending, but feared Labour would go too far. Thereafter, opinion became much more balanced between those who thought Labour would do too much and those who thought it would do too little. Second, different items have higher or lower priority, particularly if the personal consequences of higher taxes are spelt out. Brook, Hall, and Preston (1996) show in their analysis of the 1995 BSA survey that majorities remain for higher health and education spending when people are given specific tax consequences for themselves, but not for other items like the police, the environment, and defence. It is little coincidence that health and education have been Labour's spending priorities in office.

Table 7.6. *Public attitudes on the tax/spending trade-off, 1983–2002, GB*

Option	% favouring different options					
	1983	1987	1991	1995	1999	2002
Higher tax/more spending on health, education, and social benefits	32	50	65	61	58	63
Status quo	54	42	29	31	35	31
Lower tax/less spending on health, education, and social benefits	9	3	3	5	4	3
Base	*1,761*	*2,847*	*2,918*	*1,234*	*3,143*	*3,435*

Sources: Taylor-Gooby and Hastie (2002: Table 4.1) and Park et al. (2003: 290), based on British Social Attitudes survey.

7.4.2 *The Hypothecation Debate*

Such findings raise the general question of whether specific kinds of tax should be earmarked or 'hypothecated' for particular kinds of spending. If people would like particular kinds of public spending to be higher, but are reluctant to give politicians a blank cheque to spend in what might be other ways, there is a kind of political market failure. One solution might be hypothecation, so that people knew exactly where any increased revenue was going. In a survey in 2000, only 40 per cent of respondents backed a one-penny increase in the rate of income tax for unspecified public spending, but 80 per cent backed it if the revenue were to go specifically to the NHS, and 68 per cent if it were to go to education (Commission on Taxation and Citizenship 2000: Table 2.3). Analysing the 2001 British Social Attitudes survey, Taylor-Gooby and Hastie (2002) found very large majorities for even a three pence in the pound increase in income tax rates, if the revenue was specifically tied to health or education spending (see Table 7.7).[10] The numbers favouring a one penny tax increase for the top four items were greater than the 59 per cent agreeing to an increase in tax for *general* spending on 'health education and social benefits' in that year's survey in response to the question used shown in Table 7.6. For the NHS and schools, the majorities were greater, even when a three pence increase was suggested. The eventual electoral reaction to recent tax policies, including the increase in National Insurance Contributions in 2003–04 in order to fund higher health spending, will be a test of whether these kinds of findings mean anything when it comes to actual taxation rather than to hypothetical survey questions.

The findings also raise the issue of whether more of the tax system should be organized in this way, not just for this rather weak form of hypothecation—the political marketing of tax changes—but with actual spending budgets directly dependent on the revenue from particular sources. Arguments for this have come from both left and right. From the right, hypothecation—perhaps with US state-style referendums on tax levels, item by item—has been seen as a way of reining in public spending by making it harder for government to raise taxes. But from the left, it has been seen as a possible way of *reducing* the tax constraint on governments, solving the political market failure problem by allowing people to choose higher taxation for particular purposes when it would be rejected for general ones. For instance, the Commission on Taxation and Citizenship (2000) argued that in principle such a move could help 'connect' citizens to their taxes and decisions on them in a way that was lacking at present. While recognizing the problems involved (some of which are discussed below), a majority of the Commission favoured splitting off about half of income tax to become a designated 'NHS tax'.

---

[10] Respondents were told that a 1p increase would mean on average an extra £100 from each taxpayer, and a 3p increase would mean an extra £300. Different parts of the sample were asked about the two tax levels.

Table 7.7. *Public attitudes to hypothecated tax increases, 2001, GB*

	1 penny increase		3 pence increase	
	All in favour (%)	(of which 'strongly')	All in favour (%)	(of which 'strongly')
NHS	84	(41)	79	(25)
Schools	73	(19)	61	(12)
Retirement pension	65	(19)	57	(13)
Policing	61	(13)	50	(9)
Public transport	43	(8)	31	(5)
Unemployment benefits	16	(2)	11	(2)
Base	*1,657*	*1,657*	*1,630*	*1,630*

Source: Taylor-Gooby and Hastie (2002: Table 4.8), based on British Social Attitudes survey.

There are, however, problems with this approach, most of them illustrated by the largest hypothecated tax that Britain actually has, National Insurance Contributions.[11] It can be argued that National Insurance is not a very good example of hypothecation (see, for instance, Le Grand 2003: 157–60), and that cleaner systems could be devised. But it can be equally argued that the pressures that have made National Insurance so imperfect would apply to other hypothecated taxes as well.

First, despite the complications of having an earmarked tax, it might not actually be understood by the public, negating its purpose. For instance, when asked about what NICs are used for, the first thing which discussion groups came up with was the health service, even though only a tenth of NIC revenues were actually being used in that way at the time, with most of the revenue actually paying for state pensions (Stafford 1998).

Second, if spending is financed only from one source, the amount of money available for it will go up and down with those tax revenues. Even a very broad tax such as income tax moves with national income (indeed, it moves in a more exaggerated way than national income). But the need for spending may not move in that way—for instance, some national insurance benefits, such as non-means-tested Jobseeker's Allowance, tend to rise in recessions, just as revenue is falling.

To cope with this, two mechanisms can be used. The first is for the spending programme to have some form of stabilization fund—and, indeed, there is, on paper at least, a 'National Insurance Fund'. When revenues are buoyant, the fund can grow, to be run down when they do not grow as fast as spending needs.

---

[11] Other examples include the BBC licence fee; 'congestion charges' levied by local government and spent on local public transport; and the 'windfall tax' on privatized utilities brought in by the Chancellor of the Exchequer, Gordon Brown, in 1997 to fund the first years of the 'New Deal' welfare-to-work measures.

But this implies a need to dedicate scarce revenues to building up—initially at least—a substantial fund to cope with future bad times. If separate from the rest of government finance, this has a resource (and possibly an efficiency) cost but, if integrated into government finances (for example, by being 'invested in government bonds'), the idea of a strict link between spending and the particular tax rate is easily lost or subverted.

This is an even greater danger if 'stabilization' is achieved through a system of top-ups and reclaims from general government revenue—in the case of National Insurance, this used to take the form of the 'Treasury Supplement' to the fund. By manipulating the level of such top-ups, central government can entirely subvert the supposed link between the specified tax and spending item. In the 1980s, the Conservative government was able to reduce income tax rates through cutting out the payments into the National Insurance Fund, so NIC rates had to rise without any improvement in benefits paid out.

Third, if revenue is tied to a particular spending item, it becomes easier to argue that those who do not benefit from it should be exempted in some way—for instance, those with private pensions can 'contract out' of receiving some of the State Second Pension, and pay a lower rate of National Insurance Contributions in return. Under, say, an 'NHS tax' replacing part of income tax, there could be strong pressure for those with private medical insurance to pay a lower rate of tax. This would be welcomed and seen as only fair by some, but it would also mean both lower revenue for the NHS and a reduction in the progressivity of the overall mix of tax and public spending.

There is a further issue for the rest of public spending. If a popular form of spending such as the NHS is allocated the most buoyant revenue source, that could make it harder to fund less charismatic forms of spending. The popular item would act as a 'cuckoo in the nest', crowding out others. Again, from some perspectives this would be desirable, and simply an expression of the public's preferences. But it would certainly make it harder to trade-off in a coherent way the relative advantages and pressures on particular budgets given the resources available—which is one reason why the UK Treasury has always resisted (not always successfully) calls for hypothecation.

7.4.3 *Progressivity of the System*

When asked about their general views on the shares of income that people should pay in 'various taxes', two-thirds of respondents to the 2001 British Social Attitudes survey agreed with the 'progressive principle', that those with higher incomes should pay a larger *share* of their incomes (Table 7.8). Very few thought that the share should be smaller. The proportion saying the share should be larger is, however, slightly down from the three-quarters who said the share should be larger in surveys in 1987, 1992, and 1999 (Bromley 2003: Table 4.11). In particular, only one in nine in 2001 thought that the share of income taken

Table 7.8. *Public attitudes to relative shares of income paid in tax, 2001, GB (% of respondents)*

	Share of income paid by those with high incomes compared to those with low incomes	
	Share *should* be:	Share they *do* pay:
Much larger	11	8
Larger	55	56
Same	29	21
Smaller	1	6
Much smaller	—	1
Can't choose	4	8

Source: Park et al. (2002: 315, from British Social Attitudes survey (2,821 respondents).

from those with high income should be 'much larger' than from those with low incomes, half as many as in the earlier surveys. Asked what they thought the shares paid actually were, nearly two-thirds thought that higher income people actually do pay a larger share of income in tax than those with low incomes, something which the official analysis shown in Figure 7.5 suggested is not in reality true.

A preference for greater progressivity than now can also be seen in Table 7.9, showing survey responses in 2000, when people were asked about the tax levels of different income groups: 72 per cent thought that taxes on people with annual incomes below £15,000 were too high, but only 20 per cent thought this for people with incomes above £70,000. However, the table also reveals an inconsistency with the views described earlier favouring higher taxes for higher spending overall: more than half of respondents thought that taxes on those with incomes up to £30,000—covering what is in fact the large majority of the population—were too high, and more thought that taxes were 'about right' for the (rather small) highest income group than thought they were too low. If respondents are saying that taxes should be 'higher—except on most people', one reaction would be further scepticism about the kinds of results shown in Table 7.6. Another would be that the figures illustrate the danger of divorcing discussion of tax levels from the use of revenue. In principle, we might all want lower taxes and higher spending, but in the long run that is very hard for governments to deliver, and in reality the two have to be confronted together (which is what the questions underlying Table 7.6 do). Also, the implication of the responses in Table 7.8 is that, when people are talking about what should happen to taxes for particular income groups, they may be starting from a belief that the tax system is more progressive than it really is.

Table 7.9. *Attitudes of population as a whole to tax levels of different income groups, GB (% of respondents)*

	Too high	About right	Too low	Don't know
Below £15,000	72	22	1	5
£15,000 – 30,000	53	38	2	7
£30,000 – 70,000	32	46	11	10
£70,000 and above	20	40	29	11

Source: Commission on Taxation and Citizenship (2000: Table 2.4), based on ONS omnibus survey, June–July 2000 (1,716 respondents).

7.5 SUMMARY

- Understanding the impact of either taxation or public spending requires the other to be taken into account as well. For social security, the interaction with taxation has become more important as some cash benefits have been replaced by 'tax credits'.
- By comparison with other industrialized countries, the UK has below-average levels of tax in relation to national income. Its tax ratio has moved in a fairly narrow band over the last thirty years.
- In economic terms it is possible to achieve exactly the same distributional and incentive effects though either social security benefits or tax allowances and tax credits. However, they may be perceived differently by both the general public and by those benefiting from them.
- The reforms to benefits for families with children between 1997 and 2003 reduced the worst of the 'poverty trap', improved the position of those with relatively low incomes both in and out of work, and increased the gain from working for some ranges of earnings. However, this was partly at the cost of extending somewhat milder disincentives—and the need to claim special credits—to a much larger group.
- Public attitudes have shown a preference for higher levels of taxation to fund higher public spending since the late 1980s. These preferences weaken when personal consequences are spelt out, but remain strong if the hypothetical extra spending is on health and education rather than other items.
- One suggested response to this would be to extend the amount of earmarking or 'hypothecation' of taxes for particular kinds of spending— for instance, through turning part of income tax into an 'NHS tax'. But the experience of National Insurance Contributions suggests a number of difficulties with such a move.
- Surveys of public attitudes suggest public support for a progressive tax system. However, the overall impact of the UK tax system is at best proportional, taking a similar proportion of income for all income groups apart from the poorest (where it is higher) and the richest (where it is lower). Only income tax is progressive across the income range, and indirect taxes are regressive.

FURTHER READING

Two classic texts on the tax system as a whole are *The Structure and Reform of Direct Taxation* by the Meade Committee (George Allen and Unwin, 1978) and *The British Tax System* by John Kay and Mervyn King (Oxford University Press, 5th edn., 1990). A more recent discussion of the structure of the tax system and attitudes to it can be found in *Paying for Progress: A New Politics of Tax for Public Spending* by the Commission on Taxation and Citizenship (Fabian Society, 2000).

Details of the government's decisions for the tax system each year can be found in the Treasury's 'Red Book' published each year at the time of the Budget (for example, HM Treasury 2004), available on the Treasury's website: www.hm-treasury.gov.uk.

An independent pre-Budget assessment of the tax system and options for its reform can be found in the Institute for Fiscal Studies' annual 'Green Budget' and in other documents (including a historical record of tax rates and allowances) available on its website: www.ifs.org.uk.

8

Distribution and Redistribution

8.1 ANALYSING REDISTRIBUTION

Distribution is a central issue in the appraisal of social and welfare policies. For some, it is *the* central issue when they make statements such as: 'without a National Health Service providing free medical care, the poor could not afford treatment'; or 'the primary aim of social security is preventing poverty'. Over twenty years ago, in his book *The Strategy of Equality*, Julian Le Grand (1982: 3) reached the striking conclusion that 'Almost all public expenditure on the social services benefits the better off to a greater extent than the poor'. If so, a large part of social policy had failed in what many would see as one of its main aims. This conclusion was controversial (see Powell 1995, for a discussion of some of the issues, with a response from Le Grand). As we shall see below, the answer to this kind of question depends critically on a particular series of choices in the way in which distribution is analysed. Alternative ways of looking at the problem can give different answers.

Whether redistribution is occurring or not can depend on the point of analysis. Under private insurance for, say, burglaries, a large number of people make annual payments (insurance premiums) to an insurance company, but only a small number receive payouts from the company. After the event (*ex post*) there is redistribution from the (fortunate) many to the (unfortunate) few. But, looking at the position in advance (*ex ante*), not knowing who is going to be burgled, all pay in a premium equalling their risk of being burgled, multiplied by the size of the payout if this happens (plus the insurance company's costs and profits). In 'actuarial' terms there is no redistribution—people have arranged a certain small loss (the premium) rather than the risk of a much larger loss (being burgled without insurance). Similarly, much of the welfare state is insurance against adversity. People 'pay in' through tax or National Insurance Contributions, but in return, if they are the ones who become ill or unemployed, the system is there to protect them. It does not make sense just to look at which individual happens to receive an expensive heart bypass operation this year and present him or her as the main 'gainer' from the system. All benefit to the extent that they face a risk of needing such an operation. The system is therefore often best appraised in actuarial terms; that is, in terms of the extent someone would *expect* to benefit on average. Equally, if we look at pension schemes over a single year, some people pay in contributions while others receive pensions. On this snapshot, there is apparently redistribution from the former to the latter. But, with a longer time horizon, today's pensioners may simply get back what they paid in earlier.

Assessing redistribution also depends on the aims against which services are judged. Which aim is the focus has large implications for assessing distributional effects:

- *Vertical redistribution.* If the aim is redistribution from rich to poor, the crucial question is which income groups benefit (Section 8.2). As discussed in Chapter 7, since social spending does not come from thin air, the important question may be which are the *net gainers* and *net losers*, after account is taken of who pays the taxes needed to finance it (Section 8.3).
- *Horizontal redistribution on the basis of needs.* Relative incomes are not the only criterion for receiving services. The NHS is there for people with particular medical needs: it should achieve 'horizontal redistribution' between people with similar incomes but different medical needs. Particular social security benefits are there to meet the extra needs of families with children or of disabled people. The key distributional question is, then, whether what people receive matches their needs. Analysing this is hard, since the main evidence on the extent of 'needs' is often the fact of receiving services.[1]
- *Redistribution between different groups.* An aim might be redistribution between social groups defined other than by income; for instance, favouring particular groups to offset disadvantages or 'diswelfares' elsewhere in the economy. Or the system might be intended to be non-discriminatory between groups. Either way, we may need to analyse distribution by dimensions such as social class, gender, ethnicity, location, or age rather than just by income. Section 8.5 presents some analysis by age cohort (or generation), but the rest of the analysis in this chapter is concerned with distribution by income.
- *Life cycle smoothing.* Most welfare services are unevenly spread over the life cycle. Education goes disproportionately to the young; health care and pensions to the old; while the taxes that finance them come mostly from the working generation. A snapshot picture of redistribution may be misleading— it would be better to compare how much people get out of the system, and how much they pay in, over their whole lives. But available data relate to short time periods: there are no surveys tracking use of welfare services throughout people's whole lives (and even if they did, they would show the impact of a whole series of changing systems, not the lifetime impact of today's). To answer questions about lifetime distribution requires hypothetical models— although the results from these depend greatly on the assumptions fed into them (Section 8.4).

[1] Other approaches are sometimes possible. For instance, Le Grand (1982) and others have used what people say about their own health status to measure what their needs for health care might be. Berthoud, Lakey, and McKay (1993) and Zaidi and Burchardt (2003) use indicators of the living standards of disabled people by comparison with the rest of the population to estimate the extra costs of disability, which they can then compare with the social security benefits that are designed to compensate for them (see Section 2.1).

- *Compensating for unequal distribution within the family.* Many parents do, of course, meet their children's needs, and many higher-earning husbands share their cash incomes equally with their lower-earning wives. But in other families this is not so—the members of a family may not share equally in its income. Where policies are aimed at countering this kind of problem, it may not be enough to evaluate their effects simply in terms of distribution between families; we may also need to look at distribution between individuals, that is, within families as well. Doing this is hard, but it is possible to model the effects of different assumptions as to how families share their incomes in order to compare the potential impacts of different policies (Sutherland 1997; Falkingham and Hills 1995).

The relative importance given to each aim thus affects not only the interpretation placed on particular findings but also the appropriate kind of analysis.

Beyond this, to answer the question, 'Who benefits from social spending?', one has to add 'Compared with what?'. What is the 'counterfactual' situation with which one is comparing reality? A particular group may receive state medical services worth £1,000 per year. In one sense, this is the amount by which they benefit. But if the medical services did not exist, what else would be different? Government spending might be lower, and hence tax bills, including the group's own. The net benefit, if one allows for taxes, might be much less than £1,000 per year. Knock-on effects may go further. In an economy with lower taxes, many other things might be different. At the same time, without the NHS people would make other arrangements: private medical insurance, for instance. The money paid for that would not be available for other spending, with further knock-on effects through the economy. Britain without the NHS would differ in all sorts of ways from Britain with it, and strictly it is with this hypothetical alternative country we ought to compare to measure the impact of the NHS. In practice, this is very difficult—which limits the conclusiveness of most empirical studies of the kind described below.

Closely related is the question of 'incidence': who *really* benefits from a service? Do children benefit from free education, or do their parents, who would otherwise have paid school or university fees? Are tenants of subsidized housing the true beneficiaries of the subsidies, or can employers attract labour to the area at lower wages than they would otherwise have to pay? In each case, different assumptions about who really gains may be plausible and will affect the findings.

Two further things should be borne in mind in reading this chapter. First, redistribution is not only about taxation and social spending. For instance, under the Child Support Act, the state attempts to enforce payments by absent parents (generally fathers) to parents 'with care' (usually mothers). Such payments are important distributionally, but do not pass through the government accounts, and are not part of the analysis below. The National Minimum Wage is another example of what is sometimes called 'legal welfare', which has a major impact on distribution, but with most of its effects taking place beyond the government's books (see Section 6.4 for estimates of the scale of some examples of this).

Second, social spending and taxation are not only about redistribution. As discussed in the Introduction, there are other public policy aims behind much social spending and government intervention, connected, for instance, to economic efficiency (Barr 2004; Burchardt, Hills, and Propper 1999). Where this is the motivation for state provision one might not expect to see any redistribution between income groups (or other groups). Services might be appraised according to the 'benefit principle'—how much do people receive in relation to what they pay?— so the absence of net redistribution would not be a sign of failure. On the other hand, services can have multiple aims—both equity *and* efficiency—and we would remain interested in net redistribution. Similarly, some services may be justified by 'external' or 'spill-over' benefits beyond those to the direct beneficiary. Promoting the education of even the relatively affluent may be in society's interests, if this produces a more dynamic economy for all. Appraisal of who gains ought to take account of such benefits (although in practice this is again hard to do).

8.2 CROSS-SECTIONAL REDISTRIBUTION

With such points in mind, this section presents findings from recent empirical analysis of the distribution of social spending by income. First, Figure 8.1 shows the official Office for National Statistics (ONS) estimates of the average cash social security benefits received by households in different income groups in 2001–02 (Lakin 2003). Households are arranged in order of equivalent disposable income (that is, income including cash benefits but after direct taxes like income tax, and with allowance made for the greater needs of bigger households, but before deducting housing costs).

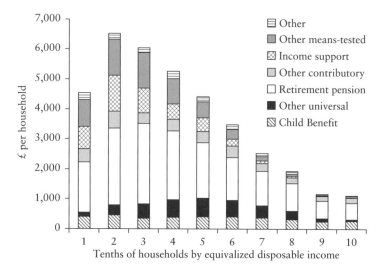

Figure 8.1. *Cash benefits by income group, 2001–02, UK*
Source: Lakin (2003: Table 14, in Appendix 1).

On average, households with incomes in the bottom half received 2.6 times as much from cash benefits as those in the top half. As a result, gross household incomes were more equally distributed than original incomes from the market (see Section 4.6). Means-tested benefits were most concentrated at the bottom: the poorest 30 per cent of households received two-thirds of all Income Support spending, as one might expect.[2] However, even 'universal' benefits are worth more to lower- than to higher-income households. For instance, the bottom half of the distribution received 2.4 times as much from the state pension as the top half. Notably, though, the poorest tenth of households received less from cash benefits than the next three groups. This is partly because households in the bottom group were slightly smaller, and partly because more of them were owner-occupiers, and so not entitled to Housing Benefit (Lakin 2003: Table 15). But it also represents a failure of the system: one reason why these households are among the poorest when ranked by disposable incomes is precisely that they have failed to take up means-tested benefits to which they might be entitled.

These results are for cash benefits. But a larger part of social spending comes in the form of benefits 'in kind', for instance, from the NHS or state education. Estimating how much people receive from them is harder than for cash benefits, as a value has to be put on the services that households use, or are entitled to use. Ideally, to know how much each household benefits from a service, we need to know how much it is worth *to it*—but we cannot usually observe this. Most studies, including those below, use the *cost* to the state of providing the service. But 'value' and 'cost' are not necessarily the same. It may *cost* a great deal to provide people with a particular service but, if offered the choice, they might prefer a smaller cash sum to spend how they liked: the cost is higher than its value to the recipients. This is, for instance, a particular problem with valuing housing subsidies where they come tied to occupying a house someone is allocated to rather than one which he or she has chosen with the ability to use the subsidy somewhere else if preferred. Similarly, the *quality* of services to different kinds of people may vary, even if the amount being *spent* by government on them is ostensibly the same—for instance, if there are greater pressures on services in particular areas than elsewhere that are not reflected in funding systems.[3]

With this proviso, Figure 8.2 adds to the cash benefits shown before, the ONS estimates of the combined value of benefits in kind from the NHS, state education, and housing subsidies. These average a total of £4,000 per household

---

[2] One reason why Income Support is not even more concentrated on the poorest is that the analysis here is by *households*. Some households may contain more than one family unit for benefit purposes, in which case household income can be high, but some of its members—for instance, a pensioner living with her children—might be entitled to the benefit.

[3] There are two particular issues relating to differences by area or neighbourhood. The first is how *needs* vary between areas. The second is how *spending* varies, depending on funding systems (Bramley, Evans, and Atkins 1998; Glennerster, Hills, and Travers 2000). The ONS analysis and that in Sefton (2002) use national figures for spending levels, applied to individual patterns of service use. These could bias the results either way, depending on whether actual spending compensates for other variations in needs.

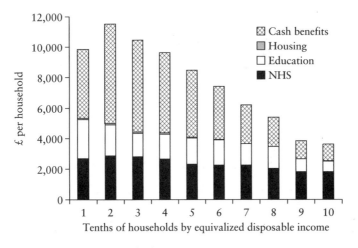

Figure 8.2. *Cash and in-kind benefits by income group, 2001–02, UK*
Source: Lakin (2003: Table 14, in Appendix 1).

(on top of total cash benefits of £3,700). They are more widely spread across the income distribution than cash benefits, so the total is somewhat less skewed to the left, but nonetheless there is a clear 'pro-poor' bias. These benefits in kind were worth an average of £5,300 for the poorest tenth of households in 2001–02 on this analysis, but only £2,500 for the richest tenth. The value of the NHS is shown here as being relatively flat across the distribution, but that of education (as families with children are poorer) and of housing subsidies to tenants of social landlords (now heavily concentrated amongst the poorest) come out as pro-poor. Thanks to the impact of cash benefits, the combined total still shows a 'humped' distribution, with the total being less for the poorest tenth than for the next two groups.

Sefton (1997, 2002) suggests that such figures need to be qualified on various grounds:

- They give each household an equal weight rather than counting each individual separately (as is, for instance, done in the main current income distribution series, *Households Below Average Income*, discussed in Chapters 2 and 3).
- They omit some important aspects of social spending, such as personal social services, as well as higher education for students living away from home (who tend to come from higher-income households).
- The way in which housing subsidies are calculated uses annual flows of subsidy in accounting terms, rather than taking account of the economic value of the properties occupied (which tends to understate benefits to low-income households).
- Perhaps most importantly, the ONS figures are based on the assumption that people of the same age and gender use services such as the NHS equally. This is not necessarily correct: as Sefton's analysis of several datasets shows,

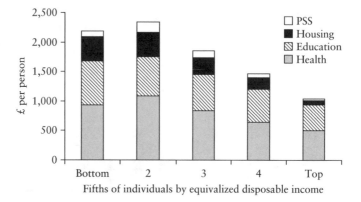

Figure 8.3. *Distribution of the social wage, 2000–01, UK*
Note: Personal Social Services (PSS) based on 1996–97 figures.
Source: Sefton (2002: Figure 1).

other characteristics, including income level, housing tenure, state of health, household type, and employment position, matter too.

With such factors taken into account, some of the results from his analysis are shown in Figure 8.3. This shows the distribution of what he calls the 'social wage' (benefits in kind from health, education, social housing, and personal social services) in 2000–01 between five income groups containing equal numbers of individuals. The services allocated average £1,700 per individual (equivalent to nearly £4,000 per household, and so close to the ONS total for that year in their analysis). Compared with the ONS results in Figure 8.2 (and remembering the change from looking at households to individuals), the total of these items is more hump-shaped, with the second fifth gaining more than the bottom fifth. Use of health services is shown as more valuable to the second and third income groups than before, and less valuable for the richest group. Education, by contrast, is shown in this analysis, which takes a greater share of higher education into account, as being less pro-poor than in the ONS figures. Housing subsidies are much more important here, as their value is estimated by comparing actual rents charged by social landlords with those which can be seen for properties with similar characteristics in the private sector.[4] It also allocates a benefit to those who have gained from buying council houses under the Right to Buy.[5]

---

[4] For comparability with earlier years, when information on uncontrolled market rents was limited, the figures shown in Figure 8.4 for 2000–01 use a somewhat different approach to estimating housing subsidy, based on an assumed return on the estimated capital values of property.

[5] Sefton allocates a benefit to households which previously exercised the Right to Buy by estimating the subsidy which they *would have been* receiving if they had stayed put (on the grounds that the value of the Right to Buy to them should be at least as great as this for them to have exercised it). An alternative would have been to allocate a large lump-sum benefit to people at the moment they exercised the Right to Buy, but that would distort comparisons between years.

Even with adjustments for such issues, the general picture is similar to that in Figure 8.2: all income groups receive significant amounts from these benefits in kind; they are less concentrated than cash benefits on the poor; but households at the bottom of the distribution still receive considerably more than those at the top. Table 8.1 looks at this in more detail. The first column shows the ratio between the estimated values of each service for people in the poorest fifth to that for the richest fifth. The overall total has a ratio of 2.1 to 1, but some services, notably residential care for the elderly, subsidies for social tenants, and state schooling for under-16s, are even more pro-poor than this. On the other hand, the richest fifth receives as much from NHS dentistry as the poorest fifth, and receives two-thirds *more* from higher education than the poorest group. In other words, higher education comes out as 'pro-rich'.

The second column shows how much of the difference between income groups occurs *over and above* what one would expect on purely demographic grounds. For instance, older people are both lower down the income distribution and

Table 8.1. *Distribution of benefits in kind by service, 2000–01, UK*

	Ratio of benefits in kind received by individuals in the bottom fifth by income relative to top fifth	
	Unadjusted	Demographically adjusted*
Health care	1.8	1.5
In-patients	2.2	1.6
Out-patients	1.4	1.2
GP consultations	1.5	1.4
Prescriptions	2.0	1.5
Dental services	1.0	0.9
Education	1.7	1.0–1.1
Schools (under 16)	2.6	1.2
Schools (over 16) and		
further education	1.6	0.8
Higher education	0.6	0.8–1.0
Housing	5.9	5.3
Social rented housing	9.7	8.1
Right to Buy	1.5	1.6
Personal Social Services	3.9	1.7
Non-residential care	1.7	1.3
Residential care	10.1	2.4
All services	2.1	1.5

* This is calculated by dividing the share of benefits in kind received by each income group by the amount it would receive if individuals in each income group were allocated the average for their age/gender group or, in the case of higher education, if spending were distributed evenly between all university-age children (for the lower figure) or all university-age children living at home (for the higher figure).

Source: Sefton (2002: Table 17).

much more likely to use public health services; families with school-age children also tend to be poorer than average, and use state schools; and so on. When this is allowed for, the pro-poor bias is reduced but not eliminated: the poorest fifth still benefit half as much again from social spending than the richest fifth, even after adjustment for demographic composition. Sefton (2002: 49) argues that the most important contributors to this include:

- the distribution of factors affecting need, such as higher incidence of long-standing illness for health and social care, and special needs for schools, for the poorer groups;
- deliberate targeting of services such as social housing on the poor;
- greater use of private alternatives such as private schools and health care by higher income groups; and
- the impact of means-tested charges (allowed for here), for instance, for residential care, prescriptions, and dental care.

However, other factors go the other way, reducing the pro-poor bias, including participation rates in further and higher education (depending on how the families of students living away from home are treated),[6] the way in which some better-off households benefited from the Right to Buy, and the impact of the way charges for residential care take into account the housing equity of even low-income owner-occupiers. Sefton also finds that 'In the case of social care and to a lesser extent health care, there seems to be an unexplained bias against potential users in the bottom quintile group [fifth], who report using fewer services in relation to needs than individuals in higher income groups'. In other words, these services are pro-poor, but not *as* pro-poor as one might have expected if people were receiving equal treatment for equal needs.

The overall pro-poor bias in the distribution of the social wage has increased over time, as can be seen from Figure 8.4, which presents comparable estimates for the total of health, education, and housing subsidies between 1979 and 2000–01. The total value increased in real terms by 48 per cent on average, and for all groups, but growth has been faster for the bottom two groups, particularly since 1996–97. Sefton (2002) suggests that this is not a result of demographic change, as the effect of the increasing concentration of children towards the bottom of the distribution has been more than offset by the growth in the number of pensioners with higher incomes. But neither is there a single overall explanation of the trend. Some of it results from conscious policy change (such as encouraging participation in further and higher education from lower socio-economic groups) or as by-product of other, not necessarily desirable, change (such as residualization of social housing). But it also reflects changing patterns of need (such as the increase in the relative proportion of those with low incomes reporting limiting long-standing illness).

---

[6] The households that students come from often look very prosperous ('empty-nesters'), but would look less so if income were adjusted to allow for inclusion of the students themselves as extra household members. When this is done, the pro-rich bias of higher education is removed, even reversed, for what becomes the poorest group (Sefton 2002: Figure 13).

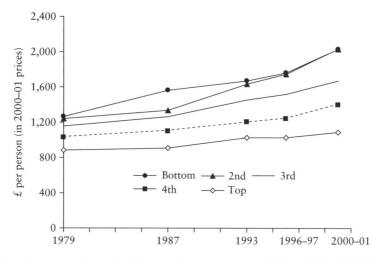

Figure 8.4. *Change in value of social wage by income group, 1979 to 2000–01, UK*
Note: For comparability over time, 2000–01 estimates differ slightly from those in Figure 8.3.
Source: Sefton (2002: Figure 7).

This increase in the pro-poor bias of social spending is not, however, enough to offset the growth in inequality of cash incomes described in Chapter 2. While social spending has become more pro-poor, it has also become smaller in scale relative to cash incomes. Disposable incomes rose in real terms, for instance by 64–72 per cent on average between 1979 and 2000–01, depending on whether they are taken before or after housing costs (DWP 2002a: Table A1 and earlier equivalents), compared with the 48 per cent increase in the social wage. In the first part of the period, 1979 to 1993, taking account of the increase in the 'equalizing' impact of the social wage would still have a moderating effect on inequality growth, equivalent to a reduction by a fifth in the growth in inequality of cash incomes (Sefton 1997: 34–5).[7] However, between 1996–97 and 2000–01, covering New Labour's first term in office, the 8 per cent increase in the real value of the social wage compared with a 12 per cent increase in cash incomes, and this slower growth almost exactly offsets the equalizing effect of it becoming more pro-poor (Sefton 2002: Table 4). Allowing for the social wage over this period would not therefore affect overall trends in income inequality.

8.3 TAKING ACCOUNT OF TAXATION

Whichever estimates are used, the absolute value of social spending whether in cash or in kind is greatest for low-income households, and much lower than

---

[7] On the assumption that productivity growth in the public sector matched the increase in the real cost of providing public services. To the extent that this was not the case, the offsetting impact on inequality growth would be reduced (or eliminated if there was none).

average for high-income families. Taxation, by contrast, is greater in absolute terms for those with higher incomes, although it is not necessarily a greater proportion of income (see Figure 7.5). Most social spending is financed from general taxation, so it is hard to be precise about *which* taxes are paying for it: if state education were abolished, would it be income tax or VAT that would fall? It is not possible to give a definitive answer. However, a clear indication of the direction and scale of the effect can be seen in Figure 8.5. This compares the total of cash and kind benefits in 2001–02 given in Figure 8.2 with the ONS's estimates of the impact of all of National Insurance Contributions (as they are earmarked, notionally at least, for social spending) and the proportion required (70 per cent) of each other tax to cover the remainder of spending. In other words, the counterfactual used here is that, in the absence of public social spending, there would be no National Insurance Contributions, and all other taxes would be reduced by 70 per cent.

The effect is clear. For the bottom five-tenths of the distribution, benefits were higher than taxes and the figures show a net gain; the sixth group roughly broke even; but for those in the top four groups taxes were higher, suggesting a net loss. The biggest 'gainers' on this basis were the second group, who received total social spending of £11,500 per household but paid less than £2,800 in tax towards the cost of this spending, giving them a net 'gain' of nearly £9,000. By contrast, the richest group received benefits and services of £3,600, only a sixth of the £20,000 they paid in tax, leaving them with a net 'loss' of more than £16,000 per household.

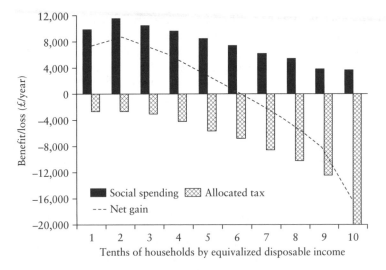

Figure 8.5. *Net impact of tax and social spending, 2001–02, UK*

Note: Taxes are NICs and proportion of other tax required to pay for social spending.

Source: Derived from Lakin (2003: Table 14, in Appendix 1).

These results suggest that, on a cross-sectional basis, the combination of welfare services and, on plausible assumptions, their financing is significantly redistributive from high- to low-income groups (although by themselves they say little about the scale of such gains in relation to 'need', such as for medical care). If the 'welfare state' were abolished and taxes reduced accordingly, society would become a great deal more unequal.

8.4 LIFE-CYCLE REDISTRIBUTION

The picture looks somewhat different over a lifetime. This is partly because income in the snapshot of a single year does not necessarily give a good measure of someone's lifetime income position. It is also because what people get out of the system is strongly linked to their age. In 2000–01, Sefton (2002: Figure 3) estimates that average in-kind benefits from health, education, housing subsidies, and personal social services ranged from over £2,500 for those under 16 and around £1,000 for those aged 16–64, to over £4,000 for those aged 75 or more (see Figure 11.2 for a finer breakdown by age for health, education, and social security). Cash benefits aimed at children and those of working age averaged around £1,000 per person in that year, but were nearly £6,000 per pensioner.[8] By contrast, the amounts paid in through taxation are much greater during people's working lives than at other times. The redistributive pattern seen in Figure 8.5 for a single year is strongly affected by these life-cycle effects.

Actually measuring 'lifetime' impacts of benefits and taxes is not possible: we do not have records covering complete lives, and systems do not stay the same for long enough. The findings in Figure 8.6, now becoming rather dated, are drawn from a computer simulation model of 4,000 hypothetical life histories (Falkingham and Hills 1995). The model built up the effects of the tax and welfare systems on a wide range of individuals on the assumption that the systems remain in a 'steady state' for their whole lives, a kind of parallel to the film *Groundhog Day*. In this case, the model individuals lived their entire lives in the world as it was back in 1985 (but using the tax and social security systems as they had evolved by 1991). Its results therefore illustrate the lifetime effects of one year's systems, not a forecast of the combined effects of different systems that may actually apply through their lives. The figures, originally calculated at 1985 prices, are adjusted in line with earnings growth to 2001 levels to give more comparability with other figures in this chapter.

The top panel of Figure 8.6 gives a 'lifetime' analogue of the cross-sectional picture in Figure 8.2 (but for only the largest services, not including housing subsidies or personal social services). The bars show total lifetime benefits from social security, education, and the NHS going to each group of model

---

[8] Social security spending in Great Britain by broad age group taken from DWP (2003*h*: Table 3) and divided by relevant population size (from DWP 2002*a*) gives averages of £1,030 per child, £900 per person of working age, and £5,870 per pensioner.

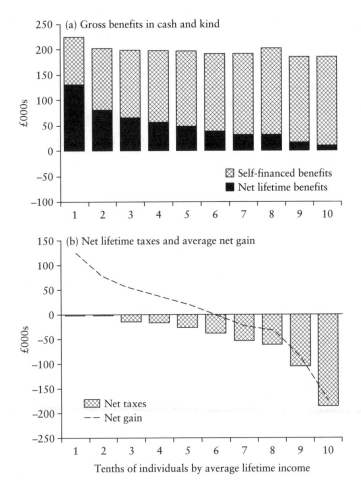

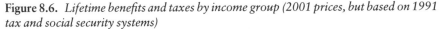
Tenths of individuals by average lifetime income

Figure 8.6. *Lifetime benefits and taxes by income group (2001 prices, but based on 1991 tax and social security systems)*

Note: Figures based on simulation of complete lifetimes from the LIFEMOD model based on 1985 population, but with the structure of taxes and benefits in 1991. Lifetime taxes based on proportionate share of lifetime incomes.

Source: Falkingham and Hills (1995: Table 7.6), adjusted by earnings growth to 2001 prices.

individuals, ordered by their average *lifetime* living standards, with the 'lifetime poorest' on the left. The 'lifetime poorest' receive somewhat more than the 'lifetime richest', but the striking feature is that the overall distribution of gross benefits is much flatter than on an annual basis. Regardless of lifetime income, *gross* receipts look much the same—around £200,000 per person (at 2001 prices).

Over their lives people both receive benefits in cash and kind, and pay taxes. Those with higher lifetime incomes pay much more tax than those with low incomes. In effect, people finance some of the benefits they receive through their *own* lifetime tax payments. However, some do not pay enough lifetime tax to pay for all of their benefits; they receive 'net lifetime benefits' from the system. These net lifetime benefits are paid for by other people, who pay more than enough tax to cover their own benefits—they pay 'net lifetime taxes' into the system.

The bars in the top panel, Figure 8.6 (a), are therefore divided between 'net' and 'self-financed' benefits, the latter being a rising proportion moving up through the income groups (although even within the highest lifetime income group there are some who pay in less than they get out—for instance, the lower-earning wives of highly paid men—so even the top group contains some 'lifetime gainers'). The bars in the lower panel, Figure 8.6 (b), show where the net lifetime taxes are coming from.[9] Net lifetime taxes also increase moving up through the income groups. Finally, the line in the lower panel—analogous to that in Figure 8.5—shows the net gain or loss from the system to each lifetime income group as a whole. The bottom five groups are again net gainers on average; the sixth group breaks even; the top four groups are net losers. In the case of the richest tenth, the taxes they pay cover not only the value of all the benefits they receive, but nearly as much again of other people's. They are 'net losers', although it should be noted that this is not nearly to as great an extent as is seen in analysis of a single year as in Figure 8.5 (where the top tenth 'get back' less than a fifth of what they 'pay in' during that year).

Thus, even from a lifetime perspective, the system does appear to redistribute from 'lifetime rich' to 'lifetime poor' (and also, importantly, from men to women, when the results are analysed by gender; see Falkingham and Hills 1995: Table 7.6). However, the diagram suggests that *most* benefits are self-financed over people's lifetimes rather than being paid for by others. On these results, nearly three-quarters of what the welfare state was doing in the late 1980s and early 1990s was like a 'savings bank', and only a quarter was 'Robin Hood' redistribution between different people (see Barr 2001 for more discussion of the 'piggy bank' role of the welfare state). Changes since 1985 will have altered this balance. For instance, although the total of health, education, and social security spending was much the same share of national income in 2001–02 as in 1985–86 (Figure 6.3), less of this takes the form of cash benefits now, and more is health spending. This would tend to push towards a smaller 'Robin Hood' effect if a similar exercise were carried out today. On the other hand, the underlying inequality of market incomes increased after 1985, and both cash benefits and the 'social wage' have become more pro-poor, which will have had the opposite impact, increasing the 'Robin Hood' effect.

[9] The figures given here are based on the assumption that welfare services and benefits are financed from taxes in general, taken to be equivalent to a fixed proportion—23 per cent here—of gross income, reflecting the roughly proportional impact of the tax system as a whole (see Figure 7.5). If, instead, financing were assumed to come only from direct taxation, lifetime redistribution—the 'Robin Hood effect'—would be somewhat larger (Falkingham and Hills 1995: 138–41).

8.5   INTERGENERATIONAL DISTRIBUTION

The analysis in the previous section looked at the impact of social spending and the taxes that pay for them on a 'steady state' basis. In reality, the size and composition of the welfare state have changed considerably over time (see Chapter 6). Given the way in which its impact varies with age, this raises the possibility that some generations, or age cohorts, may be doing better out of the system than others. One hypothesis is, for instance, that Western welfare states may favour a 'welfare generation'—which gained from the expansion of welfare services in the second half of the twentieth century but which did not have to pay much in taxes towards such services for its parents (see, for instance, Thomson 1991 for the New Zealand case, or Kotlikoff 1992 for the USA). Correspondingly, there may be later generations that are 'born to pay'—paying taxes, for instance, towards generous state pensions for their parents but getting much less back themselves. This might not happen if the welfare state were a real 'savings bank', with the earlier generation putting aside resources to pay for health care and pensions in its own retirement. In fact, however, social spending is almost entirely financed on a 'pay as you go' basis: today's taxpayers pay for the benefits and services going to today's recipients. This creates the possibility of generational inequity.

Again, establishing whether such a situation exists is not straightforward. First, to reach a conclusion on the position of any particular generation requires information on its members' positions over their complete lives. Unless we look only at generations born before, say, the First World War, this means we have to project what will happen in the future: cohorts now in their forties and fifties have already paid a great deal into the system through taxation, and will at present be out of pocket, but they can expect to get all or most of it back when they are older. We need to allow for this to compare their position with other cohorts. Second, we need a way of comparing receipts at one date with those at another. The analysis described below does this by measuring receipts and payments in terms of average incomes (GDP per capita) at the dates they take place. This is equivalent to using a real discount rate equal to the rate of economic growth. This has several attractions, but other approaches can be argued for.[10]

Table 8.2 shows the updated results of an earlier exercise that attempted to do this (Falkingham and Hills 1995: ch. 3, updated in Smithies forthcoming *a*). It shows, for cohorts of people born within successive five-year periods since 1901, the total estimated receipts from government spending on health care, education, and social security for the cohort as a whole, and the total taxes they would have paid towards those spending items as taxpayers. To get complete lifetime receipts,

---

[10] Recent real yields on long-term government indexed bonds have been around the 2 per cent level consistent with this, but were significantly higher in the 1980s and 1990s (HM Treasury 2002*b*: chart 5.3). An advantage of using the growth of average income as the discount rate is that a 'steady state' welfare state, absorbing a constant fraction of national income if age structure does not change, would be generationally neutral. Using a higher discount rate would require an ever-expanding welfare state to achieve this, which would be ultimately unsustainable.

Table 8.2. *Projected lifetime receipts from health, education, and social security,*
and taxes paid towards them by cohort, 1901–2051, GB

Cohort	Born	Age in 2001	Size when 15–19 (m)	Cumulative receipts and payments (GDP per capita per member at 15–19)			Receipts as % of tax
				Receipts	Tax	Net gain	
1	1901–06	—	4.0	9.0	7.4	1.6	122
2	1906–11	90–94	4.0	9.6	8.3	1.3	116
3	1911–16	85–89	3.9	10.8	9.1	1.7	118
4	1916–21	80–84	3.6	11.9	10.3	1.6	115
5	1921–26	75–79	3.7	12.2	11.7	0.5	104
6	1926–31	70–74	3.3	13.7	13.5	0.2	102
7	1931–36	65–69	3.1	15.3	15.1	0.2	101
8	1936–41	60–64	3.2	16.7	15.7	1.0	107
9	1941–46	55–59	3.6	18.0	16.4	1.6	110
10	1946–51	50–54	4.2	18.6	17.0	1.6	110
11	1951–56	45–49	3.7	20.5	17.8	2.8	116
12	1956–61	40–44	4.0	21.6	18.3	3.3	118
Incomplete lifetimes							
13 (to 90)	1961–66	35–39	4.5	19.4	17.9	1.5	108
14 (to 85)	1966–71	30–34	4.3	18.5	18.1	0.4	102
15 (to 80)	1971–76	25–29	3.6	17.9	18.8	–0.9	95

Sources: Smithies (forthcoming *a*), updating Falkingham and Hills (1995: Table 3.6), using actual spending by age to 2001; 2001 spending patterns after then adjusted by income growth; and population projections from GAD (2003).

the figures take account of projected receipts and payments up to 2051. The projections use the official population projections made in 2003, and are based on the assumption that 2001 spending patterns will be maintained after then in terms of spending per head at any given age in relation to GDP per capita (see Section 10.2 for discussion of the implications of this assumption and of alternatives to it).

The results show, for instance, that the earliest cohort, born between 1901 and 1906, is estimated to have benefited from education, health, and social security spending equivalent to nine year's worth of average income over their lives. However, they had to pay in only just over seven years' worth of income in tax: they got out more than 120 per cent of what they put in. The next three cohorts also gain significantly more than they put in. Later cohorts both get more out of the system and pay more in—rising to nearly 20 years' worth of income for those born since the Second World War, twice as much as for the oldest groups. For those born between 1921 and 1941, what they get out is much closer to what they will have put in, and the same is true of the youngest cohorts. However, those of us born in the 1950s come out of these projections in almost as favourable a position as the earliest cohort.

This suggests that Britain *did* have a 'welfare generation'—mostly those born between 1901 and 1921—but to only a modest extent. It also suggests that later generations do not necessarily lose out, *provided* that the system keeps going with roughly its current generosity in relative terms at any given age. Overall, the system appears fairly well-balanced between generations.[11]

The projections rest on the assumption that spending at any given age, and implicitly therefore future benefit rates, rises in line with average incomes. If this happened, overall spending on these services would rise from 22 per cent of GDP in 2001–02 to over 26 per cent by 2051 (see Table 10.2). The 1950s generation does well because the projections assume that we both benefit from increased life expectancy and, for instance, continue to receive pensions from current state pension ages with their existing levels of generosity. Official projections of long-term public spending make less generous assumptions—that benefit rates for those aged under 65 will be price-linked, and that spending on state pensions will remain a fixed share of national income—although they also incorporate more generous assumptions about future spending on the NHS (see Tables 10.1 and 10.2). Changing such assumptions would change both the projected total of social spending and the distribution between cohorts shown in Table 8.2. As one of many possible variants, if pensions spending were scaled back so that it did not rise in relation to GDP, total social spending would rise by only one percentage point of GDP by 2051. If this happened, the overall net gain for those born in the 1950s (cohorts 11 and 12 in the table) would be more than halved, and that for those born in the 1960s would be eliminated (Smithies forthcoming *a*). However, there would still be an approximate generational balance.

On the other hand, if we suddenly switched from the current system to one that expected today's workers to finance all of their own pensions and health care through private savings and private insurance *at the same time* as paying taxes for today's pensioners, there would be a severe inequity between generations. Once a country has developed a system based on pay-as-you-go principles, it is very difficult to change it without creating a 'transition generation' of losers, who are very likely to resist change.

8.6 PUBLIC ATTITUDES TO REDISTRIBUTION

We have already seen in earlier chapters (Sections 2.5 and 3.5) that a majority of the British public expresses views that the gap between rich and poor is too great (even though they underestimate its extent), that large income differences are not necessary for economic prosperity, and that poverty (perceived in a way that is consistent with a relative view of what it means) is too high. Still, the fact that

---

[11] An alternative approach, if we look at government spending more generally, using a higher discount rate, and assume that government debt would ultimately be paid off, confirms that the UK public finances are broadly neutral in their impact between generations, while systems in other countries imply losses for later-born generations (HM Treasury 2002*b*: chart 6.13; Cardarelli, Sefton, and Kotlikoff 1999).

people are concerned about inequality and poverty does not necessarily imply that they think anything can be done about it, still less that they have any idea what, and whether this should involve 'redistribution'.

On the gap between rich and poor, a majority of respondents to the British Social Attitudes survey since the 1980s have agreed that 'it is the responsibility of government to reduce the difference in income between people with high income and people with low incomes'. Fifty-eight per cent agreed with this statement in 2000, and between 51 per cent and 65 per cent did so in previous years since 1985 (Bromley 2003: Table 4.9). Asked a differently worded question in 1998 (with more options for the answer), whether 'on the whole it should be the government's responsibility to reduce income differences between the rich and poor', three-quarters of respondents said it 'definitely' (39 per cent) or 'probably' (34 per cent) was, against only a sixth who said it probably or definitely was not (Hills and Lelkes 1999). This large majority shrank somewhat when another question in the survey mentioned tax as an instrument, but more than half (53 per cent) of 1998 respondents still said that 'Government should increase taxes on the better-off to spend more on the poor', and only a sixth preferred an alternative statement that 'the better-off pay too much tax already'.

As for government's ability to do something about poverty, only 28 per cent of respondents to the 1994 survey said that 'British governments nowadays can do very little to reduce poverty', compared with 70 per cent who said that they can do 'quite a bit' (proportions that were little changed from 1986).

This does not tell us about *what* government should do, however. As Table 8.3 shows, there has been a long-running change when people are asked specifically about whether the government should 'spend more money on welfare benefits for the poor, even if it leads to higher taxes'. In 2002, the largest group, 44 per cent, agreed, but 26 per cent disagreed. As the table shows, this represented somewhat greater agreement than just two years before, when only 38 per cent agreed, but is still very different from the position at the end of the 1980s, when up to 60 per cent agreed that more should be spent and less than a fifth disagreed.

Table 8.3. *Attitudes to redistribution and welfare spending, 1987–2002, GB (%)*

	1987	1989	1991	1993	1994	1996	1998	2000	2002
Government should spend more money on welfare benefits for the poor									
Agree	55	61	58	53	50	43	43	38	44
Neither	23	23	23	25	25	29	29	31	27
Disagree	22	15	18	20	23	26	26	30	26
Government should redistribute income to the less well-off									
Agree	45	50	49	45	51	44	39	39	39
Neither	20	20	20	21	23	26	28	24	25
Disagree	33	29	29	33	25	28	31	36	34
Base	1,281	2,604	2,481	2,567	2,929	3,085	2,531	2,980	2,929

Source: British Social Attitudes survey.

The difference in trend from the evidence on attitudes to poverty discussed in Chapter 3 suggests that this may represent declining support for 'welfare benefits' rather than a decline in concern about poverty (see Section 6.5).

There has also been a change in attitudes towards the notion of 'redistribution'. The table shows that, by 2002, only 39 per cent agreed that 'the government should *redistribute* income from the better-off to those who are less well-off' (emphasis added), with 34 per cent disagreeing. This is a large change from 1994, when half thought that government should redistribute and only a quarter disagreed. Notably, as with some of the other questions discussed in earlier chapters, 1994 represented something of a peak for this kind of view, with more agreeing and fewer disagreeing then than in the late 1980s. Again, from the evidence discussed in Chapter 2, this does not seem to represent a change in people's desire for inequality to be reduced, but rather a change in *how* it should be achieved: seeing government explicitly as Robin Hood now appears less popular than it was a decade ago.

Tom Sefton (2003: Table 1.1) shows that the decline in support both for spending more on 'welfare benefits' and for government to 'redistribute income' between 1987 and 2002 occurred among those identifying with Labour, not among Conservative identifiers. These changes occurred during the period when 'New Labour', both in opposition and in government, was avoiding talking about 'redistribution', preferring instead to talk about 'fairness'. However, establishing cause and effect is not easy: has New Labour avoided using language which no longer resonates, or does it no longer resonate so much because politicians no longer use it?

It may also matter precisely how the question is put. Responses to the British Election Surveys carried out in election years to a question about whether 'income and wealth should be redistributed towards ordinary working people' show a different pattern. There was a slow decline in agreement from 54 per cent in the mid-1970s to 47 per cent in 1992, but an increase to 60 per cent at the time of the 1997 election, with only 20 per cent disagreeing. By the time of the 2001 election, there had been a sharp fall to only 34 per cent agreeing, with nearly as many, 33 per cent, disagreeing, closer to the responses shown in Table 8.3 for 2000 and 2002 (Heath, Jowell, and Curtice 2001: Table 2.9, updated from UK Data Archive). The greater volatility may reflect stronger feelings when 'wealth' is mentioned as well as income, and it may be that 'ordinary working people' were, up to 1997 at least, seen as a more deserving object of redistribution than 'those with low incomes' referred to in the BSA question.

Interestingly, despite attitudes which are more likely than elsewhere in the EU to explain poverty as being the result of 'laziness or lack of willpower' (Table 3.16), people in Britain were among the most likely to agree with the proposition put by a 2001 *Eurobarometer* survey that 'I would be ready to pay more tax if it were definitely used to improve the situation of the poor'. Just over half of respondents in Great Britain agreed with this, as many as in Denmark, the Netherlands, and Sweden, as well as Italy and Spain, and exceeded only in

Greece, where over 60 per cent agreed (Gallie and Paugam 2002: Figure 7.4). Less than a third agreed in (what had been) West Germany and in Austria.

Whatever people's explicit views of 'redistribution' in Britain, it is clear that their separate preferences for how cash benefits and taxation should be structured discussed in Chapters 6 and 7 entail *implicit* support for the government budget to be redistributive, as this is the logical consequence of even flat-rate benefits to those with particular needs, combined with proportional or progressive taxation. Some fascinating depth is added to these findings by recent exploratory qualitative research by Alan Hedges (forthcoming). He discussed issues to do with the redistributive effect of taxes and government spending (but without using such language) with focus groups of varied composition. He found that, while people did not see 'redistribution' per se as the key outcome of the taxation and spending process, there appeared to be very high levels of support for redistribution as a *by-product* of spending and taxation distributed in ways people want,[12] that is, spending which goes to people according to their needs, and taxes raised in proportion to their incomes, with the kind of distributional effect shown in Figure 8.5. As one surprised respondent put it, 'It's very communist, isn't it? Am I being a communist?', when finding that she was effectively proposing 'from each according to his means, to each according to his needs'.

8.7 SUMMARY

- There are different approaches to analysing who gains from and who pays for welfare services. Which is appropriate depends on the question being asked.
- Official analysis of annual incomes suggests that poorer households receive, as one would expect, much more from cash benefits than richer ones. This is so even for 'universal' benefits such as the state retirement pension. The poorer half of households receives more than two and a half times as much from cash benefits as those in the richer half.
- Equivalent estimates of the distribution of 'in-kind' benefits from health care, education, and housing subsidies suggest that they are more widely spread across the income distribution, but are still 'pro-poor': for instance, they are worth more than twice as much for the poorest tenth as for the richest tenth.
- Analysis which takes more factors into account confirms that the 'social wage' from in-kind benefits is pro-poor overall, but this is more marked for some services, such as residential care for the elderly, housing subsidies, and compulsory state schooling. It is not true of a few services, such as dentistry, while higher-income groups gain more from higher education on some measures.

[12] See Rothstein (1998: ch. 5) for a discussion of how collective preferences for tax and spending systems relate to the perceived legitimacy of their component parts, and to how decisions about these are reached, rather than just to their end results.

- Much, but not all, of this pattern is explained by demographic factors such as age. However, even allowing for demographic composition, the poorest fifth benefits half as much again from social spending in-kind as the richest fifth.
- Comparing who gains from welfare spending with who pays the taxes that finance it each year shows that the poorest five tenths of households are net gainers, and the richest four tenths are net losers. In 2001–02 the richest tenth paid £16,000 per household more towards the cost of welfare services than they received from them.
- If we could calculate these numbers looking across people's complete lifetimes, rather than at a snapshot of a single year, the picture would look rather different. A simulation model, based on data from the 1980s, suggested that, over complete lifetimes, all income groups would receive similar amounts on average from social security, health care, and education. However, the amounts they would pay in tax would be very different, so the impact of the system as a whole is still redistributive, with the richest tenth on a lifetime basis getting back only just over half of what they paid in over their lives.
- If one looks at the treatment of successive generations born since the start of the twentieth century, and projects what will happen to some of them into the future, those born between 1901 and 1921 appear to have gained somewhat more from the welfare state than they themselves paid in as taxpayers. Depending on the assumptions made, most later generations emerge as closer to break-even. There is little evidence in the UK case of substantial inequity between generations in the way the welfare state has developed so far.
- Three-quarters of the population believe it to be government's responsibility to reduce income differences between 'rich and poor', and nearly three-fifths to reduce them between 'those with high incomes and those with low incomes'. At the same time, explicit support for 'redistribution' towards those with low incomes as a way of achieving this has declined since the early 1990s. Qualitative research suggests, however, strong support for patterns of taxation and public spending that lead to redistribution as a by-product.

FURTHER READING

Each year the Office for National Statistics publishes official estimates of the distributional effect of taxation and of a large part of public spending, including social security and welfare services. A recent edition is 'The Effects of Taxes and Benefits on Household Income, 2001–02', by Caroline Lakin (*Economic Trends*, May 2003; available on www.statistics.gov.uk).

A more detailed examination of the distribution of benefits in kind from government spending on health, education, housing subsidies, and personal social services, taking account of variations in use by socio-economic variables beyond age and gender, can be found in *Recent Changes in the Distribution of the Social Wage* by Tom Sefton (CASE paper 62, London School of Economics, 2002; available on the CASE website: http://sticerd.lse.ac.uk/dps/case/cp/CASEpaper62.pdf).

Discussion of the life-cycle impact of welfare services and implications for policy in particular areas can be found in *The Dynamic of Welfare: the Welfare State and the Life Cycle* edited by Jane Falkingham and John Hills (Prentice Hall/Harvester Wheatsheaf, 1995); and *The Welfare State as a Piggy Bank* by Nicholas Barr (Oxford University Press, 2001).

III

WHERE DO WE GO FROM HERE?

9

New Labour, Welfare, and Distribution

9.1 WHAT'S 'NEW' ABOUT 'NEW LABOUR'?

As earlier chapters have set out, when the Blair government took office in May 1997, its inheritance included the following:

- Overall income inequality was close to its post-war high (Figure 2.9). Although the very rapid increase in income inequality seen in the 1980s had slowed considerably, the very top of the distribution (the top 1 per cent) had continued to increase its share of total income through the 1990s (Table 2.6).

- Part of this had been driven by a rapid growth in the dispersion of earnings since the late 1970s (Figure 4.3), but it was also associated with the falling relative value of social security benefits (Figure 4.11). While registered unemployment had fallen after 1993 (Figure 4.8), the proportion of the population living in households with no income from paid work continued to rise up to 1996, by which time more than a fifth of children were living in workless households (Table 4.1).

- Measured in relative terms, poverty was far higher than it had been in the 1960s and 1970s, although it had fallen from its peak in the early 1990s (Figure 3.1). Poverty in the UK, particularly child poverty, was very high by comparison with most other industrialized countries (Table 3.6). Other indicators of deprivation and social exclusion were also poor in European terms.

- Growing income inequality had not been offset by faster short-term income mobility; indeed, earnings mobility appears to have declined (Section 5.5). There also seems to have been a slowing in social and economic mobility between the generations (Section 5.7).

In terms of the policy background:

- Overall government welfare spending had been kept to around a quarter of national income since the mid-1970s (Figure 6.3). Downward pressures on spending in an attempt to reduce taxes had collided with factors pushing up the demand for social spending, resulting in a kind of stalemate in the overall total.

- An important factor in restraining spending had been the Thatcher government's decision in the early 1980s to link social security benefits to prices rather than any measure of average incomes or prosperity. Means-testing of social security benefits had become more important in both the 1970s and 1980s (Figure 6.7). Social benefits in kind (such as from health care and education) had also become somewhat more focused on those with lower incomes than in 1979 (Figure 8.4).

• The role of the private sector in welfare activity had become somewhat greater in the Conservative years, partly reflecting deliberate privatization policy. The growth of the private sector as *provider* of services had generally been more important than its growth as a source of finance (Section 6.4).

Against this background, New Labour's initial policies were rather different from what might have been expected from Labour in government in the 1960s and 1970s or in opposition in the 1980s. It is these differences that mark it out as 'new' Labour, and have led some to characterize it as following a 'third way' between the politics of the 'old left' and the 'new right' (Giddens 1998, 2000). Labour's 1997 election manifesto put little stress on poverty and inequality, explicitly pledged to stick to Conservative public spending plans in its first two years in office, and promised not increase income tax rates. The main immediate reform was to set up the 'New Deal' measures aimed at reducing youth unemployment in particular. Another of five immediate pledges (famously written on a credit card-sized card) was to reduce primary school class sizes for 5–7-year-olds, using savings from abolishing the Assisted Places scheme (which had contributed towards private school fees). But, apart from this, Labour promised very little: for instance, it abandoned the pledges of increased state pensions that had been made in election campaigns between 1983 and 1992.

This was the culmination of a strategy adopted since Tony Blair became leader in 1994 to shed Labour's 'tax and spend' image. Discussion of 'redistribution' had also been studiously avoided. The furthest the new Prime Minister had been prepared to go was to say in July 1996, 'I believe in greater equality. If the next Labour Government has not raised the living standards of the poorest by the end of its term in office, it will have failed'.[1] The goal expressed in the second part of the statement was not particularly ambitious by historical standards at times of economic growth (although, as Figure 2.7 showed, it had not been achieved between 1979 and the early 1990s on one income measure, at least).

What has followed has, however, been considerably more ambitious, as the following section discusses. What is striking overall, however, is that policies towards poverty and inequality, and towards the welfare state, have been *selective* in both target groups and in the instruments used. Most famously, in his Beveridge lecture in March 1999, Tony Blair (1999: 17) promised:

Our historic aim will be for ours to be the first generation to end child poverty, and it will take a generation. It is a 20-year mission, but I believe it can be done.

There has also been a commitment by Gordon Brown, the Labour Chancellor of the Exchequer, to 'abolish pensioner poverty in this generation',[2] but no overall promise or target for poverty as a whole. Indeed, the approach to the working-age population is summarized by the slogan 'Work for those who can, security for

---

[1] Interviewed in the *Independent*, 28 July 1996, quoted by Oppenheim (1997).
[2] Labour Party Conference speech, 29 September 2003.

those that cannot'. There has conspicuously also been no commitment to reduce overall economic inequality, particularly as related to incomes at the top of the distribution (as opposed to inequality between the bottom and the middle). Instead, the emphasis has been on equality of *opportunity*, particularly through education policies, other interventions in childhood, and initiatives from the new Social Exclusion Unit (SEU), originally reporting directly to the Prime Minister, on particular aspects of long-term disadvantage that cut across departments.

Similarly, there has not been any blanket increase in the generosity of the welfare state. Public spending has increased significantly as a share of GDP since the self-imposed constraint of the 1997 election pledge ended in 1999 but, where there has been extra spending, this has almost always been combined with some kind of structural reform. This is most clearly true of social security spending. As a default, social security benefits have remained linked to prices rather than incomes or earnings, but certain groups—families with children, low-income pensioners— have been significant beneficiaries of reform. Some parts of the 'universal' welfare state—notably health care and school education—have had increased resources, but others—such as the basic state pension—have not. Hills and Lelkes (1999) describe this combination as 'selective universalism'. The government prefers to describe its policies as 'progressive universalism', with the idea that they embody something for (almost) everyone but more for those with greatest needs.

Section 9.2 describes the policies that have been followed in more detail, while Section 9.3 looks at some of their impacts.

9.2   NEW LABOUR'S POLICIES

9.2.1   *'Work for Those who Can'*

If there were a defining word for the first phase of New Labour's social policies, it would be 'work'. One of the first actions of the government was to introduce a number of welfare-to-work measures under the banner of the 'New Deal'. These were initially financed by a one-off levy on the 'windfall' profits of various utilities that had been privatized by the Conservatives. Most of the funding has gone to measures for the under-25s, but there have also been New Deals for the long-term unemployed, for lone parents, for older workers, and for the part- ners of unemployed people. By contrast with recent US welfare reforms, these measures cover a much wider part of the population, and involve more carrots and fewer sticks. For instance, lone parents receiving welfare benefits (Income Support) are now required to attend an annual interview to discuss finding work and the help available to do so, but are not under compulsion to take up work while they have a child aged under 16 *years* old (although interviews will be more frequent once the child is 14). This contrasts starkly with US requirements for lone mothers receiving 'welfare', whereby in twenty states full-time participa- tion in work or other programmes may be required once children reach 16 *weeks* or less (Brady-Smith et al. 2001: Table 1).

Alongside the New Deal, there has been a major reorganization of the administration of benefits and other assistance for the unemployed. Following a series of pilots (obscurely known as 'One'), the functions of job centres (giving employment advice) and social security offices (paying out benefits) are being amalgamated into combined units known as Job Centre Plus. The idea of this is to switch the emphasis in the treatment of unemployed people from initial contacts being about policing benefit entitlements to being about assistance with finding work or, as the Labour leader John Smith put it in the 1980s, 'from a hand-out to a hand up'.[3]

The government also started work immediately on the first of its new tax credits, the Working Families Tax Credit (WFTC), aimed at low-paid families with children. This was eventually implemented in October 1999. In combination with Britain's first National Minimum Wage (see Section 4.2), it was described as helping to 'make work pay', reducing the disincentives caused by incomes in low-paid work for some being little higher than the incomes of those out of work. To reinforce the psychological impact of the WFTC on attitudes to work, it was originally to be paid only through the wage packet, unlike its predecessor benefit (Family Credit) that helped low-paid families with children. In the event, the Treasury conceded that couples could choose which partner received it, allowing continuing direct payments to mothers caring for children, for instance.[4]

All of this has been accompanied by a buoyant labour market and economic growth since 1997. The government claims credit for this through sound macro-economic management. It points to two particular moves: the decision to give the Bank of England operational independence in setting interest rates consistent with an inflation target of 2.5 per cent; and managing the public finances to obey the 'golden rule', that over the economic cycle, government borrowing should not exceed net investment (see Section 7.1).

9.2.2 *Tax and Benefit Reforms*

A key feature of tax and benefit reforms has been that the government has continued to adjust many benefit rates and tax allowances in line with price inflation. If nothing else had changed, this would have meant the living standards of those mainly dependent on benefits falling behind the rest of the population. It would also mean revenues from income tax rising more rapidly than economic growth through 'fiscal drag', as more of people's incomes were pulled into tax and

---

[3] Evidence from the 'One' pilots suggests that such reforms are popular with claimants because of the administrative streamlining, but did not lead to any further increases in the rate at which people found work than had already occurred following the Conservative 'active labour market' measures that had accompanied the transformation of Unemployment Benefit into 'Jobseeker's Allowance' in the mid-1990s (Green et al. 2001).

[4] In the subsequent round of reform in April 2003, payments of the new Child Tax Credit that replaced the bulk of the WFTC reverted to being made directly to the mother. Great stress was then placed on the advantages of this new approach in making it more likely that the cash would reach children.

into higher tax brackets. In fact, several parts of the tax and benefit system have been made more generous to those on low incomes, particularly families with children and pensioners.

For families with children, important elements have included:

- an increase in the real value of the universal Child Benefit, paid in respect of all children, particularly for the first child (but abolition of the special One Parent Benefit for single parents);
- phasing out of additional payments for lone parents on Income Support, but a substantial increase in the value of what were Income Support allowances for younger children;
- amalgamation of the system of child allowances paid to families who are out of work (Income Support) with payments made to those in work, but with low incomes. Under the new Child Tax Credit (CTC), from April 2003 all families with children and with incomes under £13,000 per year are entitled to the same level of CTC, whether in or out of work (depending only on the number of children). This is then reduced (with a withdrawal rate of 37 per cent of income over the threshold) until the credit reaches a flat rate amount (£545 per year in 2003–04) that goes to all but the highest-income families (see Figures 7.6 and 7.7 for an example of how the Child Tax Credit and Working Tax Credit compare with the Family Credit system in place in 1997). The flat-rate element is doubled in the first year of a child's life;
- maternity benefits have also been improved, eligibility widened, and entitlements lengthened; and
- increases in the generosity of other parts of the in-work benefit system to create the Working Tax Credit, going to parents working sixteen or more hours a week, and now to others without children working more than thirty hours per week, if they have low incomes. Associated with this, an additional tax credit also pays for up to 70 per cent of approved childcare costs.

As Table 9.1 shows, these changes have led to large real increases in certain parts of the cash benefit system for families with children.

For pensioners there has been a complex series of reforms affecting both incomes in the short-term and later entitlements to state pensions (see Hills 2004 for more details).

- Means-tested support for low-income pensioners through what used to be called Income Support (but then the 'Minimum Income Guarantee', and now the 'guarantee credit' element of the Pension Credit) has been made more generous. The minimum income that pensioners should be guaranteed (if they claim) has been increased, and the government has promised to increase it in line with earnings growth until at least the next general election.
- Since October 2003, means-tested support has been extended to those higher up the income scale through the new Pension Credit. As with the Child and Working Tax Credits, the impact of this is to reduce means-testing withdrawal rates for those who were already affected by them, to benefit those who were

Table 9.1. *Increases in benefits for families, April 1997–April 2003*

	April 97 (£/week, cash)	April 03 (£/week, cash)	Real increase (%)
Child element of Child Tax Credit (CTC)*			
–Under 11	12.05	27.75	102
–11–16	19.95	27.75	22
Child Benefit			
–First child	11.05	16.05	27
–Subsequent children	9.00	10.75	5
CTC maximum support*			
(16–29 hours work, two children under 11)	71.75	150.75	84
Income Support			
–Element for two children under 11	44.60	92.75	82
–Total, single parent, one child	81.80	109.10	17
–Total, couple, two children	121.75	179.10	29

* Equivalent under Family Credit in 1997.

Source: Author's calculations.

just above the previous cut-offs, but also to extend means-testing further up the income distribution.

- What was the State Earnings Related Pension Scheme (SERPS) has been reformed into the State Second Pension (S2P), the main change being that very low-earners will now accumulate greater rights than they would have done under the previous system.
- However, the almost universal National Insurance-based flat rate state pension has continued to be increased only in line with prices in most years,[5] and policy is that this should continue indefinitely.
- Pensioners have also benefited from a number of other payments or concessions, such as 'winter fuel allowances' for those over 60, and exemption from the flat-rate TV licence fee for older pensioners.

There have been more general tax reforms.

- The structure of National Insurance Contributions has been reformed to reduce payments by the lower-paid: for instance, raising the income level at which NICs become payable, and removing the immediate lump-sum ('entry fee') payment that used to apply to all those reaching that level.
- The initial income tax rate on a narrow band of income has been cut to 10 per cent, and the main rate of income tax was cut to 22 per cent in April 2000.

[5] Following the political furore when very low inflation led to a tiny cash increase in the basic pension—'our greatest mistake', as Tony Blair put it in the 2001 election campaign—there is a now a minimum 2.5 per cent cash increase in the basic pension each year. However, the fundamental policy remains that the real value of the basic pension will be constant, and so its value will fall in relation to average earnings.

However, various income tax allowances have been withdrawn (such as the previous across-the-board allowance for married couples and what was left of the tax relief on mortgage interest payments).

- In April 2003 rates of NICs paid by both employers and employees were each increased by one percentage point, with the revenue earmarked for higher spending on the National Health Service.
- An important source of new revenue was the withdrawal of what had amounted to tax exemption on the dividends from company profits received by pension funds announced in Gordon Brown's first Budget in July 1997.
- Various indirect taxes have been increased, most notably the Council Tax collected and set by local councils. These have tended to have a regressive effect, partly offsetting the progressive impact of the other measures described above (Sutherland, Sefton, and Piachaud 2003: section 5).

As far as the system of support for families with children is concerned, the overall effect has been a 'levelling up' in the treatment of two-parent and lone-parent families, of younger and older children, and of those out of work and in low-paid work. By contrast with US reforms (for instance, associated with the Earned Income Tax Credit), significant extra resources have gone to the *non-working* poor as well as to the working poor. The impact of these measures is discussed in more detail in the next section.

For pensioners, the overall effects in both the short-term and the long-term are to make the system of state support into one which is much more designed to achieve a minimum level of income for pensioners than to result in pensions related to previous earnings. This is most obviously seen through the decisions to increase and earnings-link the value of the means-tested minimum for pensioners, but to continue price-linking the basic pension. But it is also true of the long-run structural reforms to the State Second Pension and the Pension Credit. Figure 9.1 shows, for instance, a projection of what total state support would look like for single people retiring at three different dates having (unrealistically) spent their whole working lives with particular levels of earnings in relation to each year's adult (full-time) average:

- The solid line shows the position in 1978, before SERPS was introduced. Both the basic pension and the minimum income guaranteed by what was then Supplementary Benefit were around 25 per cent of average earnings, so state support was virtually flat-rate.
- The dotted line shows the position for those retiring in 1998, when earnings-related rights through SERPS were at their highest, but both Income Support and the basic state pension had fallen in relation to average earnings. State support had fallen for low-earners but had risen for higher-earners.[6]

---

[6] In fact, many higher earners would have 'contracted out' of SERPS and would receive part of the amount shown through their occupational pension schemes in return for having paid reduced NICs while they were working.

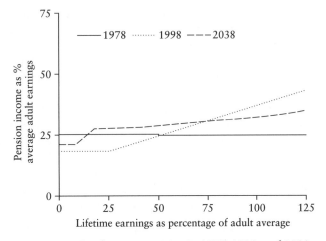

Figure 9.1. *State support: Single person retiring in 1978, 1998, and 2038*
Source: Hills (2004).

- The third (dashed) line shows a projection of state support in 2038 if current policies were continued. The minimum level of state support would, as now, be higher than in 1998 in relation to earnings. For those with lifetime earnings below three-quarters of the adult average, the level of support would also be higher than in 1998 as a result of the combined State Second Pension and Pension Credit reforms. However, for average and above-average earners, entitlements would be lower (reflecting a considerable fall in the basic pension in relation to average earnings, as well as slower accrual of rights to the State Second Pension).[7]

What perhaps stands out from the figure is the extent to which the effect of the reforms of the last few years has been to unwind the earning-related pensions introduced by Labour (and associated with Barbara Castle) in the late 1970s. They have returned the system back to giving support not so far from the original flat-rate system of 1978 (itself dating from the reforms of the Attlee government in 1948, following some of the recommendations of the 1942 Beveridge Report). The emerging system we now have does this in a far more complex way, however, with much more reliance on means-testing (the implications of which are discussed further in Section 10.4).

9.2.3 *Social Exclusion and Other Support for Children*

One of New Labour's earliest announcements was to establish the Social Exclusion Unit. Its brief has been to look at issues that cut across different government departments, except those affecting incomes, which have remained

---

[7] Again, many 'contracted-out' higher earners would actually receive less than this from the state, but would have had the offsetting advantage of lower NICs when at work.

firmly under the control of the Treasury and Department for Work and Pensions. Its reports have looked in particular at groups subject to long-term disadvantage and at contributors to it: children excluded from school; children leaving care; 16–18-year-olds not in education, employment, or training; rough sleepers; prisoners; and teenage parents. One of its main concerns has been low-income neighbourhoods, with its reports leading to the establishment of the Neighbourhood Renewal Unit with a brief to promote their revival, and to the setting of 'floor targets' for the position of low-income areas in terms of the delivery of *mainstream* services including health, education, employment, and crime prevention.

At the same time another feature of policy in New Labour's early years was a proliferation of area-based initiatives, focused on low-income neighbourhoods. For instance, Sure Start is a community-based intervention aimed at families with children aged under 4 years in low-income areas. The plan is that, by 2008, 1,700 children's centres across the country will reach more than half of all children under 4 in poverty (HM Treasury 2004: para. 5.24). The local schemes have some common elements—such as home visits to all families with new-born children—but other parts vary from area to area, depending on local preferences. Another early Treasury-led initiative, the New Deal for Communities, is spending £2 billion over ten years in thirty-nine very deprived neighbourhoods, intended to improve local employment as well as housing and the physical environment. Other area-based initiatives—'zones'—are focused on employment, education, and health.

As well as direct measures affecting family incomes, other measures to tackle underlying causes of poverty and deprivation include:

- a substantial increase (from a low base in European terms) in direct support for *childcare* for both pre-school and school-age children, as well as in indirect support through the childcare element of the new tax credits. An explicit goal of the expanded childcare provision is to raise lone mothers' employment rate to 70 per cent by 2010;
- on *early years education*, as well as Sure Start, a government promise in 1997 of at least a part-time nursery place for all 4-year-olds, to be extended to all 3-year-olds from September 2004;
- to encourage 16–17-year-olds from disadvantaged backgrounds to stay on at school, a system of *Educational Maintenance Allowances* that has been piloted and will be extended nationally from September 2004. These allowances will pay up to £30 per week to 16–17-year-olds from low-income families if they stay on at school;
- a new *Connexions* service that offers support and advice to all young people aged 13–19. Like many other recent initiatives, this started with pilot schemes in low-income areas, and was then extended across the country. Its intention is to help reduce the proportion of 16–17-year-olds who are involved in none of employment, education, or training; and

- a system of *Child Trust Funds* for all children born since September 2002. It will pay £250 into an account for all children at birth, twice this amount for those from low-income families. This will be built up with a further government endowment when children reach the age of 7, and with contributions into the tax-free accounts allowed by parents, grandparents, and others, up to an annual limit. The funds can then be drawn down when people reach the age of 18. The idea of this 'asset-based welfare' scheme is both to encourage savings and to spread asset ownership.

9.2.4 *Public spending as a Whole*

As discussed in Chapter 6, the period since New Labour was elected can be divided into two parts, so far as public social spending is concerned. In the first part, up to 1999–2000, social spending was falling as a share of GDP, from 24.5 per cent in 1996–97 to 22.9 per cent in 1999–2000 (Figure 6.3). This followed the election pledge to stick to previous Conservative spending plans for the first two years of the Parliament. This was not as rapid a fall as in public spending (Total Managed Expenditure) as a whole, so social spending grew in relation to the total (Table 6.1). Nevertheless, this was a very tight period for the public sector. Education spending fell, for instance, to its lowest share of GDP since the early 1960s (Glennerster 2002). But after 1999, social spending grew again, reaching exactly 25 per cent of GDP in 2002–03. By then, health and education spending together were their highest-ever share of GDP, 11.4 per cent. On current plans, this is intended to go further, as can be seen from Table 9.2. This shows the annual growth rates in real terms of various parts of public spending over three year periods since 1990–91. It shows the contrast between the early 1990s and the period since 1999 on the one hand, and the years just before and after the 1997 election on the other. In the middle periods, real public spending

Table 9.2. *Annual growth rates of public spending and GDP, 1990–91 to 2005–06, UK (%)*

	90–91 to 93–94	93–94 to 96–97	96–97 to 99–00	99–00 to 02–03	02–03 to 05–06 *(plans)*[a]
Health	5.0	2.0	3.2	6.9	7.6
Education	3.9	0.7	1.2	6.6	7.4
Social Protection	9.4	1.2	−0.2	3.0	1.1[b]
Defence	−2.2	−4.3	−0.6	0.7[c]	1.2
Total Managed Expenditure	4.0	1.2	0	4.3	4.3
GDP	1.1	3.3	3.1	2.1	2.6

[a] Plans from 2002 Spending Review (in resource terms).

[b] Excludes tax credits.

[c] Growth rate affected by switch to resource budgeting in 2002–03.

Sources: HM Treasury (2003*b*: Tables 3.1 and 3.3; 2002*a*: Tables B7 and A11).

grew slowly or not at all, and fell behind GDP growth. At the start of the 1990s—driven in particular by growing social security spending in the recession—it grew faster, as it did again after 1999–2000, now led by health and education spending. This is planned to continue. According to the 2002 Spending Review (HM Treasury 2002*a*), total spending will rise from 39.9 per cent to 41.9 per cent of GDP between 2002–03 and 2005–06. The bulk of the two percentage points planned increase will go to health spending (1.0 per cent of GDP extra) and education (0.7 per cent of GDP extra).

Plans do not always come to fruition, of course, but, if they did, this would take health and education spending together to 13.1 per cent of national income, compared with 10.2 per cent in 1996–97. That is an addition over and above national income growth equivalent to £32 billion at 2003–04 incomes and prices. This has been funded partly through explicit tax increases (for instance, in National Insurance Contributions in April 2003), partly through generally buoyant tax revenues (including the effects of 'fiscal drag' as well as quieter tax increases), but also through declining spending on other items, notably the parts of the social security system that remain price-linked, defence spending, and debt interest. Overall, Total Managed Expenditure would only be 0.9 per cent of GDP higher in 2005–06 than it had been in 1996–97, accounting for less than a third of the increase in resources intended for health and education.

People with low incomes are greater beneficiaries of this kind of public spending than those with higher incomes, and this 'pro-poor' bias has increased since 1996–97. Figure 8.3 suggests that public spending on health, education, and housing subsidies was 2.1 times as valuable per head to those in the poorest fifth as to those in the richest fifth in 2000–01, up from 1.9 times in 1996–97.

As well as health and education spending, a main focus has been on support for families with children and on reducing child poverty. Working out the additional resources going into the initiatives described in subsections 9.2.2 and 9.2.3 depends on what the counterfactual chosen for 'unchanged policy' would have been. For example, the Treasury (2003*a*: 107) calculates that families with children were £1,200 per year better off on average as a result of the tax and benefit reforms between 1997 and 2003 described above. The gain for those in the poorest fifth of the population is more than twice as large as the average, £2,500. This calculation is the result of comparing the actual 2003–04 system with what would have applied if the 1997–98 system had been left unchanged but simply adjusted for price inflation. In aggregate it is equivalent to a total gain to families with children of around £9 billion, or 0.9 per cent of GDP. Independent analysis suggests that, if one looks at the changes relating *only* to children (as opposed to general tax measures affecting all households), the real increase in assistance for children channelled through the tax and benefit system 1998–99 and 2003–04 amounts to £7.5 billion per year, (Figure 9.2).

However, an alternative counterfactual would be that an 'unchanged' tax and benefit system would maintain its relative generosity by adjusting benefit levels and tax brackets in line with income growth. Against this comparator, the gain

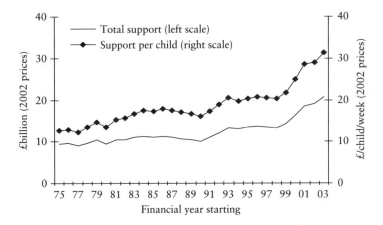

Figure 9.2. *Tax and benefit support for children, 1975–76 to 2003–04, UK*
Source: Adam, Brewer, and Reed (2002). Projected figures for 2003–04.

to families with children would be smaller. The appropriate aggregate comparison would be the change in the share of national income devoted to such assistance (in line with the health and education figures above). This comes to around 0.5 per cent of GDP for the tax and benefit measures related to children (Adam and Brewer 2004: 11). To this can be added, however, annual spending on the other measures described above: £1.5 billion on pre-school programmes; £500 million on the Connexions service; £100 million on the pilots of the Educational Maintenance Allowances (with much more to come when they are extended nationally); and £230 million on endowments for the Child Trust Funds. Overall, the change in the share of GDP since 1998 devoted to cash and services for children (excluding general education) was already 0.75 percentage points by 2003, with more to come on current plans.

9.3   POLICY OUTCOMES UNDER NEW LABOUR

The kinds of measure described in Section 9.2 are of different kinds.[8] Some might be expected to have rapid impacts—for instance, changes in the values of cash benefits—but others might only have visible impacts on life chances over many years—for instance the possible long-run effects of initiatives such as Sure Start or the Child Trust Funds. For the latter, it is clearly too early to tell whether they are having their desired effect, although there will be information relatively soon about whether their coverage is on as large a scale as planned. For the measures that affect income and living standards more directly, information is beginning to become available, and some of this is presented below. Inevitably, however, this comes from surveys and, as there is a lag in its availability, the

---

[8] This section draws heavily on analysis in Hills and Sutherland (2004).

effects of the most recent changes are not captured. Subsection 9.3.4 below contains some modelling results for potential outcomes in 2004–05 for the tax and benefit reforms implemented since 1997.

A further problem is, of course, that changes over time in the levels of outcomes such as employment or poverty are not necessarily the result of policy change. Where there is evidence that bears on this, this is also presented.

9.3.1 *Labour Market Outcomes*

The UK economy has continued to perform well under New Labour: overall unemployment (on International Labour Organization definitions) fell from over 10 per cent in 1993 and 8 per cent in 1996 to 5 per cent in 2001 and 2002; long-term unemployment fell by more than three-quarters between 1997 and 2003. By 2003 employment rates had reached 74.8 per cent, almost equalling their highest ever level (75 per cent, reached in 1990), two percentage points higher than in 1997 (DWP 2003b: 183). Within this, the employment rate of lone mothers has also increased, from about 44 per cent in 1996 to 54 per cent in 2002 (HM Treasury 2003a: chart 4.4). Note that this ten percentage point increase in the UK matches the ten percentage point increase in the labour force participation of single mothers in the USA between 1990 and 1998, but over a shorter period (Waldfogel et al. 2002). This is despite the much less coercive nature of the UK reforms. The gains in terms of the drivers of the UK's high rate of child poverty from these wider changes have been significant. For instance, the proportion of children living in workless households, which had been around 19 per cent in the first half of the 1990s, fell from 17.9 per cent in 1997 to 15.2 per cent in 2003 (DWP 2003b: 162).

These improvements cannot, however, be ascribed to the welfare-to-work initiatives by themselves: an important factor has been good macroeconomic performance. An overview of analysis of the largest New Deal programme, that for young people, concluded that total youth unemployment was 35,000–40,000 lower than it would have been without the programme, less than half of the actual fall between 1998 and 2001 (White and Riley 2002). Its *employment* effects may have been even smaller—a net increase of 17,000 on one recent estimate (Blundell et al. 2003), the difference reflecting those diverted to education or to inactivity, and those who may already have been working.

Analysis of another part of the package, the voluntary New Deal for Lone Parents, suggests that its impact was to reduce Income Support receipt by 2.5 percentage points after one year, rising to 3.3 percentage points after eighteen months (Hasluck, McKnight, and Elias 2000). A recent econometric study by Gregg and Harkness (2003) attributes five percentage points of the 6.6 percentage points increase in lone mother employment in the four years from 1998 to 2002 to the effects of policy of all kinds (not just the New Deal).

Similarly, as for 'making work pay', one econometric exercise suggests that the first stages of tax credit reform—the introduction of what was then the Working Families Tax Credit (WFTC)—led to an increase of 94,000 in employment. However, other tax and benefit reforms between 1997 and 1999 had effects mostly offsetting this, leaving a net increase in employment of 23,000, less than 0.1 per cent (Brewer, Clark, and Goodman 2003). The effect was not larger partly because incomes of those out of work were also increased, so differentials between incomes in and out of work have not increased as fast as in, say, the USA in the 1990s. The main impact of the WFTC was thus not necessarily to boost employment rates but rather to increase the incomes of those in low-paid work.

Such findings suggest that employment schemes have had positive effects, and are good value for money, but cannot be expected to transform employment rates by themselves, and are by no means the sole cause in the improvement in the labour market. What is interesting about the reform package described in Section 9.2 as a whole therefore, is perhaps that it has had the impacts on poverty outcomes described below *without preventing* the labour market improvements that have happened at the same time.

9.3.2 *Changes in Overall Inequality and Poverty*

At the time of writing, there have neither been policies directed specifically at reducing overall inequality of incomes, in terms of the gap between rich and poor, nor any evidence that such inequality is diminishing. Rather, indices of overall income inequality continued to rise between the mid-1990s and 2000–01 (Figure 2.9). As a contributor to this, the ratio between high and low earnings continued to increase up to 2002 (Figure 4.3). The share of the very richest 1 per cent of the population's share of total personal income continued to rise between 1996 and 1999 (Table 2.6).

As discussed in detail in Chapters 2 and 3, however, what has happened across the income distribution has not been uniform. While the very top has continued to move away from the middle, the bottom of the distribution has been catching up on the middle. As a result, poverty rates have begun to fall. Figure 3.2 showed the most recent data on trends in overall and child poverty in the UK against both relative and absolute standards. It illustrates the contrast between the period before and after 1996–97. In relative terms, child poverty rose from 12 per cent in 1979 (itself up from 8 per cent in the late 1960s)[9] to peak at 27 per cent (before housing costs) in the early 1990s. Since then it has fallen unevenly, down to 21 per cent in 2001–02 and 2002–03, compared with 25 per cent in 1996–97, the year before New Labour came to power. Against the fixed real threshold, despite growth of nearly 40 per cent in average incomes over the period, nearly as many, 30 per cent, of children were below the line in 1992/93 as in 1979. Numbers have fallen since then, and strikingly, between

[9] Gregg, Harkness, and Machin (1999: Figure 1), who, however, use a poverty line of *50 per cent* of *mean* income.

1996–97 and 2001–02, the proportion *more than halved*, from 25 per cent to 12 per cent.[10]

Analysing what had contributed to the fall in child poverty against a relative line over the shorter period between 1996–97 and 2000–01, Sutherland, Sefton, and Piachaud (2003) suggest that little of it was due to demographic change, and that all kinds of family with children had reduced poverty rates, particularly lone parent families and couples with three or more children. Just over half the improvement was due to the kinds of employment improvements described above (more if the income measures were taken after housing costs), and the rest to the impact of the tax and benefit reforms. Using a different approach and looking at a shorter period, Dickens and Ellwood (2003: Table 4) suggest that the benefit effect was a greater proportion of the total. They suggest that all of a three percentage point drop in child poverty between 1997 and 2000 could be accounted for by improvements in benefits, but that one percentage point of this was offset by the impact of rising real wages on median incomes, and hence the relative poverty line. Demographics had a small adverse effect, reduction in wage inequality a small positive effect, and changes in work patterns accounted for one percentage point of the fall. Subsection 9.3.3 below looks more closely at the impact of the tax and benefit reforms by themselves.

9.3.3   *Wider Indicators of Well-Being*

The figures shown in Chapter 3 (Figure 3.2) suggest that by 2001–02 overall poverty had fallen a little in relative terms, but child poverty was already falling more quickly. In absolute terms, child poverty was falling fast. Other evidence on family living standards confirms this picture. Table 9.3 presents findings from a new survey, the Families and Children Study (FACS), which asks about indicators of deprivation and financial stress. Only figures for lone parents are available on a consistent basis since 1999. The findings are startling. On all of the deprivation indicators there has been a substantial drop in the proportion reporting that they do not have and cannot afford various items.[11] The proportions of lone parents without, and unable to afford, a cooked main meal every day, a telephone, or toys and sports gear for their children more than halved between 1999 and 2002, and the proportions unable to afford the other items also dropped substantially, and between each of the four years. Similarly, the indicators of financial stress all improved markedly, again in nearly all cases

---

[10] These figures use net incomes before housing costs. On the after housing costs measure, relative child poverty fell from 34 per cent to 28 per cent between 1996–97 and 2002–03, and child poverty measured against a fixed real line from 34 per cent to 17 per cent (on the 60 per cent of median lines).

[11] Nearly all of these items, apart from a car or van, were seen as 'necessities' by a majority in a 1999 survey that asked a sample of the population whether everyone should be able to afford them (Gordon et al. 2000). They were not asked specifically about a 'best outfit' for children, or about two pairs of all-weather shoes for children, but did say that these were necessities for adults.

Table 9.3. *Trends in deprivation indicators for lone parents, 1999–2002, GB (%)*

	1999	2000	2001	2002
Without and unable to afford:				
Cooked main meal every day	7.5	5.7	4.5	3.0
Phone (including mobile)	9.0	6.7	5.1	4.0
Weatherproof coat for each child	9.0	6.9	6.3	5.0
Best outfit for children	20.1	19.0	15.2	12.8
Toys and sports gear for children	24.4	21.1	15.1	11.9
Two pairs all-weather shoes for each child	24.6	18.9	15.3	13.3
Car or van	33.7	30.4	25.9	23.8
One week holiday, not with relatives	74.0	68.5	62.1	58.1
Financial problems				
Problems with debts almost all time	14.5	13.3	10.2	12.2
Always run out of money before end of week	27.1	24.1	21.0	19.3
Not managing financially	34.7	30.1	24.1	18.3
Situation worse in past 12 months	29.0	27.1	24.2	22.6
Worried about money almost all the time	44.7	38.1	32.6	29.8
Never have money left over	47.9	40.4	34.2	17.4

Source: McKay and Collard (2003: Table 7.1).

from year to year. Most strikingly, the proportion saying that they 'never have money left over' fell from 48 per cent to only 17 per cent.

Because of more limited coverage in the earlier years, the survey does not give equivalent data for all couples with children. However, a composite index of deprivation using these and other indicators shows a *greater* drop in what the researchers call 'severe hardship' between 1999 and 2001 for non-working couples with children than for lone parents (Vegeris and Perry 2003: Figure 6.4).[12] For lone parents, the proportion classed as being in severe hardship dropped from 41 per cent to 28 per cent; for non-working couples with children, the drop was from 41 per cent to 22 per cent.

The impact of government policy towards poverty and social exclusion is being monitored through a wider range of indicators across a wider range of aspects of well-being as well. Table 9.4 compares the results from two exercises of this kind. The first of these is from the official *Opportunities for All* report, now published annually by the Department for Work and Pensions. The 2003 results shown in the table suggest a position where the majority of indicators for the population as a whole—thirty-two of the forty-four for which there are data—have been improving, not just over the most recent year for which data are available (typically around 2001 or 2002), but also over the medium term

---

[12] 'Severe hardship' is defined by the researchers as reporting three or more problems under nine indicators (three of housing problems; two of financial problems; and four reflecting levels of material deprivation, fixed over time, that would put people in the most deprived 7.5 per cent in 2001 within separate domains covering food, clothing, consumer durables, and leisure activities).

Table 9.4. *Trends in wider measures of well-being and exclusion, GB*

	Improving in medium term		Steady in medium term		Worse in medium term	
	Latest steady/ improving	Latest worse	Latest steady/ improving	Latest worse	Latest steady/ improving	Latest worse
(a) Opportunities for All indicators, 2003						
Children and young people	12	1	3	—	—	—
Working age	12	—	5	—	—	—
Older people	6	—	1	—	—	—
Communities	2	1	1	—	—	—
All	32	2	10	0	0	0
(b) New Policy Institute, *Monitoring Poverty and Social Exclusion 2003*						
Incomes	2	—	3	—	—	—
Children	4	1	2	—	1	1
Young adults	2	1	2	—	1	—
Adults, 25 to retirement	6	—	1	—	—	1
Older people	—	—	4	—	1	1
Communities	5	—	4	—	—	1
All	19	2	16	0	3	4

Sources: DWP (2003*b*); Palmer et al. (2003).

(roughly since Labour came to power). Most of the rest are steady in the medium term, and either steady or improving in the most recent year. None of the indicators chosen is now worsening in the medium term, and only two are shown as worse in the most recent year: the proportion of teenage parents not in education, employment, or training; and the rate of domestic burglaries (reversing an improving trend).

These are, of course, the results from an officially chosen set of indicators, always open to the accusation that those that were easier to achieve had been selected, or that judgements as to which were 'improving' or 'steady' were open to favourable shading. For instance, the one indicator for children (children excluded from school) that had been shown as worsening in the most recent year in the government's 2002 report has now been replaced by a different indicator (school attendance), which has been 'steady'.

The picture given by the independent analysis by the New Policy Institute (NPI) in its annual report on *Monitoring Poverty and Social Exclusion* in the second part of the table, is not quite so favourable, but is none the less encouraging. Of the 44 indicators (using official data sources, and several of them overlapping with the official set) they choose across six domains, nineteen are reported as improving and sixteen as steady in the medium term (and not worse in the latest year). The NPI suggests less favourable trends for nine indicators:

- Low birth weight children, adult obesity, help from social services for older people at home, and homelessness (households living in temporary accommodation and statutory homelessness) are all shown as worse both in the medium term and in the most recent year.
- Children in young offender institutions, problem drug use by 15–24-year-olds, and benefit take-up by older people have got worse over the medium term, although were steady in the most recent year.
- Children permanently excluded from school and young adults wanting paid work are shown as worse in the most recent year, reversing a previously improving trend.

Nonetheless, the picture is still a positive one—and can be contrasted with that given by the NPI's first exercise of this kind in 1998, when nineteen of the forty-four indicators then used were shown as improving in the medium term (up to the mid-1990s), compared with twenty-one now; eleven were steady, compared with sixteen now; and fourteen were deteriorating, compared with only seven now (Howarth et al. 1998).

9.3.4 *Projected Changes in Poverty, 1996–97 to 2004–05*

The data on poverty rates referred to in subsection 9.3.2 are, of course, retrospective, and policies have continued to develop since the period they refer to. In particular, the tax credit system was reformed and made more generous in April 2003. The government's key child poverty target relates to the year 2004–05. In order to take account of recent policy change and other economic changes, this subsection presents simulation results projecting the position in 2004–05, using the microsimulation model, POLIMOD.[13]

Table 9.5 presents projected relative poverty rates in 2004–05 (against a line of 60 per cent of the median) using the two income measures with which the government is monitoring its child poverty reduction target. Such projections are subject to significant uncertainties. In particular, not only is it hard to predict factors affecting the incomes of the poor population (such as employment rates and trends in low pay, as well as benefit rates), but also many others can affect the level of the median from which the relative poverty line is calculated.[14] The way the projections are done assumes *unchanged* population composition over the period, and so does not take account of changes resulting from, for instance,

---

[13] See Redmond, Sutherland, and Wilson (1998) for a description of POLIMOD, Sutherland (2004) and Sutherland, Sefton, and Piachaud (2003) for more detailed discussion of an earlier version of some of the projections.

[14] The projections embody, for instance, the assumption that average earnings continue to grow at the same rate as in the most recent year, at 3.7 per cent. This is a slower rate of growth in real terms than for several years. If actual earnings growth were to be faster, the relative poverty line would be higher, and with it the proportion measured as in relative poverty.

Table 9.5. *Modelled estimates of poverty in Britain, 1997 and 2004–05, GB*

	Whole population	All children	Children in lone parent families	Children in two-parent families
(a) Incomes before housing costs				
Percentage in poverty:				
1997	18	25	40	20
2004–05	14	15	22	13
Change	−4	−9	−18	−7
Number in poverty (millions):				
1997	10.2	3.2	1.2	1.9
2004–05	8.1	1.9	0.7	1.3
Change	−2.1	−1.2	−0.6	−0.7
(b) Incomes after housing costs				
Percentage in poverty:				
1997	24	33	63	24
2004–05	19	25	48	18
Change	−5	−8	−15	−6
Number in poverty (millions):				
1997	13.6	4.3	1.9	2.4
2004–05	10.9	3.3	1.5	1.8
Change	−2.7	−1.0	−0.5	−0.6

Note: Poverty line is based on modelled current incomes. 2004–05 based on projections, including parameters of 2004–05 tax-benefit system as announced up to March 2004. Modelling takes account of changes in income levels, but uses fixed composition of population (in terms of employment rates and demographic composition). Totals may not add up due to rounding.

Source: Sutherland (2004: Table 1), using POLIMOD.

changing employment rates or family composition. They are based on the levels of benefits, tax credits, and tax structure as announced up the Budget of March 2004.

They suggest that there will be further reductions in relative poverty by 2004–05 beyond those we have already seen in figures for 2001–02. For instance, from a level of 25 per cent of children in relative poverty in 1996–97 on the before housing costs measure, and 21 per cent in 2002–03 shown in Figure 3.2, the projection for 2004–05 is for a further fall to 15 per cent. Other things (such as employment rates) being equal, this would give a total fall since 1996–97 of nine percentage points, or just over a third, and a reduction of 1.2 million. This suggests that on this basis the government will hit its target of cutting child poverty by a quarter since 1998–99 (when it was slightly lower than in the base year used in the table). On the alternative after housing costs basis the reduction is eight percentage points, just under a quarter of the higher base, so in these terms the target would be marginally missed (unless there are further policy changes or other economic changes affecting 2004–05 incomes).

In an earlier exercise using a similar approach, Sutherland, Sefton, and Piachaud (2003:Table 13) suggested that the drop in child poverty by 2003–04 might be almost as much as this, eight percentage points on both income measures. That there is little difference between the projections for the two years, despite, for instance, the improvements in the Child Tax Credit for 2004–05 announced in December 2003, is partly the result of new data availability. But part of it illustrates the challenge to governments attempting to hit targets for *relative* poverty. In the absence of explicit policy change, most parts of the cash benefit system in the UK are price-linked. But if median incomes are growing in real terms, this means that those who remain mostly dependent on benefits fall behind the median, and so relative poverty rates will tend to rise. If there had *not* been improvements to tax credits in 2004–05, the government might have 'hit' its key target a year early, but then missed it, in after-housing-costs terms, at least, in the year it was set for (Brewer 2003, 2004).

Whether the target is just hit or just missed, the table shows significant improvement over the period, whether one looks at incomes before or after housing costs, particularly for children, whether in lone parent or two-parent families. This is not simply a result of part of the population being moved from just below to just above a particular poverty line. Figure 9.3 shows the modelled cumulative income distributions for the whole population and for children in relation to relative poverty lines (60 per cent of median income) in 1997 and 2004–05. In both cases, the whole distribution is shifted to the right: that is, there are fewer people with incomes below any given real level. The shift to the right at the bottom of the distribution has been faster than the growth in median incomes, and hence in the poverty line, so relative poverty rates are projected to fall.

The diagrams show the 'moving target' effect of a relative poverty line. For the whole population, 18 per cent of the 1997 distribution is shown below the 1997 poverty line. In the projection for 2004–05, 11 per cent would be below the same line. But, because of overall income growth, the 2004–05 relative poverty line will be higher, and 15 per cent are projected to remain below it. The fall in *relative* poverty is thus projected to be half that in *absolute* poverty. The lower panel shows a similar, but more dramatic, story for children: against a fixed real line, the poverty rate falls from 25 per cent to 10 per cent, but against a moving relative line the fall is only to 15 per cent.[15]

This analysis also shows what has been happening to poverty gaps, the amount by which those counted as poor fall short of the poverty line (see Section 3.2 and Table 3.3). To avoid distortions from what may be unreliable data for the very bottom of the distribution, the *median* poverty gap ratio gives the proportion of the poverty line by which the *typical* poor person falls short. On the projections used in Figure 9.3, not only is the proportion of the whole population counted as

[15] By comparison with the actual figures for 2001–02 presented in Figure 3.2, these projections therefore suggest that there are further falls in relative poverty rates to come by 2004–05, although they do not suggest much fall against a slightly higher absolute line than had already been achieved by 2002–03. This may be unduly pessimistic, resulting from the way in which the projections allow only for the changes in levels of different parts of household income between the years, but not for changes in the composition of the population (such as rising employment rates).

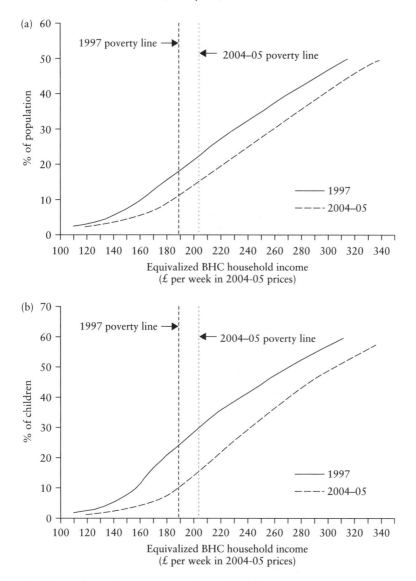

Figure 9.3. *Cumulative income distribution and relative poverty lines under 1997 and 2004–05 policies and incomes, GB (a) Whole population (b) Children*
Source: Sutherland (2004: Figure 1), using results from POLIMOD.

poor lower with 2004–05 incomes, but so is the poverty gap ratio— falling from 17 per cent in the modelled results (a little below the actual figure for 1996–97 shown in Table 3.3) with 1997 incomes to 16 per cent in 2004–05 (before housing costs; after housing costs the reduction is four percentage points, from 23 per cent to 19 per cent). For children the reduction is larger: by two and eight percentage points before and after housing costs respectively.

9.3.5 The Impact of Tax and Benefit Changes

The modelling described above also allows comparison of poverty rates under the *actual* tax and benefit system expected to apply in 2004–05 with those that would have been expected if the tax and benefit system Labour inherited in 1997 had been left unchanged (apart from price indexation of its parameters). This gives a measure of the impact of policy change by itself (against this particular counterfactual).

Figure 9.4 shows the distributional effect of the change. It shows the average percentage difference in income between the two systems for each tenth of the income distribution. The results are shown for all individuals and for children in particular (using the incomes of the households they live in). All income groups up to the eighth are better off under the 2004–05 system on average, and the gains are somewhat larger for children. The differences are far larger in percentage terms at the bottom than the top. On this basis, policy has had a very progressive effect. For instance, household incomes for children in the bottom tenth are more than 28 per cent higher than they would have been under 'unchanged policies'. Even at the median the difference is around 4 per cent. By contrast, the top tenth is slightly worse off than it would have been with the price-indexed 1997 system. The final pair of bars show that aggregate household income was about 3 per cent higher under the 2004–05 system than it would have been (over 5 per cent for children).

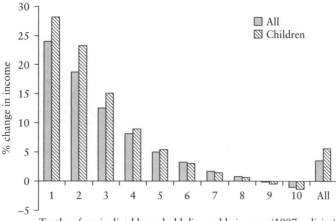

Figure 9.4. *Impact of 2004–05 tax-benefit system compared with price-indexed 1997 system, GB*

Source: Sutherland (2004: Figure 2), using results from POLIMOD.

Table 9.6 presents the effects of these policy changes on poverty rates. The projections for 2004–05 are as before in Table 9.5, but they are shown by comparison with what would have happened if the (price-indexed) tax and benefit system of 1997 had still applied in 2004–05. If this had happened, poverty rates would have been *higher* in 2004–05 than they had actually been in 1997—for example, 27 per cent of children would have been poor (before housing costs). This implies a *larger* 'policy impact'—a twelve percentage point reduction as a result of policy change—than is projected as the actual change over time. In other words, if nothing had been done, relative poverty would have increased. In fact, it is falling.

These calculations of the distributional effects of the policy changes since 1997 depend, however, on a particular specification of what the tax and benefit system would have looked like in the absence of reform. In Figure 9.4 and Table 9.6, the comparison is with a *price*-indexed version of the 1997 system.

Table 9.6. *Estimates of poverty rates in 2004–05: 2004–05 and price-indexed 1997 systems, GB*

	Individuals with income below 60% of population median			
	Whole population	All children	Children in lone parent families	Children in two–parent families
(*a*) Incomes before housing costs				
Percentage in poverty:				
1997 system	20	27	47	20
2004–05 system	14	15	22	13
Impact of reforms	−6	−12	−25	−7
Number in poverty (millions):				
1997 system	11.4	3.4	1.4	2.0
2004–05 system	8.1	1.9	0.7	1.3
Impact of reforms	−3.4	−1.5	−0.8	−0.7
(*b*) Incomes after housing costs				
Percentage in poverty:				
1997 system	26	35	68	25
2004–05 system	19	25	48	18
Impact of reforms	−7	−10	−21	−6
Number in poverty (millions):				
1997 system	14.8	4.5	2.1	2.4
2004–05 system	10.9	3.3	1.5	1.8
Impact of reforms	−3.8	−1.2	−0.6	−0.6

Note: All incomes as modelled for 2004–05. 1997 system based on parameters of tax and benefit systems as in May 1997, uprated for price inflation only. 2004–05 system based on parameters as announced up to March 2004. Totals may not add up due to rounding.

Source: Sutherland (2004: Table 2), using POLIMOD.

This is an obvious starting point, and the one which is used by the Treasury in its calculations of this kind. However, it is not the only comparator, nor even the most logical. For instance, if the key parts of the tax and benefit system are adjusted only for price inflation while real incomes are growing, three things happen. First, cash benefit levels fall further and further behind average living standards, so that, in the absence of any other change, relative poverty will tend to increase. As a corollary, social security and tax credit spending will tend to fall in relation to GDP. But, at the same time, direct tax revenues will tend to increase not only in line with income growth but actually faster than that, as, for instance, tax-free allowances cover a smaller share of people's incomes. So the price-indexed base (as Table 9.5 shows) is one where relative poverty would increase at the same time as the public sector's finances moved more and more into surplus.

An alternative comparator, and perhaps a more natural way of measuring the effects of structural reforms, would instead be the 1997 system indexed by *earnings* growth. If you like, this compares actual 'New Labour' policies in 2004–05 with what might have happened under an 'Old Labour' policy of increasing cash benefits in line with earnings growth, but without any structural reform. Figure 9.5 shows the impact of the projected 2004–05 system compared with an earnings-indexed base (earnings grew by 34 per cent over the period, compared with a 19 per cent increase in prices).

By comparison with the earnings-indexed base, the impact of New Labour's reforms is smaller than shown against the price-indexed base in Figure 9.4. First, average household income as a whole is only slightly higher under the projected 2004–05 system than it would have been with the earnings-indexed base.

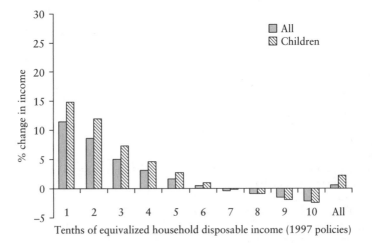

Figure 9.5. *Impact of 2004–05 tax-benefit system compared with earnings-indexed 1997 system, GB*

Source: Sutherland (2004: Figure 3), using results from POLIMOD.

Second, the gains at the bottom are smaller: for instance, individuals in the poorest tenth are only 11 per cent better-off than they would have been with earnings-indexation, rather than the 24 per cent shown in the comparison with the price-indexed base. In line with this smaller gain at the bottom, the impact of changed policies on poverty rates is also smaller. For instance, the child poverty rate would be 23 per cent under the earnings-indexed base, and so the reduction to 15 per cent under the projected 2004–05 system represents only two-thirds of the reduction compared to the price-indexed base shown in Table 9.5. Nonetheless, the reformed structure does imply lower poverty rates, particularly for children, than the earnings-indexed base. What also comes out from Figure 9.5 is that the reforms have been redistributive from higher-income households to lower-income ones: the bottom six-tenths of the distribution are better off than they would have been with earnings indexation, the top four groups worse-off.

In summary, even against the alternative comparator that takes the 1997 system and increases all benefit rates and tax thresholds in line with earnings growth, the projected 2004–05 system is more progressive in its impact, and implies lower poverty rates (particularly for children) than there would have been without the structural reforms. With the lack of public support for blanket increases in benefit rates discussed in Section 6.2 in mind, one way of describing this is to say that New Labour has achieved more through its policy mix that has gone with the grain of the more progressive aspects of public opinion than a less generally politically popular alternative would have done (Hills 2002*a*).

Whether this policy will prove to be sustainable in the longer run, and whether 'more of the same' can make further progress towards reducing child poverty, are more open questions. Chapter 10 discusses some of the constraints and challenges for future policies. Some of these relate to demography and the ageing population, some to public attitudes of the kind discussed elsewhere in the book, including towards the effective extension of means-testing that has allowed policies to have a progressive impact, with only limited effects on overall tax rates.

9.4 SUMMARY

- New Labour promised little on poverty and inequality in its 1997 election campaign, pledging to stick to tight Conservative spending plans for two years, and not to raise income tax rates. Its initial measures were focused on the labour market, introducing the New Deal welfare-to-work measures.
- Subsequently, it became much more ambitious, notably through Tony Blair's 1999 pledge to 'end child poverty' within twenty years, with a shorter-term target adopted of cutting child poverty in relative terms by a quarter by 2004–05. Its policies have remained selective, however, with neither blanket increases in social security benefits or other public spending, nor more general pledges to reduce poverty or inequality.
- A series of reforms to taxes and benefits for families with children have resulted in higher Child Benefit and in the Child Tax Credit, of equal value to

families out of work and to those in low-paid work. The system of cash support for children has been equalized upwards between one- and two-parent families, younger and older children, and those in and out of work.

- Other reforms have moved support for pensioners towards a flatter system, less related to previous earnings. In contrast to the explicitly flat-rate state pension system applying up to the late 1970s, the emerging system involves a much wider spread of means-testing.

- Overall public social spending fell from 24.5 per cent to 22.9 per cent of GDP in Labour's first two years, but had reached 25 per cent again in 2002–03, with health and education spending at their highest ever level. Current plans are for the two together to reach 13.1 per cent of GDP by 2005–06, compared with 10.2 per cent in 1996–97. Less than a third of this growth is planned to come from higher public spending in total; the rest is coming from lower spending elsewhere.

- The share of national income going on cash support for children through the tax and benefit system had risen by 0.5 per cent of GDP by 2003, with half as much again for other measures aimed at lower-income families with children.

- Overall inequality of incomes and earnings continued to rise over New Labour's first term, driven particularly by inequality at the top. However, those with low incomes began slowly to catch up on the middle, and relative poverty to fall, particularly for children. By 2001–02, relative child poverty on one measure was down to 21 per cent, compared with 25 per cent in 1996–97. Against a US-style threshold fixed in real terms, child poverty more than halved between the two years.

- Indicators of deprivation for families with children are also showing sharp reductions. The proportion of lone parents unable to afford certain key items more than halved between 1999 and 2002. The proportion that 'never have any money left over' fell from 48 per cent to only 17 per cent. One index suggests that the proportion of lone parents in 'severe hardship' dropped from 41 per cent to 28 per cent, and the proportion of non-working couples with children from 41 per cent to 22 per cent, over the two years 1999 to 2001, when improved benefits and tax credits were introduced. The great majority of a range of indicators of well-being and social exclusion have improved or remained steady since New Labour came to office.

- Projections suggest that relative child poverty may fall by eight or nine percentage points between 1997 and 2004–05, hitting the government's target of reducing it by a quarter between 1998–99 and 2004–05 (or almost hitting it on an after housing costs basis).

- A continuing issue is that, with most social security benefits indexed to prices, those remaining dependent on them tend to slip behind average incomes, and so relative poverty rises in the absence of other changes in policy or in factors such as the labour market.

- Comparing the projected 2004–05 tax and benefit system with that of 1997 adjusted for *price* inflation shows that the poorest tenth of the population are on average 24 per cent better-off than they would have been (28 per cent for children in the poorest tenth). Those in the top tenth are about 1 per cent worse-off than they would have been.

- An alternative comparator is the 1997 system indexed by *earnings* growth. Against this comparator, the structural reforms in the seven years since 1997 have a smaller impact, but are more clearly redistributive from those with high to those with low incomes. The bottom tenth is 11 per cent better off than it would have been under this alternative, but the top four-tenths are worse-off.
- One way of describing this is to say that New Labour policies have had more progressive effects overall than an alternative of uprating benefits in line with earnings growth, but without structural reform, and this has been achieved while going with the grain of public attitudes, which the alternative would not have done.

FURTHER READING

For a more comprehensive analysis of the impact of New Labour's policies towards poverty and social exclusion, see *A More Equal Society? New Labour, poverty, inequality and exclusion,* edited by John Hills and Kitty Stewart (Policy Press, forthcoming). For detailed analysis of recent developments in labour markets and employment policy, see *The Labour Market under New Labour: The State of Working Britain,* edited by Richard Dickens, Paul Gregg, and Jonathan Wadsworth (Palgrave Macmillan, 2003). Another overview of New Labour's social policies in its first term is: *Evaluating New Labour's Welfare Reforms,* edited by Martin Powell (Policy Press, 2002).

The government's own assessments of its progress can be found in a variety of documents, notably in the *Red Book* published each year at the time of the Budget, and in the *Pre-Budget Report* published later in the year. The annual *Opportunities for All* report (published by the Department for Work and Pensions) contains both assessment of progress on its selected indicators and commentary on its policies. A report by the Social Exclusion Unit, *Preventing Social Exclusion* (Cabinet Office, 2001) gives the government's view of problems and progress on social exclusion in New Labour's first term.

Independent assessments can be found in a variety of sources. These include: Holly Sutherland, Tom Sefton, and David Piachaud, *Poverty in Britain: The Impact of Policies since 1997* (Joseph Rowntree Foundation, 2003); Mike Brewer, Tom Clark, and Alissa Goodman, 'What Really Happened to Child Poverty in the UK Under Labour's First Term?' *Economic Journal,* 113 (2003), F240–57; and Mike Brewer, Tom Clark, and Matthew Wakefield, 'Social Security under New Labour: What Did the Third Way Mean for Welfare Reform?', *Fiscal Studies,* 23 (2002), 505–37.

I discuss the relationship between New Labour's policies and public attitudes in more detail in 'Following or Leading Public Opinion? Social Security Policy and Public Attitudes since 1997', *Fiscal Studies,* 23 (2002), 539–58.

10

Constraints and Pressures

10.1 AFFLUENCE AND ECONOMIC GROWTH

The pressures on social spending and on distribution do not stand still. This chapter looks at how the constraints and pressures under which policy operates may change in the coming years. First, there is an apparently obvious escape route from rising pressures on social spending: economic growth. There is a temptation to say that, while problems demanding spending may not be soluble today, a future 'growth dividend' will make life easier tomorrow, so that promises or aspirations that could not be met now could be in future. Of course, economic growth does generate more resources for government. Even if the tax ratio stays constant as the economy grows in real terms, real tax revenues will rise. For some parts of the tax system, revenues may grow even faster than the economy through 'fiscal drag'—if tax-free income tax allowances rise only with prices, for instance, a greater share of rising real incomes will end up in the tax net. Similarly, as people become better-off, they tend to spend a smaller proportion of their income on items such as food that are free of VAT, so VAT revenues may also grow relatively fast. But other taxes are less buoyant. Council tax, for instance, is charged as an amount set in pounds for properties in different bands, according to their values in 1991. Unless the amount of tax is increased each year not just with prices but with incomes, the yield of the tax will tend to fall as a share of national income. This is exactly what has happened to 'business rates', which fell from about 2.5 per cent of GDP in 1991–92 to about 1.8 per cent in 2002–03 (HM Treasury 2003a: Table C8; and earlier equivalents).

Overall, it is reasonable to assume that without too much political pain the tax ratio can remain constant, and so tax revenues will grow in line with economic growth. The problem is that the demands on government increase with economic growth as well. Public spending falls into two kinds: spending on goods and (particularly) services, such as providing health care or education; and transfer payments, such as retirement pensions, other cash benefits, and tax credits. Economic growth and rising general living standards affect demands for both kinds of spending.

For public spending on services, the big issue is public service pay. For a while, it is possible for a government to hold back public sector pay and to use higher real spending to increase, say, the numbers of nurses or teachers. In other words, the 'growth dividend' can be spent on more extensive public services. But, as Figure 10.1 illustrates, public and private sector pay rarely stay apart for

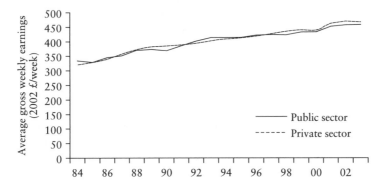

Figure 10.1. *Public and private sector pay, 1984–2003 (all full-time workers), GB*
Source: ONS (2003).

long. The comparison in the figure is a crude one, showing average weekly earnings for all employees in each sector without, for instance, any allowance for differences in qualifications, experience, or responsibility, or in benefits such as pension rights. It does not, therefore, show whether either sector is 'better' or 'worse' paid than the other after allowing for such factors. But what the remarkable way in which the two lines track each other suggests is that, if public pay does fall behind, sooner or later there tends to be a catch-up: a period when public spending on pay rises in real terms without there being any extra staff to show for it.

This may be driven either by recruitment needs or by pressure from unions and others for fairness in relative pay. For a while, relative public pay can lag behind but, if the effect of that is high staff turnover, declining morale, or exit of the most skilled staff, constant real spending may mean a declining *quality* of public services. Simply to hold quality constant real spending may have to rise. This also depends, of course, on what happens to productivity. The main reason that the economy—and real wages in the private sector—are growing will be higher productivity. To the extent that public sector workers (or those providing the services to the public sector) can also become more productive, higher real wages will go along with a better quality of service—for instance, as a result of better training or better equipment. But here there are two problems. One is that some public services are highly labour-intensive, and it can be argued that there may be limits on how much technological substitution and productivity growth there can be (Baumol 1967). Whether or not this is so, the second is perhaps more fundamental. This is that our aspirations for the quality of public services grow with affluence. Doctors, nurses, teachers, and street cleaners may all become more skilled, better equipped and more productive over time, providing a higher-quality service. But this may simply be the least that we expect—just as public sector pay keeps up in real terms, so we expect as a minimum the quality of public services to keep up as well, and are not very impressed when it does not. Matching the reasonable assumption that tax revenues can grow, other things being equal, along with economic growth, a base assumption may be that public spending to provide services will do the same, just in order to stand still in terms of public satisfaction.

From the point of view of those running the public finances, it may be worse. As we grow richer, the evidence suggests that we want to devote a greater proportion of our consumption to health care and education. This can be seen in three ways. Richer nations tend to spend a greater share of GDP on them. Second, historically their share of the economy has grown over time. As Section 6.4 showed, total 'welfare activity', public and private together, has grown rapidly as a share of national income in the last twenty years, despite the way governments have held back public spending. Third, spending patterns across households show that personal spending on health and education is 'income elastic'—spending on them rises more rapidly than income, when poorer and richer households are compared. Of course, the future may be different from the past, but the factor driving this—that other demands are becoming satisfied, while these are not—may well apply for some time to come. It certainly seems to apply in countries that are already much richer than the UK. If these services are best provided through the public sector (Barr 2004; Burchardt, Hills, and Propper 1999), this will mean continuing upward pressure on public spending, not just in real terms but as a share of national income. Instead of affluence helping reduce the pressures on public finances, it may make them worse.

Another source of pressure linked to affluence is harder to predict. Will economic growth continue to be linked to increased inequality in market incomes, and hence to greater needs for redistributive transfers if inequality in disposable incomes is not to rise too? Current conventional wisdom is that it will. For instance, the processes driving the growing wage inequality in the UK and USA described in Chapter 4 are thought of as linked to economic growth. Techno-logical change has been 'skill-biased', so that those with higher skills have seen the greatest increases in productivity and pay, while those with lower skills have found that technological change leads to reduced demand for their labour. Tech-nical advance has simultaneously led to economic growth and to greater market income inequality (Section 4.3).

However, as Chapter 4 explored, this is by no means a complete picture of what has actually happened in the last quarter-century. Other, less inexorable, factors have played their part as well. But there is no reason to assume that the future will inevitably be like the immediate past. It is not so long ago that the conventional wisdom among many economists was expressed by the 'Kuznets curve'—as soci-eties became richer beyond a certain point, their income distributions became *more* equal (see Atkinson 1975: 249, for a discussion). Economic development led to a spread of skills and resources beyond an elite and, once this had gone far enough, the effect was to compress income distributions as the bottom half of the population caught up. Simply looking at the post-war trends in income inequality shown in Figure 2.9 should give pause for thought. Someone with evidence on what had happened in the period up to the mid-1970s might incorrectly have extrapolated a continuing trend towards more equality. Someone with evidence on what had happened up to the early 1990s might incorrectly have extrapolated a continuing rapid trend towards more inequality. In 2004, the market pressures towards a richer but more unequal 'winner takes all' society look strong and may continue. But, equally, market pressures may go the other way. So far, for instance, the 'graduate premium' on wages in Britain has increased despite a large increase in the supply of graduates. But at some point the expansion of higher education may lead to graduate supply outstripping demand, and to a reduction in the relative pay of graduates. Equally, technological advance could take different forms, leading to substitution for more *skilled* labour. Highly skilled translators might become redundant as a result of combined voice recognition and translation computer software. The same might happen to other professionals such as lawyers or university lecturers, or even doctors if computer diagnosis became reliable. Equally, future trade pressures might affect workers of particular kinds in a different way from the last twenty years. The truth is that we do not know, and in thinking about the future we have to allow for the possibility that the underlying pressures towards market inequality—and through them on the public finances— might go either way.

Another aspect of the public finances is more open to control, however. This is the relative value of benefits and transfers. One way in which economic growth can help the public finances is if the real value of benefit rates is left fixed while other incomes and tax revenues grow. This was the most important way in which the lid was kept on public welfare spending under the Conservative governments in the 1980s and 1990s (see Chapter 6). Fixing the real value of some benefits has created part of the fiscal headroom used by the Labour government since 1997 substantially to increase the value of others (see Chapter 9). There is, however, a cost to this, amply illustrated in the story told in Chapters 2 and 3 of rising inequality and relative poverty. If the only aim of public policy were reduction of poverty against an absolute threshold, or to set a fixed real minimum to living standards, simply price-linking pensions, other benefits, and tax credits might be sustainable. But if poverty is seen in relative terms—as the evidence presented earlier on public attitudes suggests it is, and as is currently embodied in government targets for reducing child poverty—then constant real benefit levels will not be sustainable indefinitely.

Equally, nearly half of social security spending is explicitly on pensions, and nearly two-thirds of it goes to those over working age (Figure 6.6). Much of what social security does is about redistribution across the life cycle, helping people to smooth their living standards as they move into retirement. It is not obvious that the demand for such smoothing would necessarily be expected to fall as we become more affluent. It might even increase for the same reasons that better-off households tend to save more. But even if our objective was a constant degree of income smoothing, this would imply that pensions and other transfers to the elderly should hold their value relative to other incomes, not fall behind them. What will happen to state pensions spending is explored in more detail in Section 10.3 below.

To summarize, economic growth does much less to resolve the conflicting pressures on revenues and demands for services than is often supposed. Of itself, affluence puts upward pressure on demands both for spending on public services and for transfers, and this can absorb most of the headroom created by higher tax revenues. It may even go further than this. Of course, lack of growth can be even worse if the effect is increased unemployment, higher social security spending on the unemployed, and falling tax revenues. But relying on a 'growth dividend' to make the political problems of matching spending and revenues easier in the future than they are now is an illusion.

10.2 A DEMOGRAPHIC TIME BOMB?

In discussions about future pressures on social spending, the factor that is most often cited is not affluence but the ageing of the population and what is sometimes described as the 'demographic time bomb'. Much public spending, notably on pensions and health care, goes on the elderly. Current forecasts are that there will be many more people over the present state pension age in the future, and a very large proportionate increase in the numbers of the very elderly, who are those with the largest amounts spent on their health care and on other forms of personal or nursing care, much of which comes from the state. Putting those two together, we can expect a very large—perhaps even unsustainable—increase in social spending.

Given that, it is at first sight surprising that the Treasury's recent forecasts of the long-term state of the public finances are so reassuring. For instance, the Treasury recently published projections that allowed for the effects of changing demography on education, health, and long-term care spending, as well as for the effects of current pension policy and the rapid increase in health spending in relation to GDP that the government has committed itself to following the Wanless Review (Wanless 2002) of health spending. These projections, shown in Table 10.1, suggest that total government spending would rise from 38.6 per cent of GDP in 2001–02 to 40.6 per cent of GDP by 2011–12, and then fluctuate around that level over the following forty years. Most of that increase would in fact occur in the earliest years (see Table 9.2). On the revenue side, the Treasury's central projection is for a slight fall in revenue as a share of GDP over the next fifty years, but it argues that this is conservative, as it does not allow for several factors that may make total revenue rise as a share of GDP without a change of policy. These include real fiscal drag (as discussed above) and the tax revenues that may come from more mature private pension schemes as they pay out (taxable) pensions in future. On balance, there is little sign from these figures of either an unsustainable rise in public debt or the need for large increases in tax rates to avoid it.

Table 10.1. *Official projections of public spending, 2001–51, UK (% GDP)*

	Health	Education	Pensions	Long-term care	Other	Total
2001–02	6.3	4.6	5.0	0.9	21.7	38.6
2011–12	8.2	5.9	5.0	1.2	20.3	40.6
2021–22	8.5	5.6	4.8	1.2	19.6	39.6
2031–32	9.3	5.8	5.2	1.2	20.0	41.4
2041–42	9.7	5.7	5.0	1.2	19.3	41.5
2051–52	9.8	5.7	4.8	1.2	19.3	40.8

Source: HM Treasury (2002*b*: Table 6.1).

There are, however, two very important assumptions built into these forecasts. They do allow for health and education costs to rise with income growth as well as for demographic change (as projected in 2002, before the significant increases in projected life expectancies announced by the Government Actuary's Department in December 2003 that are used below). However, projected pensions spending (shown in more detail in Figure 10.4) is based on the assumption that key items within it, such as the level of the basic state retirement pension, continue to be indexed to prices, not to incomes. Similarly, much of the fall in 'other spending' in relation to GDP shown in the table results from the assumption that 'most non-pension social transfers will rise in line with prices after 2007–08'. Given the Treasury's other assumptions about economic growth, this implies that benefits such as Child Benefit or Income Support for the unemployed would fall considerably relative to other incomes over the period. In other words, the 'demographic time bomb' is assumed to be defused by allowing the social security system to become progressively less valuable in relative terms, with the obvious potential impacts on inequality and relative poverty.

What if this escape route were not available? Figure 10.2 shows a way of gauging the potential effect of the changing age structure of the population. The top panel shows average public spending by age group on education, health care, and social security as it was in 2001–02.[1] There is a pronounced age-related pattern: around £3,000 per head for those aged under 30, around £2,000 per head for those aged 30–59, but then a steep rise to over £8,000 for those aged over 75. The lower panel shows the proportion of the population projected to be in each five year age range in 2001 and in 2051. A smaller proportion of the population is projected to be in each age range up to 50–54 in 2051 than now, and a higher proportion in each older age range. Two and a half times the proportion of the population is projected to be over 80 (10.5 per cent) in 2051 as in 2001 (4.2 per cent).

Combining the two panels of the figure allows a simple calculation: what would be the increase in public spending on these three items as a share of

---

[1] The figures are those also used to construct the projections of spending by generation in Section 8.5 above (Smithies 2004*a*). For data reasons, all education spending on those aged 25 or more is allocated to 25–29 age group, so in reality spending for this age group is lower and for later ones it is higher.

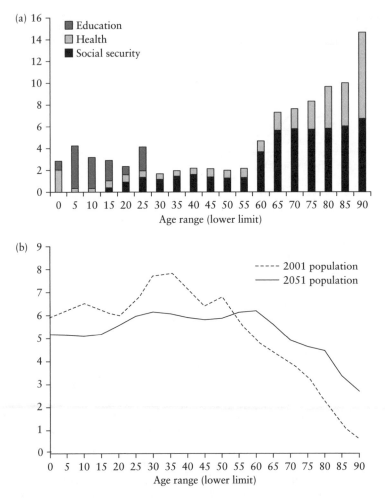

Figure 10.2. *Social spending by age (2001) and population age structure, 2001 and 2051 projection, GB*
(a) 2001 spending (£ per person) (b) Percentage of population in range
Sources: Smithies (2004a) for social spending; GAD (2003) for population structure.

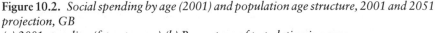

national income if we had the population structure of 2051 now, but continued to spend the same amount on each person of a given age as we did in 2001–02? This is equivalent to projecting what spending would be in 2051 if spending per head at a given age rose in line with GDP per capita. This is broadly similar to the Treasury's starting point in its calculations in Table 10.1, but without the fall in the relative value of some pensions and other benefits it incorporates.[2] The answer is that average spending per head of the total population would be

---

[2] It also differs in not allowing for the impact of the Wanless Review or any 'compression of morbidity'.

Table 10.2. *Projected social spending, 2001–51, GB (% GDP)*

	Base: Constant age-related spending (relative to GDP per capita)					Variations:		
	Health (1)	Education	Social security (under 65)	Social security (65+)	Total	Health (2)	Health (3)	Social security (under 65, price-linked)
2001	6.1	4.7	5.5	5.5	21.8	6.1	6.1	5.5
2011	6.3	4.4	5.7	6.0	22.4	8.4	9.3	4.7
2021	6.8	4.2	5.5	7.0	23.5	9.0	9.9	3.7
2031	7.3	4.1	5.4	8.2	25.0	9.7	10.7	3.0
2041	7.8	4.0	5.1	8.9	25.8	10.4	11.5	2.3
2051	8.1	3.9	5.2	9.1	26.3	10.8	11.9	1.9

Note: Health (1) assumes constant age-related spending from 2001. Health (2) takes current government spending plans up until 2007–08, then constant age-related spending from that base. Health (3) takes projected spending from the Wanless Report up to 2021, then constant age-related spending from that base. Price-linked social security based on assumed 2 per cent per year growth in real GDP per capita.

Source: Author's calculations based on age-related spending and population projections as in Figure 10.2.

£4,400, 21 per cent higher than actual spending in 2001–02. In total this corresponds to 4.5 per cent of GDP.[3] The first five columns of Table 10.2 show how this builds up over the fifty years.

This gives a first measure of the potential scale of the 'demographic time bomb'. There are two ways of looking at it. One is to say that, even if we assume that social security benefits maintain their relative values over the next fifty years, that there is no change in pension ages (which there actually will be for women in any case), and that there is no 'compression of morbidity' (so longer life expectancy does not reduce health care needs at any given age), total spending on the three main parts of social spending as a share of national income needs to increase by only just over a fifth to cope with all of the effects of ageing over the next fifty years. This is an increase of less than 0.4 per cent per year. It is only half as much again over *fifty* years as the 2.9 percentage points of GDP that the current government plans to add to health and education spending in just *six* years between 1999–2000 and 2005–06 (see Table 9.2). It is only half of the 9 per cent of GDP added to spending on education, health, and social security in the *twenty-five* years up to 1976 (Figure 6.2). If added to UK social spending as it was at the end of 1990s, it would have taken the UK's spending above the levels then spent by Portugal, Spain, and Greece, but would still have left it well below those in most other EU countries (see Figure 6.8), nearly all of which face far greater pressures from ageing over the next fifty years.

[3] Notably, the increase in life expectancies announced by the Government Actuary's Department in December 2003 contributed 1.1 percentage points of GDP to this increase. Under the previous population projections, the increase would have been 3.4 per cent of GDP. This compares with a projection made ten years ago using the same approach of an increase of 3.8 per cent of GDP over fifty years from 1991 spending levels using the then population projections for 2041 (Hills 1993: 12).

Seen in all these terms, the demographic 'time bomb' is a bit of a damp squib, and indeed the calculation does serve to put panics about the fiscal effects of ageing into perspective. There is no doubt that, as a nation, we could make the decision that we could preserve age-related public spending in this way if we wanted to do so without the costs becoming unsupportable.

The other way of looking at the calculation, however, is to ask what we would have to do to tax rates to cover such increase costs. At 2003–04 income levels, 4.5 per cent of GDP is £50 billion. If spread across all taxes (and there were no adverse effect on tax revenues), it would mean every single tax rate rising by an eighth. At the most politically alarming, if concentrated only on income tax, it would mean increasing revenues—and income tax rates—by more than two-fifths (42 per cent), increasing the basic rate from 22 per cent to 31 per cent (and others in line). An immediate increase of 9p in the basic rate of income tax would undoubtedly be political suicide for a government that proposed it, which gives another way of looking at the scale of the problem. However, this would be required gradually over a fifty year period—the political pain would be much less acute, although much more drawn out. It might also be noted that, if this were the only factor driving the overall tax ratio, the increase from its 2003–04 level of 35.8 per cent would take it to 40.4 per cent, only 1.5 per cent of GDP above its peak of just under 39 per cent reached under Mrs Thatcher in 1984 (Figure 7.1). Again, it is very hard to argue that such level is *infeasible*, if we chose it.

The calculation is the result, however, of one particular set of assumptions, which can be queried in a number of ways. First, it assumes that the cost of increased health and pension spending on the elderly is partly offset by reduced education spending on the young (as there are fewer of them). It does not allow for the kind of increased education spending per head above national income growth that many argue will be crucial to future economic success—for instance, as a result of more staying on at school after age 16, or greater participation in tertiary education. The 0.8 per cent of GDP fall in spending on education shown in Table 10.2 may well not materialize (indeed, the Treasury assumes that there will be a 1.1 per cent of GDP increase; Table 10.1).

Second, it does not allow for the increases in health spending already built into the government's spending plans following the Wanless Review (Wanless 2002). The sixth column of Table 10.2 shows what would happen to health spending if it grew across the board to 8.2 per cent of GDP by 2007–08 as currently planned, and then followed demographic changes as before. The effect is to increase 2051 spending by a further 2.7 per cent of GDP. The seventh column shows what would happen if health spending followed the full Wanless projections to reach 9.9 per cent of GDP in 2022–23, and then followed demographic change. This takes health spending to 11.9 per cent of GDP in 2051, 3.8 per cent of GDP higher than in the base projection, and nearly twice the level of 2001.

Third, on the other hand, it does not allow for any improvement in health—and so reductions in health care needs—at any given age, despite the large increase in life expectancy built into the population projections. This seems pessimistic. The Royal Commission on Long-Term Care (1999: para. 2.23) found that 'the best evidence we can find . . . suggests that the factors, which are causing us to live longer are also resulting in the extra years of life being free from severe disability . . . There is reason for optimism here but we sound a note of caution'. The Wanless Review suggested that this 'compression of morbidity' could reduce health spending by up to 10 per cent by 2022 for those aged over 65. This would by itself reduce the projected health spending shown in the sixth column of Table 10.2 by 1 per cent of GDP in 2051.

Fourth, it does not allow for current plans for the future of pensions. As discussed in Chapter 9, these have complex effects. On the one hand, the basic pension is planned to remain price-linked, and women's pension age is to rise to 65 between 2010 and 2020. Both of these would reduce costs. However, the State Second Pension will become more mature, adding to spending at any given age as time goes by. Similarly, the Pension Credit will become more important over time, partly absorbing savings from the fall in the relative value of the basic pension. Recent government forecasts (based on earlier population projections than those used in Table 10.2) suggest that on current plans government spending on pensions would remain much the same share of GDP over the next fifty years. The realism of this is discussed in Section 10.3 but, if it happened, it can be seen from the fourth column of Table 10.2 that this would remove three-quarters of the overall increase in social spending by 2051 in the base projection.

Fifth, the projections assume that all social security benefits are income-linked rather than price-linked. The final column of Table 10.2 shows that by 2051 price-linking could mean that spending on non-pensioner social security was 3.3 per cent of GDP lower than in the base projection in the third column. This is the kind of 'saving' built into the Treasury's projections of 'other' spending in Table 10.1. It would mean, however, that the relative value of benefits would be 63 per cent lower than they were in 2001 (assuming 2 per cent annual growth in real incomes). The equivalent in comparison to today's living standards would be to expect a couple receiving Income Support to live on £32 per week after housing costs (rather than the actual £86 per week). It would be likely to greatly worsen relative poverty.

Finally, the figures do not allow for one part of social spending that is very sensitive to the number of very elderly people, long-term care. The Treasury's base projection shown in Table 10.1 is that this could mean an extra 0.3 per cent of GDP of spending by 2051–52, although, if there was no compression of morbidity of the kind they and others assume, the increase could be as high as 0.8 per cent of GDP (HM Treasury 2002b: chart 6.8). Ruth Hancock et al. (2003) suggest that, with no change in policy, public spending on long-term care could rise in their base case by 0.2 per cent of GDP. There is, however, a wide 'funnel of doubt', with potential changes ranging from a *fall* of 0.1 per cent of GDP to a rise of 0.9 per cent.

It is easy, therefore, to construct scenarios in which the impact of demographic change and other policies is 3 per cent or more of GDP greater than the 4.5 per cent resulting from the crude calculation. On the other hand, favourable movements in health care needs at any given age, the working out of current pension policies, and price-linking of other parts of social security could bring the increase down closer towards the Treasury's 2.2 per cent of GDP shown in Table 10.1. On balance, the former direction seems more likely. This does not affect the fundamental point, however: the pressures from an ageing population are undoubtedly upwards, but they are taking place over a long period, and could be accommodated if we chose to do so.

10.3   AGEING AND PENSIONS

As Table 10.2 illustrates, three-quarters of the increase in social spending that would result if age-related spending remained the same while the population aged would come from pensions and other benefits for the elderly. In the lower panel of Figure 10.2, the Government Actuary Department's most recent projection (2003) suggests that the proportion of the population aged 65 or over will rise from 15.9 per cent in 2001 to 25.7 per cent in 2051. In the shorter term, the number of people over state pension age (with the planned increase in women's retirement age allowed for) per person of working age is projected to rise from 0.30 in 2002 to 0.40 by 2031. This gives a straightforward measure of the potential impact of ageing on pensions spending: within thirty years there will be a third more people over state pension age per person of working age than now. This is a result both of increased longevity and of falling fertility rates.

Another way of dramatizing the change we are facing is to put the question the other way round: what would have to happen to pension ages to keep the number of pensioners fixed? In other words, if we were prepared to support only a fixed number of pensioners, for how long would successive cohorts have to queue before they were allowed to retire? Figure 10.3 provides the answer to this thought experiment, showing the (unisex) pension age that would keep the number of pensioners stable at the number they actually were (with differential ages for men and women) in 1981 or in 2001. For the first line, a unisex pension age of 63 in 1981 would have to have risen to 65 by now, and to rise further to 72 by 2031. If we start from 2001, a unisex pension age of 63 would have to rise to 71 by 2031 to stabilize the number of pensioners at its current level. Roughly, for each four years later in the date of someone's birth, he or she would have to queue for an extra year to get a pension. This is greater than the rate of increase in life expectancy over the period. One might have expected the increase to be only a proportion of this, but this is also the period when the post-war 'baby boomers' reach retirement, so part of the lengthening queue is to cope with what would otherwise be a bulge in those reaching pension age. In subsequent years a similar, but less dramatic, effect continues as a result of later falls in fertility rates.

No one is actually suggesting such a radical solution to paying for pensions, but it does illustrate graphically the scale of the problem. At its heart, whether

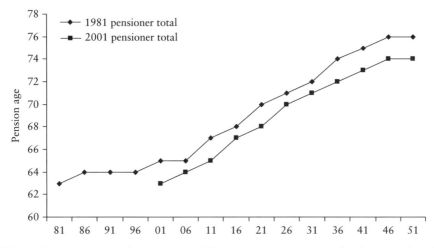

Figure 10.3. *Queuing to be a pensioner: Unisex pension age required to keep number of pensioners constant, 1981–2051, GB*

Source: Author's calculations based on GAD (2003).

we pay for pensions publicly or privately, as we live longer, there is an inescapable choice between three options (or a combination of them):

- *Spreading the jam more thinly.* We can continue to pay in the same shares of our incomes through taxes and national insurance or private pension contributions, and spread the fixed results of this over more pensioners or over a longer period, so that pensioner incomes fall in relation to other incomes.
- *Increasing the amount of jam.* We can maintain relative pensioner living standards and spend longer in retirement, but at the cost of higher taxes and/or pension contributions.[4]
- *Waiting longer for the jam.* We can decide that, as our total lives grow longer, so our working lives should lengthen by at least a proportion of the increase, and so retirement ages should rise.

Current plans for public pensions (DWP 2002*d*) are essentially based on the first of these options, although there is an element of the third, as state pension age for women will rise from 60 to 65 between 2010 and 2020. As Figure 10.4 shows, the government projects that, on its current plans, public pension spending of different kinds will remain much the same share of GDP over the next

---

[4] Another way of increasing the amount of jam is of course, to have a larger economy, that is, to organize ourselves in a way that increases future incomes. But note that if people's concern is with the *relative* incomes of pensioners, or with income smoothing as they enter retirement, higher average incomes will help less than might be hoped, as the target incomes of pensioners will increase too. This is avoided only to the extent that the higher national income does not accrue as net income to those of working age, but takes the form, say, only of productive investment.

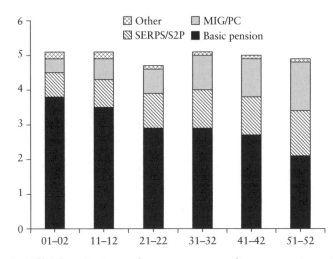

Figure 10.4. *Official projections of government spending on pensions, 2001–02 to 2051–52, UK (% GDP)*

Source: DWP (2002d: Figure A3.1).

fifty years, despite the increase in the proportion of the population over pension age. As Figure 9.1 and the discussion around it explained, this is being achieved through a rather complex series of reforms which protect the relative incomes of the poorest pensioners but which reduce the state support going to those with higher incomes. They flatten out the relationship between lifetime earnings and state support in retirement. In other words, the thinner spreading of the jam is selective, affecting those on average and higher incomes rather than those with low lifetime incomes.

A result of this is that the public finance problem facing the UK from ageing is apparently entirely different from that facing other countries in Europe. Table 10.3 shows EU projections originally made in 2001 of future public spending on pensions as a share of GDP. The UK is unique in having a projection of *lower* future spending. These projections do not take account of legislation introduced after 2000, and so do not include, for instance, the costs of Pension Credit for the UK, but even a constant share of GDP as in Figure 10.4 would be remarkable. The country with the otherwise smallest change between 2000 and its peak is Italy, with a rise from 13.8 per cent of GDP now to 15.7 per cent in 2030. In Greece, in the absence of reform, spending would virtually double from an eighth to a quarter of GDP across the period. For the EU as a whole, the projected rise is from 10.4 per cent of GDP—already nearly twice the UK level—to 13.6 per cent in 2040.

Part of the reason for the UK's position is somewhat less rapid ageing. In other European Union countries (apart from Denmark, Luxembourg, and Sweden), the number of people aged over 65 per person aged 15–64 increases even more

Table 10.3. *EU projections of public pensions spending, 2000–50 (% GDP)*

	2000	2010	2020	2030	2040	2050	Peak change
Ireland*	4.6	5.0	6.7	7.6	8.3	9.0	+4.4
UK	5.5	5.1	4.9	5.2	5.0	4.4	−1.1
Luxembourg	7.4	7.5	8.2	9.2	9.5	9.3	+2.2
Netherlands	7.9	9.1	11.1	13.1	14.1	13.6	+6.2
Sweden	9.0	9.6	10.7	11.4	11.4	10.7	+2.6
Spain	9.4	8.9	9.9	12.6	16.0	17.3	+7.9
Portugal	9.8	11.8	13.1	13.6	13.8	13.2	+4.1
Belgium	10.0	9.9	11.4	13.3	13.7	13.3	+3.7
Denmark	10.5	12.5	13.8	14.5	14.0	13.3	+4.1
Finland	11.3	11.6	12.9	14.9	16.0	15.9	+4.7
Germany	11.8	11.2	12.6	15.5	16.6	16.9	+5.0
France	12.1	13.1	15.0	16.0	15.8	n/a	+4.0
Greece	12.6	12.6	15.4	19.6	23.8	24.8	+12.2
Italy	13.8	13.9	14.8	15.7	15.7	14.1	+2.1
Austria	14.5	14.9	16.0	18.1	18.3	17.0	+4.2
EU	10.4	10.4	11.5	13.0	13.6	13.3	+3.2

* Figures are % of GNP.

Source: European Union (2003: Table 8).

rapidly than in the UK over the next fifty years (European Union 2003: Chart 3). But the main reason is the structure of public pensions. For people with lifetime earnings at most levels apart from the very lowest, UK state pensions are less generous than those elsewhere in Europe or indeed than in many other countries in the industrialized world (OECD 2001*b*: Charts 3.1–3.3). This is particularly true for those with average or above-average earnings. Unlike most other countries, the UK relies on funded private sector pension schemes (and occupational schemes for public sector workers) to provide the bulk of income replacement in retirement for most average and higher-paid workers. One of the assumptions built into current policy is that payments from private sector pension schemes will rise as a share of GDP in coming decades, helping to protect relative incomes in retirement despite the increase in the number of pensioners.[5]

That the UK does not face the increase in *public* pension costs—and hence in taxes and National Insurance Contributions—faced by other countries does not mean that it has 'solved' the pensions problem. Rather, it takes a different form. If indeed it is payments from private sector pension schemes that are to rise to cope with increasing life expectancies, then what is being paid into such schemes by employers and employees will have to rise (quite apart from any extra contributions which have to be made now to cope with the deficits that most

---

[5] The initial report of the Independent Pensions Commission, to be published in the autumn of 2004, will examine the prospects for success of this strategy.

pension funds face against their existing liabilities following the crash in the stock market values between 2000 and 2003). The scale of the required increase is not always appreciated, but follows from exactly the same logic as that which drives the projected increase in public sector pension costs elsewhere in Europe shown in Table 10.3. What makes the problem worse is that it is not obvious that public perceptions of required contribution rates have yet adjusted to cope with the changes in life expectancy that have *already* happened.

Figure 10.5 compares the ages to which people initially in the middle of their working lives, aged 45, might have expected to live to in 1981 and 2001 (under the official population projections made in 1982 and in 2003 respectively). The top panel shows the position for all people, the lower two panels that for men and women separately. Back in 1981, only 29 per cent of 45-year-olds could expect to reach the age of 85, for instance. In the most recent projections, 53 per cent of those aged 45 in 2001 can expect to do so. In 1981, the median life expectancy of a 45-year-old man was to age 75.[6] In the latest projections, half of men aged 45 in 2001 are expected to live to 84. The median expected length of survival after 65 has nearly doubled, from ten to nineteen years. For 45-year-old women, median expected survival after 65 has increased by a third, from seventeen to twenty-three years.

Even if the impact of the stock market falls between 2000 and 2003 or reduced expectations of prospective investment returns are not taken into account, such large gains in prospective lengths of retirement imply that the contribution rates required to provide a given level of pension are much larger than they were only twenty years ago (and help explain why annuity rates are much lower than they were). Table 10.4 shows illustrative calculations of the contribution rates that might be required to fund a pension from age 65 of half of (level) lifetime earnings. For simplicity, it is assumed that real net investment returns equal the rate of earnings growth and that pensions are linked to earnings growth after retirement.[7] The contribution rates shown are based on contributions being made from ages 25 to 64, and on expected survival rates up to 65 (for contributions) and then beyond for 45-year-olds, given population forecasts at the two dates. They do not allow for survivors' pensions or other common elements of actual pensions. For men, the results are particularly dramatic. Using 1981-based population projections, a combined employer and employee contribution rate of 15.4 per cent of earnings would have been enough. By 2001, this had risen to 22.5 per cent (using the 2003 projections from the Government Actuary). Over just twenty years, contribution rates should have risen by a full seven percentage points of salary. For women, with

---

[6] This median life expectancy is on a *cohort* basis, taking account of expected improvements in mortality in subsequent years. It contrasts with published *period* life expectancies, which use mortality rates at all ages at a given date. Mean period life expectancies for men aged 45 in 1981 were, for instance, 73.7.

[7] The former increases contribution rates over what more realistic assumptions might produce; the latter has the opposite effect, as very few actual pensions are so generously indexed after retirement.

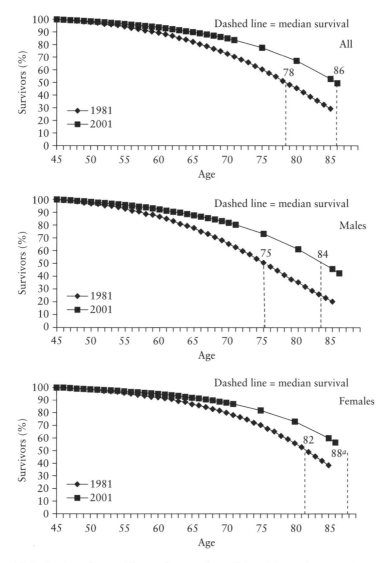

Figure 10.5. *Projected survival rates for people aged 45, 1981 and 2001, UK*

Note: [a] Estimate extrapolates beyond the range of GAD projections.

Source: GAD (2003) and earlier equivalents, and author's calculations.

longer prospective lengths of retirement even from a common age of 65, the increase would be from 22.0 per cent to 26.3 per cent. A unisex contribution rate would have to rise by something between these, or by more than five percentage points of income.

There is more to come. The 2003 population projections from the Government Actuary suggest that men aged 45 in 2021 will have median life expectancy to

Table 10.4. *Required contribution rates for earnings-linked pension from age 65 given life expectancies in year reached 45 (%)*

	Men	Women
Aged 45 in 1981	15.4	22.0
Aged 45 in 2001	22.5	26.3

Source: Own calculations using survival rates to 65 and mean (cohort) life expectancies estimated from GAD population projections (GAD 2003, and earlier equivalents). See text for basis of calculation.

age 85.7, an extra 1.5 years compared with 45-year-olds in 2001.[8] This would not be as rapid an increase in life expectancy as we have seen in the last twenty years, but contribution rates would still need to keep on rising beyond those shown in Table 10.4 to deliver as generous pensions from age 65. The implication is that, if we are hoping that funded private pensions will fill the gap left by the falling relative value of state pensions for average and higher earners, private contribution rates not only should have been increasing at least as fast as in the table but they should continue to increase further in future. The numbers involved are large, not so dissimilar to the increases in tax rates that other countries in Europe are facing to fund public pensions, for the obvious reason that they are a manifestation of the same problem.

Whether this is actually what will happen is debatable. First, there is little sign that public perceptions of the rising cost of a pension from a fixed age have adjusted as much as implied by such calculations over the last twenty years. Rather, the buoyancy of the stock market in the 1990s—and 'irrational exuberance' about its future level—lulled people into a false sense of security that pensions could be afforded without major changes in contributions. Second, the reaction of many private sector employers to the stock market crash has been to start paying in extra contributions to their pension funds to make up deficits in respect of their *existing* employees, who continue to build up rights to good 'defined benefit' pensions, based on a percentage of final salary from a fixed age. However, most such schemes are now closed to *new* members, in other words, younger workers or more recent recruits. Such employees are now within a different kind of pension scheme, one based on 'defined contributions'. Not only does this transfer a great deal of risk from employer to employee, but typically the contributions that employers make into such schemes are *lower* than the value of the promises they were making to members of the old schemes. In other words, the effective rate of contribution, far from rising to cope with increased life expectancy, is actually lower for younger workers.

---

[8] Information kindly supplied by Government Actuary's Department for cohort expectations of life consistent with the projections in GAD (2003). For women aged 45 in 2021 the comparable figure is 89.4 years, a gain of 1.1 years from 2001.

A major issue for pensions policy is that, in about twenty years time, a cohort of reasonably paid private sector workers will start reaching what they expect to be their retirement age with far smaller pension rights than their predecessors. At that point, their choices may reduce to two:[9] to carry on working if they can (in other words, a de facto increase in retirement age); or to retire on much lower incomes than their predecessors (perhaps partly augmented by increased means-tested benefits, at the cost of higher public spending). For public sector workers, final salary pension schemes have so far been retained for new as well as existing workers. Some of the lower pension ages are being raised towards 65 for new public employees, but the main impact of higher life expectancy and reduced investment returns has been an increase in actual or notional contributions paid on behalf of public sector workers. For some, this has had an immediate impact—absorbing, for instance, significant proportions of the real increases in education spending discussed in Chapter 9. For others, the impact will be delayed, with higher taxes implied in future to maintain, for instance, unfunded civil service pensions (on the assumption, of course, that the rest of the population is prepared to see taxes increase to meet such obligations).

Given all this discussion, there is an obvious solution to longer life expectancy combined with apparent unwillingness to contemplate higher future taxation or to increase private pension contribution rates, which is to postpone retirement. Although this does not solve problems such as the impact of the 'baby boom' generation hitting retirement, it would obviously help. However, it raises two further issues. The first is that it is the effective age of retirement that matters for all of this, not the official pension age. Raising the age at which people receive something called a 'pension' would make little difference to the public finances if people still stopped working at the same age and received some other form of social security payment, such as Incapacity Benefit or Income Support (although raising the age might still give an important signal to younger workers).

Second, the impact of increased pension ages would have varied impacts between different social groups, which has important political implications. The problem is illustrated by Figure 10.6. This shows ONS (2002) calculations of life expectancy beyond the age of 65 for men and women in social classes I and V at different dates.[10] These are unfortunately not available for someone in mid-life, which is what would be most relevant to thinking about political reactions to changing pension ages. However, the combination of life expectancy at birth and of those who have reached 65 tells the story. Men in social class I saw their life expectancy beyond 65 increase from seven to thirteen years (at birth), or from fourteen to nearly eighteen years for survivors to age 65, between the mid-1970s and the late 1990s. But for men in social class V the *proportionate* gains in life expectancy after 65 (measured at birth) have been much larger: from little over

[9] A third choice might, of course, be to use the political muscle of being a larger part of the voting population to change the rules of the game and to achieve higher state spending on pensions.
[10] These life expectancies are on a period basis, using current mortality rates for each age at the dates given.

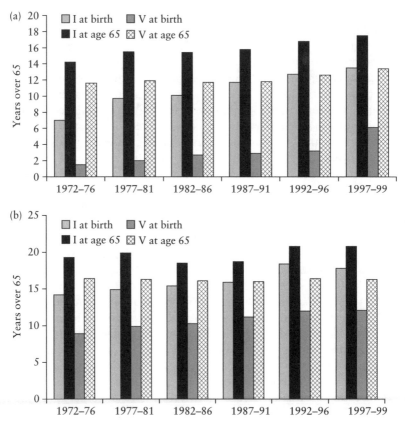

Figure 10.6. *Life expectancies beyond 65 at birth and age 65 by social class, 1972–76 to 1997–99, England and Wales (a) Males (b) Females*
Note: Life expectancies are on period basis (taking current mortality rates for all ages at each date).
Source: ONS (2002).

a year to six years (but only from eleven to thirteen years for those actually making it to 65). The effect of greater life expectancy combined with a fixed pension age has been to generate a bigger proportionate gain in potential future pensions for young men in social class V than for those in class I. The differences in trend for women are less dramatic, but class-based differences in life expectancy remain, and if anything have widened over the period.

A corollary of differential life expectancies is, however, that a simple increase in pension ages—to address the rising costs discussed above—would hit those in social class V much harder than those in social class I. For instance, an increase in pension age from 65 to 70 would, if we use these life expectancies, reduce years of receipt from eighteen to thirteen for professional man aged 65, or by a little over a quarter. But for a 65-year-old manual worker, the reduction from thirteen to eight years would be a cut of nearly two-fifths. This differential is a major political factor in considering changes to the state pension age.

10.4 INCENTIVES AND MEANS-TESTING

A different set of constraints arises from the practicalities of 'targeting' public spending on those with low incomes through means-testing of one kind or another. As Chapters 7 and 9 outlined, this has been an important part of how New Labour has achieved more redistributive policies while avoiding large increases in overall public spending and hence general taxation since 1997. This is one of the areas where policy has been out of line with what appear to be quite strongly held public beliefs, in this case against the extension of means-testing (Section 6.5). There may be limits to how much further this strategy can be pushed.

Figure 10.7 gives a first illustration of the problem. It corresponds to Figures 7.6 and 7.7, which showed the relationship between gross and net income for a family with two children aged under 11 under the tax and benefit systems of 1997–98 and 2003–04 (both at 2003–04 prices). This figure shows the implied 'effective marginal tax rates' at different gross earnings levels under the two systems: for every £1 in extra gross income, how much of this results in higher taxes or in reduced tax credits and benefits? As we saw before, the new system is considerably more generous to low-income families than the old one. It also has a shorter income range over which those in work are subject to effective marginal tax rates of nearly 100 per cent. But the diagram also shows that the cost of both of these is a much wider income range over which such a family would be facing a rate of 70 per cent. For the case shown, this extends up to £436 per week, or in other words to well beyond median adult full-time earnings (which were £394 in April 2003 for men and women combined).

This is just one case. For those without children or with fewer children, the income range affected by such high rates would be smaller, but for those with more children it would be wider. Table 10.5 shows the Treasury's calculations of the total numbers affected by effective marginal tax rates within different ranges before and after recent reforms. It shows the success of recent policy in reducing the numbers facing the very high marginal tax rates that are most likely to affect behaviour and cause the most resentment. But it also shows the increase, from 20,000 to 1,475,000, in the numbers facing rates of 'over 60 per cent', but not 'over 70 per cent' (most of which will actually be facing 70 per cent, as in Figure 10.7).[11]

This is only one aspect of the way in which recent policy has increased the effective marginal tax rates on different kinds of people. First, as discussed in Chapter 9 (see Figure 9.1 and the discussion around it), state pensions are becoming less related to people's lifetime earnings than they were in 1998. Part of what

---

[11] It is notable that, in equivalent tables published in Budget documents up to 2001, when the key rate was 69 per cent the figures were given for '70 per cent or more' rather than 'over 70 per cent' as they are now when many people face 70 per cent.

Table 10.5 *Effective marginal tax rates, working families,
1997–98 and 2004–05 tax and benefit systems, UK*

	1997–98 system	2004–05 system
Cumulative numbers		
Over 100%	5,000	0
Over 90%	130,000	50,000
Over 80%	300,000	200,000
Over 70%	740,000	270,000
Over 60%	760,000	1,745,000
Numbers in ranges		
Over 100%	5,000	0
91–100%	125,000	50,000
81–90%	270,000	150,000
71–80%	440,000	70,000
61–70%	20,000	1,475,000

Note: Figures are for families with at least one member working sixteen or more hours per week, allowing for Treasury estimates of take-up rates for mean-tested benefits.

Source: Based on HM Treasury (2003c: Table 4.2).

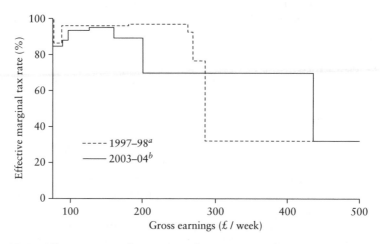

Figure 10.7. *Effective marginal tax rates under 1997–98 and 2003–04 systems*

[a] In 1997–98 system, effect of Family Credit withdrawal could be delayed up to six months.
[b] In 2003–04 system, effect of tax credit withdrawal could be delayed until next tax year (for increases in annual income above original assessment of up to £2,500).

Source: Author's calculations (see Figures 7.6 and 7.7).

many people paid in additional National Insurance Contributions used to result in higher later pensions—it was not so much a tax as a form of compulsory saving. For those contributing now, what they will get out will be less related to what they pay in, so this no longer applies so strongly.

Second, in addition, the effect of the Pension Credit reforms of October 2003 is to reduce the number of people who stand to see no gain at all from any additional pension they accumulate because they end up on the 100 per cent withdrawal rates of what was once Income Support (now the 'guarantee credit'). But it greatly increases the range of retirement incomes over which people would be benefiting from the Pension Credit, but therefore subject to its means-tested withdrawal (at 40 per cent). To start with, most recipients would be below the income tax threshold for pensioners. But over time those on higher incomes would also become entitled to Pension Credit and so subject to both its withdrawal and to income tax at 10 per cent or 22 per cent at the same time. Department for Work and Pensions and Institute for Fiscal Studies projections suggest that, by 2050, between two-thirds and four-fifths of pensioners would be entitled to Pension Credit, and potentially affected in this way (Pensions Policy Institute 2003: Chart 19).

Third, recent and proposed reforms of student finance affect rates applying to both students in later life and their parents at the time of studying. For instance, under the Higher Education Bill as published in January 2004, someone leaving university with a student loan will be expected to make payments equivalent to 9 per cent of his or her gross earnings once they exceed £14,000 (Dearden, Fitzsimons, and Goodman 2004). This will be in addition to any effect of the kind shown in Figure 10.7. At the same time, students from poorer backgrounds will pay lower fees and receive help with maintenance depending on the incomes of their parents. For instance, if parental income is £16,000 or lower (at 2006–07 prices), the total benefit will be equivalent to £3,000 per year. However, by the time parental income is over £34,000, this will have been withdrawn. This is equivalent to an additional effective marginal tax rate of 17 per cent over the income range. The higher fees go, the larger this income range will be.

Fourth, for younger students, the extension of Education Maintenance Allowances (EMAs) from September 2004 means that those with lower-income parents (that is, with incomes up to £19,000 per year) will receive help of up to £30 per week, but those with higher-income parents will receive £20 or £10 per week, and those whose parents have gross incomes of over £30,000 will receive nothing. This is equivalent to an additional marginal tax rate of about 14 per cent over the income range.

At the extreme, some people could eventually simultaneously face income tax and NICs, Child Tax Credit withdrawal in respect of their younger children, EMA withdrawal in respect of a 16-year-old, and rising fees for a student child, and still be contributing towards repaying their own student loan. Such extreme cases might be unusual, and it is not clear how all the different means-tests would interact. However, there will be many cases where tax-credit withdrawal interacts with at least one of these. For instance, a single-earner couple with two young children and a student loan to repay would face a total effective marginal tax rate of 79 per cent on annual earnings of between £13,500 and £22,500 (at 2003–04 prices). A couple with two school-age children and one at university would face a total effective marginal tax rate of 87 per cent on annual earnings of between £15,500 and £22,500.

All of this may or may not affect incentives to work and save, or public opposition to means-testing. In many cases recent reforms have replaced acute disincentives over a narrow income band with less acute ones over a wider range, so the effects overall have been ambiguous. They have also had different effects on work incentives for men and women (Bennett 2002). On balance, they appear to have increased employment slightly (Brewer et al. 2003). However, continuing with this strategy will either widen the number of people affected or push the effective marginal tax rates involved back up again, without any offsetting reductions elsewhere. Paradoxically, policies that are being followed with the aim of avoiding increases in explicit direct tax rates are having the effect of increasing implicit marginal tax rates on quite a large proportion of the population.

10.5 SUMMARY

- Economic growth is less help than often supposed in relieving the conflict between tax constraints and upward pressures on social spending. Tax revenue may well rise in real terms without policy change as the economy grows. But higher real incomes in general put upward pressure on public sector pay, and rising living standards lead to raised expectations for the quality of public services. Health care and education in particular are services for which demand appears to rise more than in proportion to income growth. At the same time, if social security policy is aimed at reducing relative poverty and at smoothing incomes across the life cycle, benefits may well have to rise along with real income growth, and so become no easier to finance as the economy grows.

- Recent official forecasts for the public finances in the long term suggest that public spending can remain broadly the same share of national income, despite the pressures from an ageing population. This is based on the assumptions, however, that public spending on pensions can be held to a constant share of GDP, and that other benefit rates are increased only in line with prices, falling by more than three-fifths relative to other incomes.

- An alternative calculation, based on applying today's levels of social spending at any given age to the forecast age structure of 2051, suggests that the total of education, health, and social security spending would be 4.5 per cent of GDP greater than it was with the age structure of 2001. This is an increase, accumulating over fifty years, that it would be perfectly feasible to accommodate, representing an increase in such spending of only 0.4 per cent per year. On the other hand, paying for it would require all tax rates to be an eighth higher than now: clearly feasible, but equally clearly painful for policy-makers to contemplate.

- Many factors could push this figure up or down. For instance, allowing for the increases in health spending already planned up to 2007–08 would add a further 2.7 per cent of GDP to the increase by 2051, although that could be reduced if we saw a 'compression of morbidity'.

- A significant part of such an increase would come from spending on people over pension age. Within thirty years there are projected to be a third more people over state pension age per person of working age than now (if we allow for the coming equalization at age 65 between men and women).

- If we were to keep the total number of pensioners fixed at that of 2001, the combined impact of longer life expectancy and the retirement of the 'baby boom' generation would mean that the unified state pension age would have to rise to 71 by 2031.
- Current pension reforms are intended to leave public pension spending fixed at much the same share of GDP for the next fifty years. This is very different from forecasts for other industrialized countries. On average across the European Union, public pension spending is already nearly twice the share of national income as in the UK, and is projected to rise by a further 3 per cent of GDP by 2040.
- In the UK it is hoped that private pension payments will meet a greater share of future retirement incomes, and so help maintain their relative value as the numbers over pension age increase. However, for this to happen, private pension contributions would have to increase substantially from those that were adequate in the past. An illustrative calculation suggests that required contribution rates for men should already have risen by 7 per cent of salary just to allow a *constant* hypothetical pension, if we allow for increases in life expectancy since 1981 (with a fixed retirement age of 65). However, many younger workers are actually now having *smaller* contributions made into occupational pensions on their behalf than the rights that are accruing to their predecessors.
- While increased pension ages are an obvious partial solution to these problems, they could have very different effects between social groups. Because post-65 life expectancies are shorter for manual than for professional workers, an equal increase in pension age would have a much larger proportionate effect on the former.
- Recent policy reforms have had the effect of making means-testing less sharp in its effects, but extending it over a wider income range. A family with two children can now face combined tax and tax credit withdrawal rates of 70 per cent over an income range that extends up to beyond median earnings.
- Pensions reforms have also reduced the number of people facing very high effective tax rates in retirement, but have increased the number facing rates of at least 40 per cent. Policies towards student finance and allowances for low-income 16-year-olds staying on at school have also extended the range and depth of means-testing. Continuation of this approach would mean either extending the income ranges affected still further or deepening the 'poverty trap' effects again.

FURTHER READING

For discussion of the way in which pressures on social spending were dealt with in the period up to 1997, see 'Welfare with the Lid on' by Howard Glennerster in *The State of Welfare: The Economics of Social Spending*, edited by Howard

Glennerster and John Hills (Oxford University Press, 1998). For the same author's discussion of how to cope with future pressures, see 'Do Public Services Have a Future?', Chapter 10 in Howard Glennerster's *Understanding the Finance of Welfare* (Policy Press, 2003).

For discussion of wider pressures in the next two decades, see *Tackling Disadvantage: A 20-Year Enterprise* by David Darton, Donald Hirsch, and Jason Strelitz (Joseph Rowntree Foundation, 2003) and associated papers on the Foundation's website: www.jrf.org.uk/bookshop/.

For particular issues related to pensions, see the initial report of the Independent Pensions Commission chaired by Adair Turner, due to be published by the Department for Work and Pensions in the autumn of 2004. See also various briefing papers published by the Pensions Policy Institute, including *The Pensions Landscape* (2003) and *Raising State Pension Age: Are We Ready?* (2002) (www.pensionspolicyinstitute.org.uk).

11

Conclusions: The Spending Pit or the Tax Pendulum?

As earlier chapters have shown, decisions on both sides of the government's accounts, spending and taxation, many taken by default rather than as the subject of day-to-day political debate, have major effects on people's lives and the resources and opportunities open to them. A recurrent theme of this book has been that the decisions we make as a society are open to choice, and are not driven by inexorable external or technological determinants. Policies matter, and we are free to choose between them. But to do this, we need to make those choices with our eyes open. Another recurrent theme has been that we are not as a society very well-informed about either how our resources are distributed or about the ways in which government affects that distribution. Some of the evidence touched on in earlier chapters may therefore come as a surprise to people across the political spectrum. To give a few examples:

1. The dramatic growth in income inequality—the gap between poor and rich— and in earnings dispersion—that between low pay and high pay—seen in the UK and the USA in the last quarter-century was not a global phenomenon.
2. The 1990s and the early years of the twenty-first century have not seen a simple continuation of the trends of the 1980s in the UK. For instance, while those with high incomes—particularly very high incomes—have continued to pull away from the middle, those with low incomes have been catching up slowly on the middle.
3. What drives income distribution is not a simple matter of earnings relativities and the impact of unemployment. Earnings dispersion has continued to widen, but relative poverty has fallen. At the same time, unemployment has fallen rapidly to its lowest level since the mid-1970s, but poverty has fallen only slowly and remains far higher than it was a generation ago.
4. New information on income dynamics—the ways in which people's incomes change over time—deepens our understanding of the situations of those with low incomes, and shows that there are few who are remorselessly poor year after year. However, most poverty is still accounted for by those who are persistently or recurrently poor.
5. Social spending as a whole has been around the same proportion of national income—a quarter—for nearly three decades. It is now lower in the UK in than in most other European countries. Similarly, the UK is now

in the lower half of the international range of tax as a share of national income.

6. People greatly overestimate the proportion of social security spending that goes to the unemployed. This contributes to the low priority given the social security budget as a whole despite the high priority given to items such as pensions that account for most of it.

7. Most people think that the tax system both should be and is progressive, with those on high incomes paying a greater fraction of their income in tax. In fact, at most income levels the proportion is actually the same, but is higher for the poorest, and lower for the richest, and so is regressive.

8. The distributional impact of New Labour's tax and social security reforms in the UK has been very different from—almost the reverse of—those followed by the Bush administration in the USA, where debt-financed tax cuts have favoured the very rich (Gale and Potter 2002). As a result, child poverty has begun to fall in the UK, even in relative terms, and its rate is no longer one of the very worst in the European Union.

9. Both the ageing of the population and the preferences of a more affluent society are likely to increase the demands on social spending. In the UK, these pressures may be of manageable scale, but would require higher taxation in the long run to accommodate them. Some of the pressures may be coped with privately, but private solutions, such as funded private pensions, neither make the problems go away nor reduce their scale.

When we review the evidence presented in earlier chapters, four themes stand out:

- the sheer scale of the change in the distribution of income in the UK in the last quarter century;
- that policy matters: the scale and structure of social spending and the taxes that pay for it have major effects on that inequality;
- that the growth in poverty and inequality is unpopular, most social spending is popular, but policy is constrained by hostility to particular items and misunderstanding of others; and
- that the dilemmas facing policy-makers are likely to become more acute, not easier, over coming decades.

THE SCALE OF INEQUALITY GROWTH

That Britain became a more unequal society in the last quarter-century is well known. Quite how large the change was may be less well-known. At the end of the 1970s, the richest tenth of the population received 21 per cent of total disposable income. This rose through the 1980s and 1990s to reach 28–29 per cent by 2002–03, as much as for the whole of the bottom half. More than half of this increase was accounted for by the top 1 per cent of taxpayers, and most of this by the top half a per cent. Whatever one's opinion of this, the numbers involved are very large: two-fifths of the total real increase in personal incomes between 1979 and 1999 went to the top 10 per cent; more than a sixth went to the top 1 per cent; and about an eighth went to the top half a per cent. Partly as a result, after two decades of stability, the distribution of wealth became sharply more unequal after 1995. By 2001, the shares of the top 1 per cent and the top 10 per cent of marketable wealth-holders appeared to be as great as at any time since the early 1970s.

The changes at the bottom were equally dramatic. At the end of the 1970s, the poorest tenth of people received about 4 per cent of disposable income. By the early 1990s this share had fallen by more than a third to between 2 per cent and 3 per cent, where it has stayed. By the early 1990s, relative poverty was twice the level it had been in the 1960s, and three times what it had been in the late 1970s. By the end of the 1990s, if one looks across fifteen industrialized countries: only the USA had and Ireland had higher relative poverty overall; only the USA had worse child poverty in relative terms; and only Ireland worse relative poverty for its pensioner population. Despite Britain's comparatively high overall income, on a fixed international poverty line (based on the purchasing power of the US poverty line), a larger proportion of children in the UK were poor (29 per cent) in the mid-1990s than in any other EU country apart from Italy and Spain (of the twelve for which figures were available).

The pattern of change over time has not been uniform (Figure 3.2). In the early 1980s poverty rose against a fixed standard as well as a relative standard. In the following decade absolute poverty fell, but relative poverty rose rapidly. For a short period in the mid-1990s both fell. Sine 1997 relative poverty has fallen a little and poverty against a fixed standard has fallen quite rapidly, particularly for children. One result has been dramatic falls since 1999 in the proportions of low-income families with children reporting various forms of material deprivation or financial stress.

The growth in inequality and poverty has resulted from a series of interlinked factors. While most of these pushed in the same way in the 1980s, the pattern since the mid-1990s has been more complicated, with some pushing one way and some the other. As a result, the pattern of change has also become more complex, with some low-income groups catching up on the middle, even at a time of growth in typical living standards, but other groups still being left behind, and the very top continuing to accelerate away from the rest.

Earnings make up two-thirds of household income, so the widening dispersion of earnings since the late 1970s has been a major driver of growing overall inequality. Even right at the bottom earnings matter: a third of the poorest fifth are in households with some member in work. There is a temptation to label the increasing returns to skill and qualifications associated with rising earnings dispersion as the emergence of a more 'meritocratic' society, and to see those widening returns as both inevitable and justified. This is, however, to miss the point of Michael Young's original satire, *The Rise of the Meritocracy*, which coined the term in 1958. Young's point was to attack both the smugness and tendency to self-perpetuation of the 'meritocrats'. On the latter he was far-sighted: the evidence from comparing what happens to the cohorts of children born in 1958 with what happens to those born in 1970 is that economic mobility appears to have *fallen* between the two. A mechanism driving this appears to be the increased importance of educational qualifications in explaining people's relative earnings, combined with the success of better-off parents in ensuring that their children gain those qualifications. But explanation is not the same as justification. Even if we agree that educational success, skill, and hard work are better reasons for above-average living standards than accidents of inherited wealth, that says nothing about how great the differences in rewards should be.

POLICY MATTERS

The state can, and does, have a major impact on distribution. To understand this, earlier chapters have argued that it is important to look at both tax and spending together. Often, both in analysis and in popular discussion, this is not done. Yet one cannot understand the distributional effect of, say, provision of health care through the National Health Service as opposed to private insurance without asking where the funds come from. Nor can one sensibly talk about the tax 'burden' without taking into account the services and transfers that it finances. This has become even more important in recent years with the replacement of what were once some social security benefits with 'tax credits', and with the restriction or abolition of some previous tax reliefs.

Once this is done, it becomes clear that the combination of state transfers and taxation does much to narrow the income distribution in the UK. The narrowing results from the combination of transfers and services that are generally *pro-poor* in their impact (worth more in absolute terms to those with lower than with higher incomes), together with a tax system that is generally *proportional* in its impact. As a result, if we take a single point in time, those on low incomes tend to be net gainers from the combination, and those on high incomes net losers.

If we look across people's whole lives, the picture is somewhat different. Most people can expect to receive much the same total benefit from social spending of one kind or another, regardless of their income. But the taxes they pay for this are much larger for those with high lifetime incomes, so the system remains redistributive in lifetime terms, even though much of what the welfare state does is to act as a form of giant 'savings bank'.

At the same time, while the size and structure of social spending has changed dramatically over the last fifty years, most generations receive—or seem likely to receive—much the same out of the system as they have paid into it. By and large, the system has evolved in a way that that is broadly fair between the generations.

The growth in inequality has reflected changes both in market income and in the way in which the state affects incomes, both through taxes and through transfers. While the impact of technological change has been identified as the main factor associated with growing inequality between the earnings of the high-skilled and those of the low-skilled in the USA and the UK, other countries have either avoided the growth in earnings inequality or have offset it though state action, so that the same widening has not occurred in their disposable incomes.

In the most recent years, the impact of policy change can be seen in Britain. While the Minimum Wage has affected relatively few men, it has led to significant increases in wages for the worst-paid women. However, income from state pensions and other benefits is 60 per cent of income for the poorest fifth, so it is the relativities between these and other incomes that are most important at the bottom. The linking of most benefits to prices rather than earnings or other incomes since the early 1980s was a crucial reason why people fell behind and why relative poverty rose. Equally, the above-inflation increases in certain benefits, pensions, and tax credits since 1999 have led to significant reductions in child poverty, and should do so in pensioner poverty (partly depending on what happens to take-up of the new Pension Credit).

GROWING INEQUALITY IS NOT POPULAR, BUT MOST SOCIAL SPENDING IS

These developments are of public concern. Large proportions of the population believe that the gap between rich and poor is too large and that it is government's responsibility to reduce it. Most people substantially underestimate the pay of highly paid occupations, but still think such pay should be lower. They also believe that the income levels that many social security benefits actually allow are too little to live on. But people are sceptical about increases in 'welfare benefits', reflecting worries about fraud and incentives, as well as overestimation of benefit levels.

Most people believe that there is 'quite a lot of real poverty' in Britain, and give views that are consistent with notions of a poverty line that rises over time as society becomes more affluent. Fewer than a quarter of the population blame 'laziness or lack of will-power' on the part of the poor for their low income (although the proportion doing so is more than in the past, and more than in any other EU country apart from Portugal, but still much less than in the USA).

The separate sides of the spending-tax equation described above appear to be widely supported. The evidence from attitude surveys suggests strong support for universal services and entitlements, and worries about the impact and fairness of means-testing. At the same time, people appear to favour a more progressive tax system than we actually have. These attitudes do not appear, however, to result from a public view of the state's main job as to be a giant Robin Hood—while people see it as government's responsibility to reduce income differences, explicit support for 'redistribution' to achieve this, while still positive, has declined since the early 1990s. Rather, two principles—to each according to his or her needs, and from each according to his or her means—are applied separately, and the redistributive effect is a *by-product* rather than people's main aim. Nonetheless, exploratory qualitative research suggests that people are content with this outcome when confronted with the result of the combination (Hedges forthcoming).

For it to be sustainable, either any formulation of public policy will have to go with the grain of public opinion or its proponents will have to persuade people to change their views. In an earlier analysis of social security policy under New Labour (Hills 2002*a*), I suggested that there were ten aspects of policy that were clearly in line with the preponderance of such public attitudes; three where policy had changed and was appearing to catch up with them; two where policy might have influenced or led public attitudes; and only five where policy remained out of line with what appeared to be majority views. As we saw in Chapter 9, this does not mean that policy has been regressive—quite the reverse—but the extent to which policy-makers have navigated within the constraints of public attitudes is striking.

These constraints are significant, and embody conflicts and contradictions. For instance, it is hard to see how inequality and relative poverty can be reduced, as people want, without the instruments including increases—as there have been for some in recent years—in social security benefits. For the most important benefits—particularly pensions—greater generosity would be popular. Yet the social security budget as whole is unpopular, largely it seems because of concerns about fraud and disincentive effects from benefits to the unemployed, combined with the misperception that these are what most of the budget is spent on. Recent reforms may change people's views of items that have new labels (for instance, as 'tax credits'), but this remains to be seen. Means-testing remains unpopular, but the alternatives are likely to be more expensive or, if less generous, less effective in tackling poverty.

On the other side, in principle people favour higher taxes to pay for higher spending, and a more progressive tax system. However, the higher taxes they want may be levied on others, better-off than themselves (although some of the questions referred to above do attempt to control for this). Even people near the top of the actual income distribution tend to think of themselves as having a 'middle income'.

IT IS NOT GOING TO BECOME ANY EASIER

These conflicts are not going to become any easier. As Chapter 10 explored, the UK is in some respects in a more favourable position than some other countries. The elderly population will grow in relation to the size of the working population, but not as rapidly as elsewhere in Europe. State pensions are much less generous than elsewhere, and the promises we have made about their future values much less ambitious. Nonetheless, we have a problem. Treasury forecasts are that the future pressures on public spending are fairly modest. But they assume that the costs of rising health spending (to raise the quality of the NHS following the Wanless Review and to cope with an ageing population) will be partly offset by a fall in the relative value of most social security benefits through continuing to link them to prices in the long term rather than increasing them in line with other incomes. It is hard to see how this could occur without relative poverty rising. At the same time it is assumed that a complex set of reforms will succeed in stabilizing the future cost of state pensions as a share of GDP, while maintaining generosity in relative terms for the poorest pensioners.

The problem of rising future costs is not insurmountable even if these comforting assumptions are not made, but thinking of how to raise taxes over even fifty years to raise four or five percentage points or more extra of GDP is certainly challenging for a country that has become used to its tax ratio remaining within a narrow band for more than a generation.

In the Edgar Allan Poe story, *The Pit and the Pendulum*, a victim of the Inquisition finds himself trapped in a cell which features a slowly descending sharp-bladed pendulum, under which he is bound in place. Even when he escapes from this, he realises that red-hot walls are gradually closing in on him, threatening to push him into a terrible pit. For policy-makers across Europe concerned with social spending, planning for the future must often feel like that (Pierson 2001). On the one hand, there are apparently inexorable pressures for increased spending on pensions, health care, education, and tackling disadvantage. On the other, the political ceiling on tax revenue seems closer every year. Ways of escape are limited, and the crunch ever nearer.

FIVE STRATEGIES

In broad terms, one can set out five strategies, each of which is being followed in the UK at present in respect of one or more aspects of social spending. Each has drawbacks of one kind or another, particularly when measured against Britain's problems of poverty and inequality on the one hand, and of public attitudes towards their solutions as discussed earlier in this book.

1. *Reduce or limit social spending in relation to national income.* For most social security benefits for the working-age population (apart from tax credits for children), current policy is to link their values to prices so that they fall back in relation to average incomes. This allows their cost, other things being equal, to fall in relation to national income. This is one reason of the reasons why the Treasury's forecasts for the long-term state of the public finances discussed in Chapter 10 are comparatively reassuring. There are, however, three difficulties:

- In the case of social security benefits, unless other developments radically reduce the proportion of the population dependent on them, this implies rising and deepening relative poverty.
- If applied to health care and education spending, the discussion in Chapter 10 suggests that even fixing spending as a share of national income would mean the quality of services such as health care and education falling behind rising expectations.

- One resolution of this might be greater private spending on such services (as we have seen in the last two decades—see Section 6.4). However, if people are spending greater proportions of their incomes on private alternatives, the tax constraint on government is likely to tighten.

2. *Maintain social spending, but concentrate it on the poor*. One way of avoiding adverse effects on poverty and of protecting those with low incomes is to concentrate the limited resources available on the poorest or on those with relatively low incomes. This is effectively the current strategy both for the funding of higher education and for the future development of state pensions. There are two, rather different, problems:

- First, in one form or another, this implies more means-testing. As we have seen in earlier chapters, this is in general unpopular. Most such systems are vulnerable to take-up problems and so leave gaps with people unprotected. They may also cause problems for incentives. While these can be exaggerated, the analysis in Section 10.4 suggests that the combination of means-tests resulting from different aspects of policy in recent years may be reaching its limits, if it has not done so already.
- Second, this strategy—of more for the poor within a fixed total—implies less for those in the middle of the distribution. At some point this may hit voter resistance and, as with reductions all round, may tighten the tax constraint as people end up paying more for private alternatives.

3. *Maintain spending for most with selective increases for the poor*. As Chapter 9 set out in detail, this has been the policy followed for tax credits and other benefits for children since 1999, with some success in reducing child poverty. The difficulties of this as a more general strategy are:

- This still involves more means-testing, with the potential problems of take-up, adverse effects on disincentives, and of general public dislike discussed above.
- Perhaps more difficult in political terms, the strategy as a general policy would imply that taxes would rise, but without improvements in services for those in the middle.

4. *Increase spending across the board to keep up with demographic and other pressures*. Recent policy towards spending on schools has effectively been to increase real spending to keep up teachers' salaries (and to cope with the increased cost of their pensions). Chapter 10 outlined some simple calculations of what this sort of policy would mean if applied to social spending across the board, given demographic changes over the next fifty years.

- First, this ultimately implies higher taxes. The evidence on social attitudes reviewed in this book suggests that this is not necessarily inherently unpopular. However, people's willingness to pay may be limited to certain services—health care in particular, but also education (and possibly pensions)—and to visible improvements in them. Also, the taxes they have in mind may be levied on others.

- Second, this strategy may involve quite large increases in spending, and hence taxes, just to 'stand still' in terms of the service (or transfer) received in any particular circumstance. This may be seen—as with the large increases in school budgets in 2003–04—as involving increased spending, but 'nothing to show for it'.

5. *Increase spending faster than the external pressures so that services can improve.* Policy towards spending on the NHS until at least 2007 is that spending should rise significantly as a share of national income, with a rate of growth that is greater than implied either by demographic pressure or by the need to keep health service salaries up with those elsewhere. As a result, both the quality of services and the amount available for given needs should improve. Taxes—in the form of National Insurance Contributions—were increased in April 2003 to contribute towards the cost of this, in effect challenging the public to put its money where its mouth had been when talking to those surveying public opinion. As of early 2004, this strategy appears to have been accepted so far, for this particular form of spending. However:

- As a general strategy—for instance, to achieve not just static but falling relative poverty—it clearly implies higher costs, and higher taxes, beyond those implied by purely demographic pressures. Again, the question is: on whom should they fall?
- In the specific case of social security benefits, while majorities favour more generous levels of benefits such as pensions that make up the bulk of the budget, this is not true of others, in particular benefits for the unemployed.

The truth is that none of these strategies is without significant political risks. At the end of the Edgar Allan Poe story, the hero is saved through two lucky events. First, rats chew through the bonds that are holding him underneath the descending pendulum, allowing him to roll free. Second, the French army arrives just in time to turn off the machinery that is pushing the red hot walls in towards him. Given the, if anything, stronger long-run pressures on social spending elsewhere in Europe, it is hard to see a French public finance army—or even an EU rapid reaction force—coming the rescue of the UK. Rather, we may need to concentrate on ways in which the political bonds holding us in place can be slackened.

First, is it true that there are no easy ways out? The most obvious—and most appealing—is to suggest that spending can be increased without tax increases, or that it can be cut back painlessly. In the short term this can, of course, be done by borrowing. While this may be necessary at times for macroeconomic reasons, in the long run the additional debt has to be repaid, or at least serviced, so longer-term pressures on the budget are worsened (see Section 7.1). In Section 10.1 it was argued that the next most popular suggestion, relying on a 'growth dividend' to make life easier, is an illusion. However, it is true that recent years have seen increases in social spending as a share of GDP without increases in the overall tax ratio, and that this has been achieved while public debt has been falling. This has been possible because social spending has taken an increasing share of total public spending (Table 6.1). Its growth has been accommodated by falls and restraint elsewhere. But what is available to squeeze elsewhere is getting smaller as social spending approaches two-thirds of the total. Will there really be much more room to squeeze transport investment or defence spending? Similarly, part of the expansion room for social spending has come from reduced debt interest payments as inflation has fallen and as public borrowing has fallen from its levels of the early 1990s. Again, it is rather hard to see this being able to contribute as much as it has over the last decade.

Second, there is the ever-popular solution of cutting out 'waste' to allow higher spending on favoured services. There are two problems. First, one person's waste may be another's valued service—we may simply be talking about different preferences. This is fine, but we then need to be explicit about what it is that will be lost. But second, while it is always possible to come up with examples of public inefficiency and waste—and improvements in public sector productivity come from identifying and eliminating them—the point is that it *is* always possible to do so, and it would be remarkably optimistic to assume that the future will be different from the past. Like painting the Forth Bridge, eliminating waste has to be a constant activity of government: as soon as organizations such as the Audit Commission have worked through one area, they need to return to where they started. This helps deliver the productivity improvements needed to keep up with public expectations, but promising an unspecified 'war on waste' as a way of solving the policy dilemmas costlessly is simply to evade the questions.

What then does this leave? First, an alternative strategy is anything that makes the underlying pressures and needs themselves smaller. If underlying market inequality is lower, the state needs to spend less to reduce it, or can achieve more from a given level of spending. This is not just a matter of pressures on the social security budget: if, for instance, poor health is linked to low income, reduced poverty may reduce some of the pressures on health services. Parts of social spending—and many recent policy changes—are intended to reduce long-run needs. Whether the investments in early-years education, schools, regeneration of low-income neighbourhoods, the New Deal, and other initiatives against social exclusion described in Chapter 9 will have the results hoped for, or whether they are of great enough scale to do so, are still open questions. But their effects in the next generation could help reduce the pressures. Similarly, regulatory action can affect spending pressures. The existence of the National Minimum Wage reduces what might otherwise be the cost of in-work tax credits, and increases in it would reduce them further. In addition, Acemoglu (2003) suggests that the effect of this kind of regulation may be to set up a dynamic of training and investment with benefits to productivity of lower-skill workers. If so, there would be further long-term help in reducing market inequality.

Equally, a second alternative strategy is that some of the pressures could be relieved by changes in behaviour that lead to 'demand reduction'. As Chapter 10 discussed, a significant part of the future pressure on social spending comes from

an assumption that we can continue to retire at the same age while life expectancies are increasing. We can—if we are prepared to pay for it. Alternatively, we
could decide to spend at least part of our increased life expectancies in working.
As discussed in Chapter 10, unless the increases in actual retirement ages were
very large, this almost certainly only *slows* the growth in the amounts we need
to pay publicly or privately for pensions rather than eliminating that growth,
but it would certainly help. Achieving such a shift without inequity between
particular social groups or generations will not, however, be straightforward,
and pensioners and those near to current pension ages will become a politically
stronger group as their numbers grow.

There may also be new, and not too unpopular, sources of tax revenue to avoid
all the strain being put on those we have at the moment. Identifying areas where
taxes or charges can be levied on activities with external costs—taxing 'bads'—
is an obvious way forward. But the amount of revenue such charges raise should
not be over-stated—after all, if they succeed in actually changing behaviour in
the way desired, they end up collecting less revenue (as the London Congestion
Charge illustrates). And if they succeed in raising significant revenues, they do
not avoid unpopularity from those who pay them (as the fuel tax protests of
2000 illustrate). Revenue could also be raised from taxing people whose
incomes are so far above the average that few voters would feel threatened. The
most frequent proposal of this kind would be a top rate of income tax of
50 pence in the pound, starting at incomes of £100,000 per year. Given the
large gains in income this group has enjoyed, many might see this as only fair.
However, because such a tax would affect only the slices of income *above*
£100,000, the revenue raised, while not at all trivial at about £5 billion per year,
is only 0.5 per cent of GDP. To start raising more significant contributions to
rising spending, higher tax rates would have to start lower down the scale and
affect more voters.

Even if these ways of slackening our bonds are successful, it would be very
optimistic to think that they avoid the need for some combination of the five
strategies described above, despite their politically unpalatable side effects. To
achieve that will need better public understanding. First, it would help if there
was better public understanding of how policy operates now—for instance, of
factors such as the domination of social security by pensions, not benefits for the
unemployed, the actual level of Income Support allowances, and the lack of
progressivity in the tax system as it actually is. But, more importantly, it will need
public understanding that these *are* the available strategies, and that a choice has
to be made between them. Howard Glennerster (2003: 199) quotes a journalist
from the *Wall Street Journal* as saying, 'The trouble with the British Electorate is
that they want European standards of public services but American levels of tax'.
We may simply need to become more grown-up about it, and for politicians
to treat us as such. If we want the state to do more, we will eventually have to
pay for it—and for many of us that means us, not some imagined richer person.
Given the strong basic support for the main elements of the welfare state and of

proportional or progressive taxes to pay for it, politicians could be braver in setting out this choice. But it will remain very difficult so long as we misunderstand what has happened to income distribution and to our place in it, and where it is that public spending really goes. Here complexity does not help; nor in the long run will obscurity. If this book has helped explain some of the former and reduce the latter, it will have succeeded in its purpose. Social spending does not disappear down a pit, and the tax pendulum does not have to swing just one way.

References

Abel-Smith, B. and Townsend, P. (1965). *The Poor and the Poorest*. London: Bell.

Acemoglu, D. (2003). 'Cross-country Inequality Trends'. *Economic Journal*, 113/485: 121–49.

Adam, S. and Brewer, M. (2004). *Supporting Families: The Financial Costs and Benefits of Children since 1975*. Bristol: The Policy Press.

——and Reed, H. (2002). *The Benefits of Parenting: Government Financial Support for Families with Children since 1975* (IFS Commentary 91). London: Institute for Fiscal Studies.

Agulnik, P. and Le Grand, J. (1998). 'Tax Relief and Partnership Pensions'. *Fiscal Studies*, 19: 403–28.

Alcock, P. (1997). *Understanding Poverty* (2nd edn.). Basingstoke: Macmillan.

——, Burchardt, T., Glennerster, H., and Hills, J. (eds.) (2001). *Welfare and Wellbeing: Richard Titmuss's Contribution to Social Policy*. Bristol: The Policy Press.

Atkinson, A. B. (1975). *The Economics of Inequality*. Oxford: Oxford University Press.

——(1998). 'Social Exclusion, Poverty and Unemployment', in A. B. Atkinson and J. Hills (eds.), *Exclusion, Employment and Opportunity* (CASEpaper4). London: London School of Economics.

——(2002a). *Top Incomes in the UK over the Twentieth Century* (Discussion Paper in Economic and Social History No. 43). Oxford: University of Oxford.

——(2002b). 'Is Rising Income Inequality Inevitable? A Critique of the "Transatlantic Consensus"', in P. Townsend and D. Gordon (eds.), *World Poverty: New Policies to Defeat an Old Enemy*. Bristol: The Policy Press.

——(2003). 'Income Inequality in OECD Countries: Data and Explanations'. *CESinfo Economic Studies*, 49: 479–513.

——, Cantillon, B., Marlier, E., and Nolan, B. (2002). *Social Indicators: The EU and Social Inclusion*. Oxford: Oxford University Press.

——, Gordon, J., and Harrison, A. J. (1986). *Trends in the Distribution of Wealth in Britain, 1923–1981* (STICERD TIDI Discussion Paper 70). London: London School of Economics.

——and Harrison, A. J. (1978). *Distribution of Personal Wealth in Britain*. Cambridge: Cambridge University Press.

——, Maynard, A., and Trinder, C. (1983). *Parents and Children: Incomes in Two Generations*. London: Heinemann Educational Books.

——and Micklewright, J. (1992). *Economic Transformation in Eastern Europe and the Distribution of Income*. Cambridge: Cambridge University Press.

——and Salverda, W. (2003). 'Top Incomes in the Netherlands and the United Kingdom over the Twentieth Century' (mimeo). Oxford: Nuffield College.

——and Voitchovsky, S. (2004). 'The Distribution of Top Earnings in the UK since the Second World War' (mimeo).

Banks, J., Blundell, R., and Smith, J. P. (2000). *Wealth Inequality in the United States and Britain* (Working Paper WP 00/20). London: Institute for Fiscal Studies.

Barclay, P. (chair) (1995). *Income and Wealth, Volume I: Report of the Inquiry Group*. York: Joseph Rowntree Foundation.

Barr, N. (2001). *The Welfare State as a Piggy Bank*. Oxford: Oxford University Press.

—— (2004). *The Economics of the Welfare State* (4th edn.). Oxford: Oxford University Press.

Baumol, W. (1967). 'Macroeconomics of Unbalanced Growth: The Anatomy of Urban Crises'. *American Economic Review*, 57: 415–26.

Bennett, F. (2002). 'Gender Implications of Current Social Security Reforms'. *Fiscal Studies*, 23: 559–84.

Berghman, J. (1995). 'Social Exclusion in Europe: Policy Context and Analytical Framework', in G. Room (ed.), *Beyond the Threshold: The Measurement and Analysis of Social Exclusion*. Bristol: The Policy Press.

Berthoud, R. (1998). *The Incomes of Ethnic Minorities*. Colchester: Institute for Social and Economic Research, University of Essex.

——, Lakey, J., and McKay, S. (1993). *The Economic Problems of Disabled People*. London: Policy Studies Institute.

Beveridge, W. (1942). *Social Insurance and Allied Services* (Cmd. 6404). London: HMSO.

Blair, T. (1999). 'Beveridge Revisited: A Welfare State for the 21st Century', in R. Walker (ed.), *Ending Child Poverty*. Bristol: The Policy Press.

Blanden, J., Goodman, A., Gregg, P., and Machin, S. (2002). *Changes in Intergenerational Mobility* (Centre for Economic Performance Discussion Paper 26). London: London School of Economics.

Blundell, R., Reed, H., Van Reenen, J., and Shephard, A. (2003). 'The Impact of the New Deal for Young People on the Labour Market: A Four Year Assessment', in R. Dickens, P. Gregg, and J. Wadsworth (eds.), *The Labour Market under New Labour: The State of Working Britain*. Basingstoke: Palgrave Macmillan.

Booth, C. (1892). *Life and Labour of the People in London*. London: Macmillan.

Bradbury, B., Jenkins, S., and Micklewright, J. (eds.) (2001). *The Dynamics of Child Poverty in Industrialised Countries*. Cambridge: Cambridge University Press.

Bradshaw, J. and Finch, N. (2003). 'Overlaps in Dimensions of Poverty'. *Journal of Social Policy*, 32: 513–25.

Brady-Smith, C., Brooks-Gunn, J., Waldfogel, J., and Fauth, R. (2001). 'Work or Welfare? Assessing the Impact of Recent Employment and Policy Changes on Very Young Children'. *Evaluation and Program Planning*, 24: 409–25.

Bramley, G., Evans, M., and Atkins, J. (1998). *Where Does Public Spending Go? Pilot Study to Analyse the Flows of Public Expenditure into Local Areas*. London: Department of the Environment, Transport, and the Regions.

Brewer, M. (2003). *What do the Child Poverty Targets Mean for the Child Tax Credit? An Update* (IFS Briefing Note 41). London: Institute for Fiscal Studies.

—— (2004). *Will the Government Hit its Child Poverty Target in 2004–05* (IFS Briefing Note 47). London: Institute for Fiscal Studies.

——, Clark, T., and Goodman, A. (2003). 'What Really Happened to Child Poverty in the UK under New Labour's First Term', *Economic Journal*, 113, F240–57.

——, ——, and Wakefield, M. (2002). 'Social Security under New Labour: What Did the Third Way Mean for Welfare Reform?'. *Fiscal Studies*, 23: 505–37.

——, Duncan, A., Shephard, A., and Suárez, M. J. (2003). *Did Working Families' Tax Credit Work? Analysing the Impact of In-Work Support on Labour Supply and Programme Participation*. London: Inland Revenue and Institute for Fiscal Studies.

——, Goodman, A., Myck, M., Shaw, J., and Shephard, A. (2004). *Poverty and Inequality in Britain: 2004* (IFS Commentary 96). London: Institute for Fiscal Studies.

Bromley, C. (2003). 'Has Britain Become Immune to Inequality?', in A. Park et al. (eds.), *British Social Attitudes: The 20th Report*. London: Sage.

Brook, L., Hall, J., and Preston, I. (1996). 'Public Spending and Taxation', in R. Jowell et al. (eds.), *British Social Attitudes: The 13th Report*. Aldershot: Dartmouth.

Burchardt, T. (1997). *Boundaries between Public and Private Welfare: A Typology and Map of Services* (CASEpaper 2). London: London School of Economics.

——(2000). *Enduring Economic Exclusion*. York: Joseph Rowntree Foundation.

——and Hills, J. (1997). *Private Welfare Insurance and Social Security: Pushing the Boundaries*. York: Joseph Rowntree Foundation.

——, ——, and Propper, C. (1999). *Private Welfare and Public Policy*. York: Joseph Rowntree Foundation.

——, Le Grand, J., and Piachaud, D. (2002*a*). 'Introduction', in J. Hills, J. Le Grand, and D. Piachaud (eds.), *Understanding Social Exclusion*. Oxford: Oxford University Press.

—— —— ——(2002*b*). 'Degrees of Exclusion', J. Hills, J. Le Grand, and D. Piachaud (eds.), *Understanding Social Exclusion*. Oxford: Oxford University Press.

——and Propper, C. (1999). 'Does the UK have a Private Welfare Class?'. *Journal of Social Policy*, 28: 643–65.

Burgess, S., Gardiner, K., and Propper, C. (2001). *Why Rising Tides Don't Lift All Boats? An Explanation of the Relationship between Poverty and Unemployment in Britain* (CASEpaper 46). London: London School of Economics.

Burrows, R. (1997). *Contemporary Patterns of Residential Mobility in Relation to Social Housing in England* (Centre for Housing Policy Research Report). York: University of York.

Campbell, N. (1999). *The Decline of Employment among Older People in Britain* (CASEpaper 19). London: London School of Economics.

Cardarelli, R., Sefton, J., and Kotlikoff, L. (1999). *Generational Accounting in the UK* (Discussion Paper 147). London: National Institute for Economic and Social Research.

Clark, T. and Taylor, J. (1999). 'Income Inequality: A Tale of Two Cycles'. *Fiscal Studies*, 20: 387–400.

Commission on Taxation and Citizenship (2000). *Paying for Progress: A New Politics of Tax for Public Spending*. London: Fabian Society.

Cowell, F. (1995). *Measuring Inequality* (2nd edn.). Hemel Hempstead: Harvester Wheatsheaf.

Darton, D., Hirsch, D., and Strelitz, J. (2003). *Tackling Disadvantage: A 20-year enterprise*. York: Joseph Rowntree Foundation.

Dearden, L., Fitzsimons, E., and Goodman, A. (2004). *An Analysis of the Higher Education Reforms* (Briefing Note 45). London: Institute for Fiscal Studies.

Dennis, N. (1997). *The Invention of Permanent Poverty*. London: Institute of Economic Affairs.

Desai, T., Gregg, P., Steer, J., and Wadsworth, J. (1999). 'Gender and the Labour Market', in P. Gregg and J. Wadsworth (eds.), *The State of Working Britain*. Manchester: Manchester University Press.

Dickens, R. (2000). 'Caught in a Trap? Wage Mobility in Great Britain 1975–94'. *Economica*, 67/268: 477–97.

——and Ellwood, D. (2003). 'Child poverty in Britain and the United States', *Economic Journal*, 113, F219–39.

276 *References*

Dickens, R., Gregg, P., and Wadsworth, J. (eds.) (2003). *The Labour Market under New Labour: The State of Working Britain*. Basingstoke: Palgrave Macmillan.

DSS (Department of Social Security) (1993). *Households Below Average Income: A statistical analysis 1979–1990/91*. London: HMSO.

—— (1995). *Households Below Average Income: A Statistical Analysis 1979–1992/93*. London: HMSO.

—— (1997). *Households Below Average Income: A Statistical Analysis 1979–1994/95*. London: TSO.

—— (1998). *New Ambitions for our Country: A New Contract for Welfare* (Cm.3805). London: TSO.

—— (2000a). *Households Below Average Income: A Statistical Analysis 1994/5–1998/9*. London: TSO.

—— (2000b). *The Changing Welfare State: Social Security Spending*. London: DSS.

DWP (Department for Work and Pensions) (2002a). *Households Below Average Income: 1994/5–2000/1*. Leeds: Corporate Document Services.

—— (2002b). *Opportunity for All: Fourth Annual Report 2002* (Cm.5598). London: TSO.

—— (2002c). 'Minister Welcomes Fall in Benefit Fraud and Error' (DWP press release). 5 September.

—— (2002d). *Simplicity, Security and Choice: Working and Saving for Retirement* (Cm.5677). London: TSO.

—— (2003a). *Households Below Average Income: An Analysis of the Income Distribution from 1994/5–2001/02*. Leeds: Corporate Document Services.

—— (2003b). *Opportunity for All: Fifth Annual Report 2003* (Cm.5956). London: TSO.

—— (2003c). *Low Income Dynamics 1991–2001*. London: DWP.

—— (2003d). *Income Related Benefits: Estimates of Take-up in 2000/2001*. London: DWP.

—— (2003e). *Measuring Child Poverty*. London: DWP.

—— (2003f). *The Pensioners' Income Series 2001/2*. London: DWP.

—— (2003g). *Abstract of Statistics for Benefits, Contributions and Indices of Prices and Earnings* (2002 edn.). London: DWP.

—— (2003h). *Benefit Expenditure Tables 2003*. London: DWP. www.dwp.gov.uk/asd/asd4/expenditure.asp.

—— (2004). *Households Below Average Income: An Analysis of the Income Distribution 1994/5–2002/03*. Leeds: Corporate Document Services.

European Union (2003). *Joint Report by the Commission and the Council on Adequate and Sustainable Pensions* (6527/2/03). Brussels: European Union.

Faggio, G. and Nickell, S. (2003). 'The Rise in Inactivity among Adult Men', in R. Dickens, P. Gregg, and J. Wadsworth, *The Labour Market under New Labour: The State of Working Britain*. Basingstoke: Palgrave Macmillan.

Falkingham, J. and Hills, J. (eds.) (1995). *The Dynamic of Welfare: The Welfare State and the Life Cycle*. Hemel Hempstead: Harvester Wheatsheaf.

Ferrera, M. (1993). *EC Citizens and Social Protection: Main Results from a Eurobarometer Survey*. Brussels: European Commission.

GAD (Government Actuary's Department) (2003). *2002-Based Population Projections*. London: GAD.

Gale, W.G. and Potter, S.R. (2002). *The Bush Tax Cut: One Year Later* (Brookings Policy Brief 101). Washington, DC: Brookings Institution.

Gallie, D., Marsh, C., and Vogler, C. (eds.) (1994). *Social Change and the Experience of Unemployment*. Oxford: Oxford University Press.

—— and Paugam, S. (2002). *Social Precarity and Social Integration*. Brussels: European Commission (Employment and Social Affairs).

Gardiner, K. (1997). 'A Survey of Income Inequality Over the Last Twenty Years—How Does the UK Compare?', in P. Gottschalk, B. Gustafsson, and E. Palmer (eds.), *Changing Patterns in the Distribution of Economic Welfare*. Cambridge: Cambridge University Press.

—— and Hills, J. (1999). 'Policy Implications of New Data on Income Mobility'. *Economic Journal*, 109/453: F91–111.

Giddens, A. (1998). *The Third Way*. Cambridge: Polity Press.

—— (2000). *The Third Way and its Critics*. Cambridge: Polity Press.

Giles, C., Johnson, P., McCrae, J., and Taylor, J. (1996). *Living with the State: The Incomes and Work Incentives of Tenants in the Social Rented Sector*. London: Institute for Fiscal Studies.

Glennerster, H. (1998). 'Welfare with the Lid on', in H. Glennerster and J. Hills (eds.), *The State of Welfare: The Economics of Social Spending*. Oxford: Oxford University Press.

—— (2002). 'United Kingdom Education 1997–2001'. *Oxford Review of Economic Policy*, 18/2: 120–36.

—— (2003). *Understanding the Finance of Welfare*. Bristol: The Policy Press.

—— and Hills, J. (eds.) (1998). *The State of Welfare: The Economics of Social Spending*. Oxford: Oxford University Press.

—— —— and Travers, T. (2000). *Paying for Health, Education, and Housing: How Does the Centre Pull the Purse Strings?* Oxford: Oxford University Press.

Glyn, A. (2001). 'Inequalities of Employment and Wages in OECD Countries'. *Oxford Bulletin of Economics and Statistics*, 63 (special issue): 697–713.

Goldthorpe, J. H. and Mills, C. (forthcoming). 'Trends in Intergenerational Class Mobility in Britain in the Late Twentieth Century', in R. Breen (ed.), *National Patterns of Social Mobility: Convergence or Divergence?*. Oxford: Oxford University Press.

Goode, J., Callendar, C., and Lister, R. (1998). *Purse or Wallet: Gender Inequalities and Income Distribution Within Families on Benefits*. London: Policy Studies Institute.

Goodin, R., Heady, B., Muffels, R., and Driven, H.-J. (1999). *The Real Worlds of Welfare Capitalism*. Cambridge: Cambridge University Press.

Goodman, A., Johnson, P., and Webb, S. (1997). *Inequality in the UK*. Oxford: Oxford University Press.

—— and Webb, S. (1994). *For Richer, For Poorer: The Changing Distribution of Income in the United Kingdom, 1961–91*. London: Institute for Fiscal Studies.

Gordon, D. and Pantazis, C. (eds.) (1997). *Breadline Britain in the 1990s*. Aldershot: Ashgate.

——, Adelman, L., Ashworth, K., Bradshaw, J., Levitas, R., Middleton, S., Pantazis, C., Patsios, D., Payne, S., Townsend, P., and Williams, J. (2000). *Poverty and Social Exclusion in Britain*. York: Joseph Rowntree Foundation.

Green, H., Marsh, A., Connolly, H., and Payne, J. (2001). *The Final Effects of ONE: Part One* (DWP Research Report 183). Leeds: Corporate Document Services.

Gregg, P. and Harkness, S. (2003). *Welfare Reform and Lone Parents' Employment in the UK* (CMPO Working Paper 03/072). Bristol: University of Bristol.

——, Harkness, S., and Machin, S. (1999). *Child Development and Family Income*. York: Joseph Rowntree Foundation.

—— and Wadsworth, J. (2001). 'Everything You Ever Wanted to Ask About Measuring Worklessness and Polarization at the Household Level But Were Afraid to Ask'. *Oxford Bulletin of Economics and Statistics*, 63 (special issue): 777–806.

Gregg, P. and Wadsworth, J. (2003). 'Workless Households and the Recovery', in R. Dickens, P. Gregg, and J. Wadsworth (eds.), *The Labour Market under New Labour: The State of Working Britain*. Basingstoke: Palgrave Macmillan.

Hall, J., Emmerson, C., and Brook, L. (1998). *Attitudes to Local Tax and Spending* (IFS Commentary 68). London: Institute for Fiscal Studies.

Hancock, R. (1985). *Explaining Changes in Families' Relative Net Resources: An Analysis of the Family Finances and Family Resources Surveys* (STICERD TIDI Working Paper No. 84). London: London School of Economics.

——, Comas-Herrera, A., Wittenberg, R., and Pickard, L. (2003). 'Who Will Pay for Long-Term Care in the UK? Projections Linking Macro- and Micro-Simulation Models'. *Fiscal Studies*, 24: 387–426.

Harkness, S., Machin, S., and Waldfogel, J. (1996). 'Women's Pay and Family Incomes in Britain, 1979–91', in J. Hills (ed.), *New Inequalities: The Changing Distribution of Income and Wealth in the United Kingdom*. Cambridge: Cambridge University Press.

—— and Waldfogel, J. (2003). 'The Family Gap in Pay: Evidence from Seven Industrialized Countries'. *Research in Labor Economics*, 22: 369–414.

Hasluck, C., McKnight, A., and Elias, P. (2000). *Evaluation of the New Deal for Lone Parents: Early Lessons from the Phase One Prototype—Cost Benefit and Econometric Analysis* (DSS Research Report 110). Leeds: Corporate Document Services.

Heath, A. and Curtice, J. (1998). 'New Labour, New Voters?'. Paper presented to the Political Studies Association Annual Conference, April.

——, Jowell, R., and Curtice, J. (2001). *The Rise of New Labour: Party Policies and Voter Choices*. Oxford: Oxford University Press.

—— and Payne, C. (2000). 'Social Mobility', in A. H. Halsey with J. Webb (eds.), *Twentieth Century British Social Trends*. Basingstoke: Macmillan.

Hedges, A. (forthcoming). *Perceptions of Redistribution: Report on Qualitative Research* (forthcoming CASE paper). London: London School of Economics.

Hills, J. (1992). *Does Britain Have a 'Welfare Generation'? An Empirical Analysis of Intergenerational Equity* (Welfare State Programme Discussion Paper 76). London: London School of Economics.

——(1993). *The Future of Welfare: A Guide to the Debate*. York: Joseph Rowntree Foundation.

——(1995). *Income and Wealth, Volume 2: A Survey of the Evidence*. York: Joseph Rowntree Foundation.

——(ed.) (1996a). *New Inequalities: The Changing Distribution of Income and Wealth in the United Kingdom*. Cambridge: Cambridge University Press.

——(1996b). 'Tax Policy: Are There Still Choices?', in D. Halpern et al. (eds.), *Options for Britain: A Strategic Policy Review*. Aldershot: Dartmouth.

——(1998a). *Income and Wealth: The Latest Evidence*. York: Joseph Rowntree Foundation.

——(1998b). 'Housing: A Decent Home Within the Reach of Every Family?', in H. Glennerster and J. Hills (eds.), *The State of Welfare: The Economics of Social Spending*. Oxford: Oxford University Press.

——(2001). 'Poverty and Social Security: What Rights? Whose Responsibilities?', in A. Park et al. (eds.), *British Social Attitudes: The 18th Report*. London: Sage.

——(2002a). 'Following or Leading Public Opinion? Social Security Policy and Public Attitudes since 1997'. *Fiscal Studies*, 23: 539–58.

——(2002*b*). 'Does a Focus on "Social Exclusion" Change the Policy Response?', in J. Hills, J. Le Grand, and D. Piachaud (eds.), *Understanding Social Exclusion*. Oxford: Oxford University Press.

——(2003). *Inclusion or Insurance? National Insurance and the Future of the Contributory Principle* (CASEpaper 68). London: London School of Economics.

——(2004). 'Heading for Retirement? National Insurance, State Pensions, and the Future of the Contributory Principle in the UK'. *Journal of Social Policy*, [33: 347–72].

——, Le Grand, J., and Piachaud, D. (eds.) (2002). *Understanding Social Exclusion*. Oxford: Oxford University Press.

——and Lelkes, O. (1999). 'Social Security, Selective Universalism, and Patchwork Redistribution', in R. Jowell et al. (eds.), *British Social Attitudes: The 16th Report*. Aldershot: Ashgate.

——and Stewart, K. (eds.) (forthcoming). *A More Equal Society? New Labour, poverty, inequality and exclusion*. Bristol: The Policy Press.

——and Sutherland, H. (2004). 'Ending Child Poverty in a Generation? Policies and Prospects in the UK'. Paper presented at conference on Supporting Children: English-Speaking Countries in International Context, Princeton University, 7–9 January.

Hillyard, P., Kelly, G., McLaughlin, E., Patsios, D., and Tomlinson, M. (2003). *Bare Necessities: Poverty and Social Exclusion in Northern Ireland*. Belfast: Democratic Dialogue.

HM Customs and Excise (1997). *Annual Report 1996–1997: 88th Report of the Commissioners of Her Majesty's Customs and Excise for the Year ended 31 March 1997* (Cm.3776). London: TSO.

HM Treasury (1997*a*). *Budget 97: Equipping Britain for our Long-term Future* (HC85). London: TSO.

——(1997*b*). *Public Expenditure: Statistical Analyses 1997–98* (Cm.3601). London: TSO.

——(2000). *Budget 2000: Prudent for a Purpose* (HC346). London: TSO.

——(2002*a*). *2002 Spending Review: Opportunity and Security for All* (Cm.5570). London: TSO.

——(2002*b*). *Long-term Public Finance Report: An Analysis of Fiscal Sustainability*. London: HM Treasury.

——(2003*a*). *Budget 2003: Building a Britain of Economic Strength and Social Justice* (HC500). London: TSO.

——(2003*b*). *Public Expenditure: Statistical Analyses 2003* (Cm.5901). London: TSO.

——(2003*c*). *Pre-Budget Report: The Strength to Take the Long-Term Decisions for Britain* (Cm.6042). London: TSO.

——(2004). *Budget 2004: Prudence for a Purpose* (HC301). London: TSO.

Howarth, C., Kenway, P., Palmer, G., and Street, C. (1998). *Monitoring Poverty and Social Exclusion: Labour's Inheritance*. York: Joseph Rowntree Foundation.

Inland Revenue (1997). *Inland Revenue Statistics 1997*. London: HMSO.

——(2003*a*). *Inland Revenue Statistics 2003*. London: Inland Revenue.

——(2003*b*). *Working Families Tax Credit: Estimates of Take-up Rates in 2001–2*. London: Inland Revenue.

Jarvis, S. and Jenkins, S. (1997*a*). 'Income Dynamics in Britain: New Evidence from the British Household Panel Study', in P. Gregg (ed.), *Jobs, Wages and Poverty: Patterns of Persistence and Mobility in the Flexible Labour Market*. London: Centre for Economic Performance, London School of Economics.

Jarvis, S. and Jenkins, S. (1997*b*). 'Low Income Dynamics in 1990s Britain'. *Fiscal Studies*, 18: 123–42.

——— (1997*c*). *Marital Splits and Income Changes: Evidence for Britain* (ESRC Research Centre on Micro-social Change Working Paper 97–4). Colchester: University of Essex.

Jenkins, S. (1995). 'Accounting for Inequality Trends: Decomposition Analyses for the UK, 1971–86'. *Economica*, 62/245: 29–63.

—— (1998). 'Income Mobility and Poverty Dynamics', in A. Lee and J. Hills (eds.), *New Cycles of Disadvantage?* (CASEreport No. 1). London: London School of Economics.

—— and Cowell, F. (1993). *Dwarfs and Giants in the 1980s: Trends in the UK Income Distribution* (Department of Economics Discussion Paper 93–03). Swansea: University of Swansea.

—— and Rigg, J. (2001). *The Dynamics of Poverty in Britain* (DWP Research Report 157). Leeds: Corporate Document Services.

Jowell, R., Curtice, J., Park, A., Thomson, K., Jarvis, L., Bromley, C., and Stratford, N. (eds.) (2000). *British Social Attitudes: The 17th Report*. London: Sage.

Kay, J. and King, M. (1980). *The British Tax System* (2nd. edn.; 5th. edn. 1990). Oxford: Oxford University Press.

Kotlikoff, L. (1992). *Generational Accounting: Knowing Who Pays, and When, for What we Spend*. New York: Free Press.

Laing and Buisson (1995). *Care of Elderly People: Market Survey 1995*. London: Laing and Buisson.

Lakin, C. (2003). 'The Effects of Taxes and Benefits on Household Income, 2001–02'. *Economic Trends*, May: www.statistics.gov.uk/articles/economictrends.

—— (2004). 'The Effects of Taxes and Benefits on Household Income, 2002–03'. *Economic Trends*, May. www.statistics.gov.uk/cci/article.asp?id = 895.

Layte, R., Nolan, B., and Whelan, C.T. (2000). 'Targeting Poverty: Lessons from Monitoring Ireland's National Anti-Poverty Strategy'. *Journal of Social Policy*, 29: 553–75.

Le Grand, J. (1982). *The Strategy of Equality*. London: George Allen and Unwin.

—— (2003). *Motivation, Agency, and Public Policy: Of Knights and Knaves, Pawns and Queens*. Oxford: Oxford University Press.

Lilley, P. (1996). 'Equality, Generosity and Opportunity: Welfare Reform and Christian Values' (speech in Southwark Cathedral, 13 June). Mimeo, Department of Social Security.

Lister, R. (2004). *Poverty*. Cambridge: Polity Press.

Low Pay Commission (2003). *The National Minimum Wage: Building on Success* (Fourth Report, Cm.5768). London: TSO.

Lupton, R. (2003). *Poverty Street: The Dynamics of Neighbourhood Decline and Renewal*. Bristol: The Policy Press.

Machin, S. (1998). 'Childhood Disadvantage and Intergenerational Transmissions of Economic Status', in *Persistent Poverty and Lifetime Inequality: The Evidence* (CASEreport 5/HM; Treasury Occasional Paper 10). London: London School of Economics/HM Treasury.

—— (1999). 'Wage Inequality in the 1970s, 1980s, and 1990s', in P. Gregg and J. Wadsworth (eds.), *The State of Working Britain*. Manchester: Manchester University Press.

—— (2001). 'The Changing Nature of Labour Demand in the New Economy and Skill-Biased Technology Change'. *Oxford Bulletin of Economics and Statistics*, 63 (special issue): 753–76.

——(2003). 'Wage Inequality since 1975', in R. Dickens, P. Gregg, and J. Wadsworth (eds.), *The Labour Market under New Labour: The State of Working Britain*. Basingstoke: Palgrave Macmillan.

Mack, J. and Lansley, S. (1985). *Poor Britain*. London: George Allen and Unwin.

McKay, S. (2002). *Low/moderate-income Families in Britain: Work, Working Families' Tax Credit and Childcare in 2000* (DWP Research Report 161). Leeds: Corporate Document Services.

——and Collard, S. (2003). *Developing Deprivation Questions for the Family Resources Survey* (Working paper 13). Bristol: Personal Finance Research Centre, University of Bristol.

——, Walker, R., and Youngs, R. (1997). *Unemployment and Jobseeking before Job-seeker's Allowance* (DSS Research Report 73). London: TSO.

McKnight, A. (2000). *Trends in Earnings Inequality and Earnings Mobility, 1977–1997: The Impact of Mobility on Long-Term Inequality* (DTI Employment Relations Research Series No. 8). London: Department of Trade and Industry.

——(2002). 'Low-paid Work: Drip-Feeding the Poor', in J. Hills, J. Le Grand, and D. Piachaud (eds.), *Understanding Social Exclusion*. Oxford: Oxford University Press.

Marsh, A., McKay, S., Smith, A., and Stephenson, A. (2001). *Low-income Families in Britain* (DSS Research Report 138). Leeds: Corporate Document Services.

Meade Committee (1978). *Structure and Reform of Direct Taxation*. London: George Allen and Unwin.

Middleton, S., Ashworth, K., and Braithwaite, I. (1997). *Small Fortunes: Spending on Children, Childhood Poverty and Parental Sacrifice*. York: Joseph Rowntree Foundation.

Mishel, L. and Bernstein, J. (1994). *The State of Working America 1994–95*. New York: M. E. Sharpe.

Mitchell, D. (1991). *Income Transfers in Ten Welfare States*. Aldershot: Avebury.

Mumford, K. and Power, A. (2003). *East Enders: Family and Community in East London*. Bristol: The Policy Press.

Neuburger, H. (1989). *Direct and Indirect Taxation: A Socialist Approach* (Fabian Taxation Review Background Paper 5). London: Fabian Society.

Nickell, S. (2001). 'Introduction'. *Oxford Bulletin of Economics and Statistics*, 63 (special issue): 617–27.

Nolan, B. and Whelan, C.T. (1996). *Resources, Deprivation, and Poverty*. Oxford: Oxford University Press.

OECD (Organization for Economic Cooperation and Development) (1997). 'Earnings Mobility: Taking a Longer Run View'. *Employment Outlook*, July: 27–61.

——(2001*a*). *Education at a Glance 2001*. Paris: OECD.

——(2001*b*). *Ageing and Income: Financial Resources and Retirement in 9 OECD Countries*. Paris: OECD.

——(2003). *Revenue Statistics*. Paris: OECD.

ONS (Office for National Statistics) (1997). *United Kingdom National Accounts—The Blue Book 1997*. London: TSO.

——(1999). *New Earnings Survey 1999*. London: TSO.

——(2002). *Trends in Life Expectancy by Social Class, England and Wales*. London: ONS.

——(2003). *New Earnings Survey 2003*. London: TSO.

Oppenheim, C. (1997). 'The Growth of Poverty and Inequality', in A. Walker and C. Walker (eds.), *Britain Divided: The Growth of Poverty and Social Exclusion in the 1980s and 1990s*. London: Child Poverty Action Group.

Oppenheim, C. and Harker, L. (1996). *Poverty: The Facts* (3rd edn.). London: Child Poverty Action Group.

Oxley, H., Dang, T.-T, and Antolín, P. (1999). *Poverty Dynamics in Six OECD Countries*. Paris: OECD.

Palmer, G., North, J., Carr, J., and Kenway, P. (2003). *Monitoring Poverty and Social Exclusion 2003*. York: Joseph Rowntree Foundation.

Park, A., Curtice, J., Thomson, K., Jarvis., L., and Bromley, C. (eds.) (2002). *British Social Attitudes: The 19th Report*. London: Sage.

—————————(eds.) (2003). *British Social Attitudes: The 20th Report*. London: Sage.

Pensions Policy Institute (2002). *Raising State Pension Age: Are We Ready?* London: PPI.

——(2003). *The Pensions Landscape*. London: PPI.

Pierson, P. (ed.) (2001). *The New Politics of the Welfare State*. Oxford: Oxford University Press.

PIU (Performance and Innovation Unit) (2001). *Social Mobility: A Discussion Paper*. London: Cabinet Office.

Powell, M. (1995). 'The Strategy of Inequality Revisited'. *Journal of Social Policy*, 24/2: 163–85.

——(ed.) (2002). *Evaluating New Labour's Welfare Reforms*. Bristol: The Policy Press.

Pudney, S., Hernandez, M., and Hancock, R. (2002). *The Welfare Cost of Means-testing: Pensioner Participation in Income Support* (Discussion Paper in Economics 03/2). Leicester: University of Leicester.

Redmond, G. and Sutherland, H. (1995). *How Has Tax and Social Security Policy Changed Since 1978? A Distributional Analysis* (Microsimulation Unit Research Note 9508). Cambridge: University of Cambridge, Department of Applied Economics.

————and Wilson, M. (1998). *The Arithmetic of Tax and Social Security Reform: A User's Guide to Microsimulation Models and Analysis*. Cambridge: Cambridge University Press.

Reich, R. (1991). *The Work of Nations*. London: Simon and Schuster.

Review Body on Senior Salaries (2000). *Twenty-Second Report on Senior Salaries* (Report 45, Cm.4567). London: TSO.

——(2001). *Review of Parliamentary Pay and Allowances—Volume 2: Independent Study on Pay and Allowances* (Report 48, Cm.4997-II). London: TSO.

Rigg, J. and Sefton, T. (2004). *Income Dynamics and the Life Cycle: Evidence from Ten Waves of the British Household Panel Survey*(CASEpaper 81). London: London School of Economics.

Room, G. (1999). *Social Exclusion, Solidarity and the Challenge of Globalisation* (Social Policy Papers 27). Bath: University of Bath.

Rothstein, B. (1998). *Just Institutions Matter: The Moral and Political Logic of the Universal Welfare State*. Cambridge: Cambridge University Press.

Rowntree, B. S. (1901). *Poverty: A Study of Town Life*. London: Macmillan.

——(1941). *Poverty and Progress: A Second Social Survey of York*. London: Longmans Green and Co.

Royal Commission on Long-Term Care (1999). *With Respect to Old Age* (Cm.4192-I). London: TSO.

Sefton, T. (1997). *The Changing Distribution of the Social Wage* (STICERD Occasional Paper 21). London: London School of Economics.

——(2002). *Recent Changes in the Distribution of the Social Wage* (CASEpaper 62). London: London School of Economics.

——(2003). 'What We Want From the Welfare State', in A. Park et al. (eds.), *British Social Attitudes: The 20th Report*. London: Sage.

SEU (Social Exclusion Unit) (1997). *Social Exclusion Unit* (brochure). London: Cabinet Office.

——(2001). *Preventing Social Exclusion*. London: Cabinet Office.

Smithies, R. (forthcoming *a*). *Intergenerational Equity and the Changing Welfare State in the UK* (forthcoming CASEpaper). London: London School of Economics.

——(forthcoming *b*). *Public and Private Welfare Activity 1979–1999* (forthcoming CASEpaper): London: London School of Economics.

Stafford, B. (1998). *National Insurance and the Contributory Principle* (DSS Social Research Branch In-house Report 39). London: DSS.

Stewart, K. (2003). 'Monitoring Social Inclusion in Europe's Regions'. *Journal of European Social Policy*, 13: 335–56.

Strategy Unit (2001). *Ethnic Minorities and the Labour Market: Interim Analytical Report*. London: Cabinet Office.

Sutherland, H. (1997). 'Women, Men and the Redistribution of Income'. *Fiscal Studies*, 18: 1–22.

——(2004). *Poverty in Britain: The Impact of Government Policy since 1997. An Update to 2004–5 using Microsimulation* (Microsimulation Unit Research Note 44). Cambridge: University of Cambridge.

——, Sefton, T., and Piachaud, D. (2003). *Poverty in Britain: The Impact of Policies since 1997*. York: Joseph Rowntree Foundation.

Taylor-Gooby, P. (1995). 'Comfortable, Marginal and Excluded: Who Should Pay Higher Taxes for a Better Welfare State?', in R. Jowell et al. (eds.). *British Social Attitudes: The 12th Report*. Aldershot: Ashgate.

——and Hastie, C. (2002). 'Support for State Spending: Has New Labour got it Right?', in A. Park et al. (eds.), *British Social Attitudes: The 19th Report*. London: Sage.

Thomson, D. (1991). *Selfish Generations? The Ageing of New Zealand's Welfare State*. Wellington: Bridget Williams Books.

Townsend, I. (2002). *The Burden of Taxation* (House of Commons Research Paper 02/43). London: House of Commons.

Townsend, P. (1979). *Poverty in the United Kingdom*. Harmondsworth: Penguin.

UNICEF (United Nations Children's Fund) (2000). *A League Table of Child Poverty in Rich Nations* (Innocenti Report Card 1). Florence: Innocenti Research Centre.

Vegeris, S. and Perry, J. (2003). *Families and Children 2001: Living Standards and the Children* (DWP Research Report 190). Leeds: Corporate Document Services.

Veit-Wilson, J. (1998). *Setting Adequate Standards: How Governments Define Minimum Incomes*. Bristol: The Policy Press.

Wakefield, M. (2003). *Is Middle Britain Middle-Income Britain?* (IFS Briefing Note 38). London: Institute for Fiscal Studies.

Waldfogel, J., Danziger, S. K., Danziger, S., and Seefeldt, K. (2002). 'Welfare Reform and Lone Mothers' Employment in the US', in J. Millar and K. Rowlingson (eds.), *Lone Mothers, Employment and Social Policy: Cross-national Comparisons*. Bristol: The Policy Press.

Walker, R. (ed.) (1999). *Ending Child Poverty*. Bristol: Policy Press.

Walker, R. with Howard, M. (2000). *The Making of a Welfare Class? Benefit Receipt in Britain*. Bristol: The Policy Press.

Wanless, D. (2002). *Securing Our Future Health: Taking a Long-term View—Final Report*. London: HM Treasury.

White, M. and Riley, R. (2002). *Findings from the Macro-evaluation of the New Deal for Young People* (DWP Research Report 168). Leeds: Corporate Document Services.

Wilkinson, D. (1998). 'Towards Reconciliation of the NES and LFS Earnings Data'. *Labour Market Trends*, 106: 223–31.

Wood, A. (1994). *North-South Trade, Employment and Inequality: Changing Fortunes in a Skill-driven World*. Oxford: Oxford University Press.

Young, M. (1958). *The Rise of the Meritocracy 1870–2033*. London: Thames and Hudson.

Zaidi, A., and Burchardt, T. (2003). *Comparing Incomes when Needs Differ: Equivalisation for the Extra Costs of Disability in the UK* (CASEpaper 64). London: London School of Economics.

Index